BUSINESS OF TOURISM

BUSINESS OF TOURISM

Vikash Choudhary

CENTRUM PRESS
NEW DELHI-110002 (INDIA)

CENTRUM PRESS
H.O.: 4360/4, Ansari Road, Daryaganj,
New Delhi-110002 (India)
Tel: 23278000, 23261597, 23255577, 23286875
B.O.: No. 1015, Ist Main Road, BSK IIIrd Stage,
IIIrd Phase, IIIrd Block, Bangalore-560085 (INDIA)
Tel: 080-41723429
Email: centrumpress@gmail.com
Visit us at: www.centrumpress.com

Business of Tourism

First Edition, 2010

PRINTED IN INDIA

Printed at Mehra Offset Press, Delhi

Contents

Preface *vii*

1. Defining and Analysing Tourism and its Impact 1
2. Development and Growth of Tourism to the Mid 20th Century 41
3. The Era of Popular Tourism: 1950 to the 21st Century 83
4. The Demand for Tourism 121
5. The Economic Impact of Tourism 143
6. The Sociocultural Impact of Tourism 155
7. The Environmental Impact of Tourism 197
8. Tourist Destinations 233
9. The Hospitality Sector 283

Bibliography 337

Index 341

Preface

Tourism is travel for recreational, leisure or business purposes. The World Tourism Organization defines tourists as people who "travel to and stay in places outside their usual environment for more than twenty-four (24) hours and not more than one consecutive year for leisure, business and other purposes not related to the exercise of an activity remunerated from within the place visited". Tourism has become a popular global leisure activity. In 2008, there were over 922 million international tourist arrivals, with a growth of 1.9% as compared to 2007. International tourism receipts grew to US$944 billion (euro 642 billion) in 2008, corresponding to an increase in real terms of 1.8%.

As a result of the Late-2000s recession, international travel demand suffered a strong slowdown beginning in June 2008, with growth in international tourism arrivals worldwide falling to 2% during the boreal summer months, and this negative trend intensified as international tourist arrivals fell by 8% during the first four months of 2009. Thereafter this declining trend was exacerbated in some regions due to the outbreak of the influenza AH1N1 virus.

Businesses and public organizations are increasingly interested in the economic impacts of tourism at national, state, and local levels. One regularly hears claims that tourism supports X jobs in an area or that a festival or special event generated Y million dollars in sales or income in a community. "Multiplier effects" are often cited to capture secondary effects of tourism spending and show the wide range of sectors in a community that may benefit from tourism.

Tourism's economic benefits are touted by the industry for a variety of reasons. Claims of tourism's economic significance give the industry greater respect among the business community, public officials, and the public in general. This often translates into decisions or public policies that are favourable to tourism. Community support is important for tourism, as it is an activity that affects the entire community. Tourism businesses depend extensively on each other as well as on other businesses, government and residents of the local community.

Economic benefits and costs of tourism reach virtually everyone in the region in one way or another. Economic impact analyses provide tangible estimates of these economic interdependencies and a better understanding of the role and importance of tourism in a region's economy.

Hospitality and tourism is a vastly important and fast-growing industry. Planning and development issues of tourism and hospitality extend from the macro to the micro level, from global concerns to those associated with the individual organisations and companies, from multivariate forecasting to the more creative endeavours of menu planning and property design/development. The book is designed to provide students, researchers, practitioners, individuals and organisations, a broad overview of planning and development issues in hospitality and tourism industry.

—*Vikash Choudhary*

1

Defining and Analysing Tourism and its Impact

An Introduction to Tourism

Tourism is travel for recreational, leisure or business purposes. The World Tourism Organization defines tourists as people who "travel to and stay in places outside their usual environment for more than twenty-four hours and not more than one consecutive year for leisure, business and other purposes not related to the exercise of an activity remunerated from within the place visited". Tourism has become a popular global leisure activity. In 2008, there were over 922 million international tourist arrivals, with a growth of 1.9% as compared to 2007. International tourism receipts grew to US$944 billion (euro 642 billion) in 2008, corresponding to an increase in real terms of 1.8%. As a result of the Late-2000s recession, international travel demand suffered a strong slowdown beginning in June 2008, with growth in international tourism arrivals worldwide falling to 2% during the boreal summer months, and this negative trend intensified as international tourist arrivals fell by 8% during the first four months of 2009. Thereafter this declining trend was exacerbated in some regions due to the outbreak of the influenza AH1N1 virus.

Tourism is vital for many countries, such as the U.A.E, Egypt, Greece and Thailand, and many island nations, such as The Bahamas, Fiji, Maldives and the Seychelles, due to the large intake of money for businesses with their goods and services and the opportunity for employment in the service industries associated with tourism. These service industries include transportation services, such as airlines, cruise ships and taxis, hospitality services, such as accommodations, including hotels and resorts, and entertainment venues, such as amusement parks, casinos, shopping malls, various music venues and the theatre.

Definition

Hunziker and Krapf, in 1941, defined tourism as people who travel "the sum of the phenomena and relationships arising from the travel and stay of non-residents, insofar as they do not lead to permanent residence and are not connected with any earning activity." In 1976, the Tourism Society of England's definition was: "Tourism is the temporary, short-term movement of people to destination outside the places where they normally live and work and their activities during the stay at each destination. It includes movements for all purposes." In 1981, the International Association of Scientific Experts in Tourism defined tourism in terms of particular activities selected by choice and undertaken outside the home.

The United Nations classified three forms of tourism in 1994, in its "Recommendations on Tourism Statistics: Domestic tourism", which involves residents of the given country travelling only within this country; Inbound tourism, involving non-residents travelling in the given country; and Outbound tourism, involving residents travelling in another country. The UN also derived different categories of tourism by combining the three basic forms of tourism: Internal tourism, which comprises domestic tourism and inbound tourism; National tourism, which comprises domestic tourism and outbound tourism; and International tourism, which consists of inbound tourism and outbound tourism. *Intrabound tourism* is a term coined by the Korea Tourism Organization and widely accepted in Korea. Intrabound tourism differs from domestic tourism in that the former encompasses policy making and implementation of national tourism policies.

Recently, the tourism industry has shifted from the promotion of inbound tourism to the promotion of intrabound tourism, because many countries are experiencing tough competition for inbound tourists.

World Tourism Statistics and Rankings

The World Tourism Organization reports the following ten countries as the most visited in between 2006 and 2008 by number of international travellers. When compared to 2006, Ukraine entered the top ten list, surpassing Russia, Austria and Mexico, and in 2008 surpassed Germany. In 2008 the U.S. displaced Spain from the second place. Most of the top visited countries continue to be on the European continent.

International Tourism Receipts

In 2008, there were over 922 million international tourist arrivals, with a growth of 1.9% as compared to 2007. International tourism receipts grew to US$944 billion (euro 642 billion) in 2008, corresponding to an increase in real terms of 1.8% on 2007. When the export value of international passenger transport receipts is accounted for, total receipts in 2008 reached a record of US$1.1 billion, or over US$3 billion a day. The World Tourism Organization reports the following countries as the top ten tourism earners for the year 2008. It is noticeable that most of them are on the European continent, but the United States continues to be the top earner.

International Tourism Expenditures

The World Tourism Organization reports the following countries as the top ten biggest spenders on international tourism for the year 2008. For the fifth year in a row, German tourists continue as the top spenders.

History

Wealthy people have always travelled to distant parts of the world, to see great buildings, works of art, learn new languages, experience new cultures and to taste different cuisines. Long ago, at the time of the Roman Republic, places such as Baiae were popular coastal resorts for the rich. The word *tourism* was used by 1811 and *tourist* by 1840. In 1936, the League of Nations defined *foreign tourist* as "someone travelling abroad for at least twenty-four hours". Its successor, the United Nations, amended this definition in 1945, by including a maximum stay of six months. The earliest forms of leisure tourism can be traced as far back as the Babylonian and Egyptian empires. A museum of "historic antiquities" was open to the public in the sixth century BC in Babylon, while the Egyptians held many religious festivals attracting not only the devout, but many who came to see the famous buildings and works of art in the cities. The local towns accommodated tourists by providing services such as: vendors of food and drink, guides, hawkers of souvenirs, touts and prostitutes.

From around the same date, Greek tourists travelled to visit the sites of healing gods. Because the independent city-states of ancient Greece had no central authority to order the construction of roads, most of these tourists travelled by water, hence seaports prospered. The lands of the Mediterranean Sea produced a remarkable evolution in travel. People travel for trade, commerce, religious purposes, festivals, medical treatment, or education developed at an early date.

Guidebooks became available as early as the fourth century BC, covering a vast area of destinations, i.e. Athens, Sparta and Troy. Pausanias, a Greek travel writer, produced a noted "description of Greece" between AD 160 and 180, which, in its critical evaluation of facilities and destinations, acted as a model for later writers. Advertisements, in the form of signs directing visitors to wayside inns, are also known from this period. However, under Romans rule is where international travel became first important. With no foreign borders between England and Syria, and with the seas safe from piracy due to the Roman patrols, conditions favouring travel had arrived. Roman coinage was acceptable everywhere, and Latin was the common language. Romans travelled to Sicily, Greece, Rhodes, and Troy, Egypt and from the third century AD, to the Holy Land.

Domestic tourism also flourished within the Roman Empire. Second homes were built by the wealthy within easy travelling distance of Rome, occupied particularly during the springtime social season. Naples attracted the retired and the intellectuals.

Before the sixteenth century, those who sought to travel had three modes in which to do so. They could walk, ride a horse or they could be carried, either on a little or on a carrier's wagon. The development of the sprung coach was a huge advance for those who regularly travelled, and by the mid 1600's, coaches were operating regularly in Britain. In the eighteenth century the introduction of turnpike roads, which provided improved surfaces for which tolls would be charged. The later introduction of the metal, leaf spring suspension also added to comfort.

Travel also requires accommodation, and at that time, it was basic. To accommodate the new demand for travel inns was provided. They provided fresh horses, and lodgings were available for rent to visitors when they arrived at their destination.

From the early seventeenth century, a new form of tourism developed as a direct outcome of the freedom and quest for learning heralded by the Renaissance. Young men who wanted positions at court were encouraged to travel to the Continent to finish their education. Others soon adopted this practice in the upper echelons of society, and it soon became customary for the education of a gentleman to be completed by a "Grand tour" of major cultural centres of Europe, accompanied by a tutor and often-lasting three years or more. The appeal soon became social, and leisure seeking young men travelled, predominantly to France and Italy, to enjoy the rival cultures and social life of cities such as Paris, Venice, or Florence. By the end of the eighteenth century, the custom had become institutionalised for the gentry.

Passports have their origins in the medieval testimonial. A letter from an ecclesiastical superior given to a pilgrim to avoid the latter's possible arrest on charges of vagrancy. Later, papers of authority to travel were more widely issued by the state, particularly during periods of warfare with neighbouring European countries.

Spas were already well established during the time of the Roman Empire, but their popularity, based on the supposed medical benefits of the waters, lapsed in the subsequent centuries. Renewed interest in the therapeutic qualities of mineral waters has been ascribed to the influence of the Renaissance in Britain, and elsewhere in Europe.

Leisure Travel

Leisure travel was associated with the Industrial Revolution in the United Kingdom – the first European country to promote leisure time to the increasing industrial population. Initially, this applied to the owners of the machinery of production, the economic oligarchy, the factory owners and the traders. These comprised the new middle class. Cox & Kings was the first official travel company to be formed in 1758.

The British origin of this new industry is reflected in many place names. In Nice, France, one of the first and best-established holiday resorts on the French Riviera, the long esplanade along the seafront is known to this day as the *Promenade des Anglais*; in many other historic resorts in continental Europe, old, well-established palace hotels have names like the *Hotel Bristol*, the *Hotel Carlton* or the *Hotel Majestic* – reflecting the dominance of English customers. Many leisure-oriented tourists travel to the tropics, both in the summer and winter. Places often visited are: Cuba, the Dominican Republic, Thailand, North Queensland in Australia and Florida in the United States.

Winter Tourism

Major ski resorts are located in the various European countries.

Mass Tourism

Mass tourism could only have developed with the improvements in technology, allowing the transport of large numbers of people in a short space of time to places of leisure interest, so that greater numbers of people could begin to enjoy the benefits of leisure time. In the United States, the first seaside resorts in the European style were at Atlantic City, New Jersey and Long Island, New York.

In Continental Europe, early resorts included: Ostend, popularized by the people of Brussels; Boulogne-sur-Mer and Deauville (Calvados) for the Parisians; and Heiligendamm, founded in 1797, as the first seaside resort on the Baltic Sea.

Adjectival Tourism

Adjectival tourism refers to the numerous niche or speciality travel forms of tourism that have emerged over the years, each with its own adjective. Many of these have come into common use by the tourism industry and academics. Others are emerging concepts that may or may not gain popular usage. Examples of the more common niche tourism markets include:

1. Agritourism,
2. Culinary tourism,
3. Cultural tourism,
4. Ecotourism,
5. Heritage tourism,
6. LGBT tourism,
7. Medical tourism,
8. Nautical tourism,
9. Religious tourism,
10. Space tourism,
11. War tourism,
12. Wildlife tourism.

Recent Developments

There has been an upmarket trend in the tourism over the last few decades, especially in Europe, where international travel for short breaks is common. Tourists have higher levels of disposable income and greater leisure time and they are also better-educated and have more sophisticated tastes. There is now a demand for a better quality products, which has resulted in a fragmenting of the mass market for beach vacations; people want more specialised versions, such as Club 18-30, quieter resorts, family-oriented holidays or niche market-targeted destination hotels.

The developments in technology and transport infrastructure, such as jumbo jets, low-cost airlines and more accessible airports have made many types of tourism more affordable. Who estimates that up to 500,000 people are on planes at any time. There have also been changes in lifestyle, such as retiree-age people who sustain year round tourism. This is facilitated by internet sales of tourism products. Some sites have now started to offer dynamic packaging, in which an inclusive price is quoted for a tailor-made package requested by the customer upon impulse.

There have been a few setbacks in tourism, such as the September 11 attacks and terrorist threats to tourist destinations, such as in Bali and several European cities. Also, on December 26, 2004, a tsunami, caused by the 2004 Indian Ocean earthquake, hit the Asian countries on the Indian Ocean, including the Maldives. Thousands of lives were lost and many tourists died. This, together with the vast clean-up operation in place, has stopped or severely hampered tourism to the area.

The terms *tourism* and *travel* are sometimes used interchangeably. In this context, travel has a similar definition to tourism, but implies a more purposeful journey. The terms *tourism* and *tourist* are sometimes used pejoratively, to imply a shallow interest in the cultures or locations visited by tourists.

Sustainable Tourism

"Sustainable tourism is envisaged as leading to management of all resources in such a way that economic, social and aesthetic needs can be fulfilled while maintaining cultural integrity, essential ecological processes, biological diversity and life support systems." Sustainable development implies "meeting the needs of the present without compromising the ability of future generations to meet their own needs"

Ecotourism

When there is a significant price difference between countries for a given medical procedure, particularly in Southeast Asia, India, Eastern Europe and where there are different regulatory regimes, in relation to particular medical procedures, travelling to take advantage of the price or regulatory differences is often referred to as "medical tourism".

Educational Tourism

Educational tourism developed, because of the growing popularity of teaching and learning of knowledge and the enhancing of technical competency outside of the classroom environment. In educational tourism, the main focus of the tour or leisure activity includes visiting another country to learn about the culture, such as in Student Exchange Programs and Study Tours, or to work and apply skills learned inside the classroom in a different environment, such as in the International Practicum Training Program.

Creative Tourism

Creative tourism has existed as a form of cultural tourism, since the early beginnings of tourism itself. Its European roots date back to the time of the Grand Tour, which saw the sons of aristocratic families travelling for the purpose of mostly interactive, educational experiences.

More recently, creative tourism has been given its own name by Crispin Raymond and Greg Richards, who as members of the Association for Tourism and Leisure Education (ATLAS), have directed a number of projects for the European Commission, including cultural and crafts tourism, known as sustainable tourism. They have defined "creative tourism" as tourism related to the active participation of travellers in the culture of the host community, through interactive workshops and informal learning experiences. Meanwhile, the concept of creative tourism has been picked up by high-profile organizations such as UNESCO, who through the Creative Cities Network, have endorsed creative tourism as an engaged, authentic experience that promotes an active understanding of the specific cultural features of a place.

More recently, creative tourism has gained popularity as a form of cultural tourism, drawing on active participation by travellers in the culture of the host communities they visit. Several countries offer examples of this type of tourism development, including the United Kingdom, the Bahamas, Jamaica, Spain, Italy and New Zealand.

Dark Tourism

One emerging area of special interest tourism has been identified by Lennon and Foley (2000) as "dark" tourism. This type of tourism involves visits to "dark" sites, such as battlegrounds, scenes of horrific crimes or acts of genocide, for example: concentration camps. Dark tourism poses severe ethical and moral dilemmas: should these sites be available for visitation and, if so, what should the nature of the publicity involved be. Dark tourism remains a small niche market, driven by varied motivations, such as mourning, remembrance, macabre curiosity or even entertainment. Its early origins are rooted in fairgrounds and medieval fairs.

Growth

The World Tourism Organization (UNWTO) forecasts that international tourism will continue growing at the average annual rate of 4 %. With the advent of e-commerce, tourism products have become one of the most traded items on the internet. Tourism products and services have been made available through intermediaries, although tourism providers can sell their services directly. This has put pressure on intermediaries from both online and traditional shops.

It has been suggested there is a strong correlation between tourism expenditure per capita and the degree to which countries play in the global context. Not only as a result of the important economic contribution of the tourism industry, but also as an indicator of the degree of confidence with which global citizens leverage the resources of the globe for the benefit of their local economies. This is why any projections of growth in tourism may serve as an indication of the relative influence that each country will exercise in the future. Space tourism is expected to "take off" in the first quarter of the 21st century, although compared with traditional destinations the number of tourists in orbit will remain low until technologies such as a space elevator make space travel cheap.

Technological improvement is likely to make possible air-ship hotels, based either on solar-powered airplanes or large dirigibles. Underwater hotels, such as Hydropolis, expected to open in Dubai in 2009, will be built. On the ocean, tourists will be welcomed by ever larger cruise ships and perhaps floating cities.

Latest Trends

As a result of the Late-2000s recession, international arrivals suffered a strong slowdown beginning in June 2008. Growth from 2007 to 2008 was only 3.7% during the first eight months of 2008. The Asian and Pacific markets were affected and Europe stagnated during the boreal summer months, while the Americas performed better, reducing their expansion rate but keeping a 6% growth from January to August 2008. Only the Middle East continued its rapid growth during the same period, reaching a 17% growth as compared to the same period in 2007.

This slowdown on international tourism demand was also reflected in the air transport industry, with a negative growth in September 2008 and a 3.3% growth in passenger traffic through September. The hotel industry also reports a slowdown, as room occupancy continues to decline. As the global economic situation deteriorated dramatically during September and October as a result of the global financial crisis, growth of international tourism is expected to slow even further for the remaining of 2008, and this slowdown in demand growth is forecasted to continue into 2009 as recession has already hit most of the top spender countries, with long-haul travel expected to be the most affected by the economic crisis. This negative trend intensified as international tourist arrivals fell by 8% during the first four months of 2009, and the decline was exacerbated in some regions due to the outbreak of the influenza AH1N1 virus.

Tourist Product

A product may be defined as the sum of the physical and psychological satisfaction it provides to the buyer. For a tourist, the product covers the complete experience from the time he leaves home to the time he returns back. Tourist products include a comprehensive range of package and travel facilities. Three basic components of the product are attractions of the destination, facilities at the destination and accessibility to the destination.

A tourism product can be defined as the sum of the physical and psychological satisfaction it provides to tourists during their travelling en route to the destination. The tourist product focuses on facilities and services designed to meet the needs of the tourist. It can be seen as a composite product, as the sum total of a country's tourist attractions, transport, and accommodation and of entertainment which result in customer satisfaction. Each of the components of a tourist product is supplied by individual providers of services like hotel companies, airlines, travel agencies, etc. The tourist product can be analysed in terms of its attraction, accessibility and accommodation.

Attractions

Of the three basic components of a tourist product, attractions are very important. Unless there is an attraction, the tourist will not be motivated to go to a particular place. Attractions are those elements in a product which determine the choice made by particular tourist to visit one particular destination rather than another. The attractions could be cultural, like sites and areas of archaeological interest, historical buildings and monuments, flora and fauna, beach resorts, mountains, national parks or events like trade fairs, exhibitions, arts and music festivals, games, etc. Tourist demands are also very much susceptible to changes in fashion. Fashion is an important factor in the demand for various tourist attractions and amenities. The tourist who visits a particular place for its natural beauty may decide to visit some other attractions due to a change in fashion. Peter has drawn up an inventory of the various attractions which are of significance in tourism.

Inventory of Tourist Attractions

Cultural: Sites and areas of archaeological interest, Historical buildings and Monuments, Places of historical significance, Museums, Modern Culture, Political and Educational institutions, Religious Institutions

Traditions: National Festivals, Arts and Handicrafts, Music, Folklore, Native life and Customs.

Scenic: National Parks, Wildlife, Flora and Fauna, Beach Resorts, Mountain Resorts.

Entertainment: Participation and Vicwing sports, Amusement and Recreation Parks Zones and Oceanariums, Cinemas and Theatres, Night Life and Cuisine.

Others: Climate, Health resorts or Spas, Unique characteristics not available elsewhere.

However, the attractions of tourism are, to a very large extent, geographical in character. Location and accessibility (whether a place has a coastal or inland position and the ease with which a given place can be reached) are important. Physical space may be thought of as a component for those who seek the wilderness and solitude. Scenery or landscape is a compound of landforms; water and the vegetation and has an aesthetic and recreative value. Climate conditions, especially in relation to the amount of sunshine, temperature and precipitation, are of special significance. Animal life may be an important attraction, firstly in relation to, bird watching or viewing game in their natural habitat and secondly, for sports purposes, e.g. fishing and hunting. Man's impact on the natural landscape in the form of his settlements, historical monuments and archaeological remains is also a major attraction. Finally, a variety of cultural features-ways of life, folklore, artistic expressions, etc. provide valuable attractions to many. Accessibility It is a means by which a tourist can reach the area where attractions are located. Tourist attractions of whatever type would be of little importance if their locations are inaccessible by the normal means of transport. A Tourist in order to get to his destination needs some mode of transport. This mode may be a motor car, a coach, an aeroplane, a ship or a train which enables him to reach his predetermined destination. If tourist destinations are located at places where no transport can reach or where there are inadequate transport facilities, they become of little value. The tourist attractions, which are located near the tourist-generating markets and are linked by a network of efficient means of transport, receive the maximum number of tourists.

The distance factor also plays an important role in determining a tourist's choice of a destination. Longer distances cost much more in the way of expenses on travel as compared to short distances. An example can be that of India. About two and a half million tourist arrivals for a country of the size of India may look rather unimpressive. However if one looks at certain factors like the country's distance from the affluent tourist markets of the world such as the United States, Europe, Canada, Japan and Australia, one may conclude that the long distance is one of the factors responsible for low arrivals. It costs a visitor from these countries, quite a substantial amount, to visit India for a holiday. It has been stated earlier that Europe and North America continue to be the main generating and receiving areas for international tourism, accounting for as much as 70% and 20% respectively, of international tourist arrivals. Easy accessibility, thus is a key factor for the growth and development of tourist movements.

Accommodation

The accommodation and other facilities complement the attractions. Accommodation plays a central role and is very basic to tourist destinations. World Tourism Organization in its definition of a tourist has stated that he must spend at least one night in the destination visited, to qualify as a tourist. This presupposes availability of some kind of accommodation. The demand for accommodation away from one's home is met by a variety of facilities. The range and type of accommodation is quite varied and has undergone considerable change since the last half century. There has been a decline in the use of boarding houses and small private hotels.

Larger hotels are increasing their share of holiday trade, especially in big metropolitan areas and popular spots. In more traditional holiday and seaside resorts in Europe and elsewhere, big hotels are keeping their share of holiday resorts. In recent years, some changes have been reflected in the type of accommodation. There has been an increasing demand for more non-traditional and informal types of accommodation. The latest trends in accommodation are holiday villages. In recent years there has been an increase in the popularity of such accommodation.

Accommodation may in itself be an important tourist attraction. In fact, a large number of tourists visit a particular destination or town simply because there is a first class luxury hotel or resort which provides excellent services and facilities. Some countries like Switzerland, Holland, France, Austria, and Belgium have gained a reputation for providing excellent accommodation with good cuisine. Many hotel establishments elsewhere in various countries, especially the resort hotels, have gained a reputation for their excellent cuisine, services and facilities. The French government for instance, paved the way for tourist development of Corsica by launching a big hotel development programme.

Amenities

Facilities are a necessary aid to the tourist centre. For a seaside resort, facilities like swimming, boating, yachting, surf-riding, and other facilities like dancing, recreation and other amusements are important for every tourist centre. Amenities can be of two types; natural, e.g. beaches, sea-bathing, possibilities of fishing, opportunities for climbing, trekking, viewing, etc. and man-made, e.g. various types of entertainment and facilities which cater to the special needs of the tourists.

Excellent sandy beaches, sheltered from sunshine with palm and coconut trees and offering good bathing conditions form very good tourist attractions. Certain other natural amenities such as spacious waters for the purpose of sailing, or the opportunities for fishing and hunting are also very important.

Characteristics of Tourism Product

By now, you must have understood what a tourism product is. Now let us look at some of its characteristics:-

1) *Intangible:* Unlike a tangible product, say, a motor car or refrigerator, no transfer of ownership of goods is involved in tourism. The product here cannot be seen or inspected before its purchase. Instead, certain facilities, installations, items of equipment are made available for a specified time and for a specified use. For example, a seat in an aeroplane is provided only for a specified time.

2) *Psychological:* A large component of tourism product is the satisfaction the consumer derives from its use. A tourist acquires

experiences while interacting with the new environment and his experiences help to attract and motivate potential customers.

3) *Highly Perishable:* A travel agent or tour operator who sells a tourism product cannot store it. Production can only take place if the customer is actually present. And once consumption begins, it cannot be stopped, interrupted or modified. If the product remains unused, the chances are lost i.e. if tourists do not visit a particular place, the opportunity at that time is lost. It is due to this reason that heavy discount is offered by hotels and transport generating organizations during off season.

4) *Composite Product:* The tourist product cannot be provided by a single enterprise unlike a manufactured product. The tourist product covers the complete experience of a visit to a particular place. And many providers contribute to this experience. For instance, airline supplies seats, a hotel provides rooms and restaurants, travel agents make bookings for stay and sightseeing, etc.

5) *Unstable Demand:* Tourism demand is influenced by seasonal, economic political and others such factors. There are certain times of the year which see a greater demand than others. At these times there is a greater strain on services like hotel bookings, employment, the transport system, etc.

6) *Fixed supply in the short run:* The tourism product unlike a manufactured product cannot be brought to the consumer; the consumer must go to the product. This requires an in-depth study of users' behaviour, taste preferences, likes and dislikes so that expectations and realities coincide for the maximum satisfaction of the consumer. The supply of a tourism product is fixed in the short run and can only be increased in the long run following increased demand patterns.

7) *Absence of ownership:* When you buy a car, the ownership of the car is transferred to you, but when you hire a taxi you buy the right to be transported to a predetermined destination at a predetermined price (fare). You neither own the automobile nor the driver of the vehicle. Similarly, hotel rooms, airline tickets, etc. can be used but not owned. These services can be bought for consumption but ownership remains with the provider of the service. So, a dance can be enjoyed by viewing it, but the dancer cannot be owned.

8) *Heterogeneous:* Tourism is not a homogeneous product since it tends to vary in standard and quality over time, unlike a T.V set or any other manufactured product. A package tour or even a flight on an aircraft can't be consistent at all times. The reason is that this product is a service and services are people based. Due to this, there is variability in this product. All individuals vary and even the same individual may not perform the same every time. For instance, all air hostesses cannot provide the same quality of service and even the same air hostess may not perform uniformly in the morning and evening. Thus, services cannot be standardised.
9) *Risky:* The risk involved in the use of a tourism product is heightened since it has to be purchased before its consumption. An element of chance is always present in its consumption. Like, a show might not be as entertaining as it promises to be or a beach holiday might be disappointing due to heavy rain.
10) *Marketable:* Tourism product is marketed at two levels. At the first level, national and regional organisations engage in persuading potential tourists to visit the country or a certain region. These official tourist organisations first create knowledge of its country in tourist –generating markets and persuade visitors in these markets to visit the country. At the second level, the various individual firms providing tourist services, market their own components of the total tourist product to persuade potential tourists to visit that region for which they are responsible.

Forms of Tourism Product

By now you must be aware of what a tourism product is and what its peculiar features are. It is necessary to understand the components of the tourist product from the point of view of the consumer. The product for the tourist covers the complete experience from the time he leaves home to the time he returns. The tourist product today is developed to meet the needs of the consumer and techniques like direct sales, publicity and advertising are employed to bring this product to the consumer. The tourist product is the basic raw material, be it the country's natural beauty, climate, history, culture and the people, or other facilities necessary for comfortable living such as water supply, electricity, roads, transport, communication and other essentials. The tourist product can be entirely a man-made one or nature's creation improved upon by man. A consumer can combine individual products in a large number of ways. There would be many possible destinations, each with a number of hotels, each to be reached by more than one airline. Thus, the potential choice facing the consumer is very large. The large number of tourist destinations have placed at the disposal of a tourist a very large variety of tourist products in abundant quantity from a large number of competing destinations. This eventually, has led to the adoption of the new concept i.e., the marketing concept in tourism by various countries promoting tourism. Tourism, basically, is an infrastructure based service product. The nature of the service here is highly intangible and perishable offering a limited scope for creating and maintaining the distinctive competitive edge. The effective marketing of tourism needs constant gearing up of infrastructure to international standards and presupposes in its coordination with the tourism suppliers. In strategic terms, it calls for the action of an integrated approach to management and marketing. In operational terms, it means the implementation of a better defined, better targeted market-driven strategy for realizing the defined objectives.

The important point to note here is that marketing is applied to situations where the choice can be limited to a relatively small number of brands giving the consumer a reasonable choice. The process of selection thus becomes easier. In the field of tourism this process is taking place by the increased use of 'package tours'. A package tour is a travel plan which includes most elements of vacation, such as transportation, accommodation, sightseeing and entertainment. The tourist product is a composite product, whether it is sold as a package or assembled by the individual himself or his travel agent.

There are many tourism products that are available to the consumer today. In modern times these products, whether traditional in nature like culture and pilgrimage, or modern like adventure, conventions and conferences, health, medical, etc. are being packaged, promoted and priced appropriately to woo as many tourists as possible.

Tourism products can be classified as under for a better understanding of each of their peculiar characteristics, so that they can be marketed and positioned appropriately:

Natural Tourism Products

These include natural resources such as areas, climate and its setting, landscape and natural environment. Natural resources are frequently the key elements in a destination's attraction. Let us look at some examples:

1) Countryside,
2) Climate-temperature, rains, snowfall, days of sunshine,
3) Natural Beauty-landforms, hills, rocks, gorges, terrain,
4) Water-lakes, ponds, rivers, waterfalls, springs,
5) Flora and Fauna,
6) Wildlife,
7) Beaches,
8) Islands,
9) Spas,
10) Scenic Attractions.

The climate of a tourist destination is often an important attraction. Good weather plays an important role in making a holiday. Millions of tourists from countries with extreme climates visit beaches in search of fine weather and sunshine. The sunshine and clear sea breeze at the beaches have attracted many people for a very long time. In fact, development of spas and resorts along the sea coasts in many countries were a result of the travellers, urge to enjoy good weather and sunshine. In Europe, countries like France, Italy, Spain and Greece have developed beautiful beach resorts. North Europeans visit the Mediterranean coast searching for older resorts like Monte Carlo, Nice and Cannes on the Riviera and new resorts in Spain and Italy. Beautiful beaches of India, Sri Lanka, and Thailand, Indonesia and Australia and some other new destinations are more examples of how good weather can attract tourists. All these areas capitalise on good weather.

Destinations with attractive winter climates, winter warmth and sunshine are also important centres of tourist attraction. Many areas have become important winter holiday resorts attracting a large number of tourists.

Around these winter resorts, winter sport facilities have been installed to cater to the increasing needs of tourists. People from warm climates travel especially to see snowfall and enjoy the cold climate. In countries with tropical climates, many upland cool areas have been developed as 'hill stations'. Hence climate is of great significance as a tourism product. The scenery and natural beauty of places has always attracted tourists. Tourists enjoy nature in all its various forms. There are land forms like mountains, canyons, coral reefs, cliffs, etc. One of the great all time favourite tourist destination is the Grand Canyon, Arizona. Mountain ranges like the Himalayas, Kilimanjaro, and Swiss Alps, etc. There are water forms like rivers, lakes waterfalls, geysers, glaciers, etc. The Niagara Falls shared by Canada and the United States is an example of how scenic waterfalls attract tourists. Lake Tahoe in California and the, deserts of Egypt are other examples of great tourist products. Other great natural wonders that attract tourists are the Giants Causeway of Northern Ireland, the Geysers of Iceland, the glaciers of the Alps, the forests of Africa etc. Vegetation like forests, grasslands, moors deserts, etc. has all been developed as tourist products.

Flora and Fauna attract many a tourist. Tourists like to know the various types of plants and trees that they see and which trees are seen in which seasons. There are many plants which are specific to certain regions and many times students and travellers visit those areas especially to see those varieties of plants. Thick forest covers, attract tourists who enjoy trekking and hunting activities. Fauna attracts tourists who like to watch birds, wild mammals, reptiles and other exotic and rare animals. Countries in South East Asia have crocodile gardens, bird sanctuaries, and other tourist products that display the fauna of their region.

Spas are gaining popularity as modern tourism products all over the world. While most parts of the world have their own therapies and treatments that are effective in restoring the wiliness and beauty of people. New kinds of health tours that are gaining popularity are spa tours. Spas offer the unique advantages of taking the best from the West and the East, combining them with the indigenous system and offering best of the two worlds. For example Swedish massages work well with the Javanese Mandy, lulur, aromatherapy, reflexology and traditional ayurvedic procedures. Now various spa products are being combined with yoga, meditation, and pranayama, giving a holistic experience to tourists. Spa treatments are now combined with other medical treatments to treat blood pressure, insomnia, depression, paralysis and some other diseases. People are now travelling to spas and clinics for curative baths and medical treatment. In some countries like Italy, Austria and Germany, great importance is given to spa treatments. In Russia along the Black Sea coast and in the foothills of the Caucasus Mountains, there are many world famous sanatoria where millions of Russians and international tourists throng every year.

Beach tourism is very popular among the tourists today. Tourists of all age groups, backgrounds, cultures and countries enjoy this tourism product. Besides attraction and saleability, beach holidaying has lead to overall development of tourism in many parts of the world. The basic importance of beaches is that they provide aesthetic and environmental value of the beach such as beautiful natural scenery with golden sands, lush green vegetation and right blue sky. The water should be clear, free of currents and underwater rocks. Beach tourism activities include water and land resource use. The water usage involves swimming, surfing, sailing, wind surfing, water scootering, Para-sailing, motorboat rides, etc. The land use has multifacets like sunbathing, recreational areas for tourists (parks, playgrounds, clubs, theatre, amusement parks, casinos, cultural museums, etc.), accommodation facilities, car and bus parking areas, entertainment and shopping complexes, access roads and transportation network. Due to its multidimensional requirements the beach product needs special care. A beach resort needs to be developed as an integrated complex to function as a self-contained community. Environmental management should also ensure the availability of necessary infrastructure in the immediate hinterland to the coastal region in support of the development on the coast to maintain its ecosystem.

Islands abound with natural beauty, with the rare flora and fauna and tribes. This makes islands an ideal place for adventure, nature and culture lovers to visit. This tourist product has great scope as these islands are being developed as tourist paradises. For example, Hawaii, Maldives, Mauritius, Tahiti, Andaman and Nicobar Islands, etc. has developed with tourism activity over the past few decades. The topography is generally undulating and they offer natural scenic beauty with exotic flora and fauna. Most of these islands have places of worship like churches, temples, etc. As an added attraction some of these islands have developed as tax havens thereby encouraging commercial development of these economies. They offer social and cultural attractions as tourists can experience the local lifestyle, local food, fairs and festivals, etc. Scenic attractions, like good weather, are very important factors in the development of tourism. Breathtaking mountain scenery and the coastal stretches exert a strong fascination on the tourist the magnificent mountain ranges provide an atmosphere of peace and tranquillity. Tourists visiting the northern slopes of the Alps in Switzerland and Austria and the southern slopes in Italy and also the Himalayan slopes of India and Nepal for the first time, cannot but be charmed by their physical magnificence.

Man-Made Tourism Products

Man-made tourism products are created by man for pleasure, leisure or business. Man-made tourism products include:

(a) Culture,

(b) Sites and areas of archaeological interest,

(c) Historical buildings and monuments,

(d) Places of historical significance,

(e) Museums and art galleries,

(f) Political and educational institutions,

(g) Religious institutions.

Cultural tourism is based on the mosaic of places, traditions, art forms, celebrations and experiences that portray the nation and its people, reflecting the diversity and character of a country. Garrison Keillor, in an address to the 1995 White House Conference on Travel & Tourism, best described cultural tourism by saying, "We need to think about cultural tourism because really there is no other kind of tourism. It's what tourism is...People don't come to America for our airports, people don't come to America for our hotels, or the recreation facilities. They come for our culture: high culture, low culture, middle culture, right, left, real or imagined — they come here to see America." Two significant travel trends will dominate the tourism market in the next decade.

- Mass marketing is giving way to one-to-one marketing with travel being tailored to the interests of the individual consumer.
- A growing number of visitors are becoming special interest travellers who rank the arts, heritage and/or other cultural activities as one of the top five reasons for travelling.

The combination of these two trends is being fuelled by technology, through the proliferation of online services and tools, making it easier for the traveller to choose destinations and customize their itineraries based on their interests. Today we can witness large masses of people travelling to foreign countries to become acquainted with the usages and customs, to visit the museums and to admire works of art. One way of hastening the beneficial effects resulting from tourism is to bring the cultural heritage into the economic circuit, thus justifying the investments made at the cost of the national community, for its preservation.

Taking an economic view of the cultural heritage of a nation may not altogether be justified, considering that the preservation of its culture is one of the basic responsibilities of any community. But considering the financial obstacles especially for the developing countries, this may appear to be a rational approach. Hence mass tourism can contribute unique benefits to the exploiting of the cultural heritage of a nation and can serve indirectly to improve the individual cultural levels of both citizens and travellers.

Cultural resources have another specific characteristic, which many tourists want to experience the exotic. There will be a great urge on the part of the tourist to visit and become acquainted with the ancient civilization in their quest for novel human knowledge. Culture means the prospect of contact with other civilizations, their original and varied customs and tradition with their distinct characteristics. This entire process creates a powerful motivator towards travel.

Various Museums also attract tourists like Madame Tussauds Museum in London, the Louvre Museum in Paris, Smithsonian Washington Museum, Museums of famous painters like Salvador Dali, Pablo Picasso, Natural History Museum, British Museum, Museum of Modern Art are also popular tourist products. Sites of archeological interest like remains of Mohenjodaro and Harappan civilizations, museums for fossils and dinosaurs.

Sites for historical interest like city of Hiroshima and Nagasaki, sites of holocaust in Germany, tombs of various leaders and emperors. Historical buildings like Warwick Castle, Tower of London, Stratford-on-Avon which is Shakespeare's birthplace, the Roman Baths are all popular with tourists. Even historical cities like Varanasi in India get a lot of tourists due to its status as one of the oldest cities of the world. Stonehenge in United Kingdom, The White House, Buckingham Palace and other places of political significance, are also great tourist draws.

Traditions Pilgrimages

- Fairs and festivals,
- Arts and handicrafts,
- Dance,
- Music,
- Folklore,
- Native life and customs.

A pilgrimage is a term primarily used for a journey or a search of great moral significance. Sometimes, it is a journey to a sacred place or shrine of importance to a person's beliefs and faith. Members of every religion participate in pilgrimages. A person who makes such a journey is called a pilgrim. Secular and civic pilgrimages are also practiced, without regard for religion but rather of importance to a particular society. For example, many people throughout the world travel to the City of Washington in the United States for a pilgrimage to see the Declaration of Independence and the Constitution of the United States. British people often make pilgrimages to London to witness the public appearances of the monarch of the United Kingdom. A large number of people have been making pilgrimages to sacred religious places or holy places. This practice is widespread in many parts of the world. In the Christian world, for instance, a visit to Jerusalem or the Vatican is considered auspicious. Among Muslims, a pilgrimage to Mecca is considered a great act of faith. In India there are many pilgrimage centres and holy places belonging to all major religions of the world.

India is among the richest countries in the world as far as the field of art and craft is concerned. Tourists like to visit and see the creative and artistic treasures of various countries. Every country has certain traditional arts like soap sculptures and batik of Thailand; gems and jewellery, tie and dye works, wood and marble carving in Indonesia; ivory, glasswork, hand block printing, sandalwood, inlay work; are some of the examples of traditional art that attract tourists.

Modern forms include Blues, Rock, Pop, Jazz, Rap, Techno and Hip-Hop. Music also adds to the attraction of a destination. Fairs and Festivals capture the fun loving side and bring out the joyous celebrations of the community. Festivals like Christmas, Easter, Thanksgiving, Eid, Ramadan, Diwali, and Holi and so on, also bring people to destinations where the celebration can be enjoyed. Some popular Fairs which cater to fun and work are Pushkar Mela in Rajasthan, Pret fair in Paris, Magic Fair in Vegas for garments, Hong Kong Fashion Week and various job fairs where people are recruited.

Entertainment

* Amusement and recreation parks,
* Sporting events,
* Zoos and oceanariums,
* Cinemas and theatre,
* Night life,
* Cuisine.

Tourist products that have entertainment as their main characteristic are many. Just to name a few there are amusement and recreational parks like Disneyworld in United States, Hong Kong, Paris, Singapore and theme parks in various countries and cities like Appu Ghar and Fun and Food Village in Delhi, Essel World in Mumbai and so on. Tourists may come to attend sports events and it is also an opportunity to explore the country. The fundamental concept is that all tourist activities have an influence on providing economic benefits and have a powerful influence in some definite locality, like the Olympics in Athens has given immense benefit to all in tourism business in Athens in particular and Greece in general. Many countries organise year round sports events like swimming meets, athletic meets, weight lifting events, cricket matches, baseball and football events and many more such events which encourage tourism. India will be hosting the Common-Wealth Games on 2010 and it is anticipated to give the tourism industry a big boost. Night Life is one of the prime attractions in a holiday. Tourists like to especially visit areas in cities where the night life activity is promoted. These areas are usually lit up with street stalls like flea markets and food areas. Bars, night clubs, casinos and very often open air bands attract and add to the psychological satisfaction and experience of tourists.

Cuisine is very often an understated but highly important part of any holiday. Nowadays there is cuisine from all areas of the world which is found at most tourist destinations. Speciality restaurants serve Indian, Continental, Chinese, Italian, Japanese, Thai, Indonesian, Fast food, Mexican, Mediterranean, and Arabic and so on. However, tourists usually like to eat the local food of the areas they visit.

Business

- conventions.
- conferences.

People who travel in relation to their work come under the category of business tourism. However such travel for business purposes is also linked with tourist activity like visiting places of tourist attraction at the destination, sight seeing and excursion trips. Business travel is also related to what is termed today as convention business, which is a rapidly growing industry in hospitality and tourism.

A business traveller is important to the tourism industry as it involves the usage of all the components of tourism. He travels because of different business reasons-attending conventions and conferences, meetings, workshops etc. Participants have a lot of leisure time at their disposal. The conference organisers make this leisure time very rewarding for participants by organising many activities for their pleasure and relaxation. The spouses and families accompanying the participants are also well looked after by the organisers. The organisers plan sight seeing tours and shopping tours for the participants and their families. In India, cooking classes for learning Indian food cooking from the various states, visits to the craft bazaars where tourists see how artisans make clay pots and other handicrafts, they visit tie and dye units to see Indian printing e.g. Batik printing etc. Women tourists enjoy henna demonstrations. Conferences are events which require meticulous planning and efficient implementation, co-coordinating various activities so that the right things happen at the right time. There are a number of players in the convention business. On one hand are the customers or the consumers and on the other hand are the principle suppliers like hotels, transporters, convention centres, tour operators and travel agencies, tourism departments, exhibition organisers, sponsors etc.

Symbiotic Tourism Products

Some tourism products do not fall into the above categories. Wildlife sanctuary, Marine parks, Aero products and Water sports, Flower festivals are the example of tourism products which are a blending of nature and man. Nature has provided the resource and man has converted them into a tourism product by managing them. National parks for example, are left in their natural state of beauty as far as possible, but still need to be managed, through provision of access, parking facilities, limited accommodation, litter bins etc. Yet the core attraction is still nature in this category of product. These products are symbiosis of nature and man.

In case of adventure sports tourists can be participants. The basic element of adventure is the satisfaction of having complete command over one's body, a sense of risk in the process, an awareness of beauty and the exploration of the unknown. Adventure tourism can be classified into aerial, water based and land based.

Aerial adventure sports include the following activities-

(A) Parachuting, which involves jumping off from an aircraft or balloon and descending by means of a parachute. The infrastructure required, includes an aircraft, parachutes and large landing zones.

(B) Sky Diving, which involves a sky diver jumping off an aircraft or balloon at a much greater height without deploying his parachute initially and opening it after some interval at a predetermined height.

(C) Hang Gliding, which involves running off a mountain or being towed by a winch and essentially flying like a glider where the directional control is achieved by a shift in his own weight by the pilot.

(D) Para Gliding, is the latest aero-sport which has taken the world by storm. A Para Glider is a specially designed square parachute, along with a harness attached by lines.

(E) Para Sailing is a simple sport that involves towing a parachutist to a height of a few hundred feet in the air and then descending by means of a parachute. As a year round activity, Para sailing can be done on land and water.

(F) Bungee Jumping, which requires no equipment except a 'bungee cord' made of nylon fibre of enough elasticity to be able to absorb the shock at the end of the jump. The jumper makes a headlong jump into empty space and the resultant rush of adrenalin makes the experience very exhilarating.

(G) Ballooning, where a balloon is attached to a basket by steel wire ropes. By regulating hot and cold air, the pilot can steer the balloon along any charted course.

Water based adventure sports include the following-

(A) White water rafting which is one of the most important and exciting water sports, which involves riding down water rapids in an inflatable raft which is used to negotiate fast flowing rivers.

(B) Canoeing and Kayaking are adventure sports which begin upstream where the water is wild and white. The gradient best suited for canoeing is the stage near the river's entry into the plains where the trip can be combined with a natural holiday in a forest. Kayaking is appealing as it enables innovation on the river by one or two oarsman seated in tandem.

(C) Adventure sports in the waters of the sea like wind surfing, scuba diving, snorkelling, yachting, water skiing, etc. also offer thrilling activities to the tourists.

Land based adventure tourist products include the following-

(A) Rock climbing which originated as a means of practising techniques for ascending high mountains. It was earlier provided as training to mountaineers but has now evolved into a highly developed sport. The climber moves up, using knowledge of rope handling, climbing, securing one to another, etc. Very sophisticated techniques and equipments are used nowadays to ascend or descend on very steep terrain.

(B) Mountaineering requires trained physical ability and suitable equipment. The higher peaks need better equipment which is also costly. The challenges which mountains like the Indian Himalayas pose attract mountaineers from various countries.

(C) Trekking the mighty Himalayas which spread across five Indian states form a sweeping arc and compress in its expanse a wide geographical variety and contrasting cultures.

(D) Skiing is the practice of sliding over snow on runners, called skis, attached to each foot. There are three types of ski resorts, the first are large towns, second type are alpine villages and the third resorts built for skiing.

(E) Heli skiing is a type of alpine skiing where the skier is dropped to the top of a mountain by a helicopter and then he slides down on his own.

(F) Motor Rally is a sport that tests the navigational skills of man and his endurance with the machine. Motor rallies, grand prix racing, hill climbing rallies, vintage car rallies, sports car racing, etc. are some forms of this tourism product.

(G) Safaris were earlier taken on camel, horse and elephants as an excursion for hunting or a journey. As a modern tourist product now safaris are taken on jeeps and in the form of caravans. Viewing and enjoying nature, meeting the local villagers, seeing their traditions, customs and lifestyle, entertainment and camp fires are some of the characteristics of modern safaris. E.g, Egypt desert safaris. Horse and elephant safaris are arranged in most of the national parks and wildlife sanctuaries.

Event Based Tourism Products

Where an event is an attraction, it as an event based tourist product. Events attract tourists as spectators and also as participants in the events, sometimes for both. The Ocktoberfest organised in Germany, Dubai and Singapore shopping festivals, the camel polo at Jaisalmer, Kite flying in Ahmedabad attracts tourists, both as spectators and participants. Whereas in case of the Snake Boat race of Kerala can be enjoyed witnessing it. Event attractions are temporary, and are often mounted in order to increase the number of tourists to a particular destination. Some events have a short time scale, such as the Republic Day Parade, others may last for many days, for example Khajuraho Dance Festival or even months like the Kumbh Mela. A destination which may have little to commend it to the tourist can nevertheless succeed in drawing tourists by mounting an event such as an unusual exhibition.

Site Based Tourism Products

When an attraction is a place or site then it is called a site based tourist product. Site attractions are permanent by nature, for example Taj Mahal, The Great Wall of China, The Grand Canyon in Arizona, Eiffel Tower, Statue of Liberty, Temples of Khajuraho, etc. A site destination can extend its season by mounting an off season event or festival. A large number of tourists are attracted every year by the great drawing power of Stratford on Avon in England because of its association with Shakespeare, the city of Agra in India with its famous Taj Mahal, Pisa in Italy for its famous Leaning Tower. Some new features have been added to the same product to keep the tourist interest alive in the products. For example now visitors can see Taj by night, music shows have been organised with Taj as the backdrop so that there are repeat tourists.

Other Tourism Products

Health Tourism

Holidaying is generally considered as an investment in health, a subject that presents opportunities of cost-benefit analysis. The medical expertise of various countries has added a new product to the existing tourism products.

People are travelling to various countries for treatment of various ailments and medical procedures like Cardio care, Bone Marrow Transplant, Dialysis and Kidney transplant, Neuro surgery, Joint Replacement Surgery, Urology, Osteoporosis, and numerous other diseases. Even cosmetic surgery, alternative medicines like homeopathy, acupressure, ayurvedic medicines and naturopathy are also becoming tourism products wherein travel companies are offering Yoga and Rejuvenation packages. Tourists travel for what is illegal in one's own country, e.g. abortion, euthanasia; for instance, euthanasia for noncitizens is provided by Dignitas in Switzerland. Tourists travel also for advanced care that is not available in one's own country, in the case that there are long waiting lists in one's own country or for use of free or cheap health care organisations.

Ecotourism

Tourism that combines local economic development, protection of the quality of the environment and promotion of the natural advantages and the history of an area. The combination of all or some of the above mentioned kinds of tourism could contribute significantly to the development of tourism in any country. The availability of tourist packages involving gastronomy, entertainment and information about the cultural wealth of a country should be regarded as a priority issue for tourist agents, as it will reduce the concentration of tourist activity in certain areas and will improve and enrich the tourist.

Rural Tourism

Any form of tourism that showcases the rural life, art, culture and heritage at rural locations, thereby, benefiting the local community economically and socially as well as enabling interaction between the tourists and the locals for a more enriching tourism experience an be termed as rural tourism. It is multifaceted and may entail farm/agricultural tourism, cultural tourism, nature tourism, adventure tourism, and ecotourism.

The stresses of urban lifestyles have lead to this counter-urbanisation approach to tourism. There are various factors that have lead to this changing trend towards rural tourism like increasing levels of awareness, growing interest in heritage and culture and improved accessibility and environmental consciousness, Tourists like to visit villages to experience and live a relaxed and healthy lifestyle.

Ethnic Tourism

Ethnic tourism is travelling for the purpose of observing the cultural expressions of lifestyles of truly exotic people. Such tourism is exemplified by travel to Panama to study the San Blas Indians or to India to observe the isolated hill tribes of Assam. Typical destination activities would include visits to native homes, attending traditional ceremonies and dances, and possibly participating in religious rituals.

Senior Citizen Tourism

A newly emerging trend in tourism, basically for senior citizens or old people who live in isolation, especially in the west, because of daily busy schedules of their children and more importantly the attitudes. The characteristic feature of this type of tourism is that the senior people are less demanding in the form of facilities and services, besides leaving minimum impact on the destination community and their main consideration is on personalised service.

Spiritual Tourism

Many people when living under conditions of stress turn to spirituality. The Eastern world is considered to be very spiritual with many of the new age Gurus and their hermitages. This takes the form of another tourism product, that is, spiritual tourism. Tourists visit places to attend spiritual discourses and meditation workshops. For example, The Osho Foundation, Art of Living Foundation which have centres all over the world, Buddhist Monasteries and Ashrams.

Golf Tourism

Golf has been enjoyed by many for a long time. Earlier it was enjoyed as a sport but in recent times it has developed into a hot tourism product. Many tourist organizations plan promotional packages to woo the golf tourist especially from Japan where the green fees are very high. These tourists take exclusive golfing holidays wherein their accommodation is also arranged near the course and they return after serious golf playing.

Nature of Tourism

The United Nations classified three forms of tourism in 1994 in its Recommendations on Tourism Statistics: Domestic tourism, which involves residents of the given country travelling only within this country; Inbound tourism, involving non-residents travelling in the given country; and Outbound tourism, involving residents travelling in another country.

The UN also derived different categories of tourism by combining the 3 basic forms of tourism: Internal tourism, which comprises domestic tourism and inbound tourism; National tourism, which comprises domestic tourism and outbound tourism; and International tourism, which consists of inbound tourism and outbound tourism.

Intrabound tourism is a term coined by the Korea Tourism Organization and widely accepted in Korea. Intrabound tourism differs from domestic tourism in that the former encompasses policy-making and implementation of national tourism policies.

Recently, the tourism industry has shifted from the promotion of inbound tourism to the promotion of intrabound tourism because many countries are experiencing tough competition for inbound tourists. Some national policy makers have shifted their priority to the promotion of intrabound tourism to contribute to the local economy. Examples of such campaigns include "See America" in the United States, "Get Going Canada" in Canada, and "Guseok Guseok" (corner to corner) in South Korea.

Before people are able to experience tourism they usually need disposable income; time off from work or other responsibilities; leisure time tourism infrastructure, such as transport and accommodation; and legal clearance to travel.

Individually, sufficient health is also a condition, and of course the inclination to travel. Furthermore, in some countries there are legal restrictions on travelling, especially abroad. Certain states with strong governmental control over the lives of citizens (notably established Communist states) may restrict foreign travel only to trustworthy citizens. The United States prohibits its citizens from travelling to some countries, for example Cuba.

Tourist Destination

A tourist destination is a city, town, or other area that is dependent to a significant extent on the revenues accruing from tourism. It may contain one or more tourist attractions and possibly some "tourist traps (A tourist trap is an establishment, or group of establishments, that has been created with the aim of attracting tourists and their money. Tourist traps will typically provide services, entertainment, souvenirs and other products for tourists to purchase, and these will often be at inflated prices.

While the term may have negative connotations for some, such establishments may be viewed by tourists as fun and interesting diversions. The term is somewhat ambiguous; the sort of tourist trap common in the US, for example, is slightly different from that found in Europe.

Tourism is distinguishable from travel undertaken in the past by its mass character, and is now not a luxury only for the upper classes.

Tourism is a luxury, with most people in the developed world and increasing numbers of people living in developing countries engaging in tourism at some time in their lives. Tourism is accepted and accustomed, and has become a good indicator of economic status and is considered necessary for good health and personal being.

Defining Tourism

Tourism is a productive activity that encompasses human behaviour, use of resources, and interaction with other people, economies and environments. It involves physical movement of tourists to locations other than their normal place of living. It involves consumption of goods and services provided by organizations in the process, and generate a mass productive activity, employment and income.

Tourism is a highly complex productive activity. It involves the activities and interests not only of large transport undertakings, owners of tourist sites and attractions, and of various tourist services at the destination but also of all levels of government. Each of these serves the resident population and visitors. For countries delivering the tourist product it makes a significant contribution to GDP, employment, investment and forex earnings. It is a major catalyst for economic growth and structural change. It also diversifies employment prospects.

Tourism is dependant on a large number of economic activities supplying inputs to the industries that directly cater for tourists and producing consumer durables used for tourist activity.

Characteristics of tourism are:

- Constantly operating industry, seasonal fluctuations,
- Labour-intensive industry,
- Lack of barriers to entry,
- Small business predominates,
- Important medium for educational and cultural exchange,
- Sheer numbers,
- Growing levels of consumer expenditure,
- A few producers dominate,
- New tourist attractions are regularly opening,
- Mass tourists products have little differentiation.
- The impacts of tourism are broad ranging (economic, social, environmental)

Two forms of tourism:

- International Tourism.

Travel to country outside residence.

- Domestic Tourism.

Travel within tourist country.

Spatial Pattern

Travel and tourism is the world largest industry. Western Europe and North America dominate global tourist flows. Total world tourism grew throughout the 1980s and 1990s at around 4% per annum. The range of destinations now encompasses virtually all countries in the developed world and many of those in the developing world. There has been spectacular growth in the Asia-Pacific region. Countries which are good destinations have sufficient environmental safeguards and a trained work force.

Tourism has developed in many contexts. Modern mass tourism has origins in affluence of industrialized countries of West Europe, North America, and Japan. Tourism has also expanded significantly in East Europe, Asia, Africa and the Caribbean. It has developed in liberal and western societies and in a variety of physical environments. Tourism has also developed in a wide variety of physical environments, with many different environments within a country becoming favourable tourist destinations. These environments may include:

- Islands,
- Alpine,
- Coasts,
- Countryside.

Factors Affecting Tourism

The tourism industry is multi faceted. Many components of tourism are inextricably bound to other economic sectors, and other forms of accommodation to commercial development. The spatial interaction that arises out of the tourist's movement from origin to destination and factors affecting it lend themselves to analysis.

The Biophysical and Built Environment

- A countries biophysical environment, cultural heritage and artistic life represent integral components of its tourist industry. Various types of tourism have differing requirements for favourable development and some countries will be more favourable for development than others.
- The industry is ultimately located according to the spatial distribution of attractions and access to them, which is largely determined by environmental factors. The tourist destination must offer tings the tourist seeks and needs.

- Tourist behaviour patterns are influenced by environment conditions, and they may place constraints on types of developments. Natural characteristics are highly desirable and should complement infrastructure and attractions.
- Climate is a special consideration, and favourable weather conditions are essential. For each tourist activity there is an optimal climate, and climate often determines the length and profitability of the holiday season at a resort.

Technological Change

- One of the most important variables affecting tourism is technological change. In the twentieth century, transport technology allowed the spread of mass tourism to a widespread array of destinations, which were previously not reachable by rail or ship.
- Manufacturers are constantly developing the capabilities of vehicles. Such developments influence places which can be reached, in terms of social and cost constraints.
- The development of wide-bodied long haul jets i.e. Boeing 747 was a major impetus to the growth of tourism.

Sociocultural Influences

- Participation in tourism is affected by a number of demographic and social factors, such as age distribution, family life cycle, level of education, occupation structure, and population concentration. Demographic and social changes should profoundly affect the propensity of populations to indulge in tourism in the future.
- Increased life expectancy and changing work force composition is also important. Increasing participation rates of women have provided a boost to tourism, because two income families have higher discretionary income. There is also a growing number of DINK's who frequently travel.

Economic Factors

- Tourism is among the strongest performing sectors of the global economy. Tourism is a major source of employment with the provision of accommodation, catering, transport, entertainment and other service industries important. There is also an enormous amount of productive activity generated indirectly by tourism. It is an important instrument for facilitating economic growth because of its wide multiplier effects.

- Tourism is Australia contributes 17.3Bn in export earnings to the Australian economy.
- Changing economic circumstances largely determine the magnitude of the tourist industry. With higher levels of development, the employment structure changes, and a more affluent society creates a demand for tourists products.

Cultural Influences

- Features of historical or cultural interest exert a powerful attraction for tourists. Three major forms of culture attract visitors:
- Forms of culture that are inanimate such as monuments.
- Forms of culture reflected in the normal daily lives of a destination.
- Forms of culture at are especially animated and may involve events such as festivals.
- Tourism is often accompanied by cultural exchanges and cultural enrichment. These contacts can have harmful effects where native cultures and traditional ways of life are weakened or destroyed.

Political Influences

- Governments at all levels and of all persuasions have recognized that while tourism is basically private sector, its impact requires government involvement.
- Government profoundly affects the economic climate in which tourism operates. The government's principal role is to foster the development of the industry that can best prosper consistent with broad economic, social and environmental objectives.

The Relationship Between Production and Consumption

Tourism as a productive activity consists of three major components: the country of origin of tourists; destinations; and routes travelled between locations.

Tourism Generating areas

Represent homes of tourists. These areas represent the main tourist markets in the world and major marketing functions of tourism are found here.

Tourism Destination Areas

Attract tourists by offering what isn't available at home.

Transit routes link these two areas of productive activity and are key elements. They are the main transport component of productive activity. As tourists travel they acquire an experience made up of many different parts. These activities are extremely interdependent.

The Changing Nature of the Production Process

The growth of tourism throughout the twentieth century was closely associated with rising living standards in the developed world. In the first half of the twentieth century the opportunity to travel remained largely the privilege of the wealthier people in society, but periods of rapid growth following WW2 enabled more people to travel. The car and aircraft became the main mode of transport.

A number of important changes are associated with the development on the industry:

- Internationalization of tourism: Tourism has become globalised. The global transportation infrastructure is rapidly becoming an interconnected pathway all over the world. The level of globalization has increased as more countries participate in international travel.
- Organizational developments: The organization of tourism comes from two sources: the government and private sectors.

Recognizing the contribution tourism makes towards a countries economic and social well being nearly all governments have organizations to promote tourism. The extents of their responsibilities vary.

The opportunities which exist in tourism give rise to a mix of large and small scale operations catering for all the tourist needs from origin to destination. As with other productive activities there has been a significant growth of corporate involvement in tourism. Much of the growth in large tourism companies arises from the very competitive nature of many tourist markets and destinations and a drive for greater market share and economies of scale.

Social Impacts of Tourism

Tourism is driven by individual consumer decisions.

Package Tours

The package tour is sold for an all inclusive price, and this is usually cheaper bringing holidays in reach of a much larger section of the market. Consumers have a wise variety of choice. Contiki tours are a good example of a company catering for 18-35 year olds world wide. Contiki has an arrangement with Cathay Pacific.

Small Group Tours

Small group tours are a popular alternative. They utilize local resources and services wherever possible.

Individual Travel

Many tourists are actively planning their own travel experience. They prefer to individualize their own itinerary rather than be locked into a group tour. Experienced travellers are seeking to fulfil specific desires. This reflects the desire of travellers for new and different experiences. More specialized demands has seen tourism as a productive activity respond.

Economic Impacts of Tourism

Increasing the Scale of Production

The profit motive has encouraged development of large scale operations and an increase in the size of the companies involved. Increasing scale is especially evident in the accommodation sector.

The scale of operations in the hotel sector continues to expand. While large hotel chains can exploit economies of scale, the small independents can compete on the basis of cost, and personalized service.

Horizontal and Vertical Integration

Growth in the scale of production and increases in the concentration of ownership and control have generally come about through horizontal and vertical integration. A business may expand or develop by itself or seek to combine with other businesses.

Transnational Operations

Integration in tourism has continued to point where operations become multinational or transnational in nature. The pattern of multinational development varies. Clearly a global marketplace provides greater market potential and opportunities to secure a competitive advantage. Companies wishing to diversify their portfolio will expand activities overseas.

Technological Impacts of Tourism

Tourism receives substantial research funds to facilitate the development of new technology. They change every area of this productive activity.

Consumer Choice

Tourist motivation and decision making are increasingly shaped by changing technology. The Internet has allowed a wealth of information to become available to tourists. Hotel facilities, reservations, and attractions to name a few.

Transport Technologies

Aircraft

Future developments in aircraft will favour larger capacity aircraft, but still subsonic speed. The amount of power to propel aeroplanes increases with speed. Therefore new aircraft are unlikely to travel any faster than existing, but they will have a greater range and more seating reducing the costs of travel.

Land Transport

Transport is now faster and more competitive over long trips. This has come hand in hand with infrastructure development.

Sea Transport

The cruise industry is growing particularly fast. The world's cruise fleet has doubled in the last decade of the 20th century.

Keeping Track of People and Possessions

Computerization allows transport operators to work more efficiently, and generates a wealth of data which can be used for planning marketing activities. Global satellite networks have provided powerful new marketing tools. Technology has transformed the distribution process.

Political Impacts of Tourism

Most governments now actively seek to promote tourism to and within their countries and take steps to coordinate public and private tourism activities and to foster industry growth. Government support has been less forthcoming in some parts of the developed world. In many developing countries tourism is seen as a way of accelerating economic development. Some governments have also encouraged the development of international tourism to further their own political objectives.

The changing political and economic environment;

- Collapse of the soviet union and opening up Eastern Europe.
- Switch from centralized economies to free market economies in China and India.
- Creation of NAFTA.

The Nature of Government Involvement

Tourism Promotion

Primary contribution of governments is to promote tourism both to and within their country. The most direct means is to establish tourism organizations to influence the path of tourism development. Australia's ministry of tourism carries out this role, and its goals include:

- Providè government with a clear statement for future development of industry.
- Enhance community awareness of economic, environmental and cultural significance of tourism.

Facilitating Visitor Entry

Ease of access to a country is a key factor in attracting tourists. If visitor entry formalities are complicated tourism will suffer. Some countries now have visa free arrangements with certain countries.

Transport Policy

The availability, pricing and ease of transport dictates the flow of tourists both within and between countries. The distribution of transport also influences the level of dispersal of tourists. Governments are generally responsible for the provision of transportation infrastructure and equipment. Many airlines have entered into alliances that enable them to reduce costs and increase passenger load. Governments are under pressure to deregulate international airlines further.

General Economic Policy

Government policies have direct and indirect implications. For example policies imposes when governments are grappling with high levels of inflation can reduce disposable incomes thereby limiting spending on tourism. Government taxes, chares and levies increase costs to tourists.

Environmental and Social Impacts of Tourism

Two major issues threaten the long term survival of tourism: environmental degradation; and undesirable social impacts, which often accompany the growth of tourism.

Tourism and the Environment

Tourist developments tend to be located near attractive or unique features of the biophysical environment. Exploitation for tourism often places a heavy strain on such natural resources. The greatest threat is to those which are most vulnerable to natural and human-induced stress. Tourism can contribute to:

- A deterioration of air and water supplies.
- Destruction of natural landscape.
- Damage to vegetation.
- Threats to wildlife.

The challenge is to develop procedures to assess the potential environmental impacts of tourism related developments. Other mechanisms available to address the impact of tourism are regulations, the establishment and management of national parks, preservation of significant heritage sites, and enactment of legislation that helps conserve our cultural and natural resources.

The link between tourism development and environmental protection is critical for the future success of this productive activity. Uncontrolled development could well destroy attraction to visitors. With adequate planning by government the threat that environmental degradation poses to global tourism can be overcome.

Social Impacts of Tourism

Social contact between tourists and residents can be mutually beneficial:

1. Resident population can gain a greater understanding of the visitor's culture as well as demand for traditional activities thereby preserving parts of the national heritage.
2. Tourist patronage brings revenue and maintains these facilities for local use as well. The tourists may go home with a better understanding of the host country and its culture and traditions.

Tourism development may promote mutual misunderstanding, hostility and social tension as residents lifestyles are affected by tourists. This can include prostitution, crime and gambling.

Social policy and provision of community services must become an integral part of tourism planning, by tourist operators and the host government. If this is not done hostility towards visitors may emerge, which could reduce tourist flows and viability.

Future Directions

Tourism is the world largest productive activity. It is embraced by governments as a result of its potential source of income and employment. The future pace and directions of tourisms explosive growth will be determined by:

- Affordability: Propensity to travel will remain closely aligned to prevailing economic conditions.
- Accessibility: As transport technology makes long hauls more affordable, more people will be able to participate in international travel. Destinations chosen will reflect perceived security.
- Accommodation: Tourists will be drawn to destinations which best meets their needs. The tourism industry is attempting to provide travel experiences to meet every budget and situation.
- Attractions: Technology will continue to develop and enhance the tourism experience. Market research will lead operators to promote new tourist products.
- It is likely there will be few barriers to international travel. Tourists will be courted by both the developed and developing countries, for the economic developments.
- Those involved in tourism will have to assume greater responsibility. Both the tourist experience and host population should be considered as does environmental quality.
- A basic strategy in tourism development is to retain and preserve the aspects that set a destination apart. Environmental codes of ethics and development guidelines should be implemented to keep tourism sustainable and viable in the coming century.
- As national boarders open up, the population ages and becomes more affluent, and tourism is promoted increasing numbers of people will travel.
- As a productive activity, tourisms importance within the global economy will continue to grow.

2

Development and Growth of Tourism to the Mid 20th Century

The world as we know it today exists as testimony to, and evidence of, the fact that people travel. Early patterns of travel were fundamentally directed by basic human needs (finding food and shelter), exchange (trade), relationships with natural phenomena (developing new settlements, escaping droughts or floods etc.) and as a result of conquest and conflict (occupation, expulsion, forced migration and resettlement). Such factors still exert considerable influence on a large proportion of the world's population today, with contemporary pilgrimage routes relatively easy to identify, frequently building on established trading relationships and patterns of diaspora and relocation.

From the late seventeenth and well into the twentieth century, motivations such as curiosity, education and social betterment took over as 'essential' travel evolved into discretionary leisure travel, gradually moving from a pursuit of the social elite of the developed world, to a widespread activity of the masses of the developed world, supported by a highly complex network of support structures and services.

It is all too easy to dismiss contemporary international tourism as a leisure activity somehow separate and below more 'worthy' social practices. As a leisure activity, tourism is carried out in 'leisure time', as a temporary discretionary activity, and as a form of 'reward' for, or counter to, daily work. However, the value of tourism cannot be solely judged in terms of the hedonistic recompense it brings to the individual. Nor can its value be solely expressed in relation to the economic benefits that it can undoubtedly generate. Tourism is centred on the fundamental principles of exchange between peoples and is both an expression and experience of culture. Tourism is cultural, and its practices and structures are very much an extension of the normative cultural framing from which it emerges. As such it has a vital part to play in helping us to understand ourselves, and the multilayered relationships between humanity and the material and non-material world we occupy.

Introduction: The Early Years

Travel In the Middle Ages

Travel in the Middle Ages was either on land or by water.

Rich people sometimes travelled in covered wagons. They must have been very uncomfortable as they did not have suspension and roads were bumpy and rutted. Others travelled on a box between two poles. Two horses, one in front and one behind carried it. They were trained to walk at the same pace.

On land the traveller had the choice of riding on an animal-packhorse, horse, ass or donkey, or of travelling in a carriage like the one above, if he was wealthy, or in a cart. The roads were poor and not surfaced as we know them. In the towns they may have been cobbled but in the country they were dirt tracks and in the rainy weather they were quagmires of dirt and mud. In winter, villages may have been cut off for weeks on end. But people had to travel and they made the best of the conditions. But travel was extremely slow.

There were inns for travellers in most towns and some of these inns still exist today. The rivers were forded or bridged and many of these bridges still stand today such as the fourteenth century bridge at Aylesford in Kent. An alternative form of travel was by river. Barges and open boats could sail up many rivers and carry passengers to inland towns. But for travel over a long distance the only comfortable method of transport was by ship.

Travellers in the Middle Ages were not confined to their own country. The Knight, Squire, Shipman and the Wife of Bath in The Canterbury Tales had all travelled abroad. Merchants did not think twice about slipping across the Channel to the wool market in Calais or to Flanders. The soldiers of these times often fought on foreign soil, such as the soldiers who went on Crusades or the soldiers who fought at Agincourt or Crecy. It is not surprising therefore to find records of long journeys.

In the Middle Ages roads were no more than dirt tracks that turned to mud in winter. Men travelled on horseback (if they could afford a horse!). Ladies travelled in wagons covered in painted cloth. They looked pretty but they must have been very uncomfortable on bumpy roads as they had no springs. Worse, travel in the Middle Ages was very slow. A horseman could only travel 50 or 60 kilometres a day.

Some goods were carried by pack horses (horses with bags loaded on their sides) and peasants pulled along two-wheeled carts full of hay and straw.

However, whenever they could people travelled by water. It was faster and more comfortable than travelling by land. It was also much cheaper to send goods by water than by land. Some goods were taken by ship from one part of the English coast to another. This was known as the coastal trade. The main type of ship in the Middle Ages was called a cog. It had only one sail. Furthermore in the early Middle Ages ships did not have rudders. Instead they were steered by a huge oar on side of the ship. It was called the steer board. Today the right side of a ship is called the starboard. It was originally the 'steer board' side. (When you tied up a ship in port the steer board always faced outwards to sea otherwise it might be crushed between the ship and the quay. The left side of a ship always faced the quay so it was the 'port' side). The rudder was invented at the end of the 13th century.

In the Middle Ages people believed they would gain favour with God if they went on long journeys called pilgrimages to visit shrines. Geoffrey Chaucer (1340-1400) wrote the Canterbury Tales about a group of pilgrims who go to Canterbury to visit the burial place of Thomas Becket. They tell each other tales to pass the time.

Development in Road Transport in 17th to Early 19th Century

History

The first methods of road transport were horses, oxen or even humans carrying goods over dirt tracks that often followed game trails. As commerce increased, the tracks were often flattened or widened to accommodate the activities. Later, the travois, a frame used to drag loads, was developed. The wheel came still later, probably preceded by the use of logs as rollers.

With the advent of the Roman Empire, there was a need for armies to be able to travel quickly from one area to another, and the roads that existed were often muddy, which greatly delayed the movement of large masses of troops. To resolve this issue, the Romans built great roads. The Roman roads used deep roadbeds of crushed stone as an underlying layer to ensure that they kept dry, as the water would flow out from the crushed stone, instead of becoming mud in clay soils. During the Industrial Revolution, and because of the increased commerce that came with it, improved roadways became imperative. The problem was rain combined with dirt roads created commerce-miring mud. John Loudon McAdam (1756-1836) designed the first modern highways. He developed an inexpensive paving material of soil and stone aggregate (known as macadam), and he embanked roads a few feet higher than the surrounding terrain to cause water to drain away from the surface. At the same time, Thomas Telford, made substantial advances in the engineering of new roads and the construction of bridges, particularly, the London to Holyhead road.

Various systems had been developed over centuries to reduce bogging and dust in cities, including cobblestones and wooden paving. Tar-bound macadam (tarmac) was applied to macadam roads towards the end of the 19th century in cities such as Paris. In the early 20th century tarmac and concrete paving were extended into the countryside.

Transportation

Transport on roads can be roughly grouped into two categories: transportation of goods and transportation of people. In many countries licencing requirements and safety regulations ensure a separation of the two industries. The nature of road transportation of goods depends, apart from the degree of development of the local infrastructure, on the distance the goods are transported by road, the weight and volume of the individual shipment and the type of goods transported. For short distances and light, small shipments a van or pickup truck may be used. For large shipments even if less than a full truckload (Less than truckload) a truck is more appropriate. In some countries cargo is transported by road in horse-drawn carriages, donkey carts or other non-motorized mode. Delivery services) are sometimes considered a separate category from cargo transport. In many places fast food is transported on roads by various types of vehicles. For inner city delivery of small packages and documents bike couriers are quite common. People (Passengers) are transported on roads either in individual cars or automobiles or in mass transit/public transport by bus/Coach (vehicle). Special modes of individual transport by road like rikshas or velotaxis may also be locally available.

Trucking and Hauling

Trucking companies (AE) or haulers/hauliers (BE) accept cargo for road transportation.

In Australia road trains replace rail transport for goods on routes throughout the centre of the country. B-doubles and semi-trailers are used in urban areas because of their smaller size. Low-loader or flat-bed trailers are used to haul containers, see containerization, in intermodal transport. Truck drivers operate either independently working directly for the client or through freight carriers or shipping agents. Some big companies operate their own internal trucking operations.

In the U.S. many truckers own their truck (rig), and are known as owner-operators. Some road transportation is done on regular routes or for only one consignee per run, while others transport goods from many different loading stations/shippers to various consignees. On some long runs only cargo for one lag of the route (to) is known when the cargo is loaded. Truckers may have to wait at the destination for the return cargo (from).

A Bill of Lading issued by the shipper provides the basic document for road freight. On cross-border transportation the trucker will present the cargo and documentation provided by the shipper to customs for inspection. This also applies to shipments that are transported out of a Free port. To avoid accidents caused by fatigue, truckers have to keep to strict rules for drivetime and required rest periods. Known in the U.S. as hours of service, and in the E.U. as drivers working hours. See e.g. "Hours of Work and Rest Periods (Road Transport) Convention, 1979" or. Tachographs record the times the vehicle is in motion and stopped. Some companies use two drivers per truck to ensure uninterrupted transportation; with one driver resting or sleeping in a bunk in the back of the cab while the other is driving.

For transport of hazardous materials truckers need a licence, which usually requires them to pass an exam. They have to make sure they affix proper labels for the respective hazard(s) to their vehicle. Liquid goods are transported by road in tank trucks (AE) or tanker lorries (BE) (also road-tankers) or special tankcontainers for intermodal transport. For unpackaged goods and liquids weigh stations confirm weight after loading and before delivery. For transportation of live animals special requirements have to be met in many countries to prevent cruelty to animals. For fresh and frozen goods refrigerator trucks or reefer (container)s are used.

Truck drivers often need special licenses to drive, known in the U.S. as a commercial driver's license. In the U.K. a Large Goods Vehicle license is required.

Modern Roads

Today roadways are principally asphalt or concrete. Both are based on McAdam's concept of stone aggregate in a binder, asphalt cement or Portland cement respectively. Asphalt is known as a flexible pavement, one which slowly will "flow" under the pounding of traffic. Concrete is a rigid pavement, which can take heavier loads but is more expensive and requires more carefully prepared subbase. So, generally, major roads are concrete and local roads are asphalt. Often concrete roads are covered with a thin layer of asphalt to create a wearing surface.

Modern pavements are designed for heavier vehicle loads and faster speeds, requiring thicker slabs and deeper subbase. Subbase is the layer or successive layers of stone, gravel and sand supporting the pavement. It is needed to spread out the slab load bearing on the underlying soil and to conduct away any water getting under the slabs. Water will undermine a pavement over time, so much of pavement and pavement joint design are meant to minimize the amount of water getting and staying under the slabs.

Shoulders are also an integral part of highway design. They are multipurpose; they can provide a margin of side clearance, a refuge for incapacitated vehicles, an emergency lane, and parking space. They also serve a design purpose, and that is to prevent water from percolating into the soil near the main pavement's edge. Shoulder pavement is designed to a lower standard than the pavement in the travelled way and won't hold up as well to traffic. (Which is why driving on the shoulder is generally prohibited.)

Pavement technology is still evolving, albeit in not easily noticed increments. For instance, chemical additives in the pavement mix make the pavement more weather resistant, grooving and other surface treatments improve resistance to skidding and hydroplaning, and joint seals which were once tar are now made of low maintenance neoprene.

Traffic Control

Nearly all roadways are built with devices meant to control traffic. Most notable to the motorist are those meant to communicate directly with the driver. Broadly, these fall into three categories: signs, signals or pavement markings. They help the driver navigate; they assign the right-of-way at intersections; they indicate laws such as speed limits and parking regulations; they advise of potential hazards; they indicate passing and no passing zones; and otherwise deliver information and to assure traffic is orderly and safe.

200 years ago these devices were signs, nearly all informal. In the late 19th century signals began to appear in the biggest cities at a few highly congested intersections.

They were manually operated, and consisted of semaphores, flags or paddles, or in some cases coloured electric lights, all modelled on railroad signals. In the 20th century signals were automated, at first with electromechanical devices and later with computers. Signals can be quite sophisticated: with vehicle sensors embedded in the pavement, the signal can control and choreograph the turning movements of heavy traffic in the most complex of intersections. In the 1920s traffic engineers learned how to coordinate signals along a thoroughfare to increase its speeds and volumes. In the 1980s, with computers, similar coordination of whole networks became possible.

In the 1920s pavement markings were introduced. Initially they were used to indicate the road's centerline. Soon after they were coded with information to aid motorists in passing safely. Later, with multi-lane roads they were used to define lanes. Other uses, such as indicating permitted turning movements and pedestrian crossings soon followed.

In the 20th century traffic control devices were standardized. Before then every locality decided on what its devices would look like and where they would be applied. This could be confusing, especially to traffic from outside the locality. In the United States standardization was first taken at the state level, and late in the century at the federal level. Each country has a Manual of Uniform Traffic Control Devices (MUTCD) and there are efforts to blend them into a worldwide standard.

Besides signals signs and markings, other forms of traffic control are designed and built into the roadway. For instance, curbs and rumble strips can be used to keep traffic in a given lane and median barriers can prevent left turns and even U-turns.

Pneumatic Tires

As the horse-drawn carriage was replaced by the car and lorry or truck, and speeds increased, the need for smoother roads and less vertical displacement became more apparent, and pneumatic tires were developed to decrease the apparent roughness. Wagon and carriage wheels, made of wood, had a tire in the form of an iron strip that kept the wheel from wearing out quickly. Pneumatic tires, which had a larger footprint than iron tires, also were less likely to get bogged down in the mud on unpaved roads.

Toll Roads in the United States

Early toll roads were usually built by private companies under a government franchise. They typically paralleled or replaced routes already with some volume of commerce, hoping the improved road would divert enough traffic to make the enterprise profitable. Plank roads were particularly attractive as they greatly reduced rolling resistance and mitigated the problem of getting mired in mud. Another improvement, better grading to lessen the steepness of the worst stretches, allowed draft animals to haul heavier loads.

A toll road in the United States is often called a turnpike. The term turnpike probably originated from the gate, often a simple pike, which blocked passage until the fare was paid at a toll house (or toll booth in current terminology). When the toll was paid the pike, which was mounted on a swivel, was turned to allow the vehicle to pass. Tolls were usually based on the type of cargo being transported, not the type of vehicle. The practice of selecting routes so as to avoid tolls is called shunpiking. This may be simply to avoid the expense, as a form of economic protest (or boycott), or simply to seek a road less travelled as a bucolic interlude.

History, Funding through Tolls

Companies were formed to build, improve, and maintain a particular section of roadway, and tolls were collected from users to finance the enterprise. The enterprise was usually named to indicate the locale of its roadway, often including the name of one of both of the termini. The word *turnpike* came into common use in the names of these roadways and companies, and is essentially used interchangeably with *toll road* in current terminology.

In the United States, toll roads began with the Lancaster Turnpike in the 1790s, within Pennsylvania, connecting Philadelphia and Lancaster.

In New York State, the Great Western Turnpike was started in Albany in 1799 and eventually extended, by several alternate routes, to near what is now Syracuse, New York.

Toll roads peaked in the mid 19th century, and by the turn of the twentieth century most toll roads were taken over by state highway departments. The demise of this early toll road era was due to the rise of canals and railroads, which were more efficient (and thus cheaper) in moving freight over long distances. Roads wouldn't again be competitive with rails and barges until the first half of the 20th century when the internal combustion engine replaces draft animals as the source of motive power.

With the development, mass production, and popular embrace of the automobile, faster and higher capacity roads were needed. In the 1920s limited access highways appeared. Their main characteristics were dual roadways with access points limited to (but not always) grade-separated interchanges. Their dual roadways allowed high volumes of traffic, the need for no or few traffic lights along with relatively gentle grades and curves allowed higher speeds.

The first limited access highways were *Parkways*, so called because of their often park-like landscaping and, in the metropolitan New York City area, they connected the region's system of parks. When the German Autobahns built in the 1930s introduced higher design standards and speeds, road planners and road-builders in the United States started developing and building toll roads to similar high standards. The Pennsylvania Turnpike, which largely followed the path of a partially-built railroad, was the first, opening in 1940.

After 1940 with the Pennsylvania Turnpike, toll roads saw a resurgence, this time to fund limited access highways. In the late 1940s and early 1950s, after World War II interrupted the evolution of the highway, the US resumed building toll roads. They were to still higher standards and one road, the New York State Thruway, had standards that became the prototype for the U.S. Interstate Highway System. Several other major toll-roads which connected with the Pennsylvania Turnpike were established before the creation of the Interstate Highway System. These were the Indiana Toll Road, Ohio Turnpike, and New Jersey Turnpike.

US Interstate Highway System

In the United States, beginning in 1956, Dwight D. Eisenhower National System of Interstate and Defence Highways, commonly called the Interstate Highway System was built. It uses 12 foot (3.65m) lanes, wide medians, a maximum of 4% grade, and full access control, though many sections don't meet these standards due to older construction or constraints. This system created a continental-sized network meant to connect every population centre of 50,000 people or more.

By 1956, most limited access highways in the eastern United States were toll roads. In that year, the federal Interstate highway program was established, funding non-toll roads with 90% federal dollars and 10%

state match, giving little incentive for states to expand their turnpike system. Funding rules initially restricted collections of tolls on newly funded roadways, bridges, and tunnels. In some situations, expansion or rebuilding of a toll facility using Interstate Highway Program funding resulted in the removal of existing tolls. This occurred in Virginia on Interstate 64 at the Hampton Roads Bridge-Tunnel when a second parallel roadway to the regional 1958 bridge-tunnel was completed in 1976.

Since the completion of the initial portion of the interstate highway system, regulations were changed, and portions of toll facilities have been added to the system. Some states are again looking at toll financing for new roads and maintenance, to supplement limited federal funding. In some areas, new road projects have been completed with public-private partnerships funded by tolls, such as the Pocahontas Parkway (I-895) near Richmond, Virginia.

The Grand Tour

The Grand Tour was the traditional travel of Europe undertaken by mainly upper-class European young men of means. The custom flourished from about 1660 until the advent of large-scale rail transit in the 1840s, and was associated with a standard itinerary. The tradition continued after rail and steamship travel made the journey less of a burden, and American and other overseas youth joined in. It served as an education rite of passage. Primarily associated with Britain (particularly the British nobility and wealthy gentry), similar trips were made by wealthy young men of Protestant Northern European nations on the Continent.

The New York Times described the Grand Tour in this way:

Three hundred years ago, wealthy young Englishmen began taking a post-Oxbridge trek through France and Italy in search of art, culture and the roots of Western civilization. With nearly unlimited funds, aristocratic connections and months (or years) to roam, they commissioned paintings, perfected their language skills and mingled with the upper crust of the Continent.

The primary value of the Grand Tour, it was believed, lay in the exposure both to the cultural legacy of classical antiquity and the Renaissance, and to the aristocratic and fashionable society of the European continent. In addition, it provided the only opportunity to view specific works of art, and possibly the only chance to hear certain music. A grand tour could last from several months to several years. It was commonly undertaken in the company of a knowledgeable guide or tutor. The Grand Tour had more than superficial cultural importance; as E.P. Thompson stated, "ruling-class control in the 18th century was located primarily in a cultural hegemony, and only secondarily in an expression of economic or physical (military) power."

History

Essentially, the Grand Tour was a scholar's pilgrimage to Rome, which was home to the Colosseum, considered one of the Wonders of the World, and Saint Peter's tomb. Catholic Grand tourists might be interested to visit the pilgrimage sites St. Thomas' body at Canterbury, and the *Shrine of the Three Kings at Cologne Cathedral*, along the way. These places were not only religious centres, but had been at various times magnets for artists, who won commissions for altarpieces or Royal portraits. Since medieval times, a tour to such places was considered essential for budding young artists to understand proper painting and sculpture techniques. The advent of the printing press and the spread of woodcuts and engravings from the 15th century onwards, had done much to popularize such trips, and following the artists themselves, the elite considered travel to such centres (outside of warzones of course) as necessary rites of passage.

In Britain, Thomas Coryat's travel book Coryat's Crudities (1611), published during the Twelve Years' Truce, was an early influence on the Grand Tour. Larger numbers of tourists began their tours after the Peace of Münster in 1648. According to the Oxford English Dictionary, the first recorded use of the term (perhaps its introduction to English) was by Richard Lassels, an expatriate Roman Catholic priest, in his book An Italian Voyage, which was published posthumously in Paris in 1670 and then in London. Lassels' introduction listed four areas in which travel furnished "an accomplished, consummate Traveller": the intellectual, the social, the ethical (by the opportunity of drawing moral instruction from all the traveller saw), and the political.

The idea of travelling for the sake of curiosity and learning was a developing idea in the 17th century. With John Locke's Essay Concerning Human Understanding (1690) it was argued, and widely accepted, that knowledge comes entirely from the external senses, that what one knows comes from the physical stimuli to which one has been exposed, thus, one could "use up" the environment, taking from it all it offers, requiring a change of place. Travel, therefore, was necessary for one to develop the mind and expand knowledge of the world. As a young man at the outset of his account of a repeat Grand Tour the historian Edward Gibbon remarked that "According to the law of custom, and perhaps of reason, foreign travel completes the education of an English gentleman." Consciously adapted for intellectual self-improvement, Gibbon was "revisiting the Continent on a larger and more liberal plan"; most Grand Tourists did not pause more than briefly in libraries.

The typical 18th century sentiment was that of the studious observer travelling through foreign lands reporting his findings on human nature for those unfortunate to have stayed home. Recounting one's observations to society at large to increase its welfare was considered an obligation; the Grand Tour flourished in this mindset.

The Grand Tour not only provided a liberal education but allowed those who could afford it the opportunity to buy things otherwise unavailable at home, and it thus increased participants' prestige and standing. Grand Tourists would return with crates of art, books, pictures, sculpture, and items of culture, which would be displayed in libraries, cabinets, gardens, and drawing rooms, as well as the galleries built purposively for their display; The Grand Tour became a symbol of wealth and freedom. Artists who especially thrived on Grand Tourists included Pompeo Batoni the portraitist, and the vedutisti such as Canaletto, Pannini and Guardi. The less well-off could return with an album of Piranesi etchings.

The "perhaps" in Gibbon's opening remark cast an ironic shadow over his resounding statement. Critics of the Grand Tour derided its lack of adventure. "The tour of Europe is a paltry thing", said one 18th century critic, "a tame, uniform, unvaried prospect". The Grand Tour was said to reinforce the old preconceptions and prejudices about national characteristics, as Jean Gailhard's *Compleat Gentleman* (1678) observes: "French courteous. Spanish lordly. Italian amorous. German clownish." The deep suspicion with which Tour was viewed at home in England, where it was feared that the very experiences that completed the British gentleman might well undo him, were epitomised in the sarcastic nativist view of the ostentatiously "well-travelled" maccaroni of the 1760s and 70s.

After the arrival of steam-powered transportation, around 1825, the Grand Tour custom continued, but it was of a qualitative difference—cheaper to undertake, safer, easier, open to anyone. During much of the 19th century, most educated young men of privilege undertook the Grand Tour. Germany and Switzerland came to be included in a more broadly defined circuit. Later, it became fashionable for young women as well; a trip to Italy, with a spinster aunt chaperon, was part of the upper-class woman's education, as in E.M. Forster's novel *A Room with a View*.

Travel Itinerary

The most common itinerary of the Grand Tour shifted across generation in the cities it embraced, but the tourist usually began in Dover, England and crossed the English Channel to Ostend, in Belgium, Calais, or Le Havre in France. From there the tourist, usually accompanied by a tutor (known colloquially as a "bear-leader") and if wealthy enough a league of servants, could rent or acquire a coach (which could be resold in any city or disassembled and packed across the Alps, as in Giacomo Casanova's travels, who resold it on completion), or opt to make the trip by boat as far as the alps, either travelling over the Seine to Paris, or the Rhine to Basel.

Upon hiring a French-speaking guide, the tourist and his entourage would travel to Paris. There the traveller might undertake lessons in French, dancing, fencing, and riding. The appeal of Paris lay in the sophisticated language and manners of French high society, including courtly behaviour and fashion. Ostensibly this served the purpose of preparing the young man for a leadership position at home, often in government or diplomacy. From Paris he would typically go to urban Switzerland for a while, often to Geneva (the cradle of the Protestant Reformation) or Lausanne. ("Alpinism," or mountaineering, was a development of the 19th century.) From there the traveller would endure a difficult crossing over the Alps into northern Italy (such as at St. Bernard Pass), which included dismantling the carriage and luggage. If wealthy enough, he might be carried over the hard terrain by servants.

Once in Italy the tourist would visit Turin (and, less often, Milan), then might spend a few months in Florence, where there was a considerable Anglo-Italian society accessible to travelling Englishmen "of quality" and where the *Tribuna* of the Uffizi gallery brought together in one space the monuments of High Renaissance paintings and Roman sculptures that would inspire picture galleries dressed with antiquities at home, with side trips to Pisa, then move on to Padua, Bologna, and Venice. The British idea of Venice as the "locus of decadent Italianate allure" made it an epitome and cultural setpiece of the Grand Tour.

From Venice the traveller went to Rome to study the ruins of ancient Rome. Some travellers also visited Naples to study music, and (after the mid-18th century) to appreciate the recently-discovered archaeological sites of Herculaneum and Pompeii and perhaps for the adventurous thrilling ascent of Mount Vesuvius. Later in the period the more adventurous, especially if provided with a yacht, might attempt Sicily (the site of Greek ruins) or even Greece itself. But Naples or later Paestum further south was the usual terminus. From here the traveller traversed the Alps heading north through to the German-speaking parts of Europe. The traveller might stop first in Innsbruck before visiting Berlin, Dresden, Vienna and Potsdam, with perhaps some study time at the universities in Munich or Heidelberg. From then travellers visited Holland and Flanders (with more gallery-going and art appreciation) before returning across the Channel to England.

Authorisation to Travel

Other Political Hindrance to Travel

Travel outside the boundaries of one's Country had always been subject to restrictions, as we have seen from some of the constraints imposed by the state under the Roman Empire. Few people travelled any great distance, and those that did so were generally involved with affairs of state. Monarchs were suspicious of intrigues and alliances with foreign states, and vetted such travel carefully, issuing letters of authority to members of court, ostensibly to facilitate travel but equally to ensure that they were aware of the movements of their subjects.

Passports have their origin in the medieval testimoniale, a letter from an ecclesiastical superior given to a pilgrim to avoid the latter's possible arrest on charges of vagrancy. Later, papers of authority to travel were More widely issued by the state, particularly during periods of warfare with neighbouring European countries. However, when Belgium sought to require visitors to present passports for inspection in 1882, there was widespread indignation in the British press. The introduction of compulsory passports as a permanent requirement in Britain is of relatively recent origin, dating only from 1916, as a result of controls during the World War I. The institution of a formal immigration service in the UK is also a twentieth-century phenomenon, being established under the Aliens Act 1905.

We should not underestimate the importance of a common currency, and the difficulties and expense incurred when changing currencies while travelling abroad. As we have seen, under the Roman Empire the universal acceptance of Roman coinage proved to be a great facilitator for travel, in contrast to the wealth of currencies even within individual countries in the Middle Ages.

Fynes Moryson, an academic who travelled extensively on the Continent, was to write in 1589 of finding over twenty different coinages in Germany, five in the Low Countries and as many as eight in Switzerland. Moneychangers cheated the visitor and were sometimes difficult to find. At a time when the European Union is planning the introduction of the Euro as a common currency throughout the Union's membership, it is worth our while considering the benefits that could accrue to tourists and the boost which this could give to tourism in the twenty-first century.

The social, political, economical and cultural upheavals in the last two centuries are due to two components: one regards the "revolution" which took place in the ideas' ground, the other one regarding the technical development and innovation. This contributed to the appearance of industrial revolution and division of labour, which rise the productivity's degree, rising the leisure time for employees. As such, countries touched by these two revolutions become more civilized and their people enjoyed a better living standard. As soon as this happened in different countries, their citizens become more and more attracted by different activities regarding the spending of their leisure time.

Tourism became a mass phenomenon. It is noteworthy to be mentioned that the transportation and communication sectors are very responsive to technical developments and innovations; they are absorbed very quickly by those two sectors and this contribute to big social, economical and political upheavals.

"In many instances the great social and political upheavals throughout history have been preceded by major advances in the technology of transportation and communications" 1954, quoted in Gilpin, 1989, p. 56). As it is a human activity with social and economical implications, tourism is touched by the transportation and communication's improvement.

Today, countries which want to enter efficiently the globalization (or regionalization) processes must develop two elements: one regards the integration of their networks with networks in other countries (or if it is possible, the creation of a international "hub" in/from that country's territory); the other one aspect regards the opening needed for receiving new ideas, new people, or put in very few words, being receptive to another people's culture for the rising of human treasury's knowledge. Here it is timely to look at Geneva's previous example. International tourism could fully serve these aims.

Tourist activity has implications on many levels:

- It has a monetary dimension (it generates revenues at destination's place);
- It has a dimension regarding the transfer of ideas—as people travel with their ideas "in their heads and souls";
- It permits cultural interaction between the tourist's (culture) and the receiver's (culture);
- This could start a process of mutual understanding between the nations to whom they belong to;
- As the people from different states understand each other (due to their contacts), the states to whom they belong to will start "rapprochement" to each other, element which in the long run will contribute to the rising of political interdependence between this countries, for the benefits of their citizens, their economy and their society, without culture playing a great role in this "game". This could be a very brave step on the way to political unification of those—until then—two separate political entities. This could be regarded as an Enlightenment characteristic, which has the vocation of universality and in this way, tourism—beside scientific cooperation and trade—could bring in the people's vision the idea of the one humanity which can surpass its specific cultural condition, through the acknowledgement of their allegiance to one global family.

The Development of the Spas

No one know exactly where the word spa comes from, but there are two main theories. One is that spa is an acronym for the Latin phrase, "salus per aquae," or "health through water."

Others believe the origin of the word "spa" comes from the Belgian town of Spa, known since Roman times for its baths. They speculate that the town was so prominent that the very word spa became synonymous in the English language with a place to be restored and pampered.

Modern spas have their roots in ancient towns famed for the healing powers of their mineral waters and hot springs. Travellers would come to "take the waters" and restore their health. The practice of bathing in hot springs and mineral waters dates at least to the Babylonians and Greeks, and knowing people, probably much sooner!

In the 19th century, Europe's great spas were destinations for the wealthy, who went there to "take the waters." Water treatments are still considered the heart of the spa experience in Europe. Today massages and facials are by far the most popular spa treatments in America. The term spa is associated with water treatment which is also known as balneotherapy. Spa towns or spa resorts (including hot springs resorts) typically offer thermal or mineral water for drinking and bathing. They also offer various health treatments. The belief in the curative powers of mineral waters goes back to prehistoric times. Such practices have been popular worldwide, but are especially widespread in Europe and Japan. Day spas are also quite popular, and offer various personal care treatments.

History

The practice of travelling to hot or cold springs in hopes of effecting a cure of some ailment dates back to prehistoric times. Archaeological investigations near hot springs in France and Czech Republic revealed Bronze Age weapons and offerings. In Great Britain, ancient legend credited early Celtic kings with the discovery of the hot springs at Bath, England.

Many people around the world believed that bathing in a particular spring, well, or river resulted in physical and spiritual purification. Forms of ritual purification existed among the native Americans, Persians, Babylonians, Egyptians, Greeks, and Romans. Today, ritual purification through water can be found in the religious ceremonies of Jews, Muslims, Christians, Buddhists, and Hindus. These ceremonies reflect the ancient belief in the healing and purifying properties of water. Complex bathing rituals were also practiced in ancient Egypt, in prehistoric cities of the Indus Valley, and in Aegean civilizations. Most often these ancient people did little building construction around the water, and what they did construct was very temporary in nature.

Bathing in Greek and Roman Times

Some of the earliest descriptions of western bathing practices came from Greece. The Greeks began bathing regimens that formed the foundation for modern spa procedures. These Aegean people utilized small bathtubs, wash basins, and foot baths for personal cleanliness.

The earliest such findings are the baths in the palace complex at Knossos, Crete, and the luxurious alabaster bathtubs excavated in Akrotiri, Santorini; both date from the mid-2nd millennium BC. They established public baths and showers within their gymnasium complexes for relaxation and personal hygiene. Greek mythology specified that certain natural springs or tidal pools were blessed by the gods to cure disease. Around these sacred pools, Greeks established bathing facilities for those desiring healing. Supplicants left offerings to the gods for healing at these sites and bathed themselves in hopes of a cure. The Spartans developed a primitive vapour bath. At Serangeum, an early Greek *balneum* (bathhouse, loosely translated), bathing chambers were cut into the hillside from which the hot springs issued. A series of niches cut into the rock above the chambers held bathers' clothing. One of the bathing chambers had a decorative mosaic floor depicting a driver and chariot pulled by four horses, a woman followed by two dogs, and a dolphin below. Thus, the early Greeks used the natural features, but expanded them and added their own amenities, such as decorations and shelves. During later Greek civilization, bathhouses were often built in conjunction with athletic fields.

The Romans emulated many of the Greek bathing practices. Romans surpassed the Greeks in the size and complexity of their baths. This came about by many factors: the larger size and population of Roman cities, the availability of running water following the building of aqueducts, and the invention of cement, which made building large edifices easier, safer, and cheaper. As in Greece, the Roman bath became a focal centre for social and recreational activity. As the Roman Empire expanded, the idea of the public bath spread to all parts of the Mediterranean and into regions of Europe and North Africa. With the construction of the aqueducts, the Romans had enough water not only for domestic, agricultural, and industrial uses, but also for their leisurely pursuits. The aqueducts provided water that was later heated for use in the baths. Today, the extent of the Roman bath is revealed at ruins and in archaeological excavations in Europe, Africa, and the Middle East.

The Romans also developed baths in their colonies, taking advantage of the natural hot springs occurring in Europe to construct baths at Aix and Vichy in France, Bath and Buxton in England, Aachen and Wiesbaden in Germany, Baden, Austria, and Aquincum in Hungary, among other locations. These baths became centres for recreational and social activities in Roman communities. Libraries, lecture halls, gymnasiums, and formal gardens became part of some bath complexes. In addition, the Romans used the hot thermal waters to relieve their suffering from rheumatism, arthritis, and overindulgence in food and drink. The decline of the Roman Empire in the west, beginning in A.D. 337 after the death of Emperor Constantine, resulted in Roman legions abandoning their outlying provinces and leaving the baths to be taken over by the local population or destroyed.

Thus, the Romans elevated bathing to a fine art, and their bathhouses physically reflected these advancements. The Roman bath, for instance, included a far more complex ritual than a simple immersion or sweating procedure. The various parts of the bathing ritual — undressing, bathing, sweating, receiving a massage, and resting — required separated rooms which the Romans built to accommodate those functions. The segregation of the sexes and the additions of diversions not directly related to bathing also had direct impacts on the shape and form of bathhouses. The elaborate Roman bathing ritual and its resultant architecture served as precedents for later European and American bathing facilities. Formal garden spaces and opulent architectural arrangement equal to those of the Romans reappeared in Europe by the end of the eighteenth century. Major American spas followed suit a century later.

Bathing in Medieval Times

With the decline of the Roman Empire, the public baths often became places of licentious behaviour, and such use was responsible for the spread rather than the cure of diseases. A general belief developed among the European populace was that frequent bathing promoted disease and sickness. Medieval church authorities encouraged this belief and made every effort to close down public baths. Ecclesiastical officials believed that public bathing created an environment open to immorality and disease. Roman Catholic Church officials even banned public bathing in an unsuccessful effort to halt syphilis epidemics from sweeping Europe. Overall, this period represented a time of decline for public bathing.

People continued to seek out a few select hot and cold springs, believed to be holy wells, to cure various ailments. In an age of religious fervour, the benefits of the water were attributed to God or one of the saints. In 1326 Collin le Loup, an ironmaster from Liege, Belgium, discovered the chalybeate springs of Spa, Belgium. Around these springs, a famous health resort eventually grew and the term "spa" came to refer to any health resort located near natural springs. During this period, individual springs became associated with the specific ailment that they could allegedly benefit.

Bathing procedures during this period varied greatly. By the 16th century, physicians at Karlsbad, Bohemia, prescribed that the mineral water be taken internally as well as externally. Patients periodically bathed in warm water for up to 10 or 11 hours while drinking glasses of mineral water. The first bath session occurred in the morning, the second in the afternoon. This treatment lasted several days until skin pustules formed and broke resulting in the draining of "poisons" considered to be the source of the disease. Then followed another series of shorter, hotter baths to wash the infection away and close the eruptions.

In the English coastal town of Scarborough in 1626, a Mrs. Elizabeth Farrow discovered a stream of acidic water running from one of the cliffs to the south of the town. This was deemed to have beneficial health properties and gave birth to Scarborough Spa. Dr. Wittie's book about the spa waters published in 1660 attracted a flood of visitors to the town. Sea bathing was added to the cure, and Scarborough became Britain's first seaside resort. The first rolling bathing machines for bathers are recorded on the sands in 1735.

Bathing in the 18th Century

In the 17th century most upper-class Europeans washed their clothes with water often and washed only their faces (with linen), feeling that bathing the entire body was a lower-class activity; but the upper-class slowly began changing their attitudes toward bathing as a way to restore health later in that century. The wealthy flocked to health resorts to drink and bathe in the waters. In 1702 Queen Anne of England travelled to Bath, the former Roman development, to bathe. A short time later, Richard (Beau) Nash came to Bath. By the force of his personality, Nash became the arbiter of good taste and manners in England. He along with financier Ralph Allen and architect John Wood transformed Bath from a country spa into the social capital of England. Bath set the tone for other spas in Europe to follow. Ostensibly, the wealthy and famous arrived there on a seasonal basis to bathe in and drink the water; however, they also came to display their opulence. Social activities at Bath included dances, concerts, playing cards, lectures, and promenading down the street.

A typical day at Bath might be an early morning communal bath followed by a private breakfast party. Afterwards, one either drank water at the Pump Room (a building constructed over the thermal water source) or attended a fashion show. Physicians encouraged health resort patrons to bathe in and drink the waters with equal vigour. The next several hours of the day could be spent in shopping, visiting the lending library, attending concerts, or stopping at one of the coffeehouses. At 4:00 P.M., the rich and famous dressed up in their finery and promenaded down the streets. Next came dinner, more promenading, and an evening of dancing or gambling.

Similar activities occurred in health resorts throughout Europe. The spas became stages on which Europeans paraded with great pageantry. These resorts became infamous as places full of gossip and scandals. The various social and economic classes selected specific seasons during the year's course, staying from one to several months, to vacation at each resort. One season aristocrats occupied the resorts; at other times, prosperous farmers or retired military men took the baths. The wealthy and the criminals that preyed on them moved from one spa to the next as the fashionable season for that resort changed.

During the 18th century a revival in the medical uses of spring water took place among some Italian, German, and English physicians. This revival changed the way of taking a spa treatment. For example, in Karlsbad the accepted method of drinking the mineral water required sending large barrels to individual boardinghouses where the patients drank physician-prescribed dosages in the solitude of their rooms. Dr. David Beecher in 1777 recommended that the patients come to the fountainhead for the water and that each patient should first do some prescribed exercises. This innovation increased the medicinal benefits obtained and gradually physical activity became part of the European bathing regimen. In 1797 in England Dr. James Currier published *The Effects of Water, Cold and Warm, as a Remedy in Fever and other Diseases.* This book stimulated additional interest in water cures and advocated the external and internal use of water as part of the curing process.

Bathing in the 19th and 20th Centuries

In the 19th century, bathing became a more accepted practice as physicians realized some of the benefits that cleanliness could provide. A cholera epidemic in Liverpool, England in 1842 resulted in a sanitation renaissance — more people bathed and washed their clothes. That same year a house in Cincinnati, Ohio, received the first indoor bathtub in the United States. Bathing, however, was still not a universal custom.

Only one year later — in 1843 — bathing between November 1 and March 15 was outlawed in Philadelphia, Pennsylvania, as a health measure, and in 1845 bathing was banned in Boston, Massachusetts, unless under the direct orders of a physician. The situation improved, however, and by 1867 in Philadelphia most houses of the well-to-do had tubs and indoor plumbing. In England, hot showers were installed in barracks and schools by the 1880s. The taboos against bathing disappeared with advancements in medical science; the worldwide medical community was even promoting the benefits of bathing. In addition, the Victorian taste for the exotic lent itself perfectly to seeking out the curative powers of thermal water.

In most instances the formal architectural development of European spas took place in the 18th and 19th centuries. The architecture of Bath, England, developed along Georgian and Neoclassical lines, generally following Palladian structures. The most important architectural form that emerged was the "crescent" — a semi-elliptical street plan used in many areas of England. The architecture of Karlsbad, Marienbad, Franzenbad, and Baden-Baden was primarily Neoclassical, but the literature seems to indicate that large bathhouses were not constructed until well into the 19th century. The emphasis on drinking the waters rather than bathing in them led to the development of separate structures known as *Trinkhallen* (drinking halls) where those taking the cure spent hours drinking water from the springs.

By the mid-19th century the situation had changed dramatically. Visitors to the European spas began to stress bathing in addition to drinking the waters. Besides fountains, pavilions, and Trinkhallen, bathhouses on the scale of the Roman baths were revived. Photographs of a 19th century spa complex taken in the 1930s, detailing the earlier architecture, show a heavy use of mosaic floors, marble walls, classical statuary, arched openings, domed ceilings, segmental arches, triangular pediments, Corinthian columns, and all the other trappings of a Neoclassical revival. The buildings were usually separated by function — with the Trinkhalle, the bathhouse, the inhalatorium (for inhaling the vapors), and the *Kurhaus* or *Conversationhaus* that was the centre of social activity. Baden-Baden featured golf courses and tennis courts, "superb roads to motor over, and drives along quaint lanes where wild deer are as common as cows to us, and almost as unafraid."

The European spa, then, started with structures to house the drinking function — from simple fountains to pavilions to elaborate

Trinkhallen. The enormous bathhouses came later in the 19th century as a renewed preference for an elaborate bathing ritual to cure ills and improve health came into vogue. European architects looked back to Roman civilizations and carefully studied its fine architectural precedents. The Europeans copied the same formality, symmetry, division of rooms by function, and opulent interior design in their bathhouses. They emulated the fountains and formal garden spaces in their resorts, and they also added new diversions. The tour books always mentioned the roomy, woodsy offerings in the vicinity and the faster-paced evening diversions. By the beginning of the 19th century the European bathing regimen consisted of numerous accumulated traditions. The bathing routine included soaking in hot water, drinking the water, steaming in a vapour room, and relaxing in a cooling room. In addition doctors ordered that patients be douched with hot or cold water and given a select diet to promote a cure. Authors began writing guidebooks to the health resorts of Europe explaining the medical benefits and social amenities of each. Rich Europeans and Americans travelled to these resorts to take in cultural activities and the baths.

Each European spa began offering similar cures while maintaining a certain amount of individuality. The 19th century bathing regimen at Karlsbad can serve as a general portrayal of European bathing practices during this century. Visitors arose at 6:00 AM to drink the water and be serenaded by a band. Next came a light breakfast, bath, and lunch. The doctors at Karlsbad usually limited patients to certain foods for each meal. In the afternoon visitors went sightseeing or attended concerts. Nightly theatrical performances followed the evening meal. This ended around 9:00 PM with the patients returning to their boardinghouses to sleep until six the next morning. This regimen continued for as long as a month and then the patients returned home until the next year. Other 19th century European spa regimens followed similar schedules.

At the beginning of the 20th century, European spas combined a strict diet and exercise regimen with a complex bathing procedure to achieve benefits for the patients. One example will suffice to illustrate the change in bathing procedures. Patients at Baden-Baden, which specialized in treating rheumatoid arthritis, were directed to see a doctor before taking the baths. Once this occurred the bathers proceeded to the main bathhouse where they paid for their baths and stored their valuables before being assigned a booth for undressing. The bathhouse supplied bathers with towels, sheets, and slippers.

The Baden-Baden bathing procedure began with a warm shower. The bathers next entered a room of circulating, 140-degree hot air for 20 minutes, spent another ten minutes in a room with 150-degree temperature, partook of a 154-degree vapour bath, then showered and received a soap massage. After the massage, the bathers swam in a pool heated approximately to body temperature. After the swim, the bathers rested for 15 to 20 minutes in the warm "Sprudel" room pool. This shallow pool's bottom contained an 8-inch (200 mm) layer of sand through with naturally carbonated water bubbled up. This was followed by a series of gradually cooler showers and pools. After that, the attendants rubbed down the bathers with warm towels and then wrapped them in sheets and covered them with blankets to rest for 20 minutes. This ended the bathing portion of the treatment. The rest of the cure consisted of a prescribed diet, exercise, and water-drinking program. The European spas provided various other diversions for guests after the bath, including gambling, horse racing, fishing, hunting, tennis, skating, dancing, golf, and horseback riding. Sightseeing and theatrical performances served as further incentives for people to go to the spa. Some European governments even recognized the medical benefits of spa therapy and paid a portion of the patient's expenses. A number of these spas catered to those suffering from obesity and overindulgence in addition to various other medical complaints. In recent years, elegance and style of earlier centuries may have diminished, but people still come to the natural hot springs for relaxation and health.

Spas in Colonial America

Some European colonists brought with them knowledge of the hot water therapy for medicinal purposes, and others learned the benefits of hot springs from the Native Americans. Europeans gradually obtained many of the hot and cold springs from the various Indian tribes. They then developed the spring to suit European tastes. By the 1760s British colonists were travelling to hot and cold springs in Connecticut, Pennsylvania, New York, and Virginia in search of water cures. Among the more frequently visited of these springs were Bath, Yellow, and Bristol Springs in Pennsylvania; Saratoga Springs, Kinderhook, and Ballston Springs in New York; and Warm Springs, Hot Springs, and White Sulphur Springs, West Virginia (now in West Virginia) in Virginia.

Colonial doctors gradually began to recommend hot springs for ailments. Dr. Benjamin Rush, American patriot and physician, praised the springs of Bristol, Pennsylvania, in 1773. Dr. Samuel Tenney in 1783 and Dr. Valentine Seaman in 1792 examined the water of Saratoga Springs in New York and wrote of possible medicinal uses of the springs. Hotels were constructed to accommodate visitors to the various springs. Entrepreneurs opened taverns where the travellers could lodge, eat, and drink. Thus began the health resort industry in the United States.

Bathing in 19th and 20th Century America

After the American Revolution, the spa industry continued to gain popularity. By the mid 1850s hot and cold spring resorts existed in 20 states. Many of these resorts contained similar architectural features. Most health resorts had a large, two-story central building near or at the springs, with smaller structures surrounding it. The main building provided the guests with facilities for dining, and possibly, dancing on the first floor, and the second story consisted of sleeping rooms. The outlying structures were individual guest cabins, and other auxiliary buildings formed a semicircle or U-shape around the large building.

These resorts offered swimming, fishing, hunting, and horseback riding as well as facilities for bathing. The Virginia resorts, particularly White Sulphur Springs, proved popular before and after the Civil War. After the Civil War, spa vacations became very popular as returning soldiers bathed to heal wounds and the American economy allowed more leisure time. Saratoga Springs in New York became one of the main centres for this type of activity. Bathing in and drinking the warm, carbonated spring water only served as a prelude to the more interesting social activities of gambling, promenading, horse racing, and dancing.

Saratoga Springs in New York had extensive architectural development by the 1830s — a time when the buildings of Hot Springs, Arkansas, were small log and frame structures without particularly distinctive detailing — just basic envelopes to keep occupants from the weather. By 1815 Saratoga had large, four-story, Greek revival hotels. The availability of train and steamship service to that destination by 1832 meant larger numbers of more sophisticated clients. With the exception of specialized baths provided in boardinghouses or small bathhouses connected with the hotels, Saratoga's development during the 19th century was based on leisure pursuits other than baths. Although Saratoga and other spas in New York centred their developments around the healthful mineral waters, their real drawing card was the complex social life — that included pursuits from gambling on racehorses to seeing the latest Paris fashions. Going to the mountains for the summer was a major exodus undertaken by urban dwellers who could afford it, and Saratoga became a hub of summer activity. Private development there featured enormous hotels with great ballrooms, opera houses, stores, and clubhouses. In 1865 the Union Hotel had its own esplanade, with fountain and formal landscaping, and two small bathhouses. Yet, during the 19th century the bathhouses were auxiliary structures and not the central features of the resort.

During the last half of the 19th century western entrepreneurs developed natural hot and cold springs into resorts — from the Mississippi River to the West Coast. Many of these spas offered individual tub baths, vapour baths, douche sprays, needle showers, and pool bathing to their guests. The various railroads that spanned the country promoted these resorts to encourage train travel. Hot Springs, Arkansas, became a major resort for people from the large metropolitan areas of St. Louis and Chicago.

The popularity of the spas continued into the 20th century. Some medical critics, however, charged that the thermal waters in such renowned resorts as Hot Springs, Virginia, and Saratoga Springs, New York, were no more beneficial to health than ordinary heated water. The various spa owners countered these arguments by developing better hydrotherapy for their patients. At the Saratoga spa, treatments for heart and circulatory disorders, rheumatic conditions, nervous disorders, metabolic diseases, and skin diseases were developed. In 1910 the New York state government began purchasing the principal springs to protect them from exploitation. When Franklin Delano Roosevelt was governor of New York, he pushed for a European type of spa development at Saratoga. The architects for the new complex spent two years studying the technical aspects of bathing in Europe. Completed in 1933, the development had three bathhouses — Lincoln, Washington, and Roosevelt — a drinking hall, the Hall of Springs, and a building housing the Simon Baruch Research Institute. Four additional buildings composed the recreation area and housed arcades and a swimming pool decorated with blue faience terra-cotta tile. Saratoga spa's Neoclassical buildings were laid out in a grand manner, with formal perpendicular axes, solid brick construction, and stone and concrete Roman-revival detailing. The spa was surrounded by a 1,200-acre (4.9 km^2) natural park that had 18 miles (29 km) of bridle paths, "with measured walks at scientifically calculated gradients through its groves and vales, with spouting springs adding unexpected touches to its vistas, with the tumbling waters of Geyser Brook flowing beneath bridges of the fine roads. Full advantage has been taken of the natural beauty of the park, but no formal landscaping". Promotional literature again advertised the attractions directly outside the spa: shopping, horse races, and historic sites associated with revolutionary war history. New York Governor Herbert Lehman opened the new facilities to the public in July 1935.

Other leading spas in the country during this period were French Lick, Indiana; Hot Springs and White Sulphur Springs, West Virginia; Hot Springs, Arkansas; and Warm Springs, Georgia. French Lick specialized in treating obesity and constipation through a combination of bathing and drinking the water and exercising. Hot Springs, Virginia, specialized in digestive ailments and heart diseases, and White Sulphur Springs, Virginia, treated these ailments and skin diseases. Both resorts offered baths where the water would wash continuously over the patients as they lay in a shallow pool. Warm Springs, Georgia, gained a reputation for treating infantile paralysis by a procedure of baths and exercise. President Franklin D. Roosevelt, who earlier supported Saratoga, became a frequent visitor and promoter of this spa.

Spa Treatment

A body treatment, spa treatment, or cosmetic treatment is non-medical procedure to help the health of the body. It is often performed at a resort, destination spa, day spa, beauty salon or school.

Typical treatments include:

- facials — facial cleansing with a variety of products.
- massage.
- waxing — the removal of body hair with hot wax.
- body wraps-wrapping the body in hot linens, plastic sheets and blankets, or mud wraps, often in combination with herbal compounds.
- aromatherapy.
- skin exfoliation — including chemical peels and microdermabrasion.
- nail care such as manicures and pedicures.
- bathing or soaking in any of the following:
  - hot spring.
    - Onsen (Japanese Hot Springs).
    - Thermae (Roman Hot Springs).
  - hot tub.

  - o mud bath.
  - o peat pulp bath.
  - o sauna.
  - o steam bath.
- nutrition and weight guidance.
- personal training.
- yoga and meditation.

Recent Trends

By the late 1930s more than 2,000 hot-or cold-springs health resorts were operating in the United States. This number had diminished greatly by the 1950s and continued to decline in the following two decades. In recent past, spas in the U.S. emphasized dietary, exercise, or recreational programs more than traditional bathing activities.

Up until recently, the public bathing industry in the U.S. remained stagnant. Nevertheless, in Europe, therapeutic baths have always been very popular, and remain so today. The same is true in Japan, where the traditional hot springs baths, known as *onsen*, always attracted plenty of visitors. But also in the U.S., with the increasing focus on health and wiliness, such treatments are again becoming popular.

Resort or Place of Treatment

- A destination spa, a resort for personal care treatments.
- A day spa, a form of beauty salon.
- A spa town, a town visited for the supposed healing properties of the water.

Medication or Equipment

- A foot spa.
- A hot tub, in United States usage.
- A soda fountain, in United States usage.
- Spa (mineral water), from the sources in Spa.
- Spas usually offer mud baths for general health, or to address a variety of medical conditions. This is also known as 'fangotherapy'. A variety of medicinal clays and peats is used.

International Spa Association Definitions

Spa-places devoted to overall well-being through a variety of professional services that encourage the renewal of mind, body and spirit.

Types of Spa

- Club spa-A facility whose primary purpose is fitness and which offers a variety of professionally administered spa services on a day-use basis.
- Cruise ship spa – A spa aboard a cruise ship providing professionally administered spa services, fitness and wiliness components and spa cuisine menu choices.
- Day spa – A spa offering a variety of professionally administered spa services to clients on a day-use basis.
- Dental spa – A facility under the supervision of a licensed dentist that combines traditional dental treatment with the services of a spa.
- Destination spa-A destination spa is a facility with the primary purpose of guiding individual spa-goers to develop healthy habits. Historically a seven-day stay, this lifestyle transformation can be accomplished by providing a comprehensive program that includes spa services, physical fitness activities, wiliness education, healthful cuisine and special interest programming.
- Medical spa-A facility that operates under the full-time, on-site supervision of a licensed health care professional whose primary purpose is to provide comprehensive medical and wiliness care in an environment that integrates spa services, as well as traditional, complimentary and/or alternative therapies and treatments. The facility operates within the scope of practice of its staff, which can include both aesthetic/cosmetic and prevention/wiliness procedures and services. These spas typically use balneotherapy, employing a variety of peloids.

"Balneotherapy treatments can have different purposes. In a spa setting, they can be used to treat conditions such as arthritis and backache, build up muscles after injury or illness or to stimulate the immune system, and they can be enjoyed as a relief from day-to-day stress."

- Mineral springs spa-A spa offering an on-site source of natural mineral, thermal or seawater used in hydrotherapy treatments.
- Resort/hotel spa-A spa owned by and located within a resort or hotel providing professionally administered spa services, fitness and wiliness components and spa cuisine menu choices.

The Rise of the Seaside Resorts

History of the Seaside Resort

The coast has always been a recreational environment, although until the mid-nineteenth century, such recreation was a luxury only for the wealthy. Even in Roman times, the town of Baiae, by the Tyrrhenian Sea in Italy, was a resort for those who were sufficiently prosperous. During the early nineteenth century, the Prince Regent popularized Brighton, on the south coast of England, as a fashionable alternative to the wealthy spa towns such as Cheltenham. Later, Queen Victoria's long-standing patronage of the Isle of Wight and Ramsgate in Kent ensured the seaside residence was a highly fashionable possession for those wealthy enough to afford more than one home. Nowadays, many beach resorts are available as far afield as Goa in India. It was in the mid-nineteenth century that it became popular for people from less privileged classes to take holidays at seaside resorts. Improvements in transport brought about by the industrial revolution enabled people to take vacations away from home, and led to the growth of coastal towns as seaside resorts.

British Seaside Resorts

The popularization of the seaside resort during this period was nowhere more pronounced than in Blackpool. Blackpool catered for workers from across industrial Northern England, who packed its beaches and promenade. Other northern towns shared in the success of this new concept, especially from trade during Wakes weeks. The concept spread rapidly to other British coastal towns including several on the coast of North Wales and notably Rhyl, and Llandudno, the largest resort in Wales and known as "The Queen of the Welsh Resorts", a title first implied as early as 1864.

Some resorts, especially those more southerly such as Bournemouth and Brighton, were built as new towns or extended by local landowners to appeal to wealthier vacationers. The south coast has many seaside towns, the most being in Sussex which has the title 'Sussex by the Sea'.

From the last quarter of the twentieth century, the popularity of the British seaside resort has declined for the same reason that it first flourished: advancements in transport. The greater accessibility of foreign holiday destinations, through package holidays and, more recently, European low-cost airlines, affords people the freedom to holiday abroad. Despite the loyalty of returning holiday-makers, resorts such as Blackpool have struggled to compete against the favourable weather of Southern European alternatives. Now, many symbols of the traditional British resort (holiday camps, end-of-the-pier shows and saucy postcards) are regarded by some as drab and outdated; the skies are imagined to be overcast (although British summers from the late 1980s onwards have often been warmer and sunnier than at any other time in living memory) and the beach windswept. This is not always true; for example Broadstairs in Kent has retained much of its old world charm with Punch and Judy and donkey rides and still remains popular being only one hour from the M25.

Many seaside towns have turned to other entertainment industries, and some of them have a good deal of nightlife. The cinemas and theatres often remain to become host to a number of pubs, bars, restaurants and nightclubs. Most of their entertainment facilities cater to local people and the beaches still remain popular during the summer months. Although international tourism turned people away from British seaside towns, it also brought in foreign travel and as a result, many seaside towns offer foreign language schools, the students of which often return to vacation and sometimes to settle.

A lot of people can also afford more time off and 'second holidays' and short breaks which still attract a lot of people to British seaside towns and a lot of young people and students are able to take short holidays and to discover the town's nightlife. A lot of seaside towns boast large shopping centres which also attract people from a wide area and a lot of day trippers still come to the coastal towns but on a more local scale than during the 19th century.

A lot of coastal towns are also popular retirement hotspots and many older people take short breaks in the autumn months.

In contrast, the fortunes of Brighton, which has neither holiday camps nor end-of-the-pier shows, have grown considerably, and, because of this, the resort is repeatedly held up as the model of a modern resort. However, unlike the *Golden Miles* of other British resorts, the sea is not Brighton's primary attraction: rather it is a backdrop against which is set an attitude of broad-minded cosmopolitan hedonism. The resulting sense of uniqueness has, coupled with the city's proximity to London, led to Brighton's restoration as a fashionable resort and the dwelling-place of the affluent.

Other English coastal towns have successfully sought to project a sense of their unique character. In particular, Southwold on the Suffolk coast is an active yet peaceful retirement haven with an emphasis on calmness, quiet countryside and jazz. Weymouth, Dorset offers itself as 'the gateway to the Jurassic Coast', Britain's only natural World Heritage Site. Newquay in Cornwall offers itself as the 'surfing capital of Britain', hosting international surfing events on its shores.

Torbay in South Devon is known is also known as the English Riviera. Consisting of the towns of Torquay, Paignton with its pier and Brixham, the bay has 20 beaches and coves along its 22-mile (35 km) coastline, ranging from small secluded coves to the larger promenade style seafronts of Torquay's Torre Abbey Sands and Paignton Sands. Northern Ireland has a number of seaside resorts, such as Portrush, situated on the north coast, with its two beaches and a world-famous golf course. Royal Portrush Golf Club. Other Northern Irish seaside resorts are Newcastle, located on the east coast at the foot of the Mourne Mountains, Portstewart, and Bangor. Bangor Marina is one of the largest in Ireland and the marina has on occasion been awarded the "Blue Flag" for attention to environmental issues.

Irish Seaside Resorts

Irish Riviera

The "Irish Riviera" features the seaside resorts of Youghal, Ardmore, Dungarvan, Cobh and Ballycotton, all set close to the south coast of Ireland. Youghal has been a favoured holiday destination for over 100 years, situated on the banks of the Blackwater river as it reaches the sea. Youghal is well known for its beaches, having been, until 2008, the only town in the Republic of Ireland with two beaches awarded EU Blue Flag status. Dungarvan is a seaside market town beneath the mountains in the centre of the Irish south coast. Kinsale is often described as a food lover's and yachting town, with a diverse range of restaurants, as well as a large and active creative community with numerous art galleries and record and book shops.

County Clare

Lahinch is a seaside resort, popular because of its long beach, golf links, promenade, and Seaworld (a leisure complex). Lahinch is also popular with surfers. Ballyvaughan is a village and small port on the southern shores of Galway Bay.

American Seaside Resorts

American seaside resorts developed along the New England coast in the late 19th century with the Mid-Atlantic region developing slightly later. Southern seaside resorts did not develop until the 1890s. In Florida, the community of Cocoanut (now Coconut) Grove began development as a resort town in the 1880s with the building of the Bayview House which closed in 1902. Visitors to the greater Miami area then flocked to Camp Biscayne (in Coconut Grove), the Royal Palm Hotel and other resort hotels in Miami, and in smaller numbers to the keys, particularly to Long Key where the Long Key Fishing Camp was particularly active in the 1910s.

Some examples of well known and sought after American seaside resort towns are:

- Carlsbad, California,
- Corona Del Mar, California,
- Coronado, California,
- Dana Point, California,
- Laguna Beach, California,
- Montecito, California,
- Newport Beach, California,
- Pebble Beach, California,
- Miami Beach, Florida,
- Palm Beach, Florida,
- Saint Augustine, Florida,
- Ocean City, Maryland,
- Provincetown, Massachusetts,
- Atlantic City, New Jersey,
- Cape May, New Jersey,
- Fire Island, New York,
- The Hamptons, New York,
- Myrtle Beach, South Carolina,
- South Padre Island, Texas,
- Virginia Beach, Virginia.

Conditions Favouring the Expansion of Travel in 19th Century

Age of Steam

When trains got started in the early 19th century, people thought that moving 20 m.p.h. might cause insanity. On the other hand, it is not speed but an enraging motionlessness — the stalled freeway, or the runway where you sit for an hour or two awaiting takeoff — that causes derangement today. We are spoiled. It has been a while since we sat back in a plane or a car and told ourselves, "Life has not many things better than this". The objective profit and loss have suffered too. Airlines explore the temptations. Amtrak staggers ahead, feckless and insolvent, through train wrecks and slowdowns. It is time to make very large changes — to rearrange the mix of the three basic modes of mass transportation: air, rail and highway.

The answer to the nation's transportation problems clearly lies neither in an expansion of aviation nor in putting more cars on additional highways. My choice would be the oldest mode of the three: rail. It is not a sentimental or nostalgic choice. The aviation industry, like the vast infrastructure for cars, is dangerously overbuilt. In recent years aviation has sucked regional boosters into ill-conceived drives for more airports and more flights, even short ones — all at immense expense.

Airplanes are indispensable for long trips over oceans, over a continent or half a continent. But air travel makes no sense over short distances. In any case, the evolution of cell phones and e-mail and the Internet and videoconferencing means that people need to travel less on business, not more. When ideas and images fly so magically, then our clumsy, inconvenient bodies need not do so — or not so much. Comparisons have been loaded to denigrate trains in favour of cars and air travel. It is true the rehabilitation of the nation's railroads would cost billions. But the arithmetic on costs and energy efficiency argues, in the long term, in favour of boldly creative, high-speed regional rail systems that would take the environmental and traffic pressures off highways and airports. Trains are two to eight times as fuel efficient as planes. As things stand, passenger trains receive only 4% as much in federal subsidies as the $13 billion given annually to the airline industry. Highways receive $33 billion in federal funds. Both airlines and highways have dedicated sources of federal funding: gasoline and ticket taxes. Rail systems should receive equivalent sources of income.

A halfhearted, partly realized plan will only validate the criticisms and doom the new railroads. What is needed is leadership of the kind that Charles de Gaulle demonstrated in backing France's immensely successful high-speed rail, and vision on the scale of President Eisenhower's push for the interstate highway system. The 21st century paradox is that it is not railroads that are old-fashioned and retrograde but rather those essentially inefficient flying machines.

Early Tourism in North America

Tourism in the United States is a large industry that serves millions of international and domestic tourists yearly. Tourists visit the US to see natural wonders, cities, historic landmarks and entertainment venues. Americans seek similar attractions, as well as recreation and vacation areas. Tourism in the United States grew rapidly in the form of urban tourism during the late nineteenth and early twentieth centuries. By the 1850s, tourism in the United States was well-established both as a cultural activity and as an industry. New York, Chicago, Washington, D.C. and San Francisco, all major US cities, attracted a large number of tourists by the 1890s. By 1915, city touring had marked significant shifts in the way Americans perceived, organized and moved around in urban environments. Democratization of travel occurred during the early twentieth century when the automobile revolutionized travel. Similarly air travel revolutionized travel during 1945–1969, contributing greatly to tourism in the United States. By 2007 the number of international tourists had climbed to over 56 million people who spent $122.7 billion dollars, setting an all time record.

The travel and tourism industry in the United States was among the first commercial casualties of the September 11, 2001 attacks, a series of terrorist attacks on the US. Terrorists used four commercial airliners as weapons of destruction, all of which were destroyed in the attacks with 3,000 casualties. In the US, tourism is either the first, second or third largest employer in 29 states, employing 7.3 million in 2004, to take care of 1.19 billion trips tourists took in the US in 2005. As of 2007, there are 2,462 registered National Historic Landmarks (NHL) recognized by the United States government. As of 2008, the most visited tourist attraction in the US is Times Square in Manhattan, New York City which attracts approximately 35 million visitors yearly.

History

19th Century: The rise of urban tourism in the United States during the late nineteenth and early twentieth centuries represented a major cultural transformation concerning urban space, leisure antural activity and as an industry. Although travel agents and package tours did not exist until the 1870s and 1880s, entrepreneurs of various sorts from hotel keepers and agents for railroad lines to artists and writers recognized the profit to be gained from the prospering tourism industry.

The rise of locomotive steam-powered trains during the 1800s enabled tourists to travel more easily and quickly. In the

United States 2,800 miles (4,500 km) of track had been completed by 1840, by 1860 all major eastern US cities were linked by rail, and by 1869 the first trans-American railroad link was completed. Yosemite Park was developed as a tourist attraction in the late 1850s and early 1860s for an audience who wanted a national icon and place to symbolize exotic wonder of its region. Photography played an important role for the first time in the development of tourist attractions, making it possible to distribute hundreds of images showing various places of interest.

New York, Chicago, Washington, D.C. and San Francisco, all major US cities, attracted a large number of tourists by the 1890s. New York's population grew from 300,000 in 1840 to 800,000 in 1850. Chicago experienced a dramatic increase from 4,000 residents in 1840 to 300,000 by 1870. Dictionaries first published the word 'tourist' sometime in 1800, when it referred to those going to Europe or making a round trip of natural wonders in New York and New England. The absence of urban tourism during the nineteenth century was in part because American cities lacked the architecture and art which attracted thousands to Europe. American cities tended to offend the sensitive with ugliness and commercialism rather than inspire awe or aesthetic pleasure. Some tourists were fascinated by the rapid growth of the new urban areas: "It is an absorbing thing to watch the process of world-making; both the formation of the natural and the conventional world," wrote English writer Harriet Martineau in 1837.

As American cities developed, new institutions to accommodate and care for the insane, disabled and criminal were constructed. The Hatford, Connecticut American School for the Deaf opened in 1817, Ossining, New York state prison in 1825, the Connecticut State Penitentiary at Wethersfield in 1827, Mount Auburn Cemetery in 1831, the Perkins School for the Blind in 1832, and the Worcester State Hospital in 1833. These institutions attracted the curiosity of American and foreign visitors. The English writer and actress Fanny Kemble was an admirer of the American prison system who was also concerned that nature was being destroyed in favour of new developments. Guidebooks published in the 1830s, 40s and 50s described new prisons, asylums and institutions for the deaf and blind, and urged tourists to visit these sights. Accounts of these visits written by Charles Dickens, Harriet Martineau, Lydia Sigourney and Caroline Gilman were published in magazines and travel books. Sigourney's *Scenes in My Native Land* (1845) included descriptions of her tour of Niagara Falls and other places of scenic interest with accounts of her visits to prisons and asylums. Many visited these institutions because nothing like them had existed before. The buildings which housed them were themselves monumental, often placed on hilltops as a symbol of accomplishment.

Early Tourism

By 1915, city touring had marked significant shifts in the way Americans perceived, organized and moved around in urban environments. Urban tourism became a profitable industry in 1915 as the number of tour agencies, railroad passenger departments, guidebook publishers and travel writers grew at a fast pace. The expense of pleasure tours meant that only the minority of Americans between 1850 and 1915 could experience the luxury of tourism. Many Americans travelled to find work, but few found time for enjoyment of the urban environment. As transportation networks improved, the length of commuting decreased, and income rose. A growing number of Americans were able to afford short vacations by 1915. Still, mass tourism was not possible until after World War II. During the nineteenth century, tourism of any form had been available only to the upper and middle classes. This changed during the early twentieth century through the democratization of travel. In 1895, popular publications printed articles showing the car was cheaper to operate than the horse. The development of automobiles in the early 1900s included the introduction of the Ford Model T in 1908. In 1900, 8,000 cars were registered in the US, which increased to 619,000 by 1911. By the time of the Model T's introduction in 1908, there were 44 US households per car. Early cars were a luxury for the wealthy, but after Ford began to dramatically drop prices after 1913, more were able to afford one.

The development of hotels with leisure complexes had become a popular development during the 1930s in the United States. The range of "club" type holidays available appealed to a broad segment of the holiday market. As more families travelled independently by car, hotels failed to cater to their needs. Kemmons Wilson opened the first motel as a new form of accommodation in Memphis, Tennessee in 1952.

Although thousands of tourists visited Florida during the early 1900s, it was not until after World War II that the tourist industry quickly became Florida's largest source of income. Florida's white sandy beaches, hot summer temperatures and wide range of activities such as swimming, fishing, boating and hiking all attracted tourists to the state. During the 1930s, architects designed Art Deco style buildings in Miami Beach. Visitors are still attracted to the Art Deco district of Miami, Florida. Theme parks were soon built across Florida. One of the largest resorts in the world, the Walt Disney World Resort, was opened in Orlando, Florida in 1971. In its first year, the 28,000-acre (110 km^2) park added $14 billion to Orlando's economy.

Late 20th Century

The revolution of air travel between 1945 and 1969 contributed greatly to tourism in the United States. In that quarter century, commercial aviation evolved from 28-passenger airliners flying at less than 200 mph (320 km/h) to 150-passenger jetliners cruising continents at 600 mph (970 km/h). During this time, air travel in the US evolved from a novelty into a routine for business travellers and vacationers alike. Rapid developments in aviation technology, economic prosperity in the United States and the demand for air travel all contributed to the early beginnings of commercial aviation in the US. During the first four decades of the twentieth century, long-haul journeys between large American cities were accomplished using trains. By the 1950s, air travel was part of everyday life for many Americans. The tourism industry in the US experienced exponential growth as tourists could travel almost anywhere with a fast, reliable and routine system. For some, a vacation in Hawaii was now a more frequent pleasure. Air travel changed everything from family vacations to Major League Baseball, as had steam-powered trains in the nineteenth and early twentieth centuries.

By the end of the twentieth century, tourism had significantly grown throughout the world. The World Tourism Organisation (WTO, 1998) recorded that, in 1950, arrivals of tourists from abroad, excluding same-day visits, numbered about 25.2 million. By 1997, the figure was 612.8 million. In 1950 receipts from international movements were US$2.1 billion, in 1997 they were $443.7 billion.

21st Century

The travel and tourism industry in the United States was among the first commercial casualties of the September 11, 2001 attacks, a series of terrorist attacks on the US. Terrorists used four commercial airliners as weapons of destruction, all of which were destroyed in the attacks with 3,000 casualties. In the first full week after flights resumed, passenger numbers fell by nearly 45 percent, from 9 million in the week before September 11 to 5 million. Hotels and travel agencies received cancellations across the world. The hotel industry suffered an estimated $700 million loss in revenue during the four days following the attacks.

The situation recovered over the following months as the Federal Reserve kept the financial system afloat. The U.S. Congress issued a $5 billion grant to the nation's airlines and $10 billion in loan guarantees to keep them flying. In the US, tourism is either the first, second or third largest employer in 29 states, employing 7.3 million in 2004, to take care of 1.19 billion trips tourists took in the US in 2005. The US outbound holiday market is sensitive in the short term, but possibly one of the most surprising results from the September 11, 2001 attacks was that by February 2002 it had bounced back for overseas travel, especially to destinations like New Zealand. This quick revival was generally quicker than many commentators had predicted only five months earlier.

The United States economy began to slow significantly in 2007, mostly because of a real-estate slump, gas prices and related financial problems. Many economists believe that the economy entered a recession at the end of 2007 or early in 2008. Some state budgets for tourism marketing have decreased, such as Connecticut which is facing soaring gas prices.

Landmarks

As of 2007, there are 2,462 registered National Historic Landmarks (NHL) recognized by the United States government. The majority of these are located in New York, California, Massachusetts and Pennsylvania. Each major US city has thousands of landmarks. For example, New York City has 23,000 landmarks designated by the Landmarks Preservation Commission. These landmarks include various individual buildings, interiors, historic districts, and scenic sites which define the culture and character of New York City.

Natural Wonders

The Grand Canyon is one of the most well known landmarks in the US. Other landmarks include Mount Rushmore, the Apalachians, the Rocky Mountains, and Stone Mountain.

Sport

Since the 1960s, sport has become an international affair, attracting a considerable amount of media attention, revenue, participants and political interest. Estimates of the US sports industry's size vary from $213 billion to $410 billion. In 1997, 25% of tourism receipts in the United States were related to sports tourism; this would have valued the market at approximately $350 billion annually. The nature of the sport's media relationship has been distinctly shaped by the emergence of American capitalism since the 1830s. Sports in the United States have attracted tourists for many decades. The 1997 New York City Marathon attracted 12,000 visitors from outside the US of 28,000 participants.

Attractions

Today, a wide range of tourist attractions exist in the United States such as amusement parks, festivals, gambling, golf courses, historical buildings and landmarks, hotels, museums, galleries, outdoor recreation, spas, restaurants and sports. In 2008, the most visited tourist sites in the US were:

Place	*Location*	*Visitors (millions)*
Times Square	New York, New York	35
Las Vegas Strip	Las Vegas, Nevada	31
National Mall and Memorial Parks	Washington, D.C.	24
Faneuil Hall Marketplace	Boston, Massachusetts	20
Magic Kingdom	Orlando, Florida	17.1
Disneyland Park	Anaheim, California	14.9
Fisherman's Wharf/Golden Gate Area	San Francisco, California	14
Niagara Falls	New York	12
Great Smoky Mountains National Park	North Carolina and Tennessee	9.4
Navy Pier	Chicago, Illinois	8.6
Lake Mead National Recreation Area	Las Vegas, Nevada	7.6
Universal Orlando Resort	Orlando, Florida	6.2
SeaWorld Orlando	Orlando, Florida	6
San Antonio River Walk	San Antonio, Texas	5.1
Salt Lake Temple	Salt Lake City, Utah	5
Delaware Water Gap National Recreation Area	New Jersey and Pennsylvania	4.8
Universal Studios Hollywood	Universal City, California	4.7
Metropolitan Museum of Art	New York City, N.Y	4.5
Waikiki Beach	Oahu, Hawaii	4.5
Grand Canyon	Arizona	4.41
Busch Gardens Africa	Tampa, Florida	4.4
Cape Cod National Seashore	Barnstable County, Massachusetts	4.35
SeaWorld San Diego	San Diego, California	4.26
American Museum of Natural History	Manhattan, New York City	4
Atlantic City Boardwalk	Atlantic City, New Jersey	4

Other Late-nineteenth-century Development

At the end of the nineteenth century, however, there began to be signs that a rapidly developing tourism industry, treated as a part of the economy, might threaten nature and culture. In 1913, Prof. Jan Gwalbert Pawlikowski, a lawyer, alpinist and one of the most active nature protectors, wrote in his prophetic work *Culture and Nature:* "Some people, moved by the beauty of nature, wanted to share their impressions with others and started to facilitate access to it by building roads, trails and shelters. A docile public understood that nature must be beautiful, for the spirit of the epoch demanded it. Seriously, modern man needs some comfort, so shelters were replaced by hotels which the catering and alcoholic beverage business eagerly supported. Would this not be in the interest of a superior level of excellence, since the public's love of nature would contribute to the national wealth? So, the trails were equipped with railings and guideposts, narrow paths were turned into roads and, eventually, engineering skill achieved a miracle: in the manner of Herostratus, it violated mountains by building railways up to their summits."

Unfortunately, subsequent development confirmed the accuracy of this diagnosis, and not only in mountain regions. The next decades were dominated by economic and consumer interests that disregarded the consequent environmental devastation. A certain disillusionment came about by the end of the 1960s, a period that can be recognized as a turning-point for the awakening of ecological consciousness on a global scale. People started to look for ways of reconciling economic development with ecological security, a quest which, in a theoretical sense, has been crowned with the World Conservation Strategy.

In terms of tourism, this change in emphasis was possible because, alongside the vast commercial tourist industry, there had continued a strong trend of traditional nature tourism, based on the knowledge, joy and satisfaction resulting from contacts with nature, historical monuments and people of different cultures-a form of tourism where physical effort is not viewed as a nuisance but as a source of satisfaction, that wonderful feeling that occurs on the top of a mountain after long hours of climbing. Tourist adventures can be experienced either alone or with companions. In the latter case, there is an additional humanistic aspect: the consciousness of a close rely. The 20th century saw a massive increase in the amount of leisure time and disposable income that the British population had. This was reflected in their sudden demand for more leisure opportunities. The public wanted bigger, better and more extreme leisure activities. Sports developed into national pastimes, as it became cheaper for people to travel around the country following football teams and rugby games.

The 20th century was also the time of great technological change. It saw cinemas, music, computers, game consoles and the internet play an even greater role in the lifestyles of both the young and the old. Not only were there now new forms of leisure, but the development of aeroplanes and the increase in holiday parks also meant that more people than ever before could afford to go on holiday, both in Great Britain and abroad.

3

The Era of Popular Tourism: 1950 to the 21st Century

During the twentieth century it grew into what is widely described as the world's largest industry and, for many destinations, it represents a vital source of income, foreign exchange and employment. More importantly, however, tourism is about people. The annual number of international arrivals reached almost 690 million by the end of the last century this figure has continued to increase into the twenty-first century – by 2006, international arrivals had exceeded 840 million. Moreover, an estimated six times that number participate in domestic tourism each year, figures which represent an enormous, yet temporary, migration of people both across international borders and within their own countries.

Tourism has had a long history. Some commentators place its origins in mediaeval pilgrimages, some in the Grand Tours of the eighteenth and nineteenth century, and others in the railway age world of the spa, mountain and seaside resort. But the real rise of tourism as a major pursuit and as a major industry begins in the post war period. UN World Tourism Organization statistics begin in 1950, when 25 million international travellers were recorded. Then the meteoric rise of the tourism industry began, with average year on year growth rates of 6.5% over the period 1950-2007. The year 2007 saw 903 million international arrivals world wide. UNWTO looks forward to 1.6 billion international arrivals by 2020. And far greater numbers holiday in their own countries: it is much easier however to count international arrivals. After 50 plus years of growth, no one working in the industry today can personally recall the pre-growth era. Growth – in numbers – in geographical impacts – in product terms – is regarded as an ongoing and given norm.

But tourism growth can have serious impacts on the environment and the world's peoples:

- It can have powerful physical impacts on places visited-farm and forest land swept away for airport and road construction, hotels and golf courses-often in scenic regions. Physical impacts can be complex and far-reaching-ski run development clearing trees can open the way to soil erosion, leading to landslides and potential major disasters. Heavily used areas can suffer erosion from sheer numbers of visitors-mountain erosion in the Alps, and Himalayas are classic examples. Whole ecosystems can be damaged.
- It can have serious cultural impacts. Tourists are wealthy and demanding guests. They can dismiss local customs, turn land values and labour markets upside down, make local languages redundant, and shift the balance of political power in favour of distant multinationals. In some scenarios tourism can bring vice and crime.
- More subtly, tourism can destroy the future it promises by rendering the destination dependent on its dollars, then declaring a spoilt destination unfashionable and redundant. This, the operation of the tourism cycle, can effect both large resorts and rural retreats, rich and poor countries alike. Tourism is a volatile, fashion industry: it needs to be understood and well managed.
- In recent years, the impacts of the transport systems that are fundamental to modern tourism growth have been increasingly recognised. They burn large quantities of fuel in a fuel hungry world; they produce large quantities of emissions in a world beset by climate change issues. Climate Change and Transport Issues are major issues that loom over the world of tourism and sustainable tourism.

Sustainable tourism was designed not to stop tourism but to manage it in the interests of all three parties involved-the host habitats and communities, the tourists and the industry itself. It seeks a balance between development and conservation. It seeks to find the best form of tourism for an area taking into account its ecology and its culture. It may mean limits to growth, or in some cases no growth at all. The precautionary principle is important here. Sustainable tourism seeks not just to plan for tourism, but to integrate tourism into a balanced relationship with broader economic development. That is the way in which sustainable tourism fulfils its requirement to think holistically, and one of its approaches to responsibility in business, the triple bottom line.

In many rural areas the watchword is that tourism should be a tool for rural conservation, service retention and diverse development-not just a business for its own sake. In many urban areas, tourism can also work with heritage conservation by using redundant historic buildings for tourism purposes, by injecting tourism expenditures into areas needing urban regeneration, and by bringing jobs and re-training to areas with unemployment/social problems.

But there is a key caveat. Sustainable development cannot be created by planning alone: it needs to work with the market and it needs to work with businesses great and small.

Progress and Problems

Sustainable tourism began as a purely reactive concept to the above issues, trying to stop negative change. Early outlines simply listed the negative impacts down the left side of the page and then had a wish list of their opposites, presumed to be positive outcomes, down the right side of the page. To be fair to their authors, there were no research findings or exemplars of successful sustainable tourism to draw on. Only gradually did sustainable tourism become pro-active, trying to create positive change. Many commentators – professional as well as amateur – enjoy criticising tourism. The key to achieving sustainable tourism is, however, to carry out analytical review and criticism, then implement effective management techniques, and then carry on a rolling review, criticism and management process.

Tourism Since World War

In 1945 there was practically no tourism. World War II sort of got in the way.

Most people who travelled did so by train or ship. Air travel was still very early in development. Since 1945 the highways have gotten better. Enter interstates. More people travel by car. Train travel (sadly) has declined in the U.S., though it remains strong in many other countries.

- Air travel has boomed. Ship travel is now largely cruise-oriented.
- Travel is more expensive in some ways, but cheaper in others.

- Many more people have travelled in 2006 than had travelled—other than through military service—in 1945.

According to the World Tourism Organization (WTO) international tourist arrivals grew from 93 million in 1963 to 284 million in 1981 *(WTO 1997)*. By 1990 arrivals had reached 456 million and are expected to double by 2010 *(WTO 1997)*. However, after the recent international terrorist events these expectations are not likely to be met. It appears that the stage is set for the continued growth of tourism in the developed world in the quaternary sector of the economy. Many developing nations are also moving towards a more service-based economy as governments begin to comprehend the potential economic magnitude of the industry. In recent years the most rapid growth of the tourism industry has been in the developing world. In these countries tourism makes up a substantial portion of their gross national and gross domestic products as well as a major portion of their foreign earnings. Many scholars feel these countries show the greatest prospects for continued growth. However, tourism is not a panacea for the economic crises of the developing world although it has become an economic fact in today's society.

Government Policy in the Mass Market Era

Marketing is indispensable part of any substantive tourism enterprise. As the market is expanding, the role of marketing as a driving force in a business endeavour is also being recognized. With growing competition, organisations in tourism business have no option but to do organised and targeted marketing. An organised approach to marketing always helps, whether it is on the tour operator end or at destinations. Guides, escorts, restaurants, hotels, transporters, shops etc. compete one another to stay ahead. A proper tourism marketing strategy calls for close cooperation between the government, tourism industry and the local population.

Evolution of Marketing

Marketing as a concept has evolved in the last 30 years. Development of marketing has three distinct stages: Production Era, Sales Era and Marketing Era. Marketing era arrived when organizations began producing what they could sell rather than trying to sell what they manufactured. While planning and designing a product, customers' needs, tastes and satisfaction were considered. Growth of competition prompted organisations to frame marketing techniques.

Change in travelling trends also made it necessary to adopt new approach. The emergence of long haul traveller prompted the need for marketing research which studied market trends, consumer behaviour and ascertained procedure to make products which satisfied the users of tourism products. Gradual social and economic development culminated in segmentation of mass market into specialized target markets. Tackling these markets needed an approach which was in tune with new times.

Selling and Marketing

Selling and Marketing are different concepts. Selling focuses on the needs of the seller while marketing concentrates on buyers' needs. A marketing oriented organisation focuses on customer needs and earns profits through customer satisfaction. Several organizations in tourism field are product oriented. They emphasise on the available services of products but ignore consumers' requirements. A marketing oriented tourist organisation has a completely different approach. They offer services around the tourists' needs.

Marketing and Travel Industry

Marketing is an important part of any tourism agency. As the market is growing, the role of marketing as a driving force in a business endeavour is also being acknowledged. With growing competition, organisations in tourism business have no option but to do organised and targeted marketing. An organised approach to marketing always helps, whether it is on the tour operator end or at destinations. Guides, escorts, restaurants, hotels, transporters, shops etc. compete one another to stay ahead. A proper tourism marketing strategy calls for close cooperation between the government, tourism industry and the local population. Marketing as a concept has evolved in the last 30 years. Development of marketing has three distinct stages: Production Era, Sales Era and Marketing Era. Marketing era arrived when organizations began producing what they could sell rather than trying to sell what they manufactured. While planning and designing a product, customers' needs, tastes and satisfaction were considered. Growth of competition prompted organisations to frame marketing techniques. Change in travelling trends also made it necessary to adopt new approach. The emergence of long haul traveller prompted the need for marketing research which studied market trends, consumer behaviour and ascertained procedure to make products which satisfied the users of tourism products. Gradual social and economic development culminated in segmentation of mass market into specialized target markets. Tackling these markets needed an approach which was in tune with new times. Selling and Marketing are different concepts. Selling focuses on the needs of the seller while marketing concentrates on buyers' needs. A marketing oriented organisation focuses on customer needs and earns profits through customer satisfaction. Several organizations in tourism field are product oriented. They emphasise on the available services of products but ignore consumers' requirements. A marketing oriented tourist organisation has a completely different approach. They offer services around the tourists' needs.

The Growing Importance of Business Travel

Despite the economic downturn, the flight cuts and the reduction of business trips, business travel to Asia is experiencing continued growth. Several airlines are profiting from business travel to Asia.

According to *Air Transport Association* analyses compiled for The New York Times, *American Airlines*' revenue for flights to and from Japan and China grew 12.8 percent for the first three months of 2008, greater growth than in any other region. That region also saw the biggest growth in average fares paid, 12.2 percent.

The report shows that 996 nonstop flights a week were scheduled in the third quarter of 2008 from the United States to Asian countries, more than ever before. Los Angeles is the most popular departure city from the United States, with 180 flights a week. Narita Airport in Tokyo is the most frequent destination, with 380 arrivals a week.

Among the factors driving this growth, there is the economic boom in China and India translating to more business travel between East and West.

However, The New York Times reports, *Mary Tabacchi*, a *Cornell University* associate professor who has tracked airline trends for 15 years, attributes this growth also to another factor, the new bigger planes used for long-haul flights. They can carry more fuel, eliminating the need for extra landings and takeoffs, which use more fuel.

The newspaper says major airlines are asking the *Department of Transportation* to negotiate with Asian countries to open traditionally restricted rights to sky routes in the East.

Gary Dorman, an airline expert and senior vice president with NERA Economic Consulting, says: "If they (the airlines) can establish brand dominance now, they will be one step ahead of their competition as conditions improve". The importance of Business Tourism continues to expand around the world, with a growing number of destinations entering the market for Conferences, Exhibitions and Incentive Travel. In most countries in the developed world, income from Business Tourism now represents between one-third and one-quarter of all tourism spending. Destinations in the developing world have also understood the potential benefits of Business Tourism, and in such countries investment in facilities for Conferences and Exhibitions is at an all-time high.

The worldwide expansion of Business Tourism has been matched by increased interest, on the part of educators and researchers, in the phenomenon of business events as an academic subject and as a field of theoretical and empirical investigation. As a result, there has been considerable growth in the number of Universities offering courses related to Business Tourism and Business Events, and research in this field is increasing.

The All-inclusive Holiday

The all inclusive vacation has become one of the most popular ways for people to take a holiday in recent years. This type of vacation offers a few advantages and disadvantages, which we'll go over, but this can be a very cost effective way to enjoy a holiday. Depending on what you look for in a trip and what needs you have, this can be an excellent choice. On the other hand, for certain kinds of vacationers an all inclusive package might not be for them.

There are two primary types of all inclusive vacations – the all inclusive resort destination and the all inclusive cruise. There are fewer all inclusive cruises because typically there will be many extra costs for port fees and other travel costs. However, there is an abundance of all inclusive holiday packages that include airfare, hotels, food, and drinks, along with some activities that are offered to tropical destinations around the world. Bermuda, the Dominican Republic, Jamaica, and Mexico are among the many places that offer these all inclusive package vacations.

The best thing about these vacations is their cost and ease. There is no hassle in booking an all inclusive vacation package since it is all completed in one fell swoop; whereas, on a normal holiday you might have to book a flight, transportation to a hotel, living accommodations, pick out restaurants, decide which activities to participate in and more, but with an all inclusive resort that is all taken care of from the outset.

Also, because of the package deal these holidays tend to be the most affordable way to go on vacation. Especially when you consider the cost of food and beverages into a holiday, you can save hundreds of dollars by going to an all inclusive resort rather than by booking a more traditional vacation.

The only downside is that you are somewhat limited to the resort, or you defeat the purpose of saving yourself that time and money. Many people simply want to lie in the sun and enjoy the pool or beach, and for them the all inclusive vacation is perfect. For those who like to get out and experience local culture and see the sites and sounds that are off the tourists' beaten path, the all inclusive vacation may not be for them. You also need to read the fine print carefully when booking your vacation. Some all inclusive packages will note that they only provide for one meal or a set number of alcoholic beverages, whereas others provide all meals and drinks regardless. Be sure you so, there are ups and downs to an all inclusive resort vacation, as there are to any type of vacation. For those who want to just enjoy themselves and to be able to afford a vacation they might not otherwise be able to, an all inclusive vacation package can be a great alternative. For travellers who prefer getting off the beaten path and immersing themselves in local culture, a more traditional vacation may be the way to go instead.

Planning a family holiday is a really difficult task, particularly when you have real money on the line. Plus, how many of us actually have relatives who work with travel agency, who will help us scout for the best holiday plan. I am sure many of us don't. Thus, it is always better for us to choose an inclusive package holiday to help us cut down the time required to do the planning.

A cheap package holiday is an all inclusive holiday and it is similar to buying items in bulk. The more you buy, the better value you will get for your money. When you are planning a holiday, it is very important that you know whether you are going to use a travel agent or you are going to do it yourself via online booking. Regardless of your decision, it is really important that you do your planning at least two weeks in advance.

When you are going on a trip, you should be thinking of its duration and how long you are going to stay. Taking the cheap buying in bulk approach, it is more beneficial for you to stay longer. But of course, the decision is yours to make. There are cheap package holidays that last for a weekend and there are some that last for at least a month.

Make your judgment call. I will provide you an example of the duration of your trip and why it is better to stay as long as possible. If you take the weekend holiday packages, you will actually spend more for fewer activities, even though entertainment and leisure are covered by the package.

Accommodation is another issue. While accommodation is already fixed in most holiday packages, you can choose one that suits your needs. For instance, will you be staying in hotels or holiday villas? If you value privacy, staying in a holiday villa is better. The opposite is true if you would like to have more convenience.

The key here is to take affordable holiday packages as a whole. In fact, companies that structure the cheap holiday package deals are playing the number game. The bigger the turnover, the more they will make. These companies are also thrilled to accommodate a group for a longer duration because it is less risky. It is better for them to have a steady income over the long term than a sporadic one from some weekend holiday deals. Even though the weekend package is cheaper, travel companies run a higher risk of making less money in the long run. So, take advantage of this and make your trip as long as possible.

The rule of thumb is to stay for at least a week. This is the most efficient way to make use of a cheap all inclusive package holiday. You will have lots of fun and you will get the most bang for your bucks if and only if you give your vacation some time. You know what you're paying for before you book your vacation.

Mass-market Tourism in its Maturity

Introduction/Background

Accordingly, one of the most important developments in the tourism markets is the growing attention for service quality from such customer's perspective. This is the consequence of the increase of the degree of dominance of the customer in the service process. This degree of dominance is high if the customer can dictate his/her demands to the service provider and is low if the service organization can dictate its demands. The latter often occurs if the service provider has specific knowledge or know-how, or if he has the power to put the customer in dependent position. There is ample growth and encouragement issues pointing to the tourism ways as these issues involve addressing some of its economic perspective that stresses changes in its market conditions which affect people's motivation to travel and the factors which influence their ability to do so, for example increased leisure time and disposable income, improved technology and travel organization, as in tourism's ability to generate income, jobs and corporate profits, bring in foreign exchange, boost tax revenues, diversify the economy and aid regional development.

The successful integration of tourism development into such destination should make the development more acceptable to local residents and existing resource users than when tourism development is imposed in a segregated and unrelated manner. Successful integration can also be a much more efficient process. To most planners, developers and managers efficiency is a goal to be achieved, and steps and processes which speed the process of completion and acceptability of development are to be welcomed. The one importance is, the fact that successful integration can avoid problems that could otherwise materialize later in the operational phase of development through achieving synergy and even symbiosis with other existing activities and resource processes rather than competition.

In the real world very few economic or social-cultural activities are equal in priority. There is normally constant state of competition or at best uneasy alliance between activities in most communities, some being in the ascendance and others stagnating or being in decline. In many parts of the world in which tourism has been introduced, traditional primary activities have had long established priority, both in terms of economic importance and because of the intricate links with cultural patterns and behaviour. Tourism is often seen as being in direct competition with these traditional activities and in such situations integration rather than imposition is essential if development is to be successful. Thus acceptance may be difficult if tourism is not carefully and appropriately fitted into the existing systems. This situation is often compounded by the fact that in the case of large-scale tourism developments, ownership and control of these developments commonly lies outside the local community, and the element of external control can make acceptance of such development much more problematic. Lack of appreciation of local preferences, patterns of activities and priorities can exacerbate such tourism market situations. These market issues may be not so much how feelings towards tourism develop over time, but whether there are opposing views at any time. There need to be policies and practices in communities to determine views towards development and to enable the community to decide what type and scale of development can be accommodated in the community before development occurs, If such processes are in place and operational, then integration of the appropriate type of development should be much more easily achieved.

Globalization has transformed the tourism product over time from domination by mass tourism to a diversified industry catering more for the individual needs of travellers. Globalization has transmitted these ideas and practices worldwide, thus making the tourism industry more diversified and putting pressure on developing countries to create targeted, niche markets. Competition has become stronger and is based increasingly on diversification, market segmentation and diagonal integration, which involves the merger and conglomeration of related business activities. An important source of tourism revenue is now based on identifying, developing and promoting niche markets. New niche markets are constantly being identified in an attempt to diversify the industry further. The changing consumer preferences of international tourists constitute another aspect of globalization that is creating new challenges for developing countries. Providers of tourism services now try to gain a competitive advantage by catering for the individual needs of travellers. Tourists are actively changing the pace and direction of the tourism industry as they become more experienced travellers and change their behaviour and values. The increased travel experience, flexibility and independent nature of tourists have been generating demand for better quality, more value for money and greater flexibility in the travel experience. The new tourism also reflects demographic changes as well as changing lifestyles, thus creating demand for more targeted and customized holidays since travellers now belong to a number of different lifestyle segments. The changing values of tourists are also generating demand for more environmentally conscious and nature-oriented holidays, which means that tourism providers have to pay more attention to the way people think, feel and behave. In recent years, the niche market has become more important factor in the tourism industry, reflecting the need to diversify and customize the industry and ensure product sustainability. The main niche markets hold great potential and are developing rapidly. The transformations that have created new tourism put pressure on basic ways of doing business and on government strategies and plans for national tourism development.

Tourism has become a global industry and is widely considered to be one of the fastest growing industries, if not the fastest growing industry in the world (WTTC, 1995). It ranks as the largest industry in the world in terms of employment and ranks in the top two or three industries in almost every country on nearly every measure. Thus, tourism industry has become a major contributor to the gross national product of many nations, with marketing tourist destinations and its products becoming a widely recognized practice for both public and private sector organizations. It provides general models, concepts and techniques for strategic marketing but there is no academic analysis of their application to the marketing of a country as a tourist destination. It is important to distinguish between strategy to improve design quality and a strategy to improve the quality of service delivery. The process of improvement and innovation in Service Company is a continuous process. To improve this process managers must know what to do, how to do it and know the appropriate methods. Certain methods and techniques are more appropriate for improving the service delivery system such as continuous collecting and analyzing the delay time of flight departures and the waiting time on the phone, analyzing complaints, mystery shopping, etc. Other methods further innovation: e.g. brainstorming, brain writing, lateral thinking, mind mapping. In this article we will discuss three methods that further innovation of the service concept as well as incremental improvement of service delivery.

Amicably, market contribution to tourism maybe undervalued by policy makers and practitioners leading in misunderstanding of nature and value of marketing discipline designed for the powerful innovation within the tourism industry. Several authors have noted the lack of detailed work in relation to strategic issues in tourism marketing and distribution processes which require a more rigorous analysis of contextual factors. Similarly, other authors have argued that the marketing concept is based on a "long-term commitment" to the satisfaction of travellers' needs and motives and for a more strategic approach to marketing instead of relying on operational measures such as marketing communication.

There are three approaches to strategy that may be used by the tourism industry. The consumer-oriented approach dominates most current discussion of international marketing strategies. Another approach focuses on competition. However, these two approaches may be insufficient for they neglect the role of intermediaries in travel and tourism. Hence, a third approach to strategy, the trade-oriented orientation of intermediaries' desires, problems and demands needs to be investigated. Although each of these three approaches to strategic marketing will be discussed in turn below, they should not be regarded as alternatives, for they may be integrated into an overall strategy.

The Consumer-oriented Approach

Undifferentiated strategic marketing focuses on the average expectations of target markets: marketing efforts concentrate on the common interests of the target segments' needs and behaviour rather than their variances. In contrast, differentiated strategic marketing aims to identify the characteristics of diverse consumer groups through the use of marketing instruments directed at specific targets in order to create and implement a marketing approach and program that suits particular segments' needs and expectations. The extent of differentiation will vary depending on prevailing market conditions (1993).

The Competitor-oriented Approach

The next approach to strategy concentrates on competition. The tourism industry is undergoing a period of rapid change and uncertainty, with new technologies and more experienced consumers being some of the opportunities and challenges facing the industry. The role of a competitive marketing strategy is to develop, maintain or defend the position of an organization. Public and private travel and tourism organizations may either strive for an overall cost/price leadership, or differentiate themselves to gain a product quality leadership. Furthermore, a concentration on market niches may lead to a successful strategic position. As a tourism market becomes more mature it will continue to segment itself. With greater maturity, niche marketing approaches appealing to particular segment seem to become the focus of, in particular, travel and tourism organizations. In addition, airlines and intermediaries may specialize in sectors other than package holidays, that is, potential niches such as ecotourism may become more important. However, charter packages may also become increasingly popular due to their low cost, such trend suggesting the growth of the mass tourism market.

The Trade-oriented Approach

The third approach to strategy focuses on intermediaries and appears to be particularly relevant to the travel and tourism industry. The distribution of travel and tourism products/services is a most important activity along the tourism chain. There are two main considerations which need to be distinguished: first, the degree to which organizations become involved in organizing and structuring the overseas distribution channel, and second, organizations' reactions and responses to marketing and distribution strategies of intermediaries in overseas markets. As a result of organizations' activeness or passiveness with regard to these two considerations, four trade-oriented strategies are possible: bypassing, cooperation, conflict, or adaptation. The tourism sector is probably the only service sector that provides concrete and quantified trading opportunities for all nations, regardless of their level of development. However, it is also a sector where there is clearly an uneven distribution of benefits, which is threatening the social, economic and environmental sustainability of tourism in some developing countries. For many developing countries tourism is one of fundamental pillars of their development process because it is one of the dominant activities in the economy, while for others, particularly by islands and some small economies, it is the only source of foreign currency and employment, and therefore constitutes the platform for their economic development.

Against this background, part I presents an overview of the most important trends and features of international tourism and the most influential factors affecting the performance, efficiency and sustainability of tourism transactions in developing countries.

Part II presents an overview and examples of the main issues affecting the viability of tourism in developing countries, including (a) the impact of the leakage effect which is adversely affecting them in taking advantage of commercial opportunities; and (b) the anti-competitive practices affecting tourism viability and performance in different segments of the tourism sector, as well as in other sectors closely linked to travel and tourism. Part III presents some reflections about the GATS 2000 negotiations as a possible turning point for making effective the increasing participation of developing countries in international tourism flows in a sustainable perspective. In this connection, some comments are provided on the impact of the proposed Annex on Tourism on the economic, social and environmental sustainability of tourism.

Salient Trends and Features of the Performance of Developing Countries in International Tourism

Trends and features of international tourism: some indicators showing the sustainability of tourism in developing countries

Overall Trends in International Tourism

"International tourism highlights 2000" of the World Tourism Organization (OMT/WTO) reports that during 1998 total tourism receipts, including those generated by international fares, were the most important export revenue worldwide. Export revenue that year amounted to an estimated US$ 532 billion, surpassing all the other international trade categories. International tourism totalled to US$ 441 billion and the international transport of passengers US$ 91 billion, which corresponded to 7.9 and 1.3 per cent respectively of worldwide exports of good and services. According to the OMT/WTO *Tourism Economic Report 1998*, tourism is one the five top export categories and the main source of foreign currency for at least 38 per cent of them.

Figure 1: Worldwide export earnings, 1998

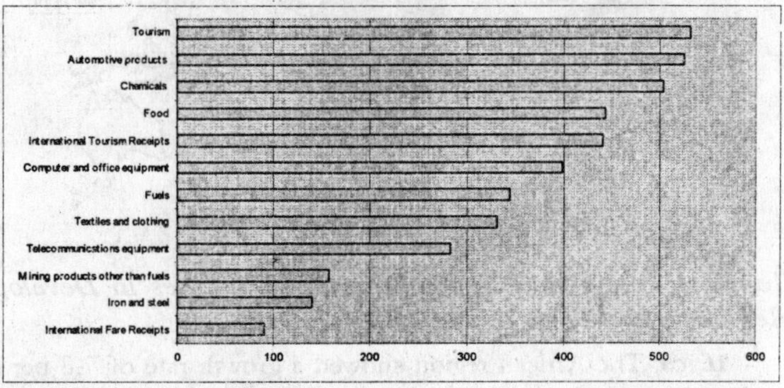

Sources: *Omt/WTO and IMF.*

Tourism Spenders

The world's top tourism spender during 1998 was by far the European Union, with an over US$ 160 billion. The most important spenders among its members were Germany (2nd world ranking), US$ 46.9 billion; the United Kingdom (4th), US$ 28.8 billion; France (5th), US$ 17.8 billion; Italy (6th), US$ 17.7; and Netherlands (7th), US$ 11.0 billion. The other members' expenses during the same year ranged between US$ 8.8 and 1.8 billion.

During the same year, the United States (1st in world ranking by individual countries) spent US$ 56.1 billion; Japan (3rd), 28.8 billion; Canada (8th) US$ 10.8 billion; China (9th), US$ 9.2 billion; Russian Federation (13th) US$ 8.3 billion; Switzerland (14th), US$ 7.1 billion; and Australia, US$ 5.4 billion. Also during the same year 45 countries reported more that US$ 1 billion in international tourism expenditure

International Tourist Arrivals

Preliminary figures for tourist arrivals for 1999 show that these arrivals totalled 664 million. The distribution and share are presented in figure 2.

Figure 2

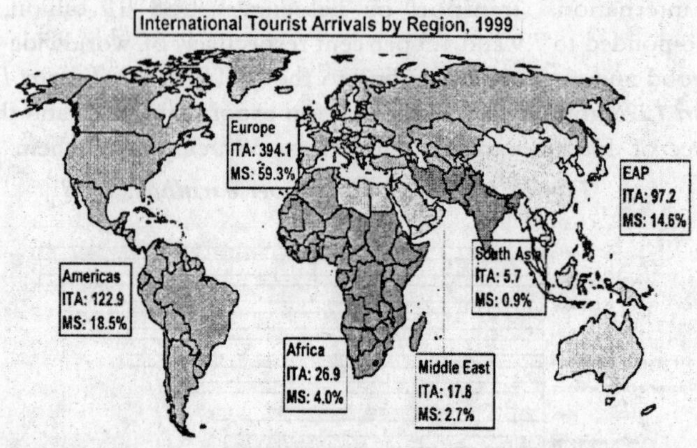

Tourism Trends and Best-performing Countries in Developing Regions Between 1997 and 1999

Africa. The African region showed a growth rate of 7.8 per cent in the number of arrivals, nearly twice the world average. There is a high concentration of international tourism arrivals in this region, bound for destinations in the north and south of the continent. The best-performing countries in terms of the increase in the number of arrivals included Morocco (18 per cent), Zimbabwe (11 per cent) and Zambia (26 per cent), while the important tourism destinations of Tunisia (3.4 per cent) and South Africa (6 per cent) continued to show steady gains.

Americas. The rate of growth for the whole region 2.4 per cent was lower than the world average, mainly owing to flat results for South American countries (-1 per cent) and Mexico (-2.9 per cent). Central America fared much better, especially Guatemala (29 per cent) and El Salvador (21 per cent). Results in the Caribbean were mixed, with Cuba (12 per cent) and the Dominican Republic (15 per cent) among the big winners and Puerto Rico (-11 per cent) among the losers.

East Asia/Pacific. After two years of decreasing tourist arrivals, East Asia and the Pacific bounced back strongly in 1999, attracting nearly 10 million more tourists than the previous record, set in 1998. Growth was widespread, with especially good results in Malaysia (43 per cent), Cambodia (29 per cent), Viet Nam (17 per cent), Singapore (11 per cent), Thailand (10 per cent), Republic of Korea (10 per cent),

China (8 per cent) and Hong Kong, China (18 per cent). Europe. Overall, tourism to Europe grew by 2.7 per cent in 1999, with results mixed according to region.

In this region some economies in transition were affected by the Kosovo crisis and instability in the Russian market, which caused problems for mature destinations in Central and Eastern Europe such as Hungary (-14 per cent), Poland (-4.4 per cent) and the Czech Republic (-1.8 per cent). However, emerging destinations managed to attract the interest of travellers, for example, Estonia (15 per cent), Kyrgyzstan (17 per cent) and Georgia (21 per cent), as well as Russian Federation (17 per cent) and Ukraine (21 per cent).

***Middle East*.** The Middle East is one of the world's smallest regions, receiving nearly 18 million tourists in 1999, but it also had the fastest growth rate with arrivals up by 16 per cent. Egypt, which represents a quarter of the regional total, recorded a spectacular growth rate of almost 40 per cent and a record number of tourist arrivals that far exceeds the totals achieved in its best year, 1997. Dubai, Lebanon and the Syrian Arab Republic also fared well, with arrivals increasing by 14, 12 and 9 per cent respectively. The Libyan Arab Jamahiriya registered an increase of 25 per cent.

***South Asia*.** Tourism increased in most countries in this region, resulting in an increase of 8.3 per cent over the previous year's results. India registered an increase of 5.2 per cent, while arrivals in the Islamic Republic of Iran rose by 16.5 per cent, in Sri Lanka by 14.4 per cent and in Maldives by 8.6 per cent.

International Tourism Receipts

Figure 3: Tourism receipts market share (%), 1998

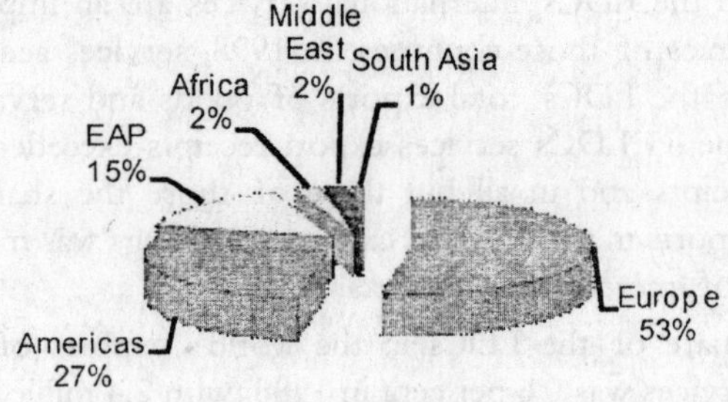

Source: OMT/WTO database.

Preliminary results processed by the OMT/WTO indicate that during 1999 tourism receipts worldwide amounted to US$ 455 billion and a further US$ 93 billion. In 59 countries the receipts amounted over US$ 1 billion. Figure 3 presents the receipts in different regions of the world during 1998.

Some Indicators about the Sustainability of International Tourism in Developing Countries

Importance and Impact of Export Revenues from Tourism for Developing Countries

During the period 1995-1998, tourism revenues were one of the five leading sources of export revenue for 69 developing countries. Among the latter, tourism revenue was the main source of foreign currency in 28 countries, its share in total exports ranging between 79 and 20 per cent; in 27 countries it accounted for between 20 and 10 per cent; and in the 24 remaining countries it was around 10 per cent.

The contribution of export revenues to gross domestic product (GDP) was equally important and accounted for between 82.29 per cent (in Maldives) and 30 per cent (in Samoa). In the second group the contribution of export revenues to GDP is between 30 and 10 per cent and in the remaining countries under 10 per cent. One aspect to be underlined is that although the contribution of tourism revenues is important in all these countries, its contribution to GDP is declining as the economies become more diversified. The best examples of this are Mauritius, the Dominican Republic and Tunisia.

The Particular 'Situation of LDCs

Although only 0.5 per cent of the world's exports of services originate in the LDCs, international services are an important part of the economies of those countries. In 1998, services accounted for 20 per cent of the LDCs' total exports of goods and services. However, in 13 of the 49 LDCs services export receipts exceeded merchandise export receipts and in all but three of those the share of tourism services exports in total foreign exchange earnings was more than twice the share of merchandise exports.

The share of the LDCs in the world's exports of international tourism services was 0.6 per cent in 1988 (with 2.4 million international tourist arrivals) and 0.8 per cent in 1998 (5.1 million). During the 1990s tourist flows to the LDCs increased more rapidly than tourist flows to the rest of the world. This growth was particularly strong in seven countries (Cambodia, Mali, Laos People's Democratic Republic, Myanmar, Samoa, Uganda, United Republic of Tanzania), which hosted over 1.2 million visitors in 1998, in comparison with 0.4 million in 1992. During that period, tourism growth was much slower in several LDCs, while a decrease was observed in a number of countries that suffered socio-political and economic instability.

The growth of international tourism receipts in the LDCs was also quite rapid during the 1990s: total receipts more than doubled between 1992 and 1998 (from US$ 1 billion to US$ 2.2 billion). There is a great degree of concentration in the distribution of tourism receipts among the LDCs: five countries (Cambodia, Maldives, Nepal, Uganda, United Republic of Tanzania) accounted for 51 per cent of the total tourism receipts of the group in 1998. Particularly strong, over the decade, was the growth in international tourists' expenditure in Cambodia, the United Republic of Tanzania, Myanmar, Bangladesh, Samoa, Uganda and Haiti. Tourism is the first source of foreign exchange earnings in the whole group of 49 LDCs, aside from the petroleum industry, which is concentrated in only three LDCs (Angola, Yemen, Equatorial Guinea): the combined tourism export receipts of all LDCs in 1998 accounted for 16.2 per cent of the total non-oil export receipts of the LDCs, thus exceeding the second and third largest non-oil export sectors (cotton and textile products) by 39 per cent and 82 per cent, respectively.

Level of Performance and Sustainability of Tourism in Developing Countries

The proper functioning of the tourism economy is linked to that of many other related economic activities, which accounts for the importance of its economic, social and environmental sustainability. As a matter of fact, the extent to which the business operations of international tourism, backward and forward are linked with other sectors will determine the level of performance and profitability of tourism, the extent of multiplier and spillover effects, and the retention of value added, i.e. the leakage effect. The sectors producing goods and services are linked backwards with tourism in catering for the needs of tourists and tourism operators, e.g. agriculture and food-processing industries, and other manufacturing industries providing furniture, construction materials and other articles required by tourism establishments. Similarly, many other services, such as transport, business services, financial services, professional services, construction design and engineering, environmental services, security services and government services, also ensure the efficient performance of tourism operators. Some of these sectors are also crucial for the proper linkage of tourism with foreign markets (forward linkages) because they constitute the platforms for "taking off" and for keeping the national tourism providers fully integrated with international tourism flows.

Many developing countries have found important to improve the linking of tourism (forward and backward) with the other sectors of the economy as one of the foundations of tourism development policies, so as to capitalize on the benefits of the globalization and internationalization of markets. Successful experiences of small economies and islands that have recently become emerging tourism destinations, such as Mauritius, Maldives, the Dominican Republic and other Caribbean islands, attest to the vital importance of the proper linkage of tourism with the rest of the economy, in their capacity of retaining value added, e.g., reducing leakages. Despite developing countries efforts to develop the most suitable domestic policy environment, the economic sustainability of tourism is being undermined by external factors beyond their control, notably the predatory behaviour of integrated suppliers which enjoy a dominant position in the originating markets of tourism flows.

Key Issues with Special Impact on the Social, Economic and Environmental Sustainability of Tourism

This part presents an overview and illustration of the main issues affecting the viability of tourism in developing countries, including (a) the leakage effect produced by their structural vulnerabilities and their difficulties in taking advantage of commercial opportunities; and (b) anti-competitive practices affecting tourism viability and performance in different segments of the tourism sector, as well as those in other sectors closely linked to travel and tourism.

Leakages from Tourism in Developing Countries

As a modality of international commerce, tourism involves not only inflows of foreign financial resources but also outflows, referred to herein as "leakages". When they exceed specific levels, these outflows can significantly neutralize the positive financial effect of international tourism. Leakage is the process whereby part of the foreign exchange earnings generated by tourism, rather than being retained by tourist-receiving countries, is either retained by tourist-generating countries or repatriated to them in the form of profits, income and royalty remittances, repayment of foreign loans, and imports of equipment, materials, capital and consumer goods to cater for the needs of international tourist and overseas promotional expenditures.

Leakages can be divided into three categories: internal leakage or the "import-coefficient" of tourism activities; external leakage or pre-leakage, depending on the commercialization mode of the tourism package and the choice of airline; and invisible leakage or foreign exchange costs associated with resource damage or deterioration.

Internal leakages can be measured by establishing "satellite accounts" within national accounting and survey procedures to detail all tourism-related economic activities. It is a normal effect present in both developed and developing countries. In principle, import-related leakages are highest where the local economies are weakest owing to sparse factor endowment or inadequate quality of goods and services. The average leakage for most developing countries today is between 40 and 50 percent of gross tourism earnings for small economies and between 10 and 20 percent for most advanced and diversified developing countries. Importantly for LDCs, tourism import-related leakages are often inferior to other economic activity leakages, including manufacturing and, in some cases, agriculture, thus confirming tourism as a choice sector of development for which they possess comparative advantages in many areas.

A first step in reducing internal leakage is to identify what levels are appropriate given the economic structure of a country and then to ensure that effective leakage remains near this objective range while strategies to build up the local supply capacity are put in place. Although restrictive trade policies can reduce the size of the market, it is important to note that import openness tends to facilitate the leakage effect unless the economy has already in place a structure capable of reacting to the competitive stimulus of imports, which is usually not the case in LDCs.

External leakage or pre-leakage is much more difficult to measure and relates to the proportion of the total value added of tourism of services actually captured by the servicing country. To the extent that developing countries have limited access to commercialization channels in their target markets, they can only offer base prices to intermediaries that capture the mark-up on those services. Observed differences between paid and received prices for developing country tourism services (lodging, food, entertainment, etc.) suggest external leakage or pre-leakage levels of up to 75 percent. In some cases, base prices do not allow for the economic sustainability of projects, and normally do not contemplate replacement costs associated with resource depletion. This leads to problems of infrastructure and environmental sustainability, which tend to be overlooked in view of the short-term importance of crucial foreign exchange inflows.

As a flow variable, leakage levels do not have a static effect. They vary in time depending on:

(a) The stage or cycle point of the tourism industry. For example, a nascent tourism industry tends to require large amounts of one-time imports, whereas loan grace periods may allow for a decrease in leakage during the first few years of operation. During a maturity phase leakage may increase as large sums are invested in marketing, rehabilitation of facilities and upgrading of products provided, etc.

(b) The evolution of the economy to provide new services and products resulting from demand from the tourism sector. The import of products and services initially not available should trigger enough entrepreneurial response to enable these to be provided locally, thus allowing for a lessening of leakage. It is therefore a main objective of leakage limitation to provide and promote these links between domestic industry and tourism. For example, in the Dominican Republic leakages diminished between 1990 and 1995 as local industry became increasingly interested in servicing the tourism market. The largest companies have now created subsidiaries specifically for this purpose.

Another factor to be evaluated in identifying appropriate leakage levels is the type of tourism being promoted. High-income tourism, because it requires the provision of very high quality and high priced goods, may actually result in increased leakage in some cases despite of the higher income it may generate. Mass tourism could have higher potential for leakage than ecological or adventure tourism because the latter value and consume local resources as part of the tourism experience. However, low-leakage tourism can also equate to low-income tourism, resulting in lower total income and therefore limiting the possibilities for expansion and development by other sectors of the receiving country's economy. In order to correctly evaluate the return on investments it is necessary to carry out a cost-of-opportunity study that will establish a "leakage break-even point" as a function of the country's economic capacity to serve different types of tourism and choose the type most suitable for a project or country.

Leakage effects on tourism net income levels are nonetheless offset by increased value added or volume. As an example of the positive outlook for LDCs, value added in tourism, measured as tourism income per tourist arrival (Yt/At) has grown by over 100 percent in 21 (almost half) of the LDCs surveyed between 1998 and 1992.

Interestingly, growth in income per tourist appears to bear no clear relationship to the level of or growth in arrivals. This suggests that growth in income per tourist is not a function of volume, and has therefore grown basically because of a favourable quality/price ratio. This also confirms the enormous diversity of situations present in LDCs and their tourism industries; but, in general, as value added grows, the *potential* for leakage lessens.

However, for varying reasons, including differing lengths of stay, very few countries have achieved income-per-tourist levels of above US$ 1000. The growth of the middle-income tourism category of US$ $500–$999 has been higher not only for arrivals (a factor of 2 versus 1.75) but also for combined income per tourist category (a factor of 4.9 versus 2). This indicates that the primary competitive segment for LDCs, as well as the segment where most opportunities for growth in value added exist, tends to be in this category of pricing.

Tourism policy should therefore be based on the premise that although leakage is an intrinsic element of international tourism, and increased value added will also benefit the economy, leakage-containment measures have multiplicative effects that will allow developing countries to maximize the financial benefits to be derived from an expansion of tourism.

A study on Indonesia showed that the tourism multiplier (1.59) was the highest of all categories, including final demand, and exhibited strong links to the agricultural sector, on which it had no direct effect at all.

To the extent that leakages lead to a definition of economic opportunities it can be useful as a strategic blueprint for further economic development. Domestic policies in developing countries against leakages from international tourism should include:

(i) the provision of incentives to reinvest profits and potential cash transfers that otherwise would be invested abroad;

(ii) the enhancement of the capacity of tourist destinations for intensifying the production of goods and services required by the tourism sector;

(iii) the provision of incentives to domestic investors to expand their participation in tourism and iv) the enforcement of domestic competition policy against anti-competitive practices by tour operators.

As regards external leakages, most issues address points of discussion under the GATS Annex on tourism in the WTO, such as:

(i) local and international competition policy, particularly with regard to market access issues and best business practices in relation to regulations on contractual practices; and

(ii) ecological and economic sustainability and the valuation and use of non-tradable resources.

Anti-competitive Practices Affecting Tourism Sustainability

The competition issue and the treatment of anti-competitive behaviour are at the core of the problems of efficiency, viability and sustainability of tourism in developing countries.

The latter's ability to deal with those two aspects and to counter their effects is a crucial matter. Firstly, this is because anti-competitive behaviour occurs largely in developed countries, as a result of the fierce competition among a few integrated dominant players with a high market share in their own market and in all segments of tourism industry supply, notably tour operators, travel agencies, hotels etc. Secondly, the pattern of globalization, which is the driving force of many of the developments in the supply of the tourism and air transport, also mostly originates and is controlled in the two leading developed economies, namely the European Union and the United States.

Consequently, what often appears to be a normal commercial relationship in a developing country may actually be the result of a network of anti-competitive practices arising from a globalized and highly integrated tourism trading environment, dominated by a few suppliers in the originating tourism markets.

Moreover, other non-behaviour-related industry issues, such as the inadequacy or absence of a domestic competition legal framework in developing countries, and the lack of multilateral disciplines and mechanisms within the GATS framework, also affect the ability of developing countries to deal with or prevent anti-competitive practices in their tourism sectors.

Why and how do anti-competitive practices threaten the viability of sustainable tourism in developing countries?

The economic and social viability of tourism in developing countries depends on sustainable growth perspectives, in terms not only of absolute values, but also of their capacity for retaining more value added in their economies, i.e. smaller leakages, an even distribution of benefits in commercial operations, elimination of all barriers to tourism, particularly to commercial presence, and the movement of tourism suppliers in both origin and destination markets, and the effective implementation of provisions enumerated in Articles IV and XIX of GATS.

The foundations for sustainable tourism are already in place in most developing countries as a result of the autonomous liberalization of the tourism sector itself and the progressive liberalization of many other services sectors. However, for those countries highly dependent on tourism revenue, the benefits of the liberalization of tourism are being threatened by the predatory practices of a few dominant tourism suppliers in the world tourism market.

The evolution of the GATS disciplines, and the consistency of future commitments of developed countries with the economic, social and environmental sustainability of tourism in developing countries in the GATS 2000 negotiations, should mark a turning point favouring more profitable tourism for all WTO members, particularly the most vulnerable small developing countries.

The predatory practices and anti-competitive behaviour in international tourism have two main effects on the economic sustainability of the tourism of developing countries: unbalanced trade benefits, and the deepening of the leakage effect. Their combined impact minimize the positive impacts of spillover and multiplier effects inherent to tourism, and undermine the financial capacity of enterprises and the ability of countries to earmark necessary resources to maintain and upgrade basic infrastructure and quality standards in order to satisfy in an adequate way competitive conditions and international demand.

Moreover, in most vulnerable and small developing economies, particularly LDCs, the foundations of tourism are threatened by unbalanced results in their business operations, which are in turn threatening the social, economic and environmental sustainability of tourism.

There is much documented evidence about the negative impact of anti-competitive behaviour of developed countries' dominant tourism suppliers on their own markets and overseas. Unfair practices, which confront developing countries' suppliers in their business operations with dominant suppliers in tourism-originating countries, are of a different nature and occur in different segments of tourism and related activities. One of the salient features that become evident in commercial relations is the uneven distribution of benefits, due to the dominant position and market power of integrated suppliers in their own markets and worldwide.

These suppliers have absolute advantages, because of their control of inbound and outbound operations in their countries and overseas, which allow them to keep consumers dependent on the offer of the products and services they supply, at the expenses of imposing onerous commercial conditions on suppliers in different tourism destinations. The huge supply capacity of dominant players in all segments of tourism, including transporters, CRS/GDS, tour operators, travel agencies and hotels, allows them to prepare holiday packages and retail them through their own business networks, as well as to impose prices and conditions on suppliers in tourism destinations.

How do the business operations of tour operators and travel agencies in the originating markets of tourism affect the sustainability of developing countries' tourism?

Tourism suppliers from developing countries e.g. hotels, inbound operators and land transport companies participate in international tourism mainly through the transactions of tour operators and travel agencies from developed countries in the developed countries' originating markets. As wholesalers of tourism products and services they assemble the holiday package by negotiating with destinations and operators in third countries.

They view the tour package as an attractive option with many advantages for them: (a) it ensures flows of tourists; (b) it reduces the international marketing costs of the destination; and (c) it increase the volume flow of package travellers, which is likely to increase investment by foreign construction companies, major tour operators and airline companies that wish to make the tourism product more attractive to consumers. However, tourism suppliers from tourism destinations in developing countries have very often underlined their weak bargaining position in business transactions, particularly with dominant suppliers of the most important originating tourism market from developed countries.

International Competition Among Tour Operators and Travel Agencies

Tour operators in originating countries manage business operations through (a) a subsidiary of a vertically integrated firm with a number of related travel interests; (b) an entirely independent firm that specializes in putting holiday packages together and selling them; (c) a subsidiary of an airline; and (d) an operator directly linked to a travel agent. The tour operator of each major market is dominated by a small number of national firms with a relatively large market share, which compete fiercely with each other.

For instance, four firms with a share of over 60 per cent dominate the United Kingdom market. This results in the larger operators having a dominant position with a very little competition, because the layer of the next competitor is too small. Consequently, the travel agencies (the retailers of tourism packages) in destination markets are almost entirely dependent on their linkages with the dominant tour operators. Also, consumers become captive in their choices of tourist package offered by dominant suppliers. The effect of this supremacy of integrated tourism suppliers in their own markets is mirrored in their dominant position in commercial relations with tourism suppliers in destination developing countries.

The benefits and costs of package tours to service suppliers in developing countries depend to a large extent on the nature and terms of the contracts between them and the tour operators from the tourism-originating countries. Accordingly, the bargaining powers of suppliers from developing countries are a central issue affecting the tourism sustainability of developing countries. Some examples of how the common practices in contractual arrangements affect the sustainability of tourism in developing countries are presented below.

Use of Monopsonistic Power Over Local Tourism Suppliers in Developing Countries

The contract between a tour operator from an originating country and the suppliers in the destination country involves a block reservation for a future period at a negotiated price and specifies the terms of risk sharing in the event that not all the packages are sold. The tour operator normally has the greater bargaining power during the contract negotiations; if it considers that the negotiating partner's offer is not attractive enough, it can choose another hotel in the same area or even another region of the same country. Tour operators thus often exercise a monopsonistic power over local tourism suppliers, such as local hotels, since for the latter the servicing of the package tour is a vital means of securing their occupancy rates.

The asymmetry of bargaining power is clearly revealed in the content of the contract. Often contracts last for one year or more, and the risk inherent in a long-term contract for a tour operator is reduced by negotiating various conditions favourable to the tour operator. A contract frequently contains the following provisions: a substantial discount is provided on rooms after the departure of the clients; no deposit is required for the booking; payment may be made long after the departure of the customers; and the tour operator retains the right to return unfilled rooms ("release-back clause") shortly before the arrival date, without any need to pay compensation.

Anti-competitive Practices Resulting from Vertical Integration

Vertical integration among tour operators and travel agencies, which is currently proceeding at a notable pace in Europe, threatens to reduce the actual number of tour operators in the market. As a result, a great deal of market power is being transferred to the intermediaries that direct consumers to specific destinations.

The consequences of this should be a major concern to developing countries' tourism destinations. The increase in the degree of concentration in the travel market in favour of mega-operators puts developing countries' suppliers and the other competitors in local markets at a clear disadvantage. It also opens the door to unfair practices, which directly affect tourist destinations. An example of this is the travel agent's "racking policy", which refers to the decision about which brochures to put on display. This has a crucial impact on the tourism destinations of developing countries, because for them the travel agent's display rack is almost an essential facility, and denial of access to it can severely restrict consumer exposure.

The threat of "deracking" (i.e. removing brochures from the shelves) is used by integrated suppliers in attempt to negotiate larger commissions, by pressuring tour operators not to supply independent travel agencies on better terms or by pushing their own holidays through in-house incentive schemes. The lasting impact of this practice is more restrictive in originating countries where tour operators are the main distribution channels, such as in Europe, where more than 60 per cent of tour packages are sold by integrated suppliers. Conversely, in the United States the possibility of "deracking" is lower because about 70 per cent of travel agencies are independent, GDS/CRS are more important as distribution channels, and the Internet is becoming a primary source of information for consumers about tourism destinations.

International Competition Among Hotels

The international hotels sector is characterized by a considerable diversity in the modalities of services provision, and by a high concentration of a very small number of large hotel groups, including hotel consortia, integrated hotel chains and tourism lodging (second homes). Their scope and focus are very often limited, either by a focus on home markets, notably through the hospitality franchising systems, or by a concentration on business travel and destinations.

One important aspect to be noted is that the intensive use of the accommodation infrastructure, particularly hotels receiving international tourists regardless of the hotel's size, requires the continuous allocation of financial resources to maintain and upgrade the quality of accommodation to meet the standards of international demand. In most developing country destinations huge investments have been made in the hospitality and accommodation sector either through investment of domestic resources or attracting foreign investors by increase of different modalities, including management contracts and franchising brand names

As in all the other segments of tourism-related activities, the importance of competition issues stems from a mix of practices through the distribution mechanisms. Anti-competitive behaviour in those mechanisms is thus most likely to have a significant effect on the ability of destinations, and of their hotel sectors, to compete effectively and to gain a fair share of the rewards of attracting tourists and travellers.

The sustainability of this sector in developing countries' tourism destinations depends on the occupancy rates (affected by seasonality) and the level of profits, which are highly influenced by the results of commercial transactions between hoteliers and tour operators from tourism-originating countries. In this connection, it has to be underlined that the accommodation sector is the one most affected by the dominant power of mega-operators, whose stringent demands in terms of quality standards are not duly compensated for with fair commercial remuneration. Another, wider impact of this predatory behaviour in the tourism economy of receiving countries is the deepening of the leakage effect and the undermining of positive inherent multipliers effects of tourism. Depending on the magnitude of these unfair compensations from dominant tour operators, some tourism destinations in developing countries might be subsidizing tourists from originating countries.

Computerized Reservation Systems (CRS) Global Distribution Systems (GDS)

The development of international tourism relies on the effective commercialization of tourism products to consumers at tourism-originating countries. World information and distribution networks play a decisive role in the international tourism sector since they bring the buyers and producers of tourism products into contact. CRS, GDS and the Internet are the backbone of world information networks, which provide the infrastructures and networking facilities for airlines, tour operators, travel agencies and other tourism operators to process and obtain information, make reservations and market tourism products.

CRS have been developed by large air carriers since the 1970s to process flight reservations. They later evolved and expanded to offer further services related to air transport, such as the storage of information on a worldwide basis, the issuance of tickets, marketing (by displaying information on fares, discounts and conditions attached to them) or the sale of products and services.

Moreover, they cover not only services provided by airlines, but also land services supplied to tourists, such as package tours, hotels and vehicle rentals. With this enlarged range of services, they became known as global distribution systems. GDS have significantly improved the efficiency of travel agents' business operations and their use is growing rapidly. They have become the main marketing and trading tool of international tourism, as well as a major source of income for the carriers which own them. Through strategic alliances and other forms of cooperation or mergers in the most important markets, these systems minimize their costs and reduce the need for a direct commercial presence. A single GDS terminal provides immediate access to all services companies which have opted to market their products through this network.

The companies (air carriers or independent commercial companies) that control CRS and GDS either partly or entirely sell access to the system to tourism operators worldwide. There are many obstacles to and measures governing GDS networks. These include (a) unfair rights of access, (b) restrictions on display, (c) costs of services influenced by monopolistic practices, (d) neutrality and regulations, and (e) the technology gap among users.

Access problems: Despite their major contribution to the development of tourism, GDS are frequently considered a barrier to market entry, mainly because they are controlled by the major carriers and because of the unfavourable access conditions for competitors. While some East Asian developing countries have participated in the establishment of a major GDS (Abacus, complemented by the strategic alliance with Worldspan), other developing countries have not been able to do likewise, leaving their carriers and other service suppliers without privileged access to any GDS.

Additionally, countries not yet seen as attractive tourist destinations, or whose hospitality sector is underdeveloped (particularly in Africa and South Asia), tend to be poorly represented, if at all, on GDS. Therefore, access to information on their tourism products is limited, thus making it difficult for them to sell their tourism services. These difficulties have meant that many smaller carriers, especially some from developing countries, have been obliged to continue using the traditional SITA CRS, which leaves them at a competitive disadvantage compared with those what are represented in the major GDS. On the other hand, in many developing countries, particularly in Africa, GDS are present as a result of joint ventures with local partners but operate within a de facto monopoly. This leads to excessive user fees and hinders their potential for developing tourism.

Display. The GDS allows a travel agent to view a wide range of information, which sometimes requires several pages on a terminal screen. In most cases, however, travel agencies only consult the information on the first page (screen); the order in which screens are displayed is thus a crucial determinant in the user's selection of products. The display may discriminate against smaller carriers which do not own a major CRS, since controllers' own flights may be better displayed on the screens than those of their competitors (this is known as "display bias"). There may also be discrimination in favour of their suppliers of land services.

Cost: The cost of having services presented GDS may be prohibitively high for SMEs, leaving them with no access to this marketing tool. Even though all service providers have to pay a fee for having their services displayed in the systems, the costs of participation for the owners of GDS are fully or partly covered by the profits generated by the systems. The cost of hardware and user fees may prevent small users from using GDS; this puts some service suppliers (particularly SMEs) from developing countries at a disadvantage compared with their larger national or international competitors.

Neutrality and regulations: In order to prevent CRS from being used as an anti-competitive tool and to ensure their neutrality, the United States, Canada and the European Union have issued regulations in recent years on GDS operations related to air services, while the International Civil Aviation Authority (ICAO) adopted a code of conduct for CRS in 1991.

However, the regulations and code have not been sufficient to resolve completely the anti-competitive bias of the systems, and particularly to address the specific problems of carriers from developing countries. The ICAO code (the only multilateral one) is non-binding and therefore there are no mechanisms to ensure its enforceability. The relevant domestic regulations are binding, but only within the territories of the countries concerned. The European Union regulations apply to CRS from countries which have similar legislation to ensure neutrality. On the other hand, although CRS have been included among the "soft" air services rights included in GATS, the commitments do not deal with their anti-competitive potential.

Technology gap: Installing and maintaining a system poses a greater problem to travel agents in developing countries, owing to deficiencies in the infrastructure necessary for such an information network, and the shortage of professionals to manage, operate and maintain the system. This not only represents a technical hindrance to the use of modern technology, but also increases the associated costs, thereby putting travel agents in developing countries at a disadvantage compared with their counterparts in developed countries.

Electronic commerce: The expansion of the use of the Internet and other forms of electronic communication opens up significant opportunities for developing countries to develop their tourism and air transport sectors. Their service suppliers can reach consumers around the world directly, offering both package tours and individual air and land services. They thereby cut out the costs of intermediaries and transaction costs and avoid the need for a direct commercial presence and its associated costs. Nevertheless, electronic marketing and trading have their own costs in terms of human and physical capital requirements. In countries where these requirements are in relatively short supply, the cost of electronic marketing and trading can be reduced if individual suppliers pool their resources. This could be coordinated, for instance, by national tourist authorities. Moreover, modern technologies are likely to be increasingly used as institutional promotion tools. If there is a minimal critical mass of information infrastructure in a given country, the new technologies can offer substantial cost savings.

Air Transport

Air access in international tourism depends on the availability and conditions of air transport connecting tourist-generating countries and destination countries. Air transport is a major factor underpinning international tourism in the vast majority of developing countries, but its importance for tourism varies considerably from one region to another. It is the means of transport used by the majority of tourists arriving in developing countries. Air transport developed as a result of the increase in demand for tourism-related travel, becoming in turn the driving force behind the development of the tourism industry. In 1998, passengers were responsible for about 75 per cent of air traffic volume and for of the total operating revenues of airlines. It is estimated that up to 40 per cent of air passenger travel is for business purposes (as opposed to leisure or personal travel) and that business travellers account for up to half of airlines' income. Like tourism, the world air transport industry has expanded at twice the rate of world output growth, and is expected to continue to do so in the next twenty years. The main recent developments affecting air transport and the industry structure are the increased international ownership of airlines and their growing concentration, worldwide moves to liberalize and deregulate the sector, the privatization of airlines and the formation of strategic alliances among firms. The main benefits of the latter are the cost reductions and efficiency gains that can be achieved by rationalizing the joint use of resources (such as check-in facilities and ground personnel), creating synergies and providing "network value" without the need to physically expand operations. The large global alliances aim at world coverage by pooling the networks of their members. The main drawback in doing this is that the alliances can restrict competition and thus negate some of these benefits, particularly if they collectively achieve a dominant position on given routes.

How the GATS 2000 Negotiations should Mark a Turning point to make Effective

How Negotiations could Support the Sustainability of Tourism Operations

The GATS 2000 negotiations mandated by the Final Act of the Uruguay Round provide developing countries with a unique opportunity to counterbalance the asymmetries imbedded in the outcome of the Uruguay Round services negotiations. In this perspective, it is the right time to take advantage of these negotiations to prepare and put forward negotiating proposals on how to make effective use of the provisions of Art IV and XIX, aimed at increasing participation of developing countries in trade in services and the expansion of their services exports including through the strengthening of their domestic services and its efficiency and competitiveness. The two-way process involves not only the refinement of offers, but also the preparation of requests from trading partners as one of the key ways to obtain substantive benefits as result of the GATS 2000 negotiations. Moreover, an active participation of developing countries in the GATS rule-making process is a contribution to building of an improved multilateral framework which would take into consideration existing asymmetries and the need for a predictable markets access for exporters of services from developing countries.

The viability of tourism, i.e. its economic, social, cultural and environmental sustainability, is at the heart of domestic policies and development concerns of developing countries. Accordingly, in the course of the present negotiations on trade in services, there is a need for similar focus on strengthening future substantive commitments on tourism by GATS members as was the case in other sector such as telecommunications and financial services. In this perspective the proposal for the Annex on Trade in Tourism Services (WT/GC/W/372), may contribute to providing a pro-competitive framework as a complementary tool which would ensure:

(a) *An adequate coverage and consistency of commitments in all tourism activities as defined by the Satellite Tourism Account:* This aspect is of paramount importance in view of specific characteristics and diversity of transactions linked to trade in tourism services, notably the heavy reliance of tourism on air transport and travel distribution systems.

(b) *The prevention of predatory behaviour and anti-competitive practices by dominant integrated suppliers in the originating markets:* This refers to disciplines to prevent anti-competitive conduct including from air transport and travel distribution systems, and to safeguard trade in tourism services from competitive exclusions, abuse of dominant and misleading or discriminatory use of information.

(c) *The effective access and use of information on a non-discriminatory basis:* It should include provisions on access to ensuring non-discrimination, transparent, reasonable and objective criteria; compliance with Art. IV of GATS and the truthfulness of the information on tourism distributed by governments (travel warning) and through GDS; the unbundling of travel distribution systems as a measure to counter vertical integration and conflicts of interest in travel agencies and the interconnection of CRS, through the portability of reservation numbers. Submitting GDS operations to effective multilateral disciplines and dispute-settlement mechanisms would have a substantial effect on trade and anti-competitive practices.

(d) *The implementation of an adequate framework for sustainable development of tourism:* Provisions on cooperation for the sustainable development of tourism are needed in recognition of the role of tourism in economic development; its need for infrastructure and development assistance; equitable trading conditions for economic sustainability; the relevance of enforcing internationally-recognized environmental and quality standards; the need for cooperation at all levels; and the importance of providing information on technologies required for competitive provision, regulation and sustainable development of tourism and all related-activities.

(e) *To preserve the environmental sustainability of tourism and the cultural heritage*: Guiding principles for national policies and trade commitments to preserve the ecological systems, the biodiversity, cultural patrimony and traditions.

Issues for Consideration by Developing Countries in Negotiating Specific Commitments in Tourism

The liberalization under the GATS 2000 will be determined on one hand, by the level of removal of barriers in the revised horizontal commitments (which affect all sectors) and on the other, the lifting of conditions and limitations applied to each sector at sector-specific level and in the four modes of supply. Accordingly the consistency between the two types of commitment is an important issue to be addressed by developing countries, seeking to obtain commercially meaningful commitments at specific sectoral level.

Improvement of Horizontal Commitments

In preparation of their positions in services negotiations, developing countries must assess to what extent the horizontal commitments of developed countries impede the liberalization of tourism and travel and related services. The major limitation in the horizontal commitments is in the lack of significant trading opportunities in mode 4, i.e. temporary movement of natural persons, since practically no commitments in this mode were made in specific services sectors.

The temporary presence of natural persons in all services sectors is undermined by the recurrence at the horizontal level to the economic needs tests, nationality and/or residence requirement and cumbersome administrative and visa procedures to be met by foreign nationals as services providers. The existing horizontal commitments by developed countries mainly refer to limitations for the establishment of the commercial presence by foreign providers to carry out the commercial operations.

Specific Tourism Sector Commitments

Majority of tourism originating countries are developed countries, which have undertaking commitment to liberalize fully or partially the supply of services in different tourism sub-sectors and modes of supply. Still, *the impact of commitments in commercial presence* in term of market value is nullified by restrictions to the commercial presence of foreign tour operators, travel agencies, restaurants and hotels, which are not listed there.

Also, the movement of natural persons engaged in the tourism supply of different services is precluded by limited horizontal commitments and the lack of specific sectoral commitments. For instance in many Members States of the EU the commercial presence of foreign tour operators from the third countries is precluded or allowed only in association with already established national firms therein. Similarly, foreigners are precluded from undertaking of the business operations in the restaurant sub-sector even for those specializing in typical national food from other countries. In addition, the level of restrictions on commercial presence is aggravated by the possibility of recourse to the economic needs test, cumbersome and discriminatory licensing requirements that foreign suppliers of tourism services must meet.

Temporary Presence of Natural Persons as Consumers and Providers of Services

It should be underlined that although the existing commitments on market access on *consumption abroad have no limitations* in the case of majority of the GATS commitments, including in the top originating countries; in real terms the freedom of movement for consumption abroad is restricted by the level of binding in other modes of supply, in particular the commercial presence of foreign suppliers in the tourism originating markets.

The movement of consumers in most of the top originating markets of tourism is captive, because the existing level of binding of commercial presence consolidates the absolute advantage of the dominant mega-tour operators and other national suppliers including the travel agencies, since the exclusive right of selling directly to travellers of holiday packages in their own markets has been consolidated in the existing commitments on commercial presence.

Moreover, under such commercial conditions, the consumers' choices are limited by the offers of holiday package by dominant tour operators, but not only them, also by the opportunities for suppliers from destination countries to reach consumer in the originating markets directly. In addition, the consumers' choices in these markets are restricted by unfair practices in the management of information systems and the "racking policies" by travel agencies, which are usually integrated with mega-tour operators.

To improve horizontal commitments on mode 4, developed countries should remove the application of the economic needs test with respect to the movement of professionals supplying tourism services. Not all the professions and occupations are equally important to the movement of persons in the context of trade in tourism services. For example, the possibility to have the waiver from the application economic needs test should be provided to individual tourism services suppliers involved in catering, maintenance services or in such areas where cultural affinities and close contacts with tourists may contribute to the quality of the services provided. To the extent that the remaining occupations would remain subject to the application of economic needs tests, efforts should be made to reduce the scope for arbitrary and discriminatory practices, provide greater transparency and introduce more neutral economic criteria. The issue of transparency in respect of the application of the GATS commitments is crucial as a tool in promoting trade in tourism services.

In that respect, commitments in mode 4 are closely linked to the implementation of the relevant immigration regulations, policies and procedures in a clear and transparent manner. Publishing of the legislation and implementing regulations which significantly affect ability of the foreign nationals or permanent residents move across borders to supply services is a general obligation, since this is the way to limit the room for discretionary and procedural rules. The lack of transparency, clarity in the existence, implementation and application of policy guidelines affecting application for and consideration of temporary work permits, residency requirements of visas impede market access, effectively violating key GATS provision.

4

The Demand for Tourism

Introduction

Tourism demand is the foundation on which all tourism-related business decisions ultimately rest. Governments and companies such as airlines, tour operators, hotels, cruise ship lines, and recreation facility providers are interested in the demand for their products by tourists. The success of many businesses depends largely or totally on the state of tourism demand, and ultimate management failure is quite often due to the failure to meet market demand.

One of the most interesting element in the tourism industry is the tourism demand. Demand as the economic concept refers to the amount of the definite products which the consumer is ready to buy, on fixed price, in the particular time and with the pointed circumstances. There is an economic rule: if the price is high, the demand for the product is lower and vice versa. But there are some exception to the rule. In general the are three main principal elements of the tourism demand. They are:

- an effective demand, which contain the amount of people who actually are participating in tourism. The commonly accepted way of measuring the actual demand is the number of travellers;
- a restrained demand, which means the amount of people, who have the desire to travel, but have no possibility to do it because of different circumstances. This type of demand is called the potential demand. If the restricting factors disappear, the potential demand becomes the effective demand;
- a deferred demand, which also can become the actual demand;
- no demand, which is characterized as the absence of desire to travel and to visit different countries.

There also a lot of the other approaches to the tourism demand. For example, the deputizing of demand, which means the substitution one activity connected with tourism for another similar activity. The another view consider the displacement of demand, which refers to the case when the geographical location of tourism interests changes. A very effective way to support and to extend the tourism demand is to open and develop new tourist centres, resorts and places of attraction. The way to attract the wide demand for these new resorts divides into three main approaches:

- to readdress the demand from the similar resorts in the area to the new places of attraction;
- to replace the demand from the absolutely dissimilar resorts to the new;
- to create the new effective demand.

The Tourist's need and Wants

Visitors want their expectations satisfied. Some will be demanding, some not. But most will be very pleased if the bathrooms are clean.

Some travellers are comforted by moving out of their comfort zones and others need substantial hand-holding throughout the journey. In most cases travellers wish to figure out how to interact with locals that is not exploitative.

Visitors have different information demands. Eco travellers want to know where the water comes from, what is growing in the fields. Many are interested in la Earlier studies acknowledged the following key motivation elements in relation to tourism. They are; the need to escape (for example a dreary home life) and to seek (new and exciting experiences). There is still acceptance of the undimentional approach to motivation on the understanding that a variety of behaviours can be explained as a response of a small number of motivational 'needs'. This appears to be the main view despite suggestions that motivation may be outdated since the decision process is a result of many experiences and knowledge of destinations. Suggests that motivation's two dimensions are lasting dispositions and object-specific elements engage and want to know the names of the trees.

General and Specific Motivation

According to some tourist motivation theories, motivations are developed as a result of 'pull' and 'push' factors. Pull factors relate to the characteristics or attractions of a travel destination. For cultural tourists visiting Australia, they include attractions such as the Sydney Opera House and Aboriginal sites. Push factors relate to the needs and wants of individuals that lead them to 'buy' particular holidays. For cultural tourism and tourism as a whole, they include the desire for social interaction and relaxation, to experience something different and to learn about themselves and the places they visit for participating in cultural activities.

Segmenting the Tourism Market

Market segmentation is essentially the process of dividing the total market into more manageable groups of people with similar buying characteristics. Avoiding a mass market approach means that sales messages can be more targeted and distribution channels tailored to the segments' needs. Segments must be discernible so you can differentiate one segment from another. Each segment also needs to be a reasonable size otherwise it won't be economically viable to target it. You should also have a product, or be able to develop one, that is appropriate to each segment you choose. It's also important to avoid making segments too large because it's much harder to develop suitable promotional messages for larger segments.

If you focus on just a few segments won't you miss out on others? Some tourism providers become concerned that by targeting only a segment of the total market, they will miss out. The reverse is usually true. The aim is to choose a limited number of segments and to understand those markets really well. This means that marketing messages are clearer and stronger. There is a ripple effect as people outside the chosen segments find these stronger messages more appealing and are also attracted to that product.

The following two diagrams demonstrate this. The first box shows the "something for everyone" approach used by many tourism providers. They don't want to exclude any markets so they try to embrace them all. But their marketing efforts and messages are rarely strong enough to reach the people at the centre of their markets so they go untapped. Market segmentation is a method of dividing a large market in to smaller groupings of consumers each having common needs or behaviour. We have two types of markets:

a) Homogenous Market: a market in which people or organisation have similar characteristics.

b) Heterogeneous Market: a market in which people or organisations have different characteristics.

Market segmentation allows a marketer to take a heterogeneous market and carve it up in to one or more homogenous markets which are made up of individuals or organisations with similar needs, wants and behavioural tendencies. In short, market segmentation in tourism helps in.

a) efficient use of marketing resources to cater to a particular type of tourists,

b) better understanding of customer needs and providing better satisfaction,

c) better understanding of the competitive situation and emerging trends, and

d) achieving accuracy in the measurement of goals and performances.

Market segmentation involves a division of the prospective market into identifiable groups. In simple words, it can be defined as the division of a market into groups of segments having similar wants. This theory is opposed to the diluting of efforts by appealing to an entire market. It is based on a realisation of the fact that a product can be sold more effectively if efforts are concentrated towards those groups which are most potential. Philip Kotter is of the view that different "competitors will be in the best position to go after particular segments of the market" and each "organisation, instead of trying to reach every one, should identify the most attractive parts of the market that it could effectively serve". At the same he mentions that this is not always the practise. The organisations, in their thinking about operating in a market have generally passed through the following three stages:

Mass Marketing: This is a marketing style where the organisation makes efforts to attract every eligible buyer to use its product which has been mass produced and will be mass distributed. Here no attention is paid to consumer preferences.

Organisation Product Mass Market

Product Differentiated Marketing: In this marketing style the organisation produces two or more products for the entire market. These products might have different characteristics but they are not designed for any different group(s). Rather they only provide alternatives to every buyer in the market.

Product

Target Marketing: Here, the organisation:

- differentiates amongst varied market segments,
- focuses on one or more of these segments (targets), and
- develops the product to meet the needs of the target market.

In tourism, the organisations practice each style of marketing though the emphasis on target marketing is gaining ground. Let us take the example of Airlines vis-a-vis the tourist market.

- Under stage-1, airlines are available for everyone to travel.
- Under stage-2, the airlines offer Royal class, J class, Business class, Economy class or one can hire charter flight or a chopper.
- Under stage-3, special airline services to pilgrim both domestic (dhams) or Vaishno Devi or international (Haj, Jerusalem) which have set target of customers from among the up budget tourist market.

This shift of emphasis is because of the benefits in market segmentation.

- By selecting the market niches, i.e., suitable markets, an organisation can exploit the market much better.
- An organisation can focus its strategies more appropriately on target groups.

Segmentation and Targeting Approaches in Tourism

It is true that product can be sold more effectively if efforts are concentrated towards those groups which are most potential. In the words of Philip Kotler, "Competitors will be in the best position to go after particular segments of the markets and each organisation instead of trying to reach everyone, should identify the most attractive parts of market that it would effectively serve". He also acknowledges that in practice marketers operating in the markets have generally passed through following three stages:

Mass Marketing

- Efforts are made to attract every eligible buyers.
- No attention is paid to consumer preferences, e.g., airline for every one who can afford, same by all airlines.

Target Marketing:

- Varied segments are differentiated.

- Focus on one or two of these segments.
- Products are developed to meet their needs, e.g., operating of short/shuttle services between popular business destinations for corporate travellers or for pilgrims. For international pilgrimages, Haj, etc. and for domestic, Vaishnodevi, Kedarnath, Ajmer, Neelkanth, etc.

Product Differentiated Segmentation;

- Organisation produces two or more products for entire market but produces specialised products for particular groups.
- Only to provide alternatives to every buyer in the market, e.g., an airline offering different classes. "J" class, "Y" class, Royal Class, etc. Some airlines provide more leg and luggage space according to their class of journey.
- the product matches the needs of that segment.

The purpose of market segmentation in tourism marketing is to:

- Segment the markets generating tourists, and
- Identify the prospective tourists according to lifestyles, socio-economic status, attitudes about travel, etc.

This is done to best qualify these tourists for high prospect customer status. This high potential prospect is defined in terms of how closely his/her vacation preferences and lifestyles match up to what the destination has to offer. In other words, the purpose is to go for cost-effective marketing. This can be achieved by designing, promoting and delivering the tourism products or services in such ways that the identical needs of the target groups are satisfied. A crucial aspect here is what is grouped in forming market segments. Consumers are not mutually exclusive categories and what is grouped together is the customers' probability of purchasing different types of product offers. Hence, it is necessary to understand what is wanted and who is going to buy it. A marketing person has to gain knowledge about this and he or she can approach this problem by asking certain questions like:

What

- factors influence the tourist demand?
- services do the tourists expect?
- is the basis for tourists comparing your product with other products?
- benefits do the tourists seek?

- risks do the tourists perceive?
- are the tastes of the tourist?

How

- do tourists buy?
- much are the tourists willing to spend?
- many vacations do the tourists take in a year?
- does promotion and advertising effect the tourists' demand?
- does the product fit into the life styles of tourists?

Where

- is the decision made by tourists to buy?
- do the tourists seek information about the product?
- do the tourists buy the product?

When

- do the tourists take a vacation?
- do the tourists make a decision to buy the product?
- is the product repurchased?

Why

- do the tourists buy your product?
- do the tourists choose one destination over the other?
- do the tourists go to a particular destination?
- do the tourists prefer one type of service and not the other?
- do the tourists buy your competitors' products?

Who

- buys your product?
- buys your competitors' products?
- are likely to buy your product?
- may not be interested in your product?

You must remember here that this list of questions is only suggestive and the nature of questions will depend on the nature of your product and certain specific situations. Besides, you will need the back up data and information for finding answers to these questions which may not always be possible. But you should not be discouraged by the limitations. Depending upon the study's purpose, various approaches are employed in the tourism industry to identify market segments. Segments can be defined either by descriptive or casual factors. Descriptive factors simply describe the characteristics of the person found in a segment. The "why" of a person's action, however, is better obtained through additional use of causal factor information which identifies the motivation behind a decision.

A practical and Actionable Segmentation requires profiling of both:

- Past visitors, and
- Prospective visitors.

This is done to ensure proper matches and to determine the actual size of each high potential segment, in terms of:

- Geographics,
- Deomgraphics
- Psychographics, and
- Travel Habits.

In other words, we can say that the:

Target for Marketing = Characteristics + Demographic profile of Consumers, Products and Services).

The studies of marketing experts like Kotler and Chisnall show that in order to make any segment actionable for marketing, each segment must be:

1) Discrete, i.e., the separate identity of the subgroup must be established by using any criteria like income, purpose, interest, etc.
2) Measurable, i.e., the characteristics that distinguish the subgroups should be measurable through the available data.
3) Viable, i.e., the projected earnings to be achieved should be more than the costs of designing the market mix.
4) Appropriate, i.e., showing the inseparability of the tourism product which should contribute to the overall image in the market.

Segmentation Factors

In practice, the ground for tourism market segmentation shall be, of course, on the basis of:

a) Geographic factors: Since tourism involves movement of millions of people across the international boundaries, it is an acknowledged fact that the tourists' needs differ according to geographic regions. For instance, tourist coming from Australasia region would have altogether different needs than a tourist coming from North America. Not only this even tourists coming from two different coasts of America have different needs, desires and attitudes. Therefore, to market successfully your product or services you must understand varied needs of the tourists coming from different geographic areas. It is only then that you can categorise your potential segments in a homogenous manner. Therefore, it is advisable that you should try to target a segment for your product which lacks that particular product/service you are marketing. For instance, you sell deserts of Rajasthan to tourists from Germany, UK or France which have no deserts. Similarly, if you are trying to sell your mountain based activities to tourist from countries who do not have such snow capped peaks. You may succeed but if you try to target tourist from Switzerland or Austria you cannot succeed. On the same pattern don't try to sell your coastal beauties to tourist from Australasia or Pacific but try to sell them to tourists who don't have such coastal attractions in their countries. Kerala started marketing "monsoon tourism to tourists from Middle East" but the same cannot be sold to tourists from North-East India. Here Kerala will have to sell beaches and back waters.

b) Demographic Profiles: This factor is a vital factor for developing tourism products and services. It means to segment your product service market on basis of income, age, sex, family size, lifestyle, family life cycle, education, religion, race and nationality and so on. If you fail to design your product or segment your market without giving due consideration to these factors then there may be serious repercussions for your product or service. It is important because:

   i) Consumer wants, preferences and usage rates are associated with demographic variables, and

   ii) this method is easy in measurement and interpretation of data.

   For instance, India being a long haul destination (average length of stay is 27.2 days) and our major markets are America, Europe, Far East and Australasia. The demographic profile of these markets will help in marketing decision making. If we look at the demographic characteristics of the European market, we see:

- Age: between 25 – 59 years,
- Sex: majority of males, alone females very few,
- Family sizes: 2 – 4 members,
- Family Life Cycle: single/married without children (DINKS) or with children below the age of 14.
- Income: Euro 7000 and above,
- Occupation: professionals, executives, teachers and professors,
- Education: Higher secondary and above,
- Nationality: German, French, Italia, Swiss, Dutch, Spanish and Swedes,
- Based on this data a marketer can develop, rejuvenate or alter his or her tourism products.

c) Psychographic Grounds: Division of groups on the basis of their social status, life styles and/or personality characteristics is very essential in tourism marketing. While using demographic parameters of income, we can divide the target segment in to upper middle class, middle class and lower middle class. Each of these sub-variable will have different tastes, likings, status, product preferences, etc. accordingly. Personality characteristics also play and important role in product development and market segmentation. For instance, if you are targeting at tourists for adventure sports related tourism, their real market segment would be tough and strong or adventure seekers only. These people shall be young and so would naturally belong to low budget or lower income.

* Another important criteria for segmenting the tourist market is on the basis of personality traits, i.e., some members of potential targeted market are allocentrics. Money wouldn't be a constraint for this segment but they want to visit a new and adventurous place every time. They don't like to repeat the same destination. They love to be called first timers or trendsetters to be followed by the masses (psycocentrics) who have a fear for unknown and who want to perform repeat visits.

* In this category, as a marketer, you should also try to identify those who are self made, successful socialite, mainstreamers, aspirers or innovator type of people because they are the ones who are most likely to purchase tours to far away countries.
* It is also advisable that you should try to segment your market with an idea that among certain categories of tourists there can be found some common attitudes. For example, people in the age group of 18-26, want to have vacation full of leisure and thrill, while others who look for adventure can form another group.

d) Behavioural Grounds: In psychological terms the whole range of generation of wants and their transformation in to buying or using decisions can be explained as behaviour. Before learning about transformation process of attitudes of tourists in to action we should know who are users and what is their base:

Foreign Tourist, Domestic Tourist, Youths, Students, Executives, Artists, Politicians, Academicians, Pilgrims, Representatives, Sportsmen;

* General Classification,
* Sex as a base,
* Male, Female,
* Region as a base,
* Urban, Rural, Cosmopolitan, Sub-urban,
* Education as a base.

Professional, Worker, Vocational, Artists, Professor, Craftsmen, business man, etc.;

* Status as a base,
* Upmarket, Budget Market, Low-Class Market,
* Occupation as a base,
* White Collar or Blue Collar Tourist.

In view of this, the marketing decision cannot be sound unless the marketers make an in-depth study of the visitors' behaviour with focused attention on customer satisfaction. Before arriving at sound marketing decisions, the marketers are required to see that users are aware or unaware; interested or intend to purchase either on trial or experimental basis; whether user is light user (non-frequent) or heavy user (frequent users).

This kind of study will help the marketers to focus their advertisements on the service sensitivity of the users. In tourism market segmentation a large number of behaviouristic variables are used. Among important ones a few are:

(I) *Occasion for travel:* You can segment your tourist market on the basis of the occasion they use for travelling. For instance, you can segment your tourist markets as business tourist market, holiday/leisure market, VFR (visiting Friends and Relations) market, adventure tourist market, heritage tourism market, or honeymooners market and so on so forth.

(II) *Benefit derivation:* Segmentation on the basis of benefits identifies the:

(i) major benefits that the customer looks for in the product;

(ii) kind of people who look for each benefit; and

(iii) major brands that deliver each benefit.

According to Kotler many products are made-up of three "core benefit segments",

(i) quality buyers – more concerned with product image rather than cost;

(ii) service buyers – product that provides good service, i.e., best value for money; and

(iii) economy buyers – who are more concerned with the cost and, therefore, would like to keep it low.

Kotler further classifies customers on the basis of behaviouristic attitudes in to four categories on the basis of behaviouristic attitudes:

(i) hard-core loyals – would never think of switching over;

(ii) soft-core loyals – may think of one or two alternatives;

(iii) shifting loyals – gradually favour one product/organisation over other; and

(iv) switchers – those who have no loyalty to any organisation.

Kotler's this classification of customers is very useful form the perspective that you can pinpoint which brands are most competitive to you. By knowing the product and market strategies of your competitor you can successfully convert your soft core loyals customers in to hard-core customers by offering them incentives like free mileage or free accommodation when they accumulate required mileage or number of nights.

(III) *Associated characteristics:* Besides the benefits sought by tourists, you can also use other associated characteristic for segmenting your market. These are:

(i) *User status:* In this category a tourist may be segmented as first time visitor or repeat visitor, past-visitor or potential visitor, etc.

(ii) *Usage rage:* This can be illustrated as frequent usage called frequent fliers for an airline or for hotels ex-numbers of night spent to earn points for complimentary services.

(iii) *Loyalty status:* This highlights the loyalty of your customer who remains loyal to you in spite of many allurements to shift to other products or service. Therefore, your company must study its own hard-core loyals and devise marketing strategies to maintain their loyalty. For example, an airline offers members of its frequent fliers scheme, quick check-in or extra baggage allowances, priority in confirmation of seats or special waiting lounge.

(IV) *Buyer-readiness stage:* This is a crucial factor for market segmentation since an in-depth study of this allows marketers to launch their product at right time. For example, if you decide to launch special packages for all family members, readiness stage would be when all the members have leisure, i.e., when they have a vacation. In another example, private domestic airlines started their services when they realised that domestic air travellers were weary of monopolistic attitude of the national carrier.

(V) *Attitudes:* No doubt tourism market can be classified by the degree of enthusiasm tourist or a potential tourist shows in buying a destination. Keeping in view this you may encounter tourists who are enthusiastic, positive, indifferent or hostile in their attitude towards the destination. It would be easier for you to sell a destination to those who are enthusiastic and positive in their attitude.

Price factor: By now you must have gathered a fair idea that tourism market constitutes of:

(i) those who are high spenders and are prepared to pay high prices and they are described as up-budget tourists;

(ii) those who want to take low priced vacation; and

(iii) those who may take a moderately priced holiday.

It is true that price range communicates to consumers the quality expectations of a product along with the producer's image. Today destinations in South Eat Asia are cheaper than travelling within India. For example, Bangkok is being sold at $25 per night, Singapore at $40 per night, etc. This is able to attract large volume of outbound tourism from India.

Other Variables

Tourism markets are also segmented on the basis of travelling habits of tourists, which include:

(a) *Distance Travelled:* Whether potential tourist segment belongs to long haul, short haul or mid haul tourist. This is classified on the basis of the distance a tourist travels. For India, tourists from Europe, Far East or USA are long haul market segments whereas Nepal or Bangladesh are short haul.

(b) *Duration of Trip:* Segmentation of tourist markets can also take place on basis of short-break holidays of 2-3 days or long trips of 20 or more days for instance to USA or Europe.

(c) *Time of Travel:* Tourist markets can also be segmented on the basis of time period when they travel. For example some tourists prefer to travel during summer holidays while some prefer to travel during winter holidays or some take a holiday in both summer and winter. In Europe, normally, longer trips are taken during summer seasons, since vacation is longer in summer than winters.

(d) *Organisation of Trips:* Marketers also segment the market on the basis of how do they travel, i.e., whether they travel individually (FIT) or in groups (GITS). On the other hand, some of your customers will buy only air tickets or in some cases only hotel bookings will be sought.

(e) *Religion as Travel Motive:* Since ancient times man has travelled for religion motives be it to have a holy dip in the revered rivers or to visit any temples devoted to their deities or even for the sake of visiting religious fairs or melas. Undoubtedly religion has always been one of the prime motive for travel. However, in present times specialise services are prepared and delivered to this niche market whether they are Muslim tourists; Hindus (Dhamyatra) or Christians. You must have noticed that there is a particular time for each of there segments to travel. For instance, Haj travellers travel between the month of January and March; Hindu tourists visit their dhams or other religious shrines like Vaishno Devi, Shirdi, Kalka, etc. during summer vacations, i.e., May to July; and, of course, Christians travel during October and December.

Motivators and Facilitators

Travel motive is an inner force which create a desire in a person to travel. Motivating factors will vary from one person to another. This unit is aimed at imparting the knowledge and understanding among learner regarding the classification of travel motivations.

1. *Physical motivators:* Physical motives are the factors which helps to improve the physical and mental well being of individuals.
2. *Cultural motivators:* Cultural motivators are factors like music, dance, architecture, folk lore, arts and crafts, customs etc. which attracts tourists to a particular destination.
3. *Interpersonal motivators:* Interpersonal motivators are the factors which create desire to visit relatives and friends, meet new people, establish new friendships etc. It also includes ethnic motives and family reasons.
4. *Status and prestige:* Some people undertake travel because they think it is fashionable. Status and prestige motivators include motives related to business and profession.

Factors Influencing Changes in Tourism Demand

Tourism has to face a challenging change in its framework conditions: The geopolitical as well as the economic situation require new strategies. Technological innovations, demographic change and a powerful customer have to be met in politics, marketing and planning. New destinations, new products with prices on a level, which would have been incredible some years ago, compete with the established tourism offer.

We may look at the "New Demand Factors" from two perspectives. On the one hand we have those factors influencing the demand, i.e. the motivation to travel and the ability to travel, directly or indirectly. They cover a wide range from the general economic situation, over politics to technological innovations, just to name some examples. On the other hand we have emerging factors, i.e. the changing face of consumer behaviour in tourism like destinations preferences, quality expectations, booking behaviour etc. But what the tourist does can not only be explained by external factors alone. The experienced and educated traveller will change his behaviour even in a constant framework. Thus, there is an endogenous dynamic within the tourist behaviour. The emerging (from external and endogenous factors) patterns characterize the tourism consumers and their behaviour within the next years.

The Situation

Holiday travel does not generally mean international travel. In most European countries domestic travel exceeds the international holiday trips. Of course, there are some exceptions like Germany or the Netherlands or – quite naturally-small countries like Luxembourg.

The total volume of European tourism demand has been quite stable, but the structure underneath showed quite a dynamic.

Vacations are not only for the fun of the travellers: Holiday tourism has become an important economic sector, a social achievement, a political Instrument, and an educational tool.

Influencing Factors

As we all experience the change around us the questions arises how these developments will have an impact on tourism demand. To name just a few categories:

- Economy,
- Politics,
- Crisis and threats,
- Demographic Change,
- Technology.

In addition we have to take into account the influences coming from general changes in consumer attitudes and, finally, the tourism industry itself, of course influencing the demand side of tourism (e.g. standardization of products, information channels, (over) capacities and price strategies).

* All these factors are linked to each other.
* How can these factors have an impact?
* Holiday demand is driven by needs, motives, and expectations, its realization depends on the individual economic situation and the freedom to travel.

Thus:

- External factors may have an impact on tourism demand by

affecting the *ability* to travel (freedom, time, money, fitness) and the *motivation* to do so.

- Consumer Behaviour is not a reaction on a single factor but on the whole *set of influencing external factors*. In addition it is driven by internal factors (e.g. motives, abilities etc.). Thus, the impact of a change in a single external factor is limited.

Most of the external factors seem to be *in favour for a sound development* of tourism demand in Europe in the years to come. However, there are no signs for a general boom.

Emerging Factors

As we can't limit our attention to a single external factor and its impacts, we look at several of the emerging factors, new trends in tourism emerging from the whole set of influences and the endogenous dynamics of tourism. These emerging trends will not change tourism over night. Trend research has shown that the future developments will most probably come as a step-by-step development, not as a revolution. Giving the global and nearly unlimited offer in tourism with capacities still on the rise at least in Europe the power in the market is clearly with the consumer. He will only choose products which fit into his motivation and expectations. Taking the efforts to reduce seasonality in tourism as an example, we clearly see that the limitations to these efforts are only partly due to e.g. school holiday regulations but predominantly due to the motivation of spending a holiday under nice weather conditions.

New Source Markets

The enlargement of the European Union in 2004 and 2007 sure is important for the whole continent. Poland, Hungary, the Czech Republic, Estonia, Latvia, Lithuania, Slovenia, Slovakia, Malta and Cyprus have joined the European Union on May 1, 2004. The EU since then embraces 25 countries. The size of the EU has grown by 25%, the population by 20%, the GDP by 5%. However, its short time effects on tourism are limited. But the general political process, under way since some 20 years, which the EU enlargement is a "natural" part of, contribute a lot to a changing tourism demand in Europe.

As destinations, the new EU-members benefit from a bonus this year: The extensive coverage in the media will influence the growing interest in these countries and the felt distances will decrease. However, for most holiday makers, almost the whole world is accessible for a vacation. For holiday destinations this means a continuously growing competition-a competition in which the new EU-member countries will have to participate as well: No guarantee for success for anybody, but chances for everybody! The dynamic in holiday tourism is based on continuous, long-term developments, not in sudden changes.

Naturally there are not only potentials and chances, but also barriers preventing a fast development in tourism. Experts mention the following reasons for Eastern Europe: Low investment rates, undeveloped traffic system, undeveloped infrastructure in the countryside, unsatisfactory quality of hotels and gastronomy, weaknesses in tourism marketing. Of course this does not go for every single destination. There are also limits on the demand side. Images are playing an important role when deciding upon a holiday destination. Closely connected to images are holiday motives. People choose holiday destinations mainly based on their suitability of fulfilling their holiday motives. Political settings or changes, like the EU-enlargement, are comparatively important.

To raise the demand for the new EU-member countries, (potential) holiday makers must be convinced that their holiday motives can very well (or better) be fulfilled in these countries. Now is the time for a powerful marketing. People are going to make use of their new freedom and the opportunities connected to rising welfare (at least those, who participate in the economic upswing).

Demographic Change

Demographic change is a constant process but has got a lot of public attention in recent years. These are major demographic changes that are already influencing society today and that are worth a closer look on how they may have an impact on holiday travel behaviour.

Examples for other important demographic trends are: Rising educational level, a more colourful society due to migration, a changing role of women in society. Research has shown that people do not change their travel behaviour just because they turn 60 or 65, or because they retire. In most cases they stick to the holiday patterns acquired till the middle of their life. This fact allows for predictions of the tourist behaviour of future senior generations: within 15 years the number of holiday tourists in the age group 70 to 80 years to rise by more than 50% (from 4,2 mn. in 2003 to 6,6 mn. in 2018) with more than 2/3 choosing a destination abroad (today: 50%; 2003 figures from RA 2004). Less dramatic are the changes in the segment of *family holidays*.

Taking again Germany as an example: The number and share of Holiday trips with children (up to 13 years) has proved to be stable in Germany for more than a decade with some 22% of all holiday trips. In 2003 this share resulted in 14.4 mn holiday trips. With an 8%.

Information Search and Travel Decisions: Skilled Consumers with Low Involvement

Along with this structural developments the consumer behaviour changes as well. One of the important fields is in the pre-trip phase the search for information and the way a decision for a certain tourist product is made. The immense tourism offer available able to fulfil the individual needs leads the way to *interchangeable products*. For the consumer it doesn't make much of a difference whether travelling to destination A or B, with the tour operator X or Y etc. Actually, with all the communication channels and the more and more detailed information available the consumer is in a state of *information overload.* Impossible to consider everything!

Thus, the holiday decision is not the final result of a comprehensive search-evaluate-choice process but a *good-enough solution* considering a few aspects of a few products (those being in the relevant set) from a few information sources. Rational arguments are not very important. This is the state consumer researcher call "*low involvement*". With basic needs fulfilled and low involvement conditions *convenience* (taking the easy way) and *experience* orientation together with *variety seeking* are getting more important. Naturally, there is nothing new about experience orientation in tourism.

Consumers' Paradox: meet the Standards & be Different

With globalization of the tourism industry, a computer based distribution, and the strive to offer high quality, *standardization* of tourism products is a must. That constitutes a risk for tourism because "standard" is nothing offering new experiences or meeting the trend for variety seeking. At the same time the tourism demand and the products get more and more *differentiated* and fragmentized, e.g. with winter sports, study trips or family holidays. The consumer expects both: *quality* and *difference.*

Standardization and *differentiation* are main trends of both the consumers' and the industry's side. Again, this is an additional challenge for the industry, because this means more efforts necessary without a growing demand or even a growing turnover.

Conclusions

Looking at the mayor trends we can summarize:

- High volume of tourism demand around Europe with a few growth potentials in some source markets.
- Source markets are different: from *close to saturated* to *offering growth potentials* and need specific treatment in marketing.
- General market conditions, skilled consumer and vast capacities in tourism are a challenge for tourism marketing, especially in the big close to saturated markets.

But holiday tourism has manifold functions. It is an economic sector (for both destinations and the travel industry), a social achievement, a political Instrument, and an educational tool. Different sectors see tourism as a tool for different objectives. The evaluation of the situation and the future perspectives may vary with the sector.

But with all the sectors is a need to focus on the customer: Holiday travel is a behaviour of individual consumers, their perception of the reality is important.

Now is the time for real marketing: Consumer behaviour in tourism is less determined by the general framework conditions than at the end of the last century. The tourists have in their decisions many degrees of freedom. Consumer research is a necessary base, not only for projections into the future, but to determine the starting point, to have an orientation to formulate own objectives and plans to reach them. Without the consumer, in tourism as in every service industry, you will go nowhere. That does not go not only for the industry and their marketing activities, but as well for politics/tourism related policies.

What do the new demand factors in tourism mean for the different sectors or functions?

For *destinations* it is of utmost importance to recognize the international competition they are in. Master plans and marketing activities need realistic objectives considering not only what one wants to reach but as well what others do, then the own resources (financial and human– which will be limited e.g. with demographic change), and – of course – the consumers' motivation and the trends in consumer behaviour in tourism.

Giving the situation of the demand and its expected future trends, it's not sufficient to have a good product. It's not sufficient either, that the consumer perceives a product as a good one. The product or the destination has to be in the consumer's *relevant set*, and to be judged a *very good choice* within this set.

The same goes for the *industry*, i.e. tour operators and travel agencies, transport companies etc. Tour operators and travel agencies may e.g. take advantage from the fact of the information overload. They can take the role of a guide in the information jungle and thus offer convenience.

Politics have not only to watch carefully the market conditions and how the consumers behave under these conditions. The time to just formulate and express good objectives like *sustainability, strengthening specific regions, support third world countries, stressing the importance of the environment, supporting the European integration through more international travel,* where everybody agrees. They have to identify the contradictions and inconsistencies arising from the whole set of objectives and to find solutions or priorities. It does not seem very useful to provide funding and financial support for everybody just because he intends to follow one of these objectives.

Another challenge for politics is to keep the *social balance* within the source markets: Some experts claim that the economic development tends to widen the distance between the poor and the rich within European societies. But tourism needs a broad base of more or less middle class people with time and money to travel.

Coming back to the tourism demand we can state that the future in a quantitative perspective seems to be quite stable: There is no boom ahead, but no bust either. Of course, the future is predictable only within close limits, and unexpected events (e.g. crisis, terror attacks, war, epidemic diseases) will always cause confusion. Still it is important (and possible) to prepare oneself for the trends that can be identified with some reliability today. Demand potentials for good products are there, but you will not be able to sell just anything to the skilled consumer.

In this way the future is open: Room to move for everybody who has a sound marketing plan or political perspective, and respects the consumer. There is a strong need for *orientation* and decision for every organization involved in tourism: Where do you want to go from now and here? What is your objective? Different paths of development are possible, so you have to decide which road to take. You may call that a vision. While elaborating your vision, you need to have a strong focus on the customer, on what other market actors are doing, and what resources are at hand. Visions will be and have to be different on different levels (pan-European, national, regional, local), and different with different destinations or other segments of the industry, but linked to some extent.

Success shall be based on safeguarding the core values (the distinctive qualities and related experiences) while constantly adapting to new market trends. A deep understanding of the consumer and his perpetual learning processes as well as the changing structure of tourism demand is a prerequisite for successful planning. A bright future for both, tourists and the tourism industry is within easy reach. Just take your responsibilities to make it real.

5

The Economic Impact of Tourism

Introduction

Businesses and public organizations are increasingly interested in the economic impacts of tourism at national, state, and local levels. One regularly hears claims that tourism supports X jobs in an area or that a festival or special event generated Y million dollars in sales or income in a community. "Multiplier effects" are often cited to capture secondary effects of tourism spending and show the wide range of sectors in a community that may benefit from tourism.

Tourism's economic benefits are touted by the industry for a variety of reasons. Claims of tourism's economic significance give the industry greater respect among the business community, public officials, and the public in general. This often translates into decisions or public policies that are favourable to tourism. Community support is important for tourism, as it is an activity that affects the entire community. Tourism businesses depend extensively on each other as well as on other businesses, government and residents of the local community.

Economic benefits and costs of tourism reach virtually everyone in the region in one way or another. Economic impact analyses provide tangible estimates of these economic interdependency and a better understanding of the role and importance of tourism in a region's economy.

Tourism activity also involves economic costs, including the direct costs incurred by tourism businesses, government costs for infrastructure to better serve tourists, as well as congestion and related costs borne by individuals in the community. Community decisions over tourism often involve debates between industry proponents touting tourism's economic impacts (benefits) and detractors emphasizing tourism's costs.

Sound decisions rest on a balanced and objective assessment of both benefits and costs and an understanding of who benefits from tourism and who pays for it. Tourism's economic impacts are therefore an important consideration in state, regional and community planning and economic development. Economic impacts are also important factors in marketing and management decisions. Communities therefore need to understand the relative importance of tourism to their region, including tourism's contribution to economic activity in the area.

A variety of methods, ranging from pure guesswork to complex mathematical models, are used to estimate tourism's economic impacts. Studies vary extensively in quality and accuracy, as well as which aspects of tourism are included. Technical reports often are filled with economic terms and methods that non-economists do not understand. On the other hand, media coverage of these studies tend to oversimplify and frequently misinterpret the results, leaving decision makers and the general public with a sometimes distorted and incomplete understanding of tourism's economic effects. How can the average person understand these studies sufficiently to separate good studies from bad ones and make informed choices? The purpose of this bulletin is to present a systematic introduction to economic impact concepts and methods. The presentation is written for tourism industry analysts and public officials, who would like to better understand, evaluate, or possibly conduct an economic impact assessment. The bulletin is organized around ten basic questions that either are asked or should be asked about the economic impacts of tourism.

The International Tourist Market

Tourism is a major source of economic revenue for countries all around the world. It sustains 200 million jobs, earns over US $1.3 billion per day, and is the biggest export earner worldwide (World Tourism Organization). Destinations invest millions of dollars into tourism research to understand their market, their competitive positioning and most importantly, how they can use this knowledge to successfully attract tourists. Yet, on September 11, 2001, everything changed. The tourism industry was dealt a mighty blow as the world reeled in the aftermath of the terrorist attacks in New York. People lacked the confidence to travel, flights were cut back, businesses closed, and jobs were lost. And the effects not only hit the immediate players of the tourism industry, but also resounded across other industries that the tourist dollar would normally support. The severity of this situation was only compounded by the War on Iraq and the existence of the SARS virus in 2003, so much so, that for the first time in over 20 years, international tourism arrivals worldwide suffered a negative growth of 0.6% or 4 million arrivals.

India's Place In World Tourism

Tourism has emerged as an instrument for employment generation, poverty alleviation and sustainable human development. Tourism promotes international understanding and gives support to local handicrafts and cultural activities. It is an important segment of the country's economy, specially in terms of its contribution towards foreign exchange earnings, generation of additional income and creation of employment opportunities. The foreign exchange earnings from tourism during the year 2000 were estimated at about Rs. 14,408 crores with an estimated direct employment of about 15 million, which is about 2.4% of the total labour force of the country. Tourism is the third largest foreign exchange earner for India. The International tourist traffic in the country is estimated to be 2.64 million during the year 2000. However, according to the World Tourism Organisation (WTO), India's share in world tourism arrivals is only 0.38%, accounting for 0.62% of the world tourist receipts. This indicates that much of the tourist potential is yet to be tapped.

With rapid advances in Science & Technology, tourism has acquired the status of an industry in all industrialised countries. The high influx of foreign tourist traffic has accelerated demand for certain economic production and distribution activities. Tourism has emerged as an industry next in importance only to Information Technology industry in the Services sector. By 2005, the contribution of Tourism to the world economy will be doubled. The economic liberalisation in India and consequent foreign investment opportunities, development of tourist facilities including expansion in airline services, etc. provide an impetus for a spurt in tourist arrivals as in South Asian regions. Domestic tourism plays a vital role in achieving the national objectives of promoting social and cultural cohesion and national integration. Its contribution to generation of employment is very high. With the increase in income levels and emergence of a powerful middle class, the potential for Domestic tourism has grown substantially during the last few years.

In its modern form since the end of the Second World War, tourism has grown into one of the world's largest industries with a growth rate in excess of 5 per cent per annum over the past twenty years. International tourism flows across frontiers in the year 2000 reached 698 million while receipts from these flows reached US$ 595 billion (including receipts from international transport fares). Estimates prepared by the World Tourism Organization indicate that global domestic tourism flows are at least ten times greater than international tourism flows indicating that there were at least 6,980 million domestic arrivals in 2000. Globally, tourism accounts for 11% of the global GDP and 8% of the world trade employment. In most countries with a large population, domestic tourism is the foundation of a viable and sustainable tourism industry. Much of the growth of global tourism has been generated by domestic tourism, which tends to be more focused On rural destinations.

With a growing interest in the intangible culture of different countries (i.e. lifestyles, cuisine, ceremonies, music, religious beliefs, traditions, customs, and history), there is a strong potential to encourage international tourism to the rural areas as well. India's share of global international tourism at 2.64 million foreign arrivals through its borders in the year 2000 is relatively small in volume (about 0.38 per cent) but almost twice as high in terms of US$ receipts (about 0.69 per cent).

On the other hand, India's share of global domestic tourism is much higher (around 4.6 per cent of estimated global domestic tourism). While the proportion of global US$ receipts from international tourism increased from 0.57 per cent in 1990 to 0.69 per cent in 2000, this compares with a share of 1.37 per cent in 1981. In contrast, India's neighbours in South and South-East Asia have more effectively utilised tourism for economic growth and employment creation. A forecasting study undertaken by the World Tourism and Travel Council estimated that in 2001, tourism would account for 10.7 per cent of global Gross Domestic Product, 207.1 million jobs; US$ 1,063.8 billion in export value, and US$ 657.7 billion in capital investment. A study on the economic impact of tourism conducted by the World Tourism and Travel Council estimated that in 2001, the consumption activity arising from domestic and international tourism will contribute 5.3 per cent of India's Gross Domestic Product. Tourism will also sustain 25 million equivalent full time jobs or 6 per cent of India's work force, and contribute more than US$ 3 billion in gross foreign exchange receipts. Separate estimates prepared by the Department of Tourism using a multiplier based on 1980 research suggests that the actual employment generation effect of (direct & indirect) tourism in India is around 42 million (includes full time/part time/casuals). The forecasting study undertaken by the World Tourism and Travel Council further indicates that between 2001 and 2011:-

- global Gross Domestic Product will increase from 10.7 per cent to 11 per cent;
- global employment contribution will increase from 207.1 million to 260.4 million jobs or 9 per cent of total global employment;
- the global value of tourism related exports will increase from US$ 1,063.8 billion to US$ 2,538.3 billion or 12.8 per cent of global export value; and
- global capital investment in tourism will increase from US$ 657.7 billion to US$ 1,434 billion or 9.3 per cent of global investment.

The Value of Economic Data

Businesses and public organizations are increasingly interested in the economic impacts of tourism at national, state, and local levels. One regularly hears claims that tourism supports X jobs in an area or that a festival or special event generated Y million dollars in sales or income in a community. "Multiplier effects" are often cited to capture secondary effects of tourism spending and show the wide range of sectors in a community that may benefit from tourism.

Tourism's economic benefits are touted by the industry for a variety of reasons. Claims of tourism's economic significance give the industry greater respect among the business community, public officials, and the public in general. This often translates into decisions or public policies that are favourable to tourism. Community support is important for tourism, as it is an activity that affects the entire community. Tourism businesses depend extensively on each other as well as on other businesses, government and residents of the local community.

Economic benefits and costs of tourism reach virtually everyone in the region in one way or another. Economic impact analyses provide tangible estimates of these economic interdependency and a better understanding of the role and importance of tourism in a region's economy.

Tourism activity also involves economic costs, including the direct costs incurred by tourism businesses, government costs for infrastructure to better serve tourists, as well as congestion and related costs borne by individuals in the community. Community decisions over tourism often involve debates between industry proponents touting tourism's economic impacts (benefits) and detractors emphasizing tourism's costs. Sound decisions rest on a balanced and objective assessment of both benefits and costs and an understanding of who benefits from tourism and who pays for it.

Tourism's economic impacts are therefore an important consideration in state, regional and community planning and economic development. Economic impacts are also important factors in marketing and management decisions. Communities therefore need to understand the relative importance of tourism to their region, including tourism's contribution to economic activity in the area.

A variety of methods, ranging from pure guesswork to complex mathematical models, are used to estimate tourism's economic impacts. Studies vary extensively in quality and accuracy, as well as which aspects of tourism are included. Technical reports often are filled with economic terms and methods that non-economists do not understand. On the other hand, media coverage of these studies tend to oversimplify and frequently misinterpret the results, leaving decision makers and the general public with a sometimes distorted and incomplete understanding of tourism's economic effects.

The Economic Impact of Tourism

- *"There are three kinds of lies: damned lies and statistics"*.

Why Statistics ?

- "The objective of a national statistical system is to provide relevant, comprehensive, accurate and objective statistical information. Generally, statistics are invaluable for monitoring the country's economic and social conditions, the planning and evaluation of government and private sector programmes and investment, policy debates and advocacy, and the creation and maintenance of an informed public."

Why Statistics ? Cont'd

Essential in:

- Official decision-making, policy formulation,
- Policy Analysis & Research,
- Academic, business, industrial & other research,
- Business planning & CRM,
- Citizens/residents being informed about performance of governments.

Why Statistics ?

- Facilitate comparison across countries/regions,
- Benchmarking,
- 'Best Practices',
- Evaluation of performance,

However, good statistics must be collected in accordance with agreed international standards using appropriate methods for data collection, processing and dissemination.

Key Tourism Statistics;

- Visitor Arrival figures,
- Tourism expenditure estimates,
- Visitor Surveys (expenditure, motivation, satisfaction etc.),
- Accommodation and Tourism Establishment Surveys,
- Tourism Satellite Account (TSA).

Typical tourism experience in regional destination can involve:

- water sports companies, golf clubs,
- destination management companies,
- yacht charter companies, marine transport companies,
- Entertainers,
- restaurants, retail outlets, local taxis, tour guides,
- telecommunications companies and casinos, etc.

Tourism Measurement Limitations

- In Caribbean absence of a reliable, thorough and internationally uniform statistical database from which one could measure the full economic impact of tourism,
- Simple analyses of arrivals, estimates of expenditure (VEMS),
- No in-depth analysis of Tourism economic impact.

Tourism Satellite Account

Overview:

- UN SNA '93 recommended TSA,
- WTO describes the TSA as the "only way to have an overall view of tourism's impact on the economy on an equal footing with all other sectors."
- Enhance ability to accurately capture economic impact of previously undefined "sectors".

- Analytical work done within existing national accounting systems.
- More flexible.
- Not overburdening CSNA.

Tourism Satellite Account

Uses:

- *Provide credible data on the impact of tourism and related employment.*
- *Serve as a standard framework for organizing statistical data on tourism.*
- *Become a new internationally accepted national accounting standard endorsed by the UN Statistical Commission.*
- *Function as a powerful instrument for designing economic policies related to tourism development.*
- *Measure tourism's contribution to GDP and its ranking in relation to other economic sectors.*
- *Provide data on tourism's impact on a country's Balance Of Payments.*
- *Provide information on tourism human resource characteristics.*
- *Measure the level of investment in tourism.*
- *Evaluate tax revenues generated by tourism industries.*
- *Measure the level of tourism's consumption of other goods and services.*

Tourism Satellite Account

Benefits:

- *Reconciliation of the demand-side data with the supply-side data within the account brings greater coherence to the definition of the industry; all partners in the industry will speak a common language.*
- *Use of a recognized accounting system brings enhanced credibility to the economic analysis of the industry.*
- *Use of an accounting framework can bring other important information into the analysis of tourism, such as data on value-added benefits of tourism, share of GDP, government revenues, human resources development or financial flows.*

Using Surveys to Assess Visitor Expenditure & Motivation, etc.

Uses of Tourism Surveys:

- demand side (visitor satisfaction, motivation, expenditure etc.),
- supply side (quality and standards of tourism establishments, employment, attitudes of residents etc.),

- Travel patterns and expenditure of regional and international visitors.

Using Surveys to Assess Visitor Expenditure & Motivation, etc.

Uses of Tourism Surveys cont'd:

1. RM/Visitor comment & feedback.
2. Evaluation of tourism promotion programmes.

Information collected from surveys used to:

- customize policies and strategies.
- redress any supply problems.
- enhance the tourism product.
- provide more competitive and attractive destination or experience for the visitor.

CTO/CRSTDP Statistics Workshop 2005;

Formula for determining Return on Investment from specific spending.

- E.g. Tourism Advertising campaign.

ROI Formula:

- Inquiries * Conversion rate * length of stay * party size * Avg. spending = Total expenditure.
- Total Advertising costs = (Costs of advertisement placement/ prod. + website development).
- ROI = Total Spending/Advertising costs.

E.g. Tourism Advertising campaign;

- Inquiries = brochures + website visits.
- In this example inquiries = 40,000 brochures+ 15,000 website visits = 55,000 inquiries.
- Conversion rate is 25% [gross conversion (# people who came, e.g. 60%) and net conversion (# people who came because of advertising, e.g. 25 %).
- Average length of stay is 6 days.
- Average party size is 2.6 people.
- Average daily expenditure is $100.
- Total Advertising costs = $100,000 (advertisement placement & production)+ $10000 (website development costs) = 110,000.

E.g. Tourism Advertising campaign;

- Total Spending = 55,000 * 25% * 6 days * 2.6 people * $50 per day = $10,725,000,
- Therefore Net ROI is: 9,750,000/110,000 = 97.5,
- For every advertising dollar spent, the return to the country was $97.50 in traveller spending.

Tourism Statistics in Macro-Economic Planning

- Accurate statistics fundamental to good economic planning !
- Planners use statistical databases, spreadsheets and modern analytical techniques to prepare reports and recommendations for governments etc.
- Analytical techniques utilized to project program costs and forecast future trends in aggregate demand (GDP), employment, housing, investment, taxation, transportation and population.

Tourism Statistics in Macro-Economic Planning cont'd.

Reliable and timely tourism statistics:

- crucial to projections & forecasting,
- vital to better planning of tourism sector and to justify its expansion,
- long-term and short-term plans for optimal land use,
- decisions on trade-offs between competing uses re: growth maximization.

Reliable and timely tourism statistics necessary for rationalizing:

- economic, political and social needs,
- traffic congestion, air, water and soil pollution,
- effects of growth and change on community *vs* potential benefits from tourism development,
- necessary to have reliable data on trends and projections in key sectors, including the tourism sector,
- not making best use of community's land and resources can be counterproductive to the particular development,
- crucial to policy framework formulation,
- informed decision-making by both public and private sectors at international, regional, national and local levels.

Policy formulation involves:

- Defining the objectives of tourism development.
- Setting growth targets for tourism.
- Determining the type of tourism to be attracted.
- Defining public and private responsibilities.
- Minimizing deleterious effects of tourism.

Economic Impacts;

- Direct (first round),
- Indirect (upstream),
- Induced (tourism $ in Dom Y),
- Negative (leakages),
- Positive (government revenues, externalities, multiplier effect).

Tourism Statistics in Business Planning & Investment Decisions

- Rapid growth of tourism necessitate more focused and informed planning and investment decisions by tourism business,
- Given massive investments and lender/shareholder demands tourism growth projections must be rigorous and as accurate as possible.

Business planning:

- involves anticipating and controlling change to maximize benefits of tourism.
- requires enterprises to rely on statistics for research, planning & design of marketing programs.
- needs reliable data for financial projections.
- demands industry and sector performance statistics for comparative analyses.

Investors

Rely on tourism statistics for:

- decision-making and financing proposals.
- evaluating performance/justifying investments.
- monitoring implementation of government policies.
- building partnerships with airlines, governments etc.
- benchmarking performance of host country vs competing destinations.

- policy advocacy in trade associations.

Accommodation Surveys

- Commercial Accommodation Classification Survey in New Zealand.
    * Survey data recorded using particular groupings (classifications) and terms.
- Classifications.

Survey provides information on groupings used Commercial Accommodation Survey Includes geographical, establishment and employee type classifications.

Classifications cont'd;

- Geographical classifications,
- Origin of guests,
- Origin of establishments.

6

The Sociocultural Impact of Tourism

Introduction

- The sociocultural impacts of tourism described here are the effects on host communities of direct and indirect relations with tourists, and of interaction with the tourism industry.
- For a variety of reasons, host communities often are the weaker party in interactions with their guests and service providers, leveraging any influence they might have.
- These influences are not always apparent, as they are difficult to measure, depend on value judgments and are often indirect or hard to identify.
- Impacts arise when tourism brings changes in value systems/ behaviour, threatening indigenous identity.
- Changes often occur in community structure, family relationships, collective traditional life styles, ceremonies and morality.
- But tourism can also generate positive impacts as it can serve as a supportive force for peace, foster pride in cultural traditions and help avoid urban relocation by creating local jobs.
- Sociocultural impacts are ambiguous: the same objectively described impacts are seen as beneficial by some groups and as negative by others.

Negative Sociocultural Impacts of Tourism

Change or Loss of Indigenous Identity or Values

Tourism can cause change/loss of local identity and values by:

- Commodification,
- Standardisation,
- Loss Of Authenticity/Staged Authenticity
- Adaptation To Tourist Demands.

Negative Sociocultural Impacts of Tourism

Commodification:

- Tourism can turn local cultures into commodities when religious rituals, traditional ethnic rites and festivals are reduced and sanitized to conform to tourist expectations, resulting in what has been called "reconstructed ethnicity."
- Once a destination is sold as a tourism product, and the tourism demand for souvenirs, arts, entertainment and other commodities begins to exert influence, basic changes in human values may occur.
- Sacred sites and objects may not be respected when they are perceived as goods to trade.

Standardization:

- Destinations risk standardization in the process of satisfying tourists' desires for familiar facilities.
- While landscape, accommodation, food and drinks, etc., must meet the tourists' desire for the new and unfamiliar, they must at the same time not be too new or strange because few tourists are actually looking for completely new things.
- Tourists often look for recognizable facilities in an unfamiliar environment, like well-known fast-food restaurants and hotel chains.

Loss of authenticity and staged authenticity:

- Adapting cultural expressions to the tastes of tourists or even performing shows as if they were "real life" constitutes "staged authenticity".
- As long as tourists just want a glimpse of the local atmosphere, a quick glance at local life, without any knowledge or even interest, staging will be inevitable.

Adaptation to tourist demands:

- Tourists want souvenirs, arts, crafts, and cultural manifestations, and in many tourist destinations, craftsmen have responded to the growing demand, and have made changes in design of their products to bring them more in line with the new customers' tastes.
- While the interest shown by tourists also contributes to the sense of self-worth of the artists, and helps conserve a cultural tradition, cultural erosion may occur due to the commodification of cultural goods.

Culture clashes :

- Because tourism involves movement of people to different geographical locations, and establishment of social relations between people who would otherwise not meet, cultural clashes can take place as a result of differences in cultures, ethnicity, religion, values, lifestyles, languages, and levels of prosperity.
- The result can be an over exploitation of the social carrying capacity (limits of acceptable change in the social system inside or around the destination) and cultural carrying capacity (limits of acceptable change in the culture of the host population) of the local community.
- The attitude of local residents towards tourism development may unfold through the stages of euphoria, where visitors are very welcome, through apathy, irritation and potentially antagonism, when anti-tourist attitudes begin growing among local people.

Cultural clashes may further arise through:

Economic Inequality

- Many tourists come from societies with different consumption patterns and lifestyles than what is current at the destination, seeking pleasure, spending large amounts of money and sometimes behaving in ways that even they would not accept at home.
- One effect is that local people that come in contact with these tourists may develop a sort of copying behaviour, as they want to live and behave in the same way.
- Especially in less developed countries, there is likely to be a

growing distinction between the 'haves' and 'have-nots', which may increase social and sometimes ethnic tensions.

- In resorts in destination countries such as Jamaica, Indonesia or Brazil, tourism employees with annual salaries of US$ 1,500 spend their working hours in close contact with guests whose yearly income is well over US$ 80,000.

Irritation due to tourist behaviour:

- Tourists often, out of ignorance or carelessness, fail to respect local customs and moral values.
- When they do, they can bring about irritation and stereotyping.
- They take a quick snapshot and are gone, and by so acting invade the local peoples' lives.
- In many Muslim countries, strict standards exist regarding the appearance and behaviour of Muslim women, who must carefully cover themselves in public.
- Tourists in these countries often disregard or are unaware of these standards, ignoring the prevalent dress code, appearing half-dressed (by local standards) in revealing shorts, skirts or even bikinis, sunbathing topless at the beach or consuming large quantities of alcohol openly.
- Besides creating ill-will, this kind of behaviour can be an incentive for locals not to respect their own traditions and religion anymore, leading to tensions within the local community.
- The same types of culture clashes happen in conservative Christian communities in Polynesia, the Caribbean and the Mediterranean.

Job level friction:

- In developing countries especially, many jobs occupied by local people in the tourist industry are at a lower level, such as housemaids, waiters, gardeners and other practical work, while higher-paying and more prestigious managerial jobs go to foreigners or "urbanized" nationals.
- Due to a lack of professional training, as well as to the influence of hotel or restaurant chains at the destination, people with the know-how needed to perform higher level jobs are often recruited from other countries.
- This may cause friction and irritation and increases the gap between the cultures.

- Even in cases where tourism "works", in the sense that it improves local economies and the earning power of local individuals, it cannot solve all local social or economic problems.
- Sometimes it substitutes new problems for old ones.

Ethical issues :

- *Crime generation:* Crime rates typically increase with the growth and urbanization of an area, and growth of mass tourism is often accompanied by increased crime.
- The presence of a large number of tourists with a lot of money to spend, and often carrying valuables such as cameras and jewellery, increases the attraction for criminals and brings with it activities like robbery and drug dealing.
- Repression of these phenomena often exacerbates social tension.
- In Rio de Janeiro, Brazil, tourists staying in beachside five star resorts close to extremely poor communities in hillside "favelas" are at risk of pickpockets and stick-ups. Security agents, often armed with machine guns, stand guard nearby in full sight, and face aggressive reactions from locals who are often their neighbours when they go home.

Child labour:

- Studies show that many jobs in the tourism sector have working and employment conditions that leave much to be desired: long hours, unstable employment, low pay, little training and poor chances for qualification.
- In addition, recent developments in the travel and tourism trade (liberalisation, competition, concentration, drop in travel fares, growth of subcontracting) seem to reinforce the trend towards more precarious, flexible employment conditions.
- For many such jobs young children are recruited, as they are cheap and flexible employees.

Prostitution and sex tourism:

- The commercial sexual exploitation of children and young women has paralleled the growth of tourism in many parts of the world.
- Though tourism is not the cause of sexual exploitation, it provides easy access to it.

- Tourism also brings consumerism to many parts of the world previously denied access to luxury commodities and services.
- The lure of this easy money has caused many young people, including children, to trade their bodies in exchange for T-shirts, personal stereos, bikes and even air tickets out of the country.
- In other situations children are trafficked into the brothels on the margins of the tourist areas and sold into sex slavery, very rarely earning enough money to escape.

Prostitution and Sex Tourism

- The UN has defined child sex tourism as "tourism organised with the primary purpose of facilitating the effecting of a commercial sexual relationship with a child".
- Certain tourism destinations have become centres for this illegal trade, frequented by paedophiles and supported by networks of pimps, taxi drivers, hotel staff, brothel owners, entertainment establishments, and tour operators who organize package sex tours.
- At the international level, there are agents who provide information about particular resorts where such practices are commonplace.
- Although sexual exploitation of children is a worldwide phenomenon, it is more prevalent in Asia than elsewhere.

How Tourism Can Contribute to Sociocultural Conservation

- Tourism can contribute to positive developments, not just negative impacts.
- It has the potential to promote social development through employment creation, income redistribution and poverty alleviation.

Other potential positive impacts of tourism include:

- Tourism as a force for peace.
- Strengthening communities.
- Facilities developed for tourism can benefit residents.
- Revaluation of culture and traditions.
- Encourages civic involvement and pride.

Tourism as a Force for Peace

- Travelling brings people into contact with each other and, as tourism has an educational element, it can foster understanding between peoples and cultures and provide cultural exchange between hosts and guests.
- Because of this, the chances increase for people to develop mutual sympathy and understanding and to reduce their prejudices.
- For example, jobs provided by tourism in Belfast, Northern Ireland, are expected to help demobilize paramilitary groups as the peace process is put in place.
- In the end, sympathy and understanding can lead to a decrease of tension in the world and thus contribute to peace.

How Tourism Can Contribute to Sociocultural Conservation

Strengthening communities:

- Tourism can add to the vitality of communities in many ways.
- One example is that events and festivals of which local residents have been the primary participants and spectators are often rejuvenated and developed in response to tourist interest.
- The jobs created by tourism can act as a vital incentive to reduce emigration from rural areas.
- Local people can also increase their influence on tourism development, as well as improve their job and earnings prospects, through tourism-related professional training and development of business and organizational skills.
- The San of Namibia and southern Africa and the aboriginal peoples of Australia have recently regained management or ownership of traditional national park lands and conservancies, operating eco-lodges and serving as guides and rangers while maintaining their heritage.

Facilities developed for tourism can benefit residents:

- As tourism supports the creation of community facilities and services that otherwise might not have been developed, it can bring higher living standards to a destination.
- Benefits can include upgraded infrastructure, health and transport improvements, new sport and recreational facilities,

restaurants, and public spaces as well as an influx of better-quality commodities and food.

Revaluation of culture and traditions:

- Tourism can boost the preservation and transmission of cultural and historical traditions, which often contributes to the conservation and sustainable management of natural resources, the protection of local heritage, and a renaissance of indigenous cultures, cultural arts and crafts.

"Tourism has forced the Balinese to reflect on their artistic output as just one cultural identifier. The presence of visitors who continually praise Balinese art and culture has given people a kind of confidence and pride in their art, and made them truly believe that their culture is glorious and thus worthy of this praise and therefore justly admired. This realization removed any possibility in the people's mind that their art was in any way inferior to the art of 'advanced' nations, and plays an important role in conserving and developing the art in general."

Tourism encourages civic involvement and pride:

- Tourism also helps raise local awareness of the financial value of natural and cultural sites and can stimulate a feeling of pride in local and national heritage and interest in its conservation.
- More broadly, the involvement of local communities in tourism development and operation appears to be an important condition for the conservation and sustainable use of biodiversity.

Conclusion

- These are some positive consequences of tourism that can arise only when tourism is practiced and developed in a sustainable and appropriate way.
- Involving the local population is essential.
- A community involved in planning and implementation of tourism has a more positive attitude, is more supportive and has a better chance to make a profit from tourism than a population passively ruled-or overrun-by tourism.
- One of the core elements of sustainable tourism development is community development, which is a process and a capacity to make decisions that consider the long-term economy, ecology and equity of all communities.

Legislation and Guidance Protecting the Tourism Destination

Tourism is a rapidly growing phenomenon and has become one of the largest industries in the world. The impact of tourism is extremely varied. On one hand, it plays an important and certainly positive role in the socioeconomic and political development in destination countries by, for instance, offering new employment opportunities. Also, in certain instances, it may contribute to a broader cultural understanding by creating awareness, respecting the diversity of cultures and ways of life. On the other hand, as a tool to create jobs, it has not fulfilled its expectations. At the same time, complaints from tourist destinations concerning massive negative impacts upon environment, culture and residents' ways of life have given rise to a demand for a more sustainable development in tourism. Different parties will have to be involved in the process of developing sustainable tourism. This section focuses on what the tourism industry itself can do in order to increase its sustainability, defines three major problems, and suggests possible tourism initiatives to help solve these problems. Other problems should also be included in the discussion for it to become exhaustive.

Industry Initiatives for Sustainable Tourism

Problems

Decreased access to natural resources for the local communities and environmental degradation: Tourism is not, as many people assert, a clean and non-polluting industry. A major problem is the lack of a common understanding of what sustainable tourism or "ecotourism" means. This ambiguity leads to violations of environmental regulations and standards. Hence, the environmental problems evolving from tourism are manifold. First of all, the tourism industry is very resource and land intensive. Consequently, the interest of the tourism sector will often be in conflict with local resource and land use practices. The introduction of tourism will imply an increased stress on resources available. An influx of tourists into the area will lead to a competition for resources. Employees working at the tourist sites compound this competition. Almost as a rule, tourists are supplied at the expense of the local population.

Tourist activities imply an intensified utilisation of vulnerable habitats. Investors and tourists do not necessarily possess awareness on how to use natural resources sustainably, and subsequently this utilisation often leads to a degradation of resources. Tourism is also a major generator of wastes. In most tourist regions of developing countries, sewage, wastewater and solid waste disposal are not properly managed or planned. Lastly, tourism is also responsible for a considerable proportion of increased volumes and mileage in global transport and hence the associated environmentally damaging pollutant emissions. The tourism industry has not shown sufficient willingness to (internalise or) compensate the cost of conservation of biodiversity in, for instance, protected areas, even though they can profit from it.

Increasing Cultural Erosion and Disrespect for Human Rights

Tourism is a powerful agent of change. International tourism acts as a catalyst for the transition from traditional ways of life to so-called modern, Western forms of society. Accordingly, tourism often brings with it the introduction of new behaviour trends and norms. Very often, these are contrary to traditional norms existing in the host community, and can come into conflict with its cultural identity and threaten the traditional value systems there. The problem is that the investors seem to have a lack of cultural understanding of the invested society. There is a need for an increased awareness that establishment of new hotels etc. will have its consequences on the society and the people who live in it.

Tourism has become associated with violation of human rights. Many destination countries have experienced an increase in criminality, prostitution, alcohol and drug abuse as a consequence of tourism. Furthermore, child labour is commonplace in the tourism industry (particularly in the informal sector). According to estimates made by ILO (International Labour Organisation), between 3 and 19 million children and teenagers work in the tourism sector. A particularly abominable form of violation of human rights is child slavery and despicable abuse of children taking place in the booming sex industry in many countries. In these countries, tourism has led to an incredible increase in prostitution and also in the exploitation of children. The tourism industry has not yet come up with a general condemnation of these violations of human rights.

Unqualified Jobs and Foreign Exchange Leakage

The tourism industry is characterised by a high degree of monopoly, which implies a concentration of services and profits into very few big transnational corporations. In many countries, tourism facilities mostly belong to foreigners. Furthermore, in local host communities in many countries a relatively small number of people are involved in the tourism industry in host communities in many developing countries. Very often, there is a lack of qualified manpower in the locality. Hence, most employees are recruited form the big cities, neighbouring countries or even from the country of origin of the investors.

Multiplier effects from tourism are less significant than is often assumed. One reason is that tourism industries purchase most of their inputs (materials, products or services) in their country of origin. As a result, a considerable amount of foreign exchange revenues leaks from the destination countries. The more goods, services, physical capital and human capital a country must import for its tourism services, the higher the leakage. Very often the investors are not approaching the local community to see what it actually can provide. In addition to this, the General Agreement on Trade in Services (GATS), with its liberalisation of global trade and services, is increasingly undermining the possibilities of individual countries and regions to control their tourism industries and the possible economic gains from tourism.

Solutions

Decreased access to natural resources for the local communities and environmental degradation.

In general, the tourism industry should engage in promoting sustainability as a hallmark for investors. More specifically, investors in tourism should strive to adopt environmentally sound technologies or other measures to minimise the consumption of local ground water. In the case of water utilisation, such measures might be water saving equipment, desalination systems and collecting and utilising rainwater. Using other types of resources in a sustainable manner is, of course, also crucial.

There is a need to use ecological materials and installation of renewable sources of energy systems (solar energy) in all new buildings and new construction. Furthermore there should be an acceleration of installation or solar/wind power in all public work projects of communities where tourism will be introduced. To prevent or minimise the impact of chemical inputs in soil, water and health, one should start utilising sound ecological methods, including IPM (Integrated Pest Management). Ecological methods need to be applied in all areas utilised for tourism, including in the maintenance of golf courts, gardens and recreational facilities.

Pollution of ground and coastal waters must be prevented, and recommendations must be made (perhaps even legislation) for tourism investors to invest in proper sewage treatment facilities. Appropriate waste disposal systems and ways to separate garbage into organic and non-organic waste should be developed. Organic waste can be composed and possibly reused on hotel gardens or even for local farming. This could be done through collaboration with local residents. Residents could organise themselves and manage the allocated dumping sites, and hence benefit from the system in receiving payment from the hotel for services rendered. A system to separate the different materials, and recycle some should be in place at the landfill site, thus reducing the waste even further.

To avoid degradation of the natural environment, tourism projects can help finance protected areas and safeguard ecologically sensitive regions against further environmental deterioration. By empowering local populations and have them participating in the entire process, sustainability will be ensured as it becomes accepted by and adjusted to the local communities. Also, a protected area might certainly be a suitable tourist-attraction, where tourists can experience amazing nature and learn about conservation and traditional uses of natural resources in the area.

Investors in tourism should always respect the traditional land tenure system in the area and the traditional user-right systems of resources. In regard to this, the communication and consultation with the local communities about resource-use is important. Tourism investors should not exclude local people from using local resources, and thus take away what they depend on for maintaining their well being. The tourism industry can and must take initiatives to implement that polluter(s) pay a principle (or other forms of internalisation of externalities) for pollution related to tourism operations. This may be organised and carried out through local tax systems or through funds established by the tourism industry for local community development. However, the paid principle should be applied for minor pollution only and should not be developed into a possibility for investors to pay a symbolic fine for imposed irreversible negative impacts on the local environment.

Inaccurate and/or mild environmental legislation in destination countries may possibly attract more foreign investors contributing to fast economic growth and development, but with environmental damage as a consequence. To avoid the dilemma, destination countries will have to choose between economic development and environmental protection international. Multinational enterprises must be committed to follow the environmental standards of their home country should these be stricter than those at the destinations.

Increasing Cultural Erosion and Disrespect for Human Rights

The tourism industry should promote projects, which are compatible with the cultural identity of the local population's way of life. Furthermore, the tourism sector should always make sure it acts in accordance with the cultural heritage, and respect the cultural integrity of tourism destinations. This might be accomplished by defining codes of conduct for the industry and hence providing investors with a checklist for sustainable tourism projects.

Establishing and developing tourist training programmes could be one way of managing codes of conducts for the tourists. Here, tourists can be informed and educated about the destination for their travel both before and after their arrival at the site. At the site, tourist information centres can be established through funding from the investor. The information given to tourists should include codes of conduct regarding appropriate behaviour and clothing. It is reasonable to assume that people's offending behaviour is largely a consequence of ignorance rather than intention. Consequently, information and facts about the destination, ways of life, history, cultural heritage is crucial to help tourists get along.

It is an absolute must that tourism investors do not engage in or promote child labour and prostitution. Moreover, it is appropriate that the industry commit themselves to a global campaign against such and any other violation of human rights. Evaluating the sustainability of the tourism development, in regards to cultural and human rights aspects, is highly recommended for those responsible for the tourism projects. As with the case mentioned earlier of preventing environmental degradation, this must be carried out through communication and consultation with the local communities.

Unqualified Jobs and Foreign Exchange Leakage

By devising local training programmes and establishing educational projects, the tourism industry can ensure that qualified local people are employed in their projects. One should train the local people instead of foreigners to become guides due to their knowledge of the area and resources. The investors should be responsive to the kind of knowledge, abilities and skills found in the local communities. Very often such knowledge and skills are well fitted to be used in tourist activities be it fishing trips, nature trails, souvenir sales or dancing courses for tourists etc.

To constrain foreign exchange leakage, those responsible for the tourism projects should ensure that local inputs are purchased for their projects. A proper examination of local resources available will be beneficial for both the industry and the local residents. Usually, there is considerable local willingness to start producing new products if a market for these products exists. The tourism sector should also adopt measures to prevent foreign exchange leakage by a commitment to reinvestment of a fair share of the locally accrued profit. We have already mentioned protected areas, training programmes on codes of conduct for tourists, or possible training of local employees, as projects in need of funds. Initiatives towards more local community development projects should also be appropriate.

The tourism industry should promote the establishment of small and medium-sized tourism enterprises which, compared to large-scale hotels etc., have far more moderate impacts on the environment. It is the industry's responsibility to act as a model for communities to show that it is possible to do business whilst protecting natural resources. The industry should also promote and support local communities to start tourism-related businesses and grant access to low interest loans. It is the responsibility of the tourism sector to ensure total transparency in all transactions, and to prevent tourism projects from being used as projects for laundering illicit money, as well as to refuse using bribes as a means to obfuscate or avoid government rules and regulations. There should be a global boycott against those investors involved in such or other types of illegal activities.

General Recommendations and Possible Solutions which Concern all three Problem Areas

Empowerment of residents at tourist destinations, through local participation, may be facilitated by providing written and legally binding contracts between local people and tourism investors. The contracts will help to avoid broken promises, which too many examples and previous experience prove to be a huge problem. In addition to the mentioned examples (providing proper information for tourists and establishing training programmes for residents), the tourism industry, through for instance the WTTC or the WTO with NGOs in the selection panels, could issue awards especially for sustainable tourism projects as an encouragement for investors.

Agents and Partnerships for Change

In this section, the focus has been on what the tourism industry itself can do in order to augment and improve its environmental, cultural, social and economic profile and make sure this is sustainable. However, the industry's effort cannot be successful without a profound collaboration with all stakeholders.

Within the industry, it is important that both small and large-scale tourism operators are included in the collaboration and that they participate in solving problems related to tourism development. As mentioned, a sustainable development of the tourism industry can only be ensured through participation of all local residents in the destination countries. There is a need for a willingness and ability for the partners to work with this kind of bottom-up approach. In this context, both environment and social NGOs have an important role to play, putting pressure on the industry and facilitating contracts and local participation for community development. Governments in both destination and countries of origin of tourists and investors are responsible for providing appropriate legislation for sustainable tourism development, and to follow up the tourism projects with sufficient monitoring and appropriate sanctioning. Exchange of successful experiences of sustainable tourism projects is an important factor in this connection. Lastly, an interdisciplinary approach to the problem is necessary: using local, regional and/or international consultative forums.

Influencing Consumer Behaviour to Promote Sustainable Tourism Problems

International tourism plays an ambivalent role in contributing to cultural exchange and sustainable development. On the one hand, it involves a highly buffered, short-term consumer experience of other locales. Tourists can pay and leave, remaining isolated from negative impacts at the local level. On the other hand, tourism may increase recognition of the importance of respecting cultural diversity and developing an identity as a world citizen. It offers opportunities to educate consumers regarding responsible tourism and sustainable development. Consumers can play a major role in the transformation of societies towards sustainability. While mass tourism in the past was rather producer-driven, the industry today is becoming increasingly consumer-driven. In highly competitive tourism markets, well informed, responsible consumers can put increasing pressure on the industry to behave more responsibly.

A number of official proclamations have affirmed every individual's right to rest and leisure including tourism. However, tourism remains an unobtainable luxury for the majority of the world's population. Tourists primarily originate from affluent industrialised societies where tourism has become a mass phenomenon. Tourists' values, attitudes and behaviour are determined by their social environment, cultural identity and way of life which may be in conflict with local customs. Tourism is heterogeneous in nature, made up of many different types of traveller, seeking a wide range of tourism products. Demand is influenced by irrational factors, e.g. fashion and trends. Demand depends on the availability of time and money, on images, perceptions and attitudes. Tourists have various needs, desires and motivations, both of a 'push' and 'pull' nature. While household incomes in major tourist-sending countries are declining, industry sales projections continue to grow, indicating increasing competition. The consumer mind is set on discount prices and "buy now/pay later" options. This poses serious threats, as prices already lag far behind any realistic accounting of tourism costs and impacts.

Many of the demand patterns in tourism reflect the unsustainable lifestyles of industrialised consumer societies. Tourism acts as an agent in exporting these life-styles and consumerist attitudes to less industrialised societies via demonstration effects and modelling. Tourism increases demand for imported consumer goods in the destinations, with detrimental effects on the environment, due to the ecological costs of transport and the high amount of waste generated. Increasing imports also reduce local/national economic gains, due to foreign exchange leakage.

The over-consumption of resources by tourists and tourism infrastructure (e.g. the excessive use of water, firewood or food) is incompatible with sustainable development. The carrying capacity of natural environments is often exceeded with the addition of tourism demands. Tourist demand for resources (land, water, energy, food) may also compete with the needs of local people and may increase social inequality, gender inequality and injustice. Tourist transport, especially air travel, is highly energy intensive and causes pollutant emissions. Many tourism activities such as skiing, boating, mountain hiking, motorised water-sports (e.g. jet skies), and trekking represent stress for fragile ecosystems.

Tourists often lack information and awareness about their impact in a different culture and environment, about their impacts on socioeconomic and sociocultural development, and about the environmental costs of tourism. While tourists may be open to learning, they are often unaware of inappropriate behaviour and have little guidance on how to improve them. Others may refuse to adapt to local lifestyles (even when informed) insisting on their freedom to behave as they want.

While the tourism industry may be willing to improve their products and services, there is a conflict between the industry's pursuit of economic gains and social and environmental responsibility. The industry lacks information on the requirements of sustainable tourism and on how to integrate economic forces with environmental and social requirements. Tourists shopping for escapism generally abide by one fundamental consumer ethic: receipt upon payment. Consumer advocates may intervene where inferior customer service is delivered. However, the sustainability of corporate practices is self-regulated. This conflict of interest within the industry, and consumers' low awareness of tourism impacts, have led to a widespread abuse of 'green' labelling.

The mass media, especially television through films and reports about events, sights, etc. in other parts of the world, are increasingly influential on travel decisions and consumer behaviour in the destinations. However, these programmes often serve primarily as advertisements, painting images of destinations, rather than providing relevant information for potential travellers. There is a lack of reliable and appropriate (e.g. age and gender segregated) research data on the determinants of tourist demand, motivation and behaviour. Few countries, whether tourist-sending or tourist-receiving, collect such data that are helpful under sustainable development criteria. Most studies of tourist behaviour focus on mainstream markets or market segments, rather than assessing or modelling sustainable alternatives. Governments in many tourist destinations and local communities have little or no information on what to expect from tourism and the incoming tourists, and how to influence and control tourism and guide tourist behaviour; They are controlled by international/global institutions, the industry and the consumers. Governments of the affluent countries are only beginning to look at the issues of outgoing tourism. They are not yet sufficiently aware of their responsibility and methods to influence tourist behaviour by political and legal guidelines/criteria and appropriate planning and policies. Trade unions have fought successfully for shorter working hours and more vacation. However, they need to take more responsibility for helping to create a leisure industry that is more sustainable.

Solutions

Consumer behaviour can and must be influenced by:

- Fighting unsustainable forms and aspects of tourism, at the various levels, by sanctioning unacceptable behaviour and discouraging inappropriate consumer behaviour.
- Promoting responsible and sustainable patterns of behaviour, at the various levels, by promoting best practises and encouraging responsible consumer behaviour. There are different types of instruments and remedial measures available:
  * Legal measures (rules, regulations, sanctions);
  * Market based instruments, such as taxes to influence market prices;
  * Promotion of and (financial) support for best practice;
  * Industry self-monitoring/codes of conduct;
  * Information, education and research.

Governmental Action

- Introduce and enforce legislation to abolish child prostitution, implement effective control mechanisms, conclude judicial assistance agreements;
- Regulate tourist access to ecologically fragile or stressed natural areas;
- Tourist-sending countries: develop policies on outgoing tourism from a development perspective;
- Provide frameworks for ecologically appropriate pricing by strictly applying the polluter-pays-principle to internalise external costs. This includes ecological tax reforms including the taxation of aviation gasoline and oil, removal of subsidies/other economic incentives with negative environmental impacts.
- Improve conditions for sustainable consumer behaviour by providing/promoting sustainable tourism facilities;
- Promote environmentally friendly modes of transport and transport concepts, reduce tourism-related traffic, shift demand to less environmentally damaging modes of transport;
- Promote renewable sources of energy (such as solar power),

reduce the use of non-renewable energy and of limited local resources, through more sustainable practices/consumption patterns.

- Develop information and education programmes in cooperation with local stakeholders ensuring all stakeholders' involvement (e.g. women's); provide information to tourists on appropriate behaviour (sensitivity, respect for/adaptation to local culture), e.g. by establishing information centres in destinations, or by including briefing material for package tours;
- Take into account the specific information needs of various market segments, provide information to the local population on the opportunities and risks from tourism and on how to influence tourist behaviour;
- Adopt, observe, implement and promote codes of conduct, e.g. the planned WTO-OMT 'Global Code of Ethics for Tourism';
- Integrate sustainable development education including tourism in the curricula of schools at all levels, universities and training institutions, involving all stakeholder groups, create and promote open networks for information and research on sustainable tourism, disseminate and implement results; 35. Tourism Industry Action
- Promote sustainable tourism products, using market related instruments and incentives, such as contests, awards, certification, model projects, culturally sensitive quality labels covering both environmental and social sustainability;
- Reduce inappropriate consumption, use local resources in preference to imports in a sustainable manner; reduce and recycle waste, ensure safe waste disposal, develop and implement sustainable transport policies and systems, e.g. efficient public transport, walking, cycling in destinations;
- Provide tourists with authentic information, enabling them to understand all environmental and related aspects (e.g. human rights situation) of tourism when selecting any destination or holiday package; educate visitors in advance of arrival and give guidance on 'dos' and 'don'ts'; make tourists aware of their potential impact on and their responsibilities towards host societies;

- Provide information on respecting the cultural and natural heritage of destination areas; employ tour guides who portray societies honestly and dispel stereotypes;
- Ensure that the marketing of 'green' tourism reflects sound environmental policy and practice; use non-exploitative marketing strategies that respect people, communities and environments of destinations, dismantle stereotyping, integrate sustainable tourism principles when creating new marketing strategies;
- Train staff to foster tourist responsibility towards the destinations, encourage multi-cultural education and exchange;
- Actively discourage exploitative sex tourism, particularly sexual exploitation of children, and tourism which causes or contributes to social problems;
- Adopt, observe, implement and promote codes of conduct.

Cultural Transgressions

The Exploitation of Indigenous Populations

Indigenous peoples are paying a high price for tourism, says Raymond de Chavez. In their drive for profits, transnational corporations which dominate the international tourist industry have, with the complicity of governments (particularly those of the Third World), devastated the lives and lifestyles of indigenous peoples. The process of globalization will only exacerbate their plight.

Globalization and tourism have become a deadly mix for indigenous peoples. Tourism's impact on indigenous peoples' way of life and on their control of and access to their resources and environment has become more pronounced with globalization of the world economy.

For several decades now, tourism has been a major source of revenue for countries, specifically in the Third World. Its growth has been nothing short of phenomenal. In the 1950s, 25 million people travelled to a foreign destination. In the 1960s, this grew to 70 million. By 1997, 617 million tourists had been reported by the Madrid-based World Tourism Organisation to have travelled to foreign countries.

The World Tourism Organisation has even predicted that by the 21st century, tourist arrivals would have reached billions annually. It foresees that by the year 2010, 1 billion tourists would have travelled abroad and by 2020, this would have increased to 1.6 billion.

In terms of revenues, this would easily translate to billions of dollars yearly. In the 1960s, for example, tourism earned 'only' US$6.8 billion. In 1997, revenues jumped to US$448 billion. By the year 2000, the WTO predicts tourism earnings to reach $621 billion and by 2010, a whopping $1.5 trillion.

Tourism is also touted as a major source of employment worldwide. According to the World Travel and Tourism Council (WTTC), an aggrupation of more than 80 chief executives of the travel and tourism industry, tourism employs directly or indirectly more than 260 million. This translates to one out of nine jobs in the world economy generated by the industry. By the coming decade, the work force is expected to increase by 100 million more jobs, 70% of these in the Asia-Pacific region.

The WTTC in fact now considers tourism as the world's biggest industry and a 'key 21st century economic and employment driver'. Its growth for the past decades has been a constant 9% annually, in spite of the economic slowdown. While acknowledging a decline in tourism activities due to the Asian financial crisis, the WTTC recommended in February 1998 that governments give continued priority to tourism to assist Asian economic recovery.

Tourism as Export Strategy

It is no wonder therefore that cash-starved Third World countries view tourism as a shortcut to rapid development. Its potential to earn billions of dollars easily has resulted in it being viewed as a panacea for debt-ridden countries. But more than this, tourism has become part and parcel of multilateral financial institutions' package for financial bail-outs for countries in distress. Tourism is now being pursued as a serious development strategy for the Third World.

The International Monetary Fund (IMF) has included tourism as part of its Structural Adjustment Programmes (SAPs). The SAPs, which are preconditions for the approval of financial assistance, require the indebted country to:

- be integrated into the global economy;
- deregulate and liberalise its economy;
- shift from an agriculture-based to a manufacturing and service industry-based economy; and
- liberalise its financial sector. In essence, these preconditions link the Third World country to the world economy. The SAP

opens up the local economy to foreign investments and multinational corporations, while eliminating subsidies and protection to local industries. Under IMF-World Bank prescriptions, tourism is classified as an export strategy. With its capacity to earn billions of dollars, tourism is being promoted by the IMF-WB as a means for Third World countries to repay their debts to them.

Third World governments have therefore tried to fulfil their commitments to these SAPs by large-scale investments in tourism-related ventures. In conjunction with financial multilateral institutions and travel and tourism transnational corporations (TNCs), they have launched infrastructure projects such as roads, hotels and tourist-promotion programmes. Worldwide, public and private investments have reached $800 billion annually, accounting for 12% of total worldwide investments.

But these IMF-WB conditionalities have proven to be insufficient to integrate and open up Third World economies. The World Trade Organisation has taken further steps to fully liberalise the world economy. The most important international agreement with direct bearing on tourism is the General Agreement on Trade in Services (GATS). Signed in Morocco in April 1994, this agreement '... sets up a legal and operational framework for the gradual elimination of barriers to international trade in services'. GATS is an offshoot of the Uruguay Round talks of the General Agreement on Tariffs and Trade (GATT), the World Trade Organisation's precursor.

In short, GATS makes it easier for big tourist and travel TNCs to invest in the local tourism industries of Third World countries. Among others, it removes restrictions on foreign corporations' abilities to transfer staff from one country to another; and enables them to use trademarks, create and operate branch offices abroad, and more importantly, to repatriate their earnings to their mother companies abroad.

Under GATS, protection to the local tourism industry would be construed as unfair practice and would thus have to be eliminated. TNCs now enjoy the same benefits as local travel and tourism agencies. This opens the local industry to competition from giant TNCs, which virtually means effectively transferring its control to them.

Other international agreements integrating the tourism industry into the global economy include the Agreement on Trade-Related

Investment Measures (TRIMs), which removes the requirement for foreign companies to utilise local input. The proposed Multilateral Agreement on Investment (MAI) also 'secure[s] for foreign investors, unfettered rights to invest in all sectors of the host country's economy and to obtain for them the same treatment as investors from the host nation'. This proposal has, however, been shelved recently as a result of intense lobbying by non-governmental organisations, indigenous peoples' organisations included.

Threat to Indigenous Peoples

But what does globalization and tourism mean for the indigenous peoples? It is already an established fact that tourism had brought pernicious and long-term damaging effects on indigenous peoples even prior to globalization. The present economic order further exacerbates and hastens these impacts.

For one, indigenous communities, which have otherwise been left untouched by traditional tourism activities, have now been targeted for tourism ventures, most specifically, ecotourism. A relatively new variant, ecotourism is described as environment-friendly, sustainable and nature-based. It came about as a response to the growing environmental awareness worldwide these past decades.

Eager to cash in on this trend, the industry promoted ecotourism as an alternative activity, ostensibly to promote tourism while protecting the environment. This activity 'involves visiting relatively undisturbed natural areas with the aim of studying, admiring and enjoying the scenery, wild plants and animals, as well as any existing cultural aspects'. It includes spelunking, mountain climbing, scuba diving, bird watching, and whale watching, among others.

This tourism sub-sector has been met with remarkable success. Today, it has become the fastest growing sub-sector, growing at a rate of 10%-15% annually. Ecotourism now accounts for 25% of all leisure trips abroad. It is important to note that ecotourism destinations are more often than not in the Third World. Tourism here has been increasing annually by 6% as compared to 3.5% in developed countries. After all, it is in these areas that relatively undisturbed and preserved natural environments and exotic areas are located. But it is also in these countries that the majority of the distinct indigenous cultures can be found.

To a large extent, therefore, indigenous communities have become targets of ecotourism in this globalised economy.

In Africa, tourism's effects on indigenous peoples have been profound: widescale eviction from their lands, economic dislocation, breakdown of traditional values, and environmental degradation. Although ecotourism is a relatively new phenomenon internationally, it has long been existing in Africa.

In the 1950s, the colonial governments of Tanzania and Kenya under the British legalised the hunting and culling of wild animals by 'white settlers', thus paving the way for mass tourism. They set up zones for the exclusive use of hunters and prevented access to local inhabitants. Lodges and campsites were established near the preserves, making them major revenue earners. Some 70% of the protected areas and wildlife preserves, however, straddled lands of the Masai tribe.

Basically pastoralists, the Masai used these lands for their economic activities and traditional practices. The ban thus dislocated them economically. Forced out of their traditional grounds, they were left with little or no support from the government. And even after independence, the government failed to provide them with social services such as education and employment.

The Masai's traditional economic activity-pastoralism-has been attacked as primitive and destructive. Yet it has been noted that 'pastoralism and conservation of nature go hand in hand'. Alienated from their main economic activity and disadvantaged from job opportunities by a lack of education, the Masai were subjected to poverty. Even the Masai's traditional sociopolitical institutions have suffered as a consequence of tourism. Lands outside the preserves where the Masai have been resettled are considered communal. In these areas, residents are registered, and land and resources are to be distributed equally by a management committee.

However, corrupt officials have registered even nonresidents who have monopolised prime lands near the preserves. Land disputes have thus arisen. Elders, traditional mediators of conflicts, have become powerless against nonresidents who are often backed by powerful persons.

Destruction of properties by wildlife has also been reported but the government has not given any compensation to affected residents. This has caused disruption in the relationship between the tribes and the animals, which are given priority because of tourism. As a consequence, the 'Masai...are coming to abhor the very wild animals they have successfully coexisted with for centuries'.

Tourism has not spared the environment and biodiversity. The rise in tourist arrivals in these preserves-more so with globalization-has increased deforestation, pollution and disruption in the ecological balance. In the Masai Mara National Park in Kenya and in the Ngorongoro Conservation Area in Tanzania, forests adjacent to lodges and camping grounds have been cut down due to the demand for firewood.

The massive influx of tourists and their vehicles has also caused destruction of grass cover, affecting plant and animal species in the area. Hotels have dumped their sewage in Masai settlement areas while campsites have polluted adjacent rivers.

Masai culture has further been threatened and commercialised. Negative Western values have influenced the Masai youth, leading to a loss of traditional values, prostitution, and the spread of AIDS.

Postcards portraying tribes in their traditional costumes abound in these preserves. It is in the interest of ecotourism to 'preserve' indigenous communities and their practices since exotic tribes with exotic practices serve as the main selling point to foreign tourists. 'There is rarely an acknowledgement-much less support-of indigenous people's struggle for cultural survival, self-determination, freedom of cultural expression, rights to ancestral lands, and control over land use and resource management.' In the Philippines, where tourism has long been considered as a major dollar-earner, ecotourism has also become a priority. Blessed with a rich biodiversity, the Philippines has developed ecotourism as a strategy to entice more foreign tourists and increase its share in world tourism revenue. Its Department of Tourism (DOT)'s Master Plan aims to develop 'sustainable' tourism while making the Philippines a leading tourist destination in Asia. In support of this thrust is the National Integrated Protected Areas System Act (NIPAS) of 1992, which classifies certain areas as protected zones. The DOT has identified 17 protected areas all over the country as suitable for ecotourism. It is important to note that the majority of these areas are territories of indigenous peoples.

In the Cordillera in the northern Philippines, tourism continues to affect adversely many of its 1.3 million indigenous population. Sagada in Mountain Province, home to the indigenous Kankanaeys, is known internationally for its cool climate, rice terraces, and caves, among others. Its people have maintained their indigenous way of life, subsistence economy and sustainable relationship with nature for centuries.

In recent years, tourism arrivals have grown tremendously, caused in part by ecotourism promotion packages advertising Sagada as a pristine community where one can commune with nature. Hotels and inns mushroomed, changing the town's landscape and straining its water resources. Pollution caused by littering and improper waste disposal has now become a major problem for the community.

Apart from environmental degradation, the influx of tourists has disrupted the Kankanaeys' traditions and practices. The solemnity and sacredness of rituals, such as those relating to the agricultural cycle and passage of life, have been affected due to the presence of curious tourists. Caves, traditionally their burial grounds, have been vandalised by graffiti, and some of the bones of their ancestors stolen.

Western influences have also taken their toll on the local community. These include the production, distribution and use of prohibited drugs such as marijuana and hashish. Taboos have been constantly broken by foreign tourists. Tourists, for example, have bathed in the nude in waterfalls, which is frowned upon by the local community. In 1995, the world-famous Ifugao Rice Terraces in Banawe, Ifugao province, was declared by the UN Educational, Scientific and Cultural Organisation (UNESCO) as a World Heritage Site.

This was part of the Philippine government's campaign to sell Ifugao as a major tourist destination in the world. The influx of tourists over the decades has similarly affected the Ifugaos, the indigenous inhabitants of the province. Foremost is the disruption of traditional economic practices of the community. The builders of the world-renowned rice terraces, the Ifugaos for centuries have subsisted on crops planted in their terraces. With the entry of tourists and hotels, the lure of money from tourist-related businesses such as selling of woodcarvings, became more attractive than subsistence farming. This has left many terraces untended and in danger of deterioration.

Commercial production of woodcarvings has also affected nearby forests. Trees have been cut down to support commercial woodcarving activities that cater to foreign as well as domestic tourist demand. This has led to the drying up of water sources much needed for irrigation.

Joan Carling of the Cordillera Peoples Alliance aptly summed up the effects of tourism on the indigenous peoples in the Cordillera when she wrote: 'The tourism industry has facilitated the further disintegration of the peoples' indigenous way of life. Cash production for the tourism industry has led to commercialism and individualism in contrast to the indigenous ways of simple living and mutual cooperation. Likewise, the commercialisation of their culture has led to undignified ways of seeking a livelihood such as allowing themselves to be photographed as souvenirs or to do their indigenous dance for a fee. This practice was never part of their culture.'

The pervasive effects of globalised tourism can also be seen in the way it has affected other indigenous peoples all over the world. In the Cook Islands in the Pacific, a 204-room hotel was built on land sacred to the local people. The construction has caused environmental damage amounting to US$1 million. In the Russian Federation's Providenskij and Tchukogskij regions, home to the indigenous Tchukchi peoples, the development of tourism in the past years has affected their source of livelihood. Known areas of walrus concentration such as those in Rugor's Bay and the isle of Arykamchechen have become ecotourism destinations. Sightseeing tour groups ride on motorboats to walruses' breeding grounds.

But a rise in such tours has affected the walrus population. Visitor arrivals have caused stress among the walruses, causing a decline in their population. This has in turn affected the quality and quantity of walrus catch, traditionally the Tchukchi peoples' source of livelihood.

Tourism's High Cost

Indigenous peoples are paying a high price for tourism. In their desire to cash in on the billion-dollar profits from this industry, governments, specifically in the Third World, and transnational corporations have disregarded the interests of indigenous peoples.

The effects have been devastating. Indigenous peoples have been evicted from their traditional lands, their control and access to their natural resources compromised. They have suffered social degradation brought about by foreign influences and the commercialisation of their culture. Even the rich biodiversity of their natural resources has suffered from pollution and environmental damage, unable to support the growing number of tourist arrivals. What few benefits indigenous peoples derive from tourism are far outweighed by the damage it has caused them. They have been made to bear the brunt of an industry over which they have neither say nor control.

With globalization, these threats have been exacerbated. International agreements that open up access to the local tourism industry by big travel and tourism TNCs will only speed up exploitation of the natural resources, culture and way of life of indigenous peoples. Ecotourism, which has been touted as the fastest growing form of tourism in the Third World, has not proven to be sustainable at all. Rather, it has targeted indigenous communities as areas of destination and exploitation in the guise of being environment-friendly.

Unless indigenous peoples have a direct participation in the planning, implementation, and regulation of tourism activities that affect them, and unless benefit-sharing mechanisms are put in place, tourism can never redound to their interest. Indigenous peoples will continue to be mere cogs in the wheel of this billion-dollar industry.

Managing Social Impact of Tourism

As one of the world's largest industries, tourism carries with it significant social, environmental, economic and political impacts. Although tourism can provide significant economic benefits for some destinations, the image of tourism as a benign and environmentally friendly industry has often been challenged. There is a clear and growing body of evidence that suggests that the effects of tourism development are far more complex than policy-makers usually suggest and that the impacts of tourism occur not just at the destination but at all stages of a tourist's trip. Furthermore, tourism does not exist in a vacuum. Broader social and environmental changes also shape the form, growth and experience of tourism development.

Bringing Economic Benefits to Locals

* Tourism generates jobs and income, and contributes to the economic health and vitality of a community or county.
* Like any development activity, tourism also generates social, economic, and environmental impacts.
* Communities often focus on only one type of impact, usually economic, that a development project might generate.

The accurate assessment of both costs and benefits helps communities avoid problems and maintain community support for growth. Planning discussions allow communities to put the whole range of impacts on the table, assess who will and will not benefit, and facilitate a compromise that results in mutual benefit. The following cost and benefit framework from the University of Minnesota Tourism Centre's Community Tourism Development Manual provides information on the "common economic, social and environmental impacts that communities face as a result of hosting visitors, as well as community strategies that can help mitigate costs."

Economic Impacts of Tourism

Economic Benefits

- Brings new money into the community.
- Helps diversify and stabilize the local economy.
- Attracts additional businesses and services to support tourism industry.
- May be a catalyst for other industries and bring capital investment to area.
- Creates local jobs and new business opportunities.
- Increases expansion and retention of existing businesses.
- Contributes to the state and local tax base.
- Helps support local businesses that might not survive on resident income alone.

Economic Costs

- Imposes organizational and operational costs to develop tourism.
- Places demands on public infrastructure that may exceed what the local tax base can support.
- May inflate property values and the price of goods and services.
- Requires customer service training of employees, business owners, and community residents.
- May be cyclical and impacted by forces outside the community's control.
- Reduces local economic benefits if developers come from outside the community.
- May cause economic and employment distortions if development is not geographically balanced.

Techniques to Minimize Economic Costs

- Use tourism development as a supplement to, not a substitute for, other sources of economic activity.
- Use local capital, goods, services, labour, and expertise whenever possible.
- Involve both public and private sectors in development process.
- Provide financial incentives and training to foster local business ownership.

- Implement tourism awareness programs for local businesses.
- Establish programs to ensure affordable housing for residents.

Environmental Impacts of Tourism

Environmental Benefits

- Fosters conservation and preservation of natural, cultural, and historical resources.
- Increases local environmental awareness.
- May encourage community beautification, revitalization, and environmental quality.
- May improve local urban/rural landscapes through facilities development.
- May simulate improvements in infrastructure (airports, roads, water, waste, sewage).
- May be cleaner than other industries.

Environmental Costs

- May cause environmental hazards due to poor land use planning and facility design.
- May create land use problems, add to urban and rural sprawl.
- May degrade quality of natural and historic sites.
- May increase water, air, and noise pollution.
- May result in visual/architectural pollution.
- May create solid waste problems.
- May bring overcrowding and traffic congestion.

Techniques to Minimize Environmental Costs

- Implement land use planning and zoning laws prior to tourism development.
- Design hotels and tourist facilities to reflect local architectural styles.
- Set standards for water, sewage, and power supplies that encourage conservation.
- Establish guidelines for local carrying capacity and limits of acceptable. change.
- Implement visitor use and management plans for cultural, historic, and natural attractions.

- Organize proper building, park, and landscaping maintenance for public areas.
- Establish conservation/protected areas to prevent growth in ecologically sensitive areas.
- Execute environmental public awareness programs for visitors and residents.

Social Impacts of Tourism

Social Benefits

- Supports development of community facilities and other local improvements.
- May enhance community's "sense of place" through cultural/historic celebration.
- Encourages civic involvement and community pride.
- May help maintain cultural identity of minority populations that are dying out.
- May facilitate renewed interest in traditional lifestyles among younger residents.
- Provides cultural exchange between hosts and guests.
- Promotes peace and understanding.

Social Costs

- May introduce lifestyles, ideas, and behaviours that conflict with those of residents.
- May create crowding, congestion, and increased crime.
- May encourage "trinketization" of local arts and crafts.
- Brings residents new competition for services and recreation opportunities.
- May create conflict among residents if benefits are unequally distributed.
- May produce a "demonstration effect" (Imitation of visitors' behaviours and spending patterns), resulting in loss of cultural pride.
- May create racial tension and resentment between hosts and guests.

Techniques to Minimize Social Costs

- Inform residents about both the benefits and costs of tourism.

- Establish quality controls to maintain authenticity of handicrafts and cultural activities.
- Plan tourism based on goals, values, and priorities identified by residents.
- Ensure residents have convenient access to tourist attractions, facilities, and services.
- Strictly control drugs, crime and prostitution.
- Use selective, target marketing to draw the right kinds of tourists.
- Educate and train local residents to work at all levels of tourism.
- Have ongoing public awareness programs about tourism.

The application of sustainable tourism in practice means understanding and addressing the costs and benefits of tourism: This also means that a community has to find the means to balance economic, social and environmental needs while minimizing negative impacts. In practice the goal is to maximize benefits and reduce the costs that tourism, like any industry, can bring to a community.

The Impact of Travel on Tourist Health

Introduction

Until 19th century, travel for recreation was only undertaken by the elite. With the advent of rail, mass travel was available for the first time and destinations such as Brighton, UK and Coney Island, NY developed. Status was then defined by the mode of travel. In 20th century status was revealed by the nature of the destinations. Travel and tourism has been going on since time immemorial, and for the 'twentieth century tourist, the world has become one large department store of countrysides and cities'. By 21st century, travel became a new economy-*tourism*-available to all with enough money.

The focus of the tourism industry has shifted from air travel, overnights, meals and so on to total experiences or fantasy worlds associated with specific destinations. This new tourism phenomenon is not only influenced by economic factors but also by new cultures and a new generation of tourists. In tourism, the different destinations compete worldwide through globalization. The paradigm shift from mass tourism (also known as *Fordian Tourism*), which was the norm for more than three decades, no longer suffices to achieve competitiveness in tourism enterprises and regions. A new paradigm, or new tourism, is gathering momentum owing to its ability to face prevailing circumstances. Modern information and communication technology development in symbiosis with the transformation of tourism demand gave rise to a *new tourism.* This paradigm shift is not easy to define but is indicative of a new type of tourist who wants a new or different product. The new tourists are more experienced, more educated, more "green", more flexible, more independent, more quality-conscious and "harder to please" than ever before. Furthermore, they are well read and know what they want and where they want to go.

The different approach of the new tourist's creates a demand for new products. The small, medium and micro entrepreneurs within the tourism industry are dependent on major tourism developments. It is essential role of these small entrepreneurs be increased to deal with the changing demands of the new tourists. In Canada, 20% of the population is truly entrepreneurial while in South Africa the role of entrepreneurs is still extremely small. Only about 4% of the South African population is truly entrepreneurial.

What is New Tourism?

New Tourism is characterised mainly by *supersegmentation of demand,* the need for flexibility of supply and distribution, and achieving profitability through diagonal integration and subsequent system economies and integrated values, instead of economies of scale. This paradigm permits the tourism industry to offer products adapted to the increasingly complex and diverse needs of demand, while being competitive with the old standardized products. These markets of experience have become global, affecting the demand as well as the supply side of the tourism industry.

The tourism industry has undergone profound changes, which have been categorized by Poon (1993) in the following groups: (a) new consumers, (b) new technologies, (c) new forms of production, (d) new management styles, and (e) new prevailing circumstances.

As a result of the super segmentation of demand there is a very strong need for *in-depth knowledge* of the market in order to identify the *clusters of consumer traits and needs.* This knowledge will enable the tourism enterprises to develop those products that will give a greater competitive edge, and to place them on the market using efficient methods of communication and distribution. *Flexibility* is also a very relevant factor since it can assist the enterprise in adapting to the new demand requirements. This factor is relevant in several areas: flexibility in the organisation and in the production and distribution of tourism products; flexibility in reservation, purchasing and payment systems; and flexibility in ways in which the tourism product is consumed. New technologies are fundamental in this respect and, in particular, in the expansion and development of new systems of tourism information.

Diagonal integration is the final basic element. Compared with vertical and horizontal integration, which characterise the mass-standardised production paradigm, this is a process by which the tourism enterprise can develop and compete not only in one activity, but also within a wider framework, seeking profitability on the basis of system economies, obtaining synergies between different products and offering services well integrated in the value systems of consumers.

Key shifts in global tourism market trends are as follows:

- In the long term, the average standard of living in western developed countries will increase, as will the amount of discretionary money available for travel;
- Rising affluence will bring with it increases in the amount of free time available. Longer weekends and increased paid holidays have helped to stimulate expansion in attraction visitation;
- There is a shift in emphasis from passive fun to active learning;
- Activity or special interest holidays are likely to gain at the expense of conventional sightseeing, visiting and other passive experiences;
- There is growing concern about the impact of modern industry, including tourism, on the physical and social environment;
- There is growing awareness of risks to personal health and safety;
- Leisure time will be used more actively, for mental development as well as physical exercise;
- People aged 45 to 64 years of age will be growing significantly in number to the year 2010. In the United States alone, this age group is forecasted to grow by 31% by the year 2000;
- The potential visitor of the future will be: older, more affluent; more demanding; more thoughtful and discriminating; and more active physically and mentally;

- Timeframes for decision-making windows will be smaller. Hence, one-stop-shopping for all-inclusive packages will continue to be appealing; and
- Consumers will increasingly seek low impact tourism facilities, consistent with environmental values and the desire not to contribute to negative impacts.

The New Tourist

The travelling consumer of today (let alone in the future) is very different from any other time in history. The most successful businesses in the travel industry are those that respond to the challenge through the use of technology, innovative marketing programs, better training of staff and by developing a closeness and understanding of its customers/guests.

The differences in travel patterns in the next century will be more related to what consumers are seeking in a travel experience than in how they travel. Today's traveller, the well-heeled or footloose back-packer, is usually informed, educated, and more often than not, fully aware of what he or she wants from their travels. For them the optimisation of time and money is the key and they prepare for their trip by researching their destination through the Web and the experiences of friends and fellow travellers. Mass media has responded to this shift and further fuelled the search for experiences through the promotion of a vast range of lifestyle/adventure programs which have evolved more recently into experiential voyeuristic docu-dramas referred to as reality programmes. Attention is being turned to exploring new frontiers or daring to go where traditional thought did not allow.

In *Tourism, Technology and Competitive Strategies*, author Auliana Poon speaks about the changes in consumer behaviour and values which are the critical driving forces for the new tourism. The new tourist is experienced, more flexible, independent, quality conscious and harder to please. "New" tourists however, are increasingly being seen to be environmentally sensitive, displaying respect for the culture of host nations and looking to experience and learn rather than merely stand back and gaze. "New" tourists are participators not spectators. Things that would never appear on the list of the "mass" tourist such as adventure, getting of the beaten track and mingling with the locals are now the foundations of the new tourist experiences. Typically these tourists are turning away from travel and prefer to have a high level of involvement in the organisation of their trip.

Comparison of Old and New Tourists

Old Tourists		New Tourists
Search for the sun	=	Experience something different
Follow the masses	=	Want to be in charge
Here today, gone tomorrow	=	See and enjoy but not destroy
Just to show that you had been	=	Just for the fun of it
Having	=	Being
Superiority	=	Understanding
Like attractions	=	Like sports
Precautions	=	Adventurous
Eat in hotel	=	Try local fare
Homogeneous	=	Hybrid

Travel is no longer a novelty to the new tourist. Studies support what industry executives have been noticing for the last few years. People expect more out of their vacations than they used to and they are more adventuresome. Surveys done by the Canadian Tourism Research Institute indicate a high degree of interest in getaway vacations, ecotourism, cultural tourism and combining a business trip with a pleasure trip.

Over the next ten years, tourism products and attractions will have to cater to visitors who are more demanding and discriminating, as well as more active and more purposeful in their choice of destination. There will be a shift in emphasis from passive fun to active learning, and the quality and genuineness of visitor experiences will be crucial to future success in a competitive market. An Acronym that is relevant to describe the 'new' tourist is REAL, which stands for:

- Rewarding,
- Enriching,
- Adventuresome,
- Learning Experience.

A key underpinning concept for REAL tourism is authenticity of experience, which is often related to the environment and culture and seen to be unaffected by "mass" tourism. The New Tourists prefer to be regarded as travellers and not tourists. Some specific points which need to be kept in mind while dealing with the New Tourist are:

- This type of traveller requires a completely different marketing approach. They avoid conventional glossy marketing mechanisms and prefer to use reliable sources such as *word of mouth referrals*, their own independent research and trusted publications;

- They desire *experiences* as opposed to products and services;
- They can be called *experiential travellers*, they extend across all age groups and traditional market segments;

New Tourism for the New Tourist

To enable new tourism attractions to stand the test of time and satisfy the demanding requirements of the evolving 'new' tourist, the following criteria should be applied to existing and proposed attractions:

- That the attraction offers a distinct, unique experience that cannot easily be replicated by competitors;
- That the attraction is value added through 'best practice' interpretation, which preferably utilises a 'human element' such as interpretive guides, seasoned veterans and/or local characters;
- That, where possible, the experience is externalised within the natural/actual setting rather than internalised within a false/reproduced setting;
- That the attraction offers an exciting, authentic, interactive and educational experience;
- That 'comfort' should not compromise the authenticity of the experience;
- That the attraction adheres to ecologically sustainable development principles;
- That the attraction avoids the over reliance on technological interpretive devices that will become quickly outdated; and
- That the attraction offers a choice in the form of interpretation offered.

Responding to the shift in market dynamics towards a "New" style of tourist, a number of initiatives need to be taken so as to fuel the growth of experiential tourism these include:

- Network tourism initiatives;
- The development of interpretive highways;
- The explosion of interpretive centres;
- The latest trend towards regional base camps.

Network Tourism Initiative: Tourism experience consists of a large number of factors, which have different levels of importance dependant on the perspective of the visitor. For experiential travellers, the experience may be strongly influenced by the experiences between attractions such as the expert commentary provided by a trained guide or the friendliness of locals along the way.

The aim of Network tourism is to package a diverse range of products and services throughout a broad region to create a quality experience that capitalises on a region's strengths and comparative advantages. This principle recognises that the combination of discreet experiences within the network creates a greater attraction than its individual components and serves to increase economic benefits and market profile for the entire region. To satisfy the diverse experiential requirements of the "new" tourist, it is imperative that a strong referral system is developed between attractions contained within the network. This therefore goes beyond current promotional attempts by the tourism agencies to promote the entire network, and rests with the individual attractions within the network themselves and the need to actively cross promote between attractions.

Interpretive Highways: Travel is seen to be a part of a network of experiences as opposed to the mere mechanism for going from point A to B. Interpretive highways have been a successful device to link a number of disparate experiences to provide a more comprehensive visitor experience. Whilst principally a tool for satisfying the travel desires of self-guided travellers, a framework should be developed that has also serves to assist experiential requirements of commercial guided tour operators. This is primarily attributed to improved interpretation offered along the travel path to break the monotony of long haul travel between attractions.

The Explosion Of Interpretive Centres: The purpose of the centre is to educate the general public and children in particular on the importance of a particular tourist site, historical monuments, natural resources, wetland ecosystems etc. These centres can contain permanent and evolving exhibit galleries, meeting space, a classroom and teaching laboratory, an auditorium, and a gift shop, along with offices and other support facilities. Indoor exhibits on natural history and other objects of tourist interest can be complemented by regular showings of multi image presentations.

The Wildlife Institute of India: United States Fish and Wildlife Services and Madhya Pradesh Forest Department collaborative programme aims to achieve long term conservation of the park by increasing awareness and appreciation towards Panna National park among visitors as well as local people through the use of interpretive centres. The main components of the programme are:

Outreach Programme: It is aimed at sensitizing the local community about the benefits of the programme to the park and eventually to them.

Resource Material: In the form of books, brochures and CD-ROMs would be developed to highlight the conservation needs. An exclusive website on Panna National Park is also planned for attracting international attention.

Interpretation Centre and Visitor Centre: They are an important component of the project and would comprise of exhibits on Panna National Park and its conservation needs. This is a means of education mainly targeted to the tourists, School children and local community.

Capacity Building: Training of local youths as guides, Park staff and tour operators on Interpretation and communication skills to enable them to run the programme.

The Latest Trend Towards Regional Base Camps: While the traditional centralised awareness centre can be thought of as a strategic hub located at a major strategic travel point, it is proposed that a 'hub and spokes' approach be the next evolutionary step. The hub can be thought of as the 'base camp' for regional exploration and provides advice, essential services, orientates the visitor, provides all the necessary supplies and equipment to enable the visitor to safely and sensitively explore the region. In delivering these services, the hub can also become an important community asset by encouraging mixed use. The spokes visit important remote sites and recognise that where possible, interpretation should be undertaken in the authentic setting. The 'hub' attempts to put the heart back into a township and revitalise the local economy.

Politico-cultural Impacts

- o Political stability and political relations influences the image of destinations in tourist-generating regions.
- o Media portrayal: books, magazines, newspapers, satellite and cable links has a substantial influence.
- o Examples of political strife that cause problematic concerns in the attraction of visitors are:

- * Warfare.
- * coups.
- * political strikes or protests.

"Any evidence of domestic turmoil is likely to result in a decision not to visit that country. " Ankomah and Crompton.

What is Political Instability?

- 'Political instability is described as a condition of a country where a government has been toppled, or is controlled by factions following a coup, or where basic functional prerequisites for social-order control and maintenance are unstable and periodically disrupted".
- Multifaceted and complex character.
- Impact in various countries worldwide is multilevel and multidimensional.

Relationship between politics and tourism

- 'The political aspects of tourism are interwoven with its economic consequences...tourism is not only a "continuation of politics" but an integral part of the world's political economy. In short, tourism is, or can be, a tool used not only for economic but for political means".

Unwillingness on the part of many decision makers both in government and in the private sector to acknowledge the political nature of tourism.

- Lack of official interest in conducting research into the politics of tourism.
- Tourism not regarded as a serious scholarly subject.

" Tourism is by now too important and a pervasive activity for governments to ignore.".

The Reasons Behind the Neglect

China-Tiananmen Square, June 4 1989;

- Prime time news coverage showed army tanks threatening the civilian population.
- After the Tianamen Square incident Hotel occupancy rates in Beijing dipped below 30 per cent.
- Tourism earnings declined by $430 million in 1989 alone.

Has tourism been affected by political instability?

Effects of Political Violence

Effects of Military Coups ;

Fiji-1987: As a result of a mainly non-Fijian government being elected.

- Two military coups occurred within four months.
- Qantas imposed a two-month ban on flights to Fiji, following the hijacking attempt of an Air New Zealand Boeing 747.
- Travel Insurance cover was withdrawn after negative Australian government travel advice.

Effects of Revolutions

- Ejtrcito Zapatista de Liberacion National (EZLN) initiated an armed rebellion against the Mexican government.
- The revolution resulted in 145 to 500 deaths.
- 1994 visitation to Mexico dropped by 70 per cent.

Effects of Civil War

Yugoslavia – 1991, Army attacks Slovenia ;

- Conflict continued for 10 days before moving to Croatia in 1991, and Bosnia-Herzegovina in 1992,
- Tour operators for Yugoslavia lost over one million bookings in 1991,
- Two years after the war, figures for Slovenian tourism are still far behind prewar figures.

Sub Saharan Africa

The most extensive of Sub-Saharan colonial wars was fought in Angola, Mozambique and Guinea Bissau. Nigeria had five successful coups since gaining independence in the 1960'

- In total, more than 20 major wars have taken place on the sub-Saharan region of Africa since the 1960s.
- Zimbabwe (formerly southern Rhodesia) was the scene of a fifteen years Liberation War of Attrition between Africans and white settlers.

Effects of Civil War

Effects of Civil War ;

- IPRA targets included senior British government officials, British military and police,

- Visitor arrivals fell from a 1967 peak of 1,080,000 to 321,000 in 1976,
- Ceasefire which began on August 31 1994 was observed until February 9 1996 when a bomb exploded in London killing two bystanders and injuring 43 people,
- 18-month ceasefire recorded a 59 per cent increase (from previous year) in inquiries, 11 per cent increase in hotel occupancy, 18 per cent increase with out-of-state visitors, and a 68 per cent increase in holiday visitors.

Effects of Terrorism

Turkey – 1974, PKK Seeks to Establish Southeastern Marxist State;

- Kurdistan Worker's Party specifically targeted Turkey's tourism industry between 1991 and 1996.
- Bombed tourist sites, hotels and kidnapped foreign tourists.
- Foreign visitor arrivals dropped eight per cent from 1992-1993.
- After self-imposed ceasefire, international arrivals reached record levels (9.5 million) in 1996.

Peru –Formation of Maoist Terrorist Group;

- Aim of replacing existing Peruvian institutions with a peasant revolutionary regime.
- Attacks led to a steep decline in tourism from 350,000 international visitors in 1989 to 33,000 in 1991.

Egypt – Late 1970s, Islamic Extremist Group Activity;

- Egyptian Islamic extremist group works toward establishing an Islamic state.
- Specifically targeted and launched attacks against Egypt's tourism industry since 1992.
- Egypt removed from programs of international tour operators.
- Experienced a 22 per cent drop in international visitors, 30 per cent drop in tourist nights and 43 per cent decrease in tourism receipts.

7

The Environmental Impact of Tourism

Introduction

It has been said many times and by many actors: Tourism is a double-edged activity. It has the potential to contribute in a positive manner to socioeconomic achievements. At the same time, its fast and sometimes uncontrolled growth can be the major cause of degradation of the environment, and loss of local identity and traditional cultures. Tourism's relationship with the environment is highly complex. There are obvious economic benefits involved for countries and societies, and obvious options for an increased interest in conservation and concern for nature and the protection of fragile environments. At the same time, there are equally obvious ecological risks of ecosystem and habitat depletion and destruction due to the pressure of growing tourism.

Tourists may, literally speaking, love nature to death. According to a much-quoted Asian saying: "Tourism is like fire-you can cook your dinner on it, or it can burn your house down". UNESCO stresses the following on tourism and the management of protected natural areas, including many biosphere reserves: "Yet tourism is ambivalent, by its very nature. On the one hand, tourism generates well-known advantages. Visitor fees, concessions, and donations provide funds for restoration and protection efforts. Visitors are recruited as 'friends' of a site and can aid in generating international support. Tour operators and hotel chains can play a role in the management of a site either with financial contributions, aiding monitoring efforts, or encouraging their clients to follow guidelines of responsible tourism. Tourists can support artisan activities and help to strengthen threatened cultural values. Tourism also generates well-known problems. Tourism growth is difficult to control.

Guiding development is a time-consuming process involving establishing policies, ongoing dialogue with stakeholders, and monitoring to determine if desired conditions are being met. Tourism activities require environmental impact assessments and carrying capacity studies. At sites with limited budgets and staff, increasing tourism can stretch scarce resources taking managers away from protection efforts. While tourism's benefits can contribute to protection and restoration efforts, it can be difficult to strike a balance between economic gain and unacceptable impacts."

Or thus summarized in a scope: (International Council for Science/ Scientific Committee on Problems of the Environment) research programme and symposium on "Placing tourism in the landscape of diversities", on the tourism–biodiversity interaction, opposition and possible symbiosis:

Interactions: The interactions between tourism and biodiversity can be both negative and positive. They are negative when tourism results in a progressive decrease of biodiversity and cultural diversity, to the point that this diminution adversely affects the potential of tourism itself. Positive interactions may include an increase or steady maintenance of biodiversity, enhancement of cultural diversity, economic growth, as well as increasing the potential for quality tourism. Most depends on the type of landscape planning and management, and of societal adaptation. When tourism implies positive interactions, one may speak of sustainable tourism. Even if interactions are more often negative in the world's tourism, there are many cases and examples of positive interactions within similar regions and ecosystems. A comparison of case studies of success and of failure of tourism, under similar geographic and ecological initial situations, is therefore a key to understand the dynamics of the process of tourism development.

Opposition: Tourism activities often originate a self-destruction cycle. As tourism becomes more massive, intensive and spread out in a region, and when there is an excessive urban growth, there is a progressive degradation of biodiversity. This negative impact is especially important concerning the diversity of landscapes, and the type of exploitation that takes place on them. It may eventually lead to a lack of quality and diversification that will no longer attract tourists. The economic profitability of tourism decreases, the return on investments is too low, and there is a progressive trend towards uniformity of both tourists and landscapes. Tourism operators are forced to lower prices to attract tourists, tourism becomes even more massive and low quality, and the self-destructive cycle is increasingly strengthened, up to the moment that tourism may eventually end.

In general, as mentioned by the World Bank, the features of the natural and sociocultural environment that are important resources for tourism attract people because of aesthetic, recreational educational/ scientific value. However, many of the same features are particularly sensitive to disturbance by human activities. Negative impacts resulting from inadequately planned and uncontrolled tourism development can easily damage the very environments on which the success of the project depended. This in turn may severely reduce project benefits. In other words, without careful attention to the balance between the volume and type of tourist activity and the sensitivities and carrying capacities of the resources being developed, tourism projects can be not only environmentally harmful but also economically self

For example, an increased number of hotels sited to attract tourists to a coral reef fail after a few years, because hotel effluents discharged offshore rapidly impair-or kill-the reef.

More specifically, the negative environmental impacts of tourism development may be the result of the following activities:

- planning tourism development and policy making,
- siting tourism facilities,
- construction of tourism infrastructure,
- maintenance and operation of tourism infrastructure,
- tourism related transport and activities,
- use by tourists of the territory.

In general, many environmental impacts in the Seychelles are due to a lack of enforcement of existing legislation and lack of obedience of existing guidelines, e.g. those of the Planning Authority.

Planning Tourism Development and Policy Making

Lack of proper integration of environmental concerns into tourism planning may result in: increasing the gap between visitors' expectations in environmental terms and their actual experience, increasing the gap between the required infrastructure and the availability of services for proper environmental management and the actual number of tourists to aceommodate, lack of attention to the shift in demands for environmental services by the tourists, lack of attention given to new promising environmentally conscious tourism customers community. Over estimating the tourism carrying capacity of the various islands will also result in negative environmental impacts. Implicitly admitting too many tourists compared with the carrying capacity will increase de facto the environmental problems generated by the tourism industry. Tourist education is not a significant part of the present tourism policy in Seychelles.

Siting Tourism Facilities

Facilities have been constructed and are being operated at distances too close to the beach and coastline, resulting in increased coastal erosion, flora and fauna destruction and more generally sensitive ecosys disturbance. As most tourism facilities are sited on coastal areas, see Guideline 2 for more on coastal zone management.

The improper siting of tourism facilities may result in:

- direct destruction of valuable ecosystems, e.g. during the land clearing operations.
- overburden to the natural environment in connection with the carrying capacity of the ecosystems.
- can either be due to high tourist concentrations in an average ecosystem, or reasonable tourist concentration in a fragile environment.

Examples of the latter in the Seychelles include most of the small islands: We have long been proud of the fact that mass-tourism has a greater impact on the world than we do, and rightly so; backpackers generally tend to stay away from the large resorts, and because we try to get off the beaten track our tourist dollars benefit those outside the more well-trodden parts of the world. Unfortunately, our numbers mean we are having a profound effect on the places we visit, and in 2007 the 119,000 British backpackers who flew to Australia created a sobering 480,000 tonnes of CO_2 through their flights.

When tourism and its environmental impact is discussed in the media, an 'industry spokesperson' will appear to reassure us that everything is being done to blah, blah, blah...but the 'tourist industry' is not an IATA or ATOL accredited travel agent in your high-street. The tourist industry is a luxury hotel in Bombay which employs cleaners for bed and board, or an Italian owned resort in Honduras which throws hundreds of empty plastic water bottles into a local landfill everyday. The tourist industry is the tourists themselves-us.

In an age where back packing and gap-year travel have become the norm, sustainable travel is not just about the impact you have personally, it all comes down to numbers. There are an awful lot of backpackers out there and we are just as capable of damaging the areas we visit as package tourists are. Rather than sticking to the illusion that we are the last of the world's explorers, it is vitally important now that we begin to see ourselves as part of the much larger group we represent. The key is to imagine that you are actually quarter of a million customers, not just one. If everyone is carrying the same guidebooks and eventually everyone reaches the same page then you're certainly not the only person buying a piece of that snake skin, and a quarter of a million bits of snake skin is more than just a couple of dead snakes. We need to get back to using our guide books as 'guides', not just the only option.

Marco Polo's been dead for 700 years and if there is anything left to be discovered it won't be done by back packers, so it's time for us to be honest. We are still pioneers, but unfortunately it's for the travel industry and a back packer centre now will be a tourist resort in ten years time. Our responsibility now is not just to be responsible travellers in what we do ourselves, but to show those parts of the world we visit that we value what they can offer us, be it virgin rainforest or a full-moon party, and that we want them to preserve not their lifestyles (a dubious idea anyway) but the environment as it exists now.

Sustainable travel is not expensive, nor is it a barrier to local people making the life for themselves that they wish-but it is a chance for us to influence how the tourist industry, as defined above, treats its local environment. We are not explorers in the Marco Polo sense of the word-the world has been mapped and is waiting for us to arrive-but we can be pioneers for a new kind of environmentally and socially sustainable travel.

Public-sector Planning for Control and Conservation

Tourism is one of the world's fastest growing industries as well as the major source of foreign exchange earning and employment for many developing countries, and it is increasingly focusing on natural environments. However, tourism is a double-edged activity. It has the potential to contribute in a positive manner to socioeconomic achievements but, at the same time, its fast and sometimes uncontrolled growth can be the major cause of degradation of the environment and loss of local identity and traditional cultures. Biological and physical resources are in fact the assets that attract tourists. However, the stress imposed by tourism activities on fragile ecosystems accelerates and aggravates their depletion. Paradoxically, the very success of tourism may lead to the degradation of the natural environment: by depleting natural resources tourism reduces the site attractiveness to tourists, the very commodity that tourism has to offer.

As far as economic benefits are concerned, tourism certainly constitutes an opportunity for economic development, economic diversification and the growth of related activities, in developing countries especially, contributing around 1.5 per cent of world gross national product. Tourism is also a major source of income and employment. Tourism based on the natural environment (ecotourism) is a vital growing segment of the tourism industry and, despite the negative impacts, and given the fact that tourism generates a large proportion of income and that a growing percentage of the activities are nature-based, tourism does present a significant potential for realizing benefits in terms of the conservation of biological diversity and the sustainable use of its components.

Among the benefits are direct revenues generated by fees and taxes incurred and voluntary payments for the use of biological resources. These revenues can be used for the maintenance of natural areas and the contribution of tourism to economic development, including linkage effects to other related sectors and job-creation. Sustainable tourism can make positive improvements to biological diversity conservation especially when local communities are directly involved with operators. If such local communities receive income directly from a tourist enterprise they, in turn, increase their evaluation of the resources around them. This is followed by greater protection and conservation of those resources as they are recognized as the source of income. Moreover, sustainable tourism can serve as a major educational opportunity, increasing knowledge of and respect for natural ecosystems and biological resources. Other benefits include the provision of incentives for maintaining traditional arts and crafts, traditional knowledge, and innovations and practices that contribute to the sustainable use of biological diversity.

In considering the role of tourism in the sustainable use of biological resources and their diversity, it is important that the potential adverse impacts of tourism are fully considered. These are roughly divided into environmental impacts and socioeconomic impacts, the latter generally being those imposed on local and indigenous communities. Although such impacts on biological resources may be less easy to quantify and analyse systematically, they may be at least as important as, if not more important than, environmental impacts in the long term.

Direct use of natural resources, both renewable and non-renewable, in the provision of tourist facilities is one of the most significant direct impacts of tourism in a given area. Land use for accommodation and infrastructure provision, the choice of the site, the use of building materials are all essential factors. Deforestation and intensified or unsustainable use of land also cause erosion and loss of biodiversity. Direct impact on the species composition and on wildlife can be caused by incorrect behaviours and unregulated tourism activities (e.g. off-road driving, plant-picking, hunting, shooting, fishing, scuba diving). Moreover, tourists and tourist transportation means can increase the risk of introducing alien species and the manner and frequency of human presence can cause disturbance to the behaviour of animals. Construction activities related to tourism can cause enormous alteration to wildlife habitats and ecosystems.

Tourism has for many years been focused on mountain and coastal areas. Pressures from tourism activities on biological resources and their diversity are enormous and includes: erosion and pollution from the construction of hiking trails, bridges in high mountains, camp sites, chalet and hotels. Tourism activities have a major impact also on the marine and coastal environment, the resources they host and the diversity of those resources. Most often, those impacts are due to inappropriate planning, irresponsible behaviour by tourists and operators and/or lack of education and awareness of the impacts by, for example, tourist resorts along the coastal zones.

Tourism is also a water-intensive activity with a large production of waste. The extraction of ground-water by some tourism activities can cause desiccation, resulting in loss of biological diversity. Moreover, the disposal of untreated effluents into surrounding rivers and seas can cause eutrophication and it can also introduce a large amount of pathogens into the water body. Disposal of waste produced by the tourism industry may cause major environmental problems.

Socioeconomic and cultural impacts of tourism include influx of people and related social degradation, impacts on local communities and on cultural values. Increased tourism activities can cause an influx of people seeking employment or entrepreneurial opportunities, but who may not be able to find suitable employment, thus causing social degradation. Sudden loss of income and jobs can also be experienced in times of downturn, if the economy is not diversified and it heavily relies on tourism. When tourism development occurs, economic benefits are usually unequally distributed among members of local communities. In the case of foreign direct investment, much of the profit may be transferred back to the home country. Therefore, tourism can actually increase inequalities in communities, and thus relative poverty.

Tourism has a highly complex impact on cultural values. Tourism activities may lead to intergenerational conflicts and may affect gender relationships. Traditional practices and events may also be influenced by the tourist preferences. Tourism development can lead to the loss of access by indigenous and local communities to their land and resources as well as sacred sites.

Sustainable tourism is therefore in everybody's interest. Given that a high percentage of tourism involves visits to naturally and culturally distinguished sites, generating large amounts of revenue, there are clearly major opportunities for investing in the maintenance and sustainable use of biological resources. Along with the efforts to maximize benefits, efforts must be made to minimize the adverse impacts of the tourism industry on biological diversity.

In this context, one the challenges for the Convention on Biological Diversity is to develop, promote and disseminate guidelines for the sustainable planning and management of tourism activities in vulnerable terrestrial, marine and coastal ecosystems and habitats of major importance for biological diversity.

The Public-private Sector Interface in Sustainable Tourism Development

The ever-growing threat to environmental support systems and the continuing lack of progress toward sustainability are ringing alarm bells. As a result, environmental issues have surged to the forefront of public consciousness, and are rewriting the rules for business, investors and consumers. Some of the rising pillars of a sustainable future include: environmental economics, environmental markets, new ways of measuring environmental impact, renewable energy technologies, eco-technologies, payments for ecosystem services, biodiversity offset schemes, innovative approaches to applied ecology in industry, and new action networks for sustainability. IUCN believes that private enterprise has a strong interest and an important role to play in securing our natural heritage and using it sustainably for human benefit.

The promise of a vibrant economy that meets human needs depends in large part on society's ability to sustain the biodiversity that underpins all economies. There is a need for stronger action on the part of governments, business and consumers to make environmental protection and poverty reduction integral to the pursuit of individual, corporate or national prosperity.

The Structure of Tourism Industry

The Tourism Chain of Distribution

Distribution (or place) is one of the four elements of marketing mix. An organization or set of organizations (go-betweens) involved in the process of making a product or service available for use or consumption by a consumer or business user. The other three parts of the marketing mix are product, pricing, and promotion.

The Distribution Channel

Chain of intermediaries, each passing the product down the chain to the next organization, before it finally reaches the consumer or end-user. This process is known as the 'distribution chain' or the 'channel.' Each of the elements in these chains will have their own specific needs, which the producer must take into account, along with those of the all-important end-user.

Channels

A number of alternate 'channels' of distribution may be available:

- Distributor, who sells to retailers,
- Retailer (also called dealer or reseller), who sells to end customers,
- Advertisement typically used for consumption goods.

Distribution channels may not be restricted to physical products alone. They may be just as important for moving a service from producer to consumer in certain sectors, since both direct and indirect channels may be used. Hotels, for example, may sell their services (typically rooms) directly or through travel agents, tour operators, airlines, tourist boards, centralized reservation systems, etc.

There have also been some innovations in the distribution of services. For example, there has been an increase in franchising and in rental services-the latter offering anything from televisions through tools. There has also been some evidence of service integration, with services linking together, particularly in the travel and tourism sectors. For exampie, links now exist between airlines, hotels and car rental services. In addition, there has been a significant increase in retail outlets for the service sector. Outlets such as estate agencies and building society offices are crowding out traditional grocers from major shopping areas.

Channel members

Distribution channels can thus have a number of levels. Kotler defined the simplest level, that of a direct contact with no intermediaries involved, as the 'zero-level' channel. The next level, the 'one-level' channel, features just one intermediary; in consumer goods a retailer, for industrial goods a distributor. In small markets (such as small countries) it is practical to reach the whole market using just one-and zero-level channels.

In large markets (such as larger countries) a second level, a wholesaler for example, is now mainly used to extend distribution to the large number of small, neighbourhood retailers or dealers. In Japan the chain of distribution is often complex and further levels are used, even for the simplest of consumer goods. In Bangladesh Telecom Operators are using different Chains of Distribution, especially 'second level'.

In IT and Telecom industry levels are named "tiers". A one tier channel means that vendors IT product manufacturers (or software publishers) work directly with the dealers. A one tier/two tier channel means that vendors work directly with dealers and with distributors who sell to dealers. But the most important is the distributor or wholesaler.

The Internal Market

Many of the marketing principles and techniques which are applied to the external customers of an organization can be just as effectively applied to each subsidiary's, or each department's, 'internal' customers.

In some parts of certain organizations this may in fact be formalized, as goods are transferred between separate parts of the organization at a 'transfer price'. To all intents and purposes, with the possible exception of the pricing mechanism itself, this process can and should be viewed as a normal buyer-seller relationship.

The fact that this is a captive market, resulting in a 'monopoly price', should not discourage the participants from employing marketing techniques. Less obvious, but just as practical, is the use of 'marketing' by service and administrative departments; to optimize their contribution to their 'customers' (the rest of the organization in general, and those parts of it which deal directly with them in particular). In all of this, the lessons of the non-profit organizations, in dealing with their clients, offer a very useful parallel. But in spite of this many, organizations prefer not to operate at a 'transfer' price because costs gradually increase as they undergo the distribution process.

Channel Decisions

- Channel strategy.
  - o Gravity.
  - o Push and Pull strategy.
- Product (or service)<>Cost<>Consumer location.

Managerial Concerns

The channel decision is very important. In theory at least, there is a form of trade-off: the cost of using intermediaries to achieve wider distribution is supposedly lower. Indeed, most consumer goods manufacturers could never justify the cost of selling direct to their consumers, except by mail order. Many suppliers seem to assume that once their product has been sold into the channel, into the beginning of the distribution chain, their job is finished. Yet that distribution chain is merely assuming a part of the supplier's responsibility; and, if they have any aspirations to be market-oriented, their job should really be extended to managing all the processes involved in that chain, until the product or service arrives with the end-user. This may involve a number of decisions on the part of the supplier:

- Channel membership.
- Channel motivation.
- Monitoring and managing channels.

Channel membership

1. Intensive distribution-Where the majority of resellers stock the 'product' (with convenience products, for example, and particularly the brand leaders in consumer goods markets) price competition may be evident.
2. Selective distribution-This is the normal pattern (in both consumer and industrial markets) where 'suitable' resellers stock the product.
3. Exclusive distribution-Only specially selected resellers or authorized dealers (typically only one per geographical area) are allowed to sell the 'product'.

Channel Motivation

It is difficult enough to motivate direct employees to provide the necessary sales and service support. Motivating the owners and employees of the independent organizations in a distribution chain requires even greater effort. There are many devices for achieving such motivation. Perhaps the most usual is 'incentive': the supplier offers a better margin, to tempt the owners in the channel to push the product rather than its competitors; or a competition is offered to the distributors' sales personnel, so that they are tempted to push the product. Dent defines this incentive as a Channel Value Proposition or business case, with which the supplier sells the channel member on the commercial merits of doing business together. He describes this as selling business models not products.

Monitoring and Managing Channels

In much the same way that the organization's own sales and distribution activities need to be monitored and managed, so will those of the distribution chain. In practice, many organizations use a mix of different channels; in particular, they may complement a direct salesforce, calling on the larger accounts, with agents, covering the smaller customers and prospects.

The supply chain comprises the suppliers of all the goods and services that go into the delivery of tourism products to consumers. It includes all suppliers of goods and services whether or not they are directly contracted by tour operators or by their agents (including ground handlers) or suppliers (including accommodation providers). It should also be considered that some tourism goods and services are supplied direct to tourists and are purchased by consumers themselves and it should not be forgotten that tour operators can influence their customers in this area too. The initiatives reviewed in this report focus on improving benefits to the destination, consumers and the tourism industry. These initiatives are focused around four main points in the tourism supply chain:

- Accommodation.
- Transport.
- Ground handlers, excursions and activities.
- Food and crafts.

These include a variety of different activities-from increasing the proportions of local goods and services used in the tourism sector, to working on environmental and sociocultural issues, such as waste management practices, employment training and combating illegal forms of tourism. Many of these initiatives are being put into practice by one or a few tourism businesses, sometimes working with partners across different points in the supply chain. We have also included some initiatives designed to support more sustainable tourism that are being undertaken at destination level.

Tourism and Supply Chain Management

The impacts of a tour operator come from the impacts of all components of the products they sell, including use of raw materials and their processing and production, as well as impacts from transport and distribution. Understanding the sustainability of each tourism product means going right back to the raw materials from which they are produced, through suppliers, and so on, right back to source, as well as ensuring that a company meets sustainability criteria in its own internal operations.

Tourism, like all other supply chains, operates through business-to-business relationships, and supply chain management can be applied to deliver sustainability performance improvements alongside financial performance, by working to improve the business operations of each supplier in the supply chain. The main differences between tourism supply chains and those of other sectors, are that tourists travel to the product, and the product that they buy has a particularly high service component-in other words, it involves a higher proportion of people in the immediate production of the holiday experience.

A good example of supply chain management from another sector is the DIY retailer, B&Q, which has developed and implemented a major supply chain management programme, first addressing environmental impacts, and now incorporating social impacts as well, for all its 40,000 products. In order to assess its overall sustainability as a retailer, B&Q analyses the sustainability of its products going right back to the raw materials from which they were produced, through suppliers, and so on, right back to source, as well as ensuring that B&Q meets sustainability criteria in its own internal operations. For B&Q, the ethics of a product-including employment and working conditions-are an important part of quality and sustainability. Supply chain management in any sector, including tourism, covers all parts of a product's 'life cycle': raw materials, processing, manufacture, distribution, retailing, customer use and final disposal. Overall, the sustainability of a tourism product, depends on issues including the environment and working conditions in destination countries; safety, including safety of customers and staff in delivering all aspects of a tourism product; and resource use and disposal, including proper handling, reuse and recycling of waste materials, and measures to increase the efficiency of resource use.

Tourism supply chains involve many components-not just accommodation, transport and excursions, but also bars and restaurants, handicrafts, food production, waste disposal, and the infrastructure that supports tourism in destinations. These all form a part of the holiday product that is expected by tourists when they purchase holidays-whether or not the suppliers of those components are directly contracted by a tour operator. Just as no tour operator would provide 1-star transport to take customers to a 5-star holiday hotel, the sustainability of a holiday, like quality, depends on performance at all the links in the tourism supply chain.

A further aspect of the tourism supply chain is the activities of customers while on holiday, particularly in relation to their behaviour, and what they source for themselves in destinations. Tour operators are marketing the whole holiday experience to customers, and this includes opportunities to experience a destination's local products and services. Tour operators can play a significant role in providing appropriate advice to their customers about local products and services, and in ensuring that local producers and service providers have access to tourists on a fair basis. Many tour operators already supply some information on these aspects, but there is scope to do more.

Transport to & from destinations: Tour operating includes advertising, purchasing, package development, marketing and sales, and purchasing. Ground operations include ground transport and excursions Some of the components of tourism products... Tour operators contract suppliers to provide some of these components directly: others are obtained by suppliers and their suppliers. All suppliers providing component goods and services that go into delivery of a tourism product are part of the supply chain for that product.

Assessment of Current Practices: Adequacy, Implementation, Motivations & Challenges

We have assessed information on tourism supply initiatives against actions and policies for sustainable tourism that have been outlined by international organisations, tourism industry organisations and NGOs. Socioeconomic and cultural issues encompass a number of aspects, including contribution to the economic development and the wellbeing of local communities; preservation of cultural identity; respect for human rights local communities' and indigenous peoples' rights.

Environmental aspects include sustainable transport development and sustainable use of resources; reducing, minimising and preventing pollution and waste (e.g. solid and liquid waste, emissions to air); conserving plants, animals, ecosystems and protected areas (biodiversity); and conserving landscapes, cultural and natural heritage. Examples of practices here include environmental auditing and management in hotels, as well as supply chain management actions. The principles embodied in the various actions and policies advocated for making tourism more sustainable, are well summarised in the definition of fair trade tourism- a "commitment to finding positive and practical solutions for the tourism industry as well as consumers, local communities and destination governments, so as to benefit local communities through trade, in preference to aid". Fair trade principles can be applied to investments, business benefits including wages and working conditions, direct tourist expenditure, and use of natural resources.

Overall, we conclude that proven examples and practical expertise to implement initiatives addressing most aspects of sustainability are already available, and that the main challenges are to apply these more widely, and in some cases to extend their breadth. We also note that widening the opportunity to implement such initiatives in mass tourism from the UK, may require a shift to business models based on destination sustainability and value-for-money, rather than price and asset yield alone, and therefore may raise issues about brand values and consumer marketing which at present often focus heavily on price.

While all the sectors reviewed have some examples of good practice, there is a significant variation between tour operators in their efforts to promote sustainability in their supply chains. The range of actions available is sufficient for all tour operators to engage at some level, although analysis indicates specific challenges in each sector:

Accommodation

Within those actions undertaken to improve the sustainability of accommodation, our research found a range of activities, but not many of these were the result of tour operator demand or support. So far it is the mass tour operators that have been able to set sustainability programmes for their accommodation suppliers, whilst small operators state that they do not have the purchasing power to change behaviour.

The emphasis of sustainable tourism activities, such as those from My Travel Northern Europe, Kuoni and Hotelplan, is on the environment, mainly focusing on the reduction of costs from energy, water and waste.

Fewer activities are evident in relation to employment conditions and staff development. Most small tour operators rely on selecting suppliers that already meet their sustainability requirements, partly because these smaller operators work with niche markets for whom many of the characteristics of sustainability (small properties, local food, host contact) are part of the product. Developments such as the AITO preferred supplier scheme and the Green Travel Market, as well as the increase of sustainability certification standards are expected to help in this respect.

Socioeconomic Issues

The accommodation sector requires considerable numbers of staff, and so has the potential to provide employment for nearby communities. However, many jobs in the accommodation sector are low paid and involve long hours and difficult shift patterns. Because of the restricted length of the tourism season in some destinations, many jobs are temporary and insecure.

There is also a tendency to employ non-local labour, especially in large hotels. Improving working conditions and pay and encouraging greater employment of local labour, are all part of improving sustainability performance, and hotels and tour operators are starting to address some of these issues. There are examples of good practice on training and employing local people in hotels (such as Serena Hotels, and the Movenpick, Carlson and Taj hotel chains), or providing education for staff families (e.g. Tongabezi Lodge in Zambia), and a range of smaller tour operators prefer to use locally-owned hotels with good standards rather than international foreign-owned hotel chains (Trips Worldwide, Explore Worldwide, MAD Adventures Guerba World Travel, Inntravel, Exodus, SNP, Worldhorseriding amongst others). Members of the TOI and other large tour operators support the ECPAT Code of Conduct against Child Sex Tourism, and deliver training modules on the Code and its implementation to all staff, including accommodation suppliers in pilot destinations, as well as including specific clauses on the issue in hotel contracts.

Environmental Issues

Action on some environmental issues, such as energy efficiency is widespread in larger hotels (e.g. Maldives, Lanzarote, Kingfisher Bay-Australia, and Mauritius), and more use is being made of renewable energy technologies, especially in remoter areas (e.g. Rottnest Island and Couran Cove-Australia, Cousin Island-Seychelles). Some also use water saving devices, and recycle wastewater ('grey water') for irrigation. Large hotel chains (e.g. Marriott, Radisson SAS, TUI Hotels and Resorts, and Accor) often include training on environmental issues as part of staff training programmes, and in other cases, tour operators may provide environmental training for hotels-examples are My Travel and Kuoni Switzerland.

In a scheme supported by members of the TOI operating in Side (Turkey), a joint action plan on waste management has been developed through a multi-stakeholder process including local hotels, the Side Tourism Association, and the Side Municipality. As part of this, waste separation bins have been introduced in approximately 100 hotels in Side (representing an overall capacity of around 20,000 beds), training provided for hotels and key workers dealing with waste management, and a waste handling and recycling scheme set up by the municipality.

Many of these actions help to reduce operating costs as well as improving environmental performance. However, little attention has so far been given to the siting and design of hotels to minimise their environmental impacts. Smaller hotels generally take less action on environmental issues, but some accommodation owners, especially in remote areas, use solar and wind energy.

Management Issues

A variety of management tools and standards are available and being applied for improving sustainability performance in the accommodation sector. These include standards and certification (including ecolabelling), auditing and environmental management systems, as well as development of action plans and designation of clear management responsibilities. Many of these tools were originally developed to manage environmental aspects of business, but can be (and in some cases have been) extended to incorporate social aspects too. Working conditions and employment aspects can be integrated into human resource management.

Some large tour operators have developed environmental standards backed by training materials to assist and encourage improvements in performance by their accommodation suppliers (Kuoni Switzerland, TUI, My Travel Northern Europe, First Choice, Hotelplan); environmental management systems are being implemented in hotel chains (Marriott, Radisson, Hilton, Accor) while a few programmes are integrated with tour operator demands or incentives such as the agreement between the Swiss tour operator Hotelplan and the Spanish hotel chain Iberostar, and some destinations are operating certification schemes to audit and reward good performance by tourism businesses on environmental aspects (Red Sea, Rimini-Italy, Alcudia-Spain, Bolivia, Seychelles, Lloret de Mar-Spain, Phuket Yacht Club-Thailand).

A number of these also provide technical advice and support to help businesses improve standards ranging from the municipality of Rimini in Italy to the nationwide Costa Rican Certificate for Sustainable Tourism.

Conservation Issues

Some hotels are developed within old and historic buildings giving them a new life and preserving a part of a destination's architectural heritage. Smaller buildings, such as former fishermen's cottages and barn conversions, traditional properties and colonial buildings are also preserved by restoring them as holiday accommodation (e.g. the Laona Project, supported by Sunvil, Cyprus, Laskarina, Inntravel, Worldhorseriding, Pure Crete, and Gites de France). As well as preserving local heritage, these also offer communities a new source of income from tourism.

Transport

Transport by air, land and sea is a major area of environmental impact for the tourism industry, and one that can only partly be managed through switching to less polluting forms of transport or upgrading to more efficient transport. The emphasis in transport has been on environmental issues, rather than on social ones and this has meant that opportunities to use airlines for instance as a communication medium to captive audiences have often been missed by operators.

Environmental Issues

Tour operators maintain that they do not have the ability to influence the sustainability of air transport and the few examples are mainly focused on offsetting carbon emissions. However, tour operators do have some choice over mode of travel, and over the operation of ground transportation that they use. A few tour operators have schemes to promote a modal change towards use of forms of transport with lower environmental impacts, such as using trains instead of planes as the preferred form of transport for their products where feasible (Studiosus, Forum Anders Reisen). SNP, the largest soft adventure tour operator in the Netherlands, always offers train transport first for all package holiday destinations under 1,000 kilometres away and offers to quote for train transport for all other destinations.

Ground transportation operators can promote greater fuel efficiency by ensuring that their fleets are well maintained, and by requiring drivers to switch off engines when vehicles are stationary (Vasco Travel). And in the Pantanal region of Brazil, World Horse Riding has supported its suppliers to replace environmentally unfriendly two-stroke boat engines with cleaner four-stroke engines and small solar-powered electric motors.

Because of the difficulties in reducing environmental costs, some tour operators use carbon offset schemes (e.g. Future Forests, Climate Care, C Level and Coolflying) which calculate carbon dioxide emissions from air transport and promote offsetting of these generally through reforestation projects, or in some cases through investment in renewable energy supplies. Some tour operators provide information on these schemes in their brochures (Kuoni Switzerland, Guerba, Trips Worldwide, Island Holidays, Naturetrek, The Adventure Company) and websites (Journey Latin America, The Gambia Experience) and encourage contributions by their customers on a voluntary basis. Other operators-usually at the higher end of the market-include contributions to these schemes in the price of the packages they sell (High and Wild, Greentours, The Expedition Company, Discovery Initiatives, Club Robinson-part of TUI, South American Experience Ltd., The Last Resort, Wildlife World, Crystal Holidays). In discussions with industry experts it was stated that these programmes won't make a real difference to the problem of climate change, but can raise awareness and lead to more advanced proposals.

Socioeconomic Issues

Some airlines deliver sustainability messages through their in-flight presentations, such as magazines and videos, and the few examples available (such as destination-specific videos produced by Tourism Concern) could be replicated. For example, Air France and Austrian Airlines show ECPAT video spots in their flights highlighting the issue of sexual exploitation of children.

Ground Handlers, Representatives, Excursions, and Activities

Most of the examples found of sustainability requirements from ground handlers come from smaller, nature and ecotourism operators, and even amongst those, there are relatively few examples of ongoing impact assessments of excursions and other products. There are however good examples of destination training, both for the operators' own representatives and those of its suppliers. In particular, it is important that tour guides and local representatives are trained in minimisation of environmental impacts, and maximisation of local economic benefit and educating customers on the social workings of a region so as to maximise positive local impact, so that they can play their part in implementing company policies. These examples however are small compared to the portfolio of excursions, since tour operators are often unwilling to deselect unsustainable and poorly managed products that are otherwise popular with customers.

Like the accommodation sector, ground handling and related activities are staff-intensive, and often provide only low-paid jobs with poor working conditions as well as suffering from the seasonality of tourism. However, there are a number of examples of good practice on sustainability issues. Most of these come from ecotourism and nature tourism companies and excursions, where experienced staff with detailed knowledge of local culture and environments are vital for delivery of quality holidays. But these are also equally relevant and applicable to mass market operators too.

Socioeconomic Issues

Our research found that some operators (e.g. Rainbow Tours, Inntravel and Guerba) emphasise the importance of selecting suppliers based on community and work force issues before environmental concerns, and/or are working on introducing responsible tourism criteria in their purchasing policies to cover these issues. Some take steps to employ local staff (Guerba, Worldhorseriding, and Andean Trails), and/or promote visits to community projects or tourism enterprises (Sunvill Africa, Dragoman, Abercrombie & Kent, Exodus, and Andean Trails). A number of mainly smaller tour operators have provided financial investment to assist their ground handlers to improve the quality of their services (Guerba, Alternative Travel Group) and, indirectly, the sustainability of their operations, or have provided basic equipment needed for specialist excursions, such as field guides, binoculars and telescopes (Naturetrek). Importantly, nearly 40 tour operators that offer trekking holidays are implementing policies on porters rights and working conditions, based on Tourism Concern's Porters' Rights Campaign. Some operators state they will stop using suppliers if standards are not met, but have never actually had to carry through this approach (Imaginative Traveller, Explore, Audley).

Environmental Issues

A variety of practical measures are available to address environmental quality issues. Some tour operators are working with their customers and local suppliers to reduce the amount of waste generated by their tours (Andante Travel, Thomas Cook, Laskarina, and Exodus), and most adventure tour operators interviewed take home all waste materials to prevent litter in the sites they visit. Some tour operators set standards for key excursion and activity suppliers operating in protected or sensitive areas such as marine environments. TOI member companies are working with Conservation International and CORAL to establish guidelines for marine recreation standards, to support resorts and tour operators in selecting more sustainable suppliers.

Conservation Issues

Nature and wildlife are key parts of some holiday packages and excursions, yet just the pressure of sheer numbers of visitors can do serious damage to wildlife and sensitive sites. Provision of information combined with simple management controls can help visitors experience the natural environment while protecting it for others to enjoy in the future. Most tour operators provide an element of customer education on conservation, especially advising customers not to buy products made from endangered species, such as from coral, shells or ivory, which are in any case protected by national and international legislation (Thomas Cook in Cuba, Jamaica and Egypt, TUI UK in Tunisia and Kenya); and in many parts of the world, tourists diving around coral reefs must first take a local induction programme on how to avoid damage to corals (e.g. Bonaire Marine Park, Accor hotel group in the Red Sea, Hotel association in Fiji). Some tour operators encourage and develop nature-based tours which can help raise awareness of the environment and conservation issues amongst tourists (e.g. TUI UK turtle appreciation excursion in Greece).

Food and Crafts

Food and crafts can generate considerable profits for the local population, when volume production and delivery at set quality standards can be met by local producers. Key issues for local sourcing of food supplies in the tourism sector are quality, reliability and quantity of supply. Promotion of local sourcing therefore requires training and technical support and investment-for example in storage and distribution facilities-to meet quality and reliability standards, as well as the development of production and distribution networks to gather supplies from different local producers into the quantities required by hotels.

Socioeconomic Issues

Few tour operators have supply chain initiatives on the production and distribution of local, sustainable food and crafts, but some work with their local suppliers to promote local sourcing of food and other local products. Small hotels are more likely to buy from local suppliers, while some large hotels have developed programmes to encourage local production at the standards they require. This generally requires constant supervision and commitment, and success is often linked to championing of local sourcing by hotel chefs. Most large hotels that have worked with local food producers have found it requires constant supervision and commitment, and success is often linked to championing of local sourcing by hotel chefs-examples include Grecotel's organic vegetable program linked to promoting local products in hotel restaurants, and the Sheraton Lombok's fish programme that has created a number of local jobs. Local sourcing and production will usually improve the contribution of tourism to the local economy, both financially and in terms of employment and may also help to preserve local skills in craft production, such as the production of local crafts in Malta, provide a source of diversification and reduce seasonality in employment.

In many cases tour operators use local food and crafts as one of the tourist attractions of their packages. There is also scope for tourists to visit local bars and restaurants to experience local produce and cuisine. Local crafts retail outlets and restaurants are often key to the holiday experience, for example the Canadian Economuseum Society opens craftmakers's workshops to visitors, and the 'Eurotext' initiative in Finland, Greece and Portugal uses the production of traditional textiles as a tourist attraction. Tour operators and representatives can play an important role in suggesting visits to appropriate places through the holiday information they provide to customers when they book, and at destination meetings. Tour operators are in a tremendous position to educate their customers about local food and crafts and to encourage their appreciation, which can help to make a real difference to the preservation of local skills and jobs. However there are few examples were available of tour operators considering the potential depletion of local food (for example fish and seafood) or the outcome of rises in prices for locals.

Destinations

In relation to the tourism supply chain and direct inputs to tourism, destinations provide infrastructure and services. Destination initiatives for sustainable tourism seek to improve the quality of infrastructure-for example, through improvements to waste management infrastructure for solid wastes and waste (e.g. Cirali and Side (Turkey), Menorca and Calvia (Balearics), Hanauma Bay (Hawaii), Cape Town, Phuket Yacht Club (Thailand), and Rio de la Plata (Uruguay)) and awareness raising programmes on waste management practices (e.g. the Maldives, Lanzarote, Lloret de Mar and Mauritius), to transport systems and to reduce vehicle impacts (Hanauma Bay (Hawaii), Tres Islas (Mexico), Alcudia, Lloret de Mar and Sant Feliu de Guíxols (Spain), Cap d´Agde (France), Rottnest Island, and Couran Cove)-and to increase the ability of the destination to gain from tourism. Several destinations have worked to improve the sustainability performance of suppliers (e.g. Red Sea Sustainable Tourism Initiative), and marketing and product developments being used by mass tourism destinations to offset seasonality in tourism (e.g. Calvia and Sant Feliu de Guixols in Spain, and Bermuda). Other initiatives include the promotion of linkages between tourism sites, and promotion of a wider range of tourism activities to encourage tourists to sample different aspects of the country and thereby diversify and spread the economic benefits of tourism.

A number of initiatives in destinations in many developing countries are designed to enhance local employment in tourism, such as by supporting the substitution of locally-grown and locally-manufactured products in place of imports in the tourism sector (Western Samoa), the establishment of investment and loan funds to assist local tourism businesses to start and expand (Zambia), or the setting up of employment bureaux to match employees with tourism jobs (Macedonia).

Some destinations have set up local quality of life and sustainability programmes using sustainability indicators to monitor environmental quality (Lanzarote and Calvia), and in some cases, biodiversity (St. Lucia Marine Park and Cousin Island), as well as monitoring visitor satisfaction and changes in tourism markets. Marketing, products and operations can then be adapted according to the monitoring information obtained.

Associated environmental initiatives often include general environmental education programmes (Rottnest Island, and Calvia), as well as various approaches to protect biodiversity, which may include the protection of a single species or site, such as turtle protection (Belek, and some Brazilian sites), establishment of environmental monitoring and restoration programmes, and environmental impact studies and indicators (Couran Cove, and the Maldives). Measures for protection of cultural heritage are also in place in a number of destinations, ranging from requirements for new developments to be of appropriate architectural designs and built of local materials (e.g. Mauritius and Tres Islas) to the development of visitor management infrastructure and encouragement for visitation to historic monuments and archaeological sites (e.g. Honduras and Turkey).

Trade Stability as Precondition to Sustainability Improvement in Supply Chains

Suppliers are more willing to adopt tour operator requirements when they have long term contracts that guarantee the return on investment. A large part of sustainable supply chains depends on first ensuring the socioeconomic sustainability of the suppliers. The move in the early 1990s towards "guaranteed" accommodation contracts, in which operators would guarantee payment regardless of occupancy, was designed to secure accommodation and to mitigate financial risk, but in fact laid the foundations of a more sustainable supply chain partnership.

A secure income stream, with stable contracts and foreseeable contracting conditions including prices is paramount, both to facilitate the necessary investments by the supplier, and to cement the trust in the relationship. Because projects require time for companies to build knowledge and develop relationships, supply chain initiatives are unlikely to produce measurable short term, quick fix results.

Tour operators interviewed reported that it is necessary to develop initiatives gradually and that results are based on solid working relationships that have been built up over time and reflect a mutual respect between both parties. Tour operators tend to require a steady and significant volume of operations with a supplier or destination if they are to make a significant contribution and expect changes in local operations, whether this is in terms of contracting local people or influencing decision-making of suppliers. Therefore three necessary conditions must to be met in the tour operator-supplier relationship:

- Long-term partnership;
- Fair pricing;
- Consistent volume of operations.

Many improvements in the supply chain are not the result of projects *per se*, but of advice and support provided to suppliers through long term working relationships and the security of a stable client. Smaller tour operators with long term links to destinations have a greater tendency to fund projects that improve local quality of life, whilst creating new tourist products that their customers can visit on excursions.

Approaches to Implementation of Good Practices

Two main types of approach can be identified. The first involves businesses working though their own internal management procedures and/or through their business networks and relationships with suppliers. The second approach involves actions outside the direct supply chain, through partnerships with stakeholders in the public sector, private and voluntary sectors, including local enterprises, host communities and destination NGOs.

Internal Management, Supplier Networks and Direct Business Relationships

A tour operator may adopt practices to reduce the environmental impacts of their office and sales operations, including addressing issues such as brochure production, energy and waste management at their premises. However, the main opportunities for improving the sustainability of their holiday products are to be found in the hotels, airlines, ground transport and other suppliers that are contracted directly. In this tour operators are in a similar position to any retailers where most of its impact as a business comes not from its internal operation, but from the products it sells.

Tour operators direct and influence the volume of tourism, the tourist destinations and facilities that are used. Through this, tour operators have enormous influence over activities throughout the tourism supply chain and the opportunity to use their influence to help in promoting general improvements in sustainability performance as part of good commercial practice.

A detailed review by the TOI of initiatives in the management of supply chain relationships by companies in partnership with their suppliers, shows that a defined series of steps are applied to supply chain management by tour operators. These steps are set out in the TOI Supply Chain Management Handbook, and comprise the following:

Establish a Sustainable Supply Chain Policy and Management System

1 Create a clear company policy on sustainability and coordinate implementation across relevant departments.

2 Conduct a baseline assessment using consultation to assess the performance of a sample of suppliers against criteria defined in the sustainability policy, and identify priority areas for improvement.

3 Prepare and implement an action plan drawing on the baseline assessment, and working with suppliers to improve their sustainability.

Support Suppliers in Reaching Sustainability Goals

1 Raise awareness on sustainability issues amongst suppliers and demonstrate why sustainability performance is important.

2 Provide suppliers with technical support on actions to improve their sustainability performance

3 Offer incentives to sustainable suppliers to recognise and reward them for improvements on key environmental, social and economic issues.

Integrate Sustainability Criteria into Suppliers' Contracts and Preferentially Contract Suppliers that Meet those Criteria

These steps are equally applicable to development of action within individual companies. Within these frameworks we have found a series of tools that are being implemented, with some overlaps in use, including:

- Standard setting and use of certification schemes.
- Performance monitoring through special surveys and through customer satisfaction questionnaires.
- Provision of a range of incentives, such as long term relationships and preferential marketing.
- Partnerships, such as investment assistance.
- Provision of technical support and advice.
- Preferred contracting.

- Avoidance or deselection of suppliers that do not meet basic requirements.

The successful implementation of sustainability management systems relies on systematic data gathering. For tour operators that are not already doing this, there are a variety of tools available that offer frameworks that they can use. These include the GRI reporting indicators for tour operators, the socioeconomic and environmental indicators that form part of the IHEI's Benchmark tool for accommodation, and the forthcoming supply chain management handbook, and marine purchasing guidelines from the Tour Operators' Initiative for Sustainable Tourism Development (TOI).

It would be valuable to encourage use these or similar tools in order to gather baseline information which can then be used by tour operators in setting clear objectives and programmes for implementation of sustainability improvements in their internal operations and in their supply chains, which together make up the mainstream business activities of tour operators.

The basic methodology for information gathering can be developed around existing expertise with sustainability indicators, including the work of the GRI and TOI on sustainability reporting indicators for tour operators, and the TFIU's Integrated Responsible Tourism Programme which includes a section on assessing the impact of products and services.

It would be possible for information gathering to be done collectively, for example through the TF or the FTO, or to be done or commissioned by individual tour operators for specific destinations. Whichever approach is adopted, it is essential that tour operators buy into the process, as it is they who will primarily act upon the information gathered.

Financing for supply chain initiatives based on internal management and business-to-business relationships of this type generally comes from the budgets of the businesses concerned, and can be obtained from budgetary reallocations, as well as through cost savings that may be made in some areas of sustainability implementation.

The majority of actions taken through this approach are self-financing, although in some cases external funding support may also be provided, for example through programmes funded by governments or by overseas development aid that are aimed at improving various aspects of business performance linked to sustainability.

Partnerships Involving the Public, Private and Voluntary Sectors

When the World Tourism Organization analysed 49 sustainable tourism good practices, they found that, irrespective of whether they were in developed or developing countries, the success of these projects is linked to local community involvement in the planning, development and management of the projects in over 40% of examples. Partnerships such as that in Side supported by the TOI, or Tourism Concern's work to develop its Porters' Rights campaign are critical to ensure that a good understanding is built up between all those who need to take action in a supply chain or in a destination, and that common actions with clear responsibilities are established from the outset of a project aimed at creating sustainability improvements. It should also be noted that NGOs can and do play an important role in drawing attention to some supply chain issues-the Porters' Rights campaign being a good example.

Partnerships involving two or more groups of stakeholders are the second main approach used to promote sustainability in tourism supply chains. The stakeholders involved in these initiatives can include national and local government organisations, business associations (such as the Caribbean Alliance for Sustainable Tourism and the Caribbean Hotels Association), local communities (often through community associations), and NGOs. Some of these projects incorporate components that are directly aimed at assisting the private sector to improve performance in some aspects of sustainability. One example is the programme of environmental auditing for hotels-EAST; Environmental Audits for Sustainable Tourism-that has been set up in Jamaica.

A number of these partnerships deal with infrastructure for environmental and resource management at destination level-particularly solid and liquid waste management, and water quality and supply-through supporting investment and through establishment of improved management systems.

Other partnership projects deal with a range of areas covering:

- Marketing, ecolabelling and certification.
- Promotion of economic development and employment, including development of economic linkages between tourism and other local economic activity.
- Legislation enforcement and standard raising.
- Training and awareness raising.
- Protection and restoration of natural and cultural heritage.

Financing for initiatives based on partnerships often comes mainly from national governments and overseas development aid, with varying degrees of contributions from the private sector and local government. Some initiatives-generally smaller schemes-can also involve funding from NGOs or are self-financed by tourism enterprises.

The recent work of the Association of Independent Tour Operators (AITO) is a good example of partnership approach to using market mechanisms to promote sustainable suppliers, by developing a system to promote the use of sustainable suppliers for AITO members' new product development.

Details of tourism service suppliers that have met sustainability criteria will be stored in a database and directory, which AITO members can search when preparing new packages. Current suppliers of these tour operators will be encouraged to demonstrate that they meet the criteria to be included in the database, while the service will be promoted to other suppliers with good sustainability credentials that aim to work with AITO tour operators.

As a multi-stakeholder organisation, the TF is well placed to encourage partnerships that integrate a number of tour operators working in the same destination, as this reflects specific TF aims, to which TF Forum members have signed up to through the UK Sustainable Tourism Initiative Commitment, in which they have undertaken to:

- "develop a policy and associated strategy to integrate and implement sustainable tourism practices into their mainstream business activities with indicators to track progress and to engage with other stakeholders to achieve the goals of the initiative."
- "work together in a process of continuous improvement in sustainable tourism practice."
- "Implementation of preferred codes of practice supported by practical tools that allow continuous improvement in the environmental and social performance of supply chain partners in destinations."
- "Building multi-stakeholder partnerships in destinations to identify and address priority areas in promoting sustainable tourism practice."
- "Developing a communication process that will engage consumers and other stakeholders in sustainable tourism issues.

Business Issues and Motivations

Good practice covers both what a business aims to achieve, and the processes and approaches by which it seeks to implement such aims. The cases reviewed for this report demonstrate a range of good practices, which have potential to be applied widely across the industry by tour operators and their supply chain partners. However, at present, apart from some basic environmental technologies, such as use of energy efficient lighting, few of the good practices recorded in this report are being applied very widely.

Tour operators make strict health and safety demands in their supplier contracts, but they tend not to set local labour and employment conditions, even though these can also contribute to the quality of their customers' holiday experience, by encouraging the development of high quality local staff. Some of the actions are tokenistic and short term and use philanthropic actions to make up for an inability of internalising sustainability in core business operations.

Most suppliers are chosen on overall quality, but at present the tourism sector only rarely includes sustainability issues as part of the quality equation. Sustainability issues are most evident as a quality issue amongst smaller and specialist tour operators. The mass tourism sector is just at the very early stages of incorporating sustainability as a product quality issue, focusing mainly on environmental issues, but now starting to address a few social issues such as working against child sex tourism through implementation of the ECPAT code. However despite examples such as Serena Hotels, specific action to improve employment and working conditions within mass tourism businesses is still a rarity.

Yet good practices recorded in this report are clearly viable as part of the business practices of those businesses that have adopted them, and indeed provide a range of business benefits that maintain and increase competitiveness. These include gains from brand reputation, to better staff morale and retention, to stronger long term business relationships with key suppliers. This suggests that there is huge scope for good practices to be adopted by tourism businesses throughout the supply chain on both social and environmental aspects of sustainability.

However there are some very good examples that genuinely incorporate sustainability into supply chain management and contractual relationships: these need to be encouraged. Pro-active, forward looking tourism firms have much to gain from selecting, developing and retaining sustainable and responsible suppliers. The TOI members and the World

Travel and Tourism Council have separately reported similar benefits from corporate social leadership and actions to improve sustainability performance. Seven categories of business benefit have been identified by the TOI from a series of case studies of good practices by TOI members:

- Retention of your clients, as there they increasingly expect responsible behaviour even from those not willing to pay for it.
- Increased revenue.
- Reduced costs and improved operational efficiency, remaining competitive to assess and respond to risks and opportunities in the market.
- Management of risks and staying ahead of legislative requirements.
- Enhanced staff performance, achievement of better recruitment and staff retention, as satisfied staff are a key asset.
- Protection of the core assets of the business (environment and culture).
- Enhanced brand value, reputation and market share, protecting image and status, particularly for companies publicly quoted on stock markets.

These business benefits match those highlighted by the WTTC in their 2002 report "Corporate Social Leadership".

Promoting Sustainable Suppliers: Green Travel Market

The Green Travel Market (GTM) is a business to business service launched in 2003 to help European and North American tour operators become more aware of sustainable products, integrate them into the packages they offer, and reach relevant markets. GTM offers a range of services: a network of over 500 tour operators aiming to promote sustainability amongst their suppliers; a matchmaking service to support new product development for tour operators and for tourist destination firms to seek new markets, promotion at key European travel fairs, consumer marketing, information know-how and training materials.

Central to GTM is a database of tourism suppliers with information and credentials on their sustainability performance. This project benefits from the over 1000 European accommodation providers certified by one of the ecolabels under the VISIT initiative. Information included on the database includes receipt of sustainable or environmental awards, being members of key industry associations with sustainability codes of conduct and a solid track record of implementation, or having undergone a screening process from GTM. The list of suppliers in the GTM database ranges from organic farms in Eastern Europe, to car-free resorts in the Alps, community projects in Costa Rica and incoming tour operators from Latin America.

Providing Benefits and Developing Skills for the Local Community: Klein's Camp

Klein's Camp in Tanzania is one of the Conservation Corporation Africa's (CC Africa) group of small safari lodges and it is committed to CC Africa's core principle "Care of the Land, Care of the Wildlife, Care of the People". Klein's Camp is set against the most breathtaking scenery in Tanzania adjacent to the northern boundary of the Serengeti. Klein's Camp – CC Africa and the Ololosokwan (Maasai) community have reached a land lease agreement under which Klein's Camp can only use 3,000 acres while the remaining 22,000 acres are shared by the camp for safari operations and the locals for their needs. Under this agreement a joint management committee has been established consisting of equal number of members from both the local community and the Klein's Camp lodge, and which is responsible for making all land-related decisions. The agreement gives the Maasai unrestricted access to water and the salt licks.

Following the land agreement Klein's Camp and the CC Africa have launched a number of initiatives that support the Ololosokwan community and its environment. Klein's Camp helped the development of the Ololosokwan Community clinic and employs a medical assistant who treats staff and community members. Apart from medical facilities, Klein's Camp helps the communities to build and fully equip classrooms and provides skills training such as carving, building, weaving and ironmonger that help the locals not only to improve their lives but also to increase their revenue by selling handicrafts to guests. Klein's Camp supported locals to establish vegetable gardens, and this project has proved so successful that the garden keepers now supply not only Klein's camp, but all the Serengeti camps and two local villages.

Other initiatives include AIDS education, scholarship sponsored, employment opportunities in the camp and reintroduction and re-establishment of endangered wildlife populations. A significant portion of the revenue from Klein's Camp is given to the community and to the local conservation authority in order to care for the local people and wildlife.

Environmental Standards for Accommodation Suppliers: Kuoni Switzerland

Kuoni Switzerland developed in 2000 an in-house scheme, the Green Planet Award, to encourage and reward environmental management for its beach accommodation suppliers. In assessing candidates for the award, Kuoni focuses on how hotels deal with energy, waste and water. In order to achieve this Kuoni developed a questionnaire to provide measurable data.

The key issues of the questionnaire are the quantity and quality of the information the hotel provides on its energy consumption, its waste and waste-water management and its use of water resources. Great importance is also given to details on aspects such as information provided to guests on each hotel's environmental efforts, and on training provided to the staff on how to operate their duties in more environmentally-friendly ways. Space is also provided for further information about their future environmental development goals.

The initiative was launched in the summer of 2000 in all seaside resort-destinations where Kuoni does business: since then, 641 beach resort hotels have been approached and by May 2002, 43 of these had met the criteria and were presented with the award. Kuoni conducts its survey once a year and publicises the winners in its catalogues and on its webpage, enabling its customers to select their holiday accommodation in line with their environmental principles. Each hotel that receives the award can retain it for one year only and has to prove each year that it still meets the criteria through participating in Kuoni's annual survey. Through this Kuoni's accommodation partners can demonstrate systematic environmental management, their willingness to innovate and put environmental action into day-to-day practice.

The award enables Kuoni to work with its partners to achieve more sustainable tourism development. Through this, both parties-accommodation suppliers and the tour operator-not only can acquire new clients but also to increase customer loyalty as a result of the strong reputation they built through the award. Through the Green Planet Award Kuoni has achieved to build its suppliers' environmental awareness and motivated them to implement better practices. By receiving this award a hotel can develop a distinctive profile that can be used for promotional purposes and also gains competitive advantage in the market, as well as benefiting from long term cost savings by implementing water and energy conservation strategies.

Tour Operator and Destination Partnership for New Product Development: Pantanal Association of Nature Tour Operators

Pantanal is a protected area in Brazil covers 2.3 million hectares of mainly private land in 197 different Fazendas, as well as some land owned by local and regional authorities. A partnership approach has been used to plan the use of tourism as a tool for sustainable development, with the involvement of seven selected specialist tour operators through a familiarisation trip that involved stays in several pousadas (ranches) starting tourism businesses to complement their traditional sources of income. After the trip a two day workshop brought together pousada-owners and tour operators for feedback on both activities and accommodations offered, including comments and suggestions for improvement. The tour operators were invited by the Pantanal Park as the area considers it needs tourism income to maintain its protected area qualities.

The tour operators provided expertise in new product development, designed guide training programmes in nature interpretation and other concepts, and are currently providing a supportive network for local landowners to adapt their facilities and services to meet the requirements the specialised western ecotourism market. The Pantanal Association for Nature Tour Operators is now a unit working together with the Park and Association of Pousadas for connecting the local providers with parts of the international market, creating a feeling of fellowship between the Tour Operators, and creating a group-synergy around the Pantanal both as a destination and as a project, something that can further develop the local providers' products and future income.

The Pousadas have gained invaluable knowledge on not only the ecotourism market but the value as well as the limitations of their resources, as well as gaining a small but secure market that allows targeted investments. These pousadas are receiving some tourists through tour operators that are supportive of a learning environment, and the pousadas are gaining skills such as responding to tour operator requirements, pricing, quality assurance, logistics and other elements of the incoming tour operator's job. As a result of the familiarisation trip, the new products developed in conjunction with the pousadas are high-end incentive trips for CEOs, riding holidays, jungle trips, ecotours, back packer trails, and wildlife and birdwatching tours, by Adventura

AB, World Horse Riding, JungleTrekker, Worldwide EcoLodges Viventura, Saïga and Discovery Initiatives.

Developing Environmental Management Systems for Resorts: Red Sea Sustainable Tourism Initiative

The Sinai Peninsula and Red Sea Coast benefit from a USAID funded program to support Egypt's Tourism Development Authority (TDA) to plan and manage sustainably for tourism growth. The focus of the Red Sea Sustainable Tourism Initiative (RSSTI) is to highlight best practice and raise sustainable tourism awareness through awareness campaigns, and in particular to train and implement Environmental Impact Assessment and monitoring and Environmental Management Systems.

Within this program eight resorts have implemented a resort-wide Environmental Management Systems (EMS) which resulted in significant savings, as well as the development of local examples for other resorts to follow. The EMS programme covers a range of issues such as energy and water efficiency, solid waste management, landscape design and planting. To support the implementation of an EMS, the program includes training courses for hotel senior management leading to a recognised certificate, the development of practical manuals and awareness campaigns, the preparation of self-auditing checklists and the potential to access independent certification of the properties through Green Globe. The Steigenberger Golf Resort and The Oberoi Sahl Hasheesh received this certificate by amongst other actions conserving energy and water, reducing their solid waste through separation and recycling.

Production and Distribution of Food to meet the Requirements of Large Purchasers: Sandals St. Lucia

Sandals St. Lucia has been working to improve their supply chain by supporting a local farmers organisation and distribution company, with support from Oxfam UK. The Caribbean islands suffer from production of only a limited range of produce which is grown locally and not well-planned in relation to market requirements. The lack of a common Caribbean-wide market and protective national policies towards other Caribbean states, means that most goods for resorts like Sandals are in fact flown in from Miami. Oxfam UK chose to work with St. Lucia because they perceived there was a positive national government agenda, policy framework and desire to act, as well as a formalised agricultural sector, and with local food production because it could contribute to tackling poverty in ways that heritage and environmental conservation could not. Other locations where similar work could be considered are the Dominican Republic and Mexico. Oxfam is providing support focusing on bridging the institutional gaps that exist between small farmer producers to reach potential markets. This requires linking individual farmers in groups through planned production beyond monocrops, by introducing the necessary skills and equipment. Local producers need to focus on health and safety primarily in supplying meat and fish produce, while for most fruit and vegetables the producers need training on washing and packaging, and on quality standards set at a national level.

Common-interest Organizations

UNWTO is the Largest Tourism Organization

Originated for the International Congress of Official Traffic Associations, the World Tourism Organization is a United Nations agency that deals with tourism related issues. As of 2005, its membership included more than 350 affiliate members, 145 countries, and 7 territories and representing educational institutions, private sector, and tourists associations. The UNWTO is located in Madrid, Spain.

Goals and Points of Concern of Air Highways Magazine

Launched in 1995, Air Highways Magazine emerged as a result of the publishing of a series of travel maps displaying diverse models of transportation. Thousands of copies of the magazine were distributed by the company's customers Avis Rent A Car and Best Western Hotels to their clients in North America. This resulted in the assignment by Canada's Government to create a supermap of air routes, as travellers were interested in how to get to various destinations in fast and convenient manner.

Luxury and Sophistication of American Hotels

The most famous American hotels have gained their reputation and renown by hosting some important events and celebrities and providing top quality services. Many hotels have entered into the consciousness by popular culture and are also frequented by celebrities. To these belong such famous hotels as the Beverly Hills Hotel and the Chateau Mountain in California and the Plaza Hotel and the Hotel Chelsea and many more hotels.

8

Tourist Destinations

Introduction: What Defines a Destination

A tourist destination is a city, town, or other area that is dependent to a significant extent on the revenues accruing from tourism. It may contain one or more tourist attractions and possibly some "tourist traps."

Coastal Tourism

Coastal Tourism is based on a unique resource combination at the border of land and sea environments: sun, water, beaches, outstanding scenic views, rich biological diversity (birds, whales, corals etc.), sea food and good transportation infrastructure. Based on these resources, various profitable services have been developed in many coastal destinations such as well maintained beaches, diving, boat-trips, bird watching tours, restaurants or medical facilities. The coastal zone is an area that has attracted considerable interest from scholars in a number of disciplines including marine policy, coastal zone management, marine policy, conservation, ecology and heritage. Surprisingly, there has been little recognition of the significance of the coastal zone in the tourism literature. In recent decades and paralleling the growing importance of the coastal zone as a centre for economic activity, coastal cities are now exerting an increasingly significant influence on the shape and expression of cultural, economic, spatial and social structures of the regions and nations where they are located.

Urban Tourism

Tourism has been conceptualised in many different ways within the discipline of social science. Up to fairly recently literature relating to urban tourism has seen a formidable growth. However, within urban tourism there has been little critical engagement with the subject. At the end of the twentieth century a tendency to replace secondary economic sector by tertiary sector was observed in European cities. There were also changes in service sector as, apart from transport and trade functions, information, financial, medical and entertainment services became more important. According to these changes cities are described not only as places of industrial production but also as "increasingly as centres of control, interaction, creativity and enjoyment"

Definitions and Scope of Urban Tourism

The term "urban tourism" describes tourism activity which occurs in metropolitan areas and involves interactions between visitors and urban environments, characterised by close concentrations of population. Visitors to urban areas are motivated by a range of purposes including business, conference, VFR, and leisure and special interest such as sport, education or culture. Though cities have existed for almost as long as human civilisation, the blossoming of urban tourism has coincided with the de-industrialisation of cities, and the rise of the information economy. Much urban tourism is now associated with "post-modern" cities with their growing emphasis on spectacle, image and lifestyle.

The commercial impetus towards the staging of televised events and the apparently insatiable interest amongst both residents and tourists explains the move by many cities towards a closer alignment between their tourism and major events strategies.

Determinants of Supply and Demand

Since major urban tourism precincts function as attractions for locals as well as for outof-town visitors, the supply side of tourism in urban areas typically involves a role for or participation by city residents. Tourism must compete for attention with an array of other urban functions, impacting upon the lives of locals. Within cities there is limited scope to develop or construct exclusive tourist environments such as resorts. Particular locales may be predominantly frequented by tourists but the issue of contested use between locals and visitors is ever present. Spectacles and special events offer an opportunity to target both residents and visitors in a complementary manner. Until recently studies of tourism demand rarely focused on urban areas as destinations.

The conventional view depicted urbanisation as having led to alienation and a desire for escape. This began with the mass exodus during holiday periods from the newly expanding and industrialising cities of the Victorian era to the newly established seaside resorts. The process of post-industrialisation has led to an improvement in the urban environment and to the appeal of cities as destinations. Urban and non-urban dwellers are attracted equally by the "bright lights" of the city and by the concentration of social activities. The increasing practice in the developed world to take multiple "short break" holidays has also worked in favour of city locations because they offer easy accessibility and a range of readily available activities. The internationalisation of major events (propelled by the influence of global television rights) has added to the appeal of cities and has prompted city and state authorities to pursue event-based strategies as a means of increasing visitation.

Key Urban Planning and Development Issues

Outside urban areas, planning and development issues often focus around the natural environment with pressure to locate tourism developments close to the most attractive scenic areas. The pressures are different in the case of cities. Because of high land prices and the more concentrated population, different commercial pressures impact upon proposed tourism developments. Up-scale leisure-only hotel properties in inner urban areas are relatively rare since properties which are able to attract the higher yield corporate market are favoured. Much of the pressure in urban areas focuses on the desire or otherwise to preserve significant elements of the built environment. The process of deciding whether to demolish and rebuild or to restore historic constructs affects urban planning generally and urban of tourism in particular. Events and spectacles can provide a mechanism for bringing outsiders into the city without the need for lavish tourism-only investment. However in the case of a city such as Perth, where many of the city centre historic buildings were demolished during earlier phases of development, the capacity of events to overcome these losses remains largely untested.

The difficulty of developing and applying a universally applicable model to cities is highlighted. The four cities referred to in the title are the largest in the UK outside London. However because of the overwhelming dominance of London and the centralisation of power in a unitary state such as the United Kingdom, these major cities are correctly labelled "provincial". Equivalent cities in Australia are generally the capitals of their respective states and enjoy considerable political autonomy from the Commonwealth Government. The term "provincial" is less applicable in this context Perth positioned itself as the "Western Gateway to Australia" for the Olympics. One could not envisage the local government of Britain's provincial cities being able to adopt such an approach because of the extent of centralisation in London and its predominance as an international gateway.

This provides a different dynamic in assessing the role and prospects of Australian cities as centres for international profile events. Kozak and Rimmington (1999) applied the concept of industry competitiveness to city destinations. Competitiveness is often a rationale given by city government representatives for the development of event strategies. A study by Faulkner, Oppermann and Fredline (1999) on South Australia concluded that the state capital of Adelaide, was not perceived as a strength. Only two of the state's eight "core" attractions were in Adelaide and both of these were located outside the inner urban area. Urban regeneration in Australian cities has emerged as an issue of both public debate and in the academic literature.

Hall and Hamon's work on casinos and regeneration has relevance to Melbourne in particular where a previously industrial area (Southbank) was redeveloped as the site for a casino and entertainment centre (1996). The use of the term "entertainment " is indicative of the desire to position the casino complex as an events centre and "happening place." The site is adjacent to the Melbourne Exhibition and Convention Centre which has assisted emerging success as a setting for major events. The increasing inner city residential populations have emerged as an particularly in Sydney and Melbourne and to some extent in Perth. Australian cities do not have the tradition of inner urban living that is common in Europe.

Tourism is, however, emerging as a catalyst for enhancing the liveliness of the inner city. Growing inner urban populations are also beginning to offer event organisers with a population base, conveniently located. When Melbourne's Docklands stadium was first built there was a minimal population base nearly. The proliferation of apartments has changed this. Tourists visit cities for a range of reasons including shopping, eating, culture, special events, theatre and gambling. There is, however, less understanding about whether event strategies are sustainable as a means of positioning destinations effectively and sustainably. Perth and Melbourne do not necessarily provide answers to these questions as yet, but some observations may be made about progress in linking their respective tourism and events strategies.

A special event may be defined as a one-time or infrequently occurring event of limited duration that provides consumers with a leisure and social opportunity beyond their everyday experience. The number of special events appears to have been increasing and continues to do so. It has been claimed that the special events segment is one of the fastest growing segments of the tourism industry, influencing both day trip and overnight visitation. Events can supplement a city's range of tourist attractions and provide a focus for media coverage of the destination, leading to the prospect of repeat visitation.

Events have become an important part of the tourism strategies of many cities. Those less well endowed with natural or man-made attractions may use events as the basis for attracting tourists and for creating the reputation of being as a "happening place". In the case of cities that have an existing range of attractions, events can stimulate repeat visitation much sooner than would have otherwise have been the case. The expression 'event tourism' first gained currency during the 1980s in recognition of the growing link between events and tourism. It involves "the systematic planning, development and marketing of festivals and special events as tourist attractions, catalysts and image builders". Event tourism is not a new phenomenon, but its scale is unprecedented, prompting many cities to pursue a strategy of specialising in the creation and hosting of special events. The economic benefits of special events for cities are well documented. Events can also enhance the image of a city, thereby prompting longer-term visitation. Larger scale events often require the development of additional infrastructure and such projects are often located in rundown districts of the inner city. The facilities and stadiums developed to stage larger events become available for the staging of subsequent events and may help either to establish tourism precincts, or to provide recreational opportunities for the local community. Such benefits have flowed in the case of the Olympic Games in Barcelona and Atlanta, the World Expo in Brisbane and the Americas Cup in Fremantle. In these cases, the resulting urban regeneration has played a part in transforming the image of the cities, has prompted the formation of tourism precincts and has provided for longer-term recreational use.

Following the staging of a successful event which promotes the city externally, enhanced community pride is often evident amongst residents. After Adelaide successfully hosted the Formula One Grand Prix in 1995, residents showed greater support for the pursuit of opportunities to host other events. Since patronage for special events in cities is derived predominantly from the local community, involvement by the local community in the planning and conduct of special events is essential for their long-term future. Most of the longer established festivals and special events, were celebrations of certain aspects of life within a community. Tourists are increasingly seeking authentic experiences, which involve some engagement with local people. Where a strong connection is evident with the community events can assist in this process. Many of the most successful special events and festivals provide visitors with insights into the local community.

The Impact of Hosting Events on Supply and Demand

Major events generally make use of existing city infrastructure. Mega events, such as the Olympics are an exception since they usually involve substantial new investments. Events often stimulate greater than normal use of existing venues, accommodation, shops and restaurants. By staging events during quieter times of the year and attracting visitors when facilities would otherwise be under-utilised, cities can reduce the extremes of seasonality, increase aggregate visitor numbers and generate greater revenues for individual business. To avoid the temptation of staging events exclusively during peak periods, substantial planning is required. All too often, key events are staged during peak times, which makes it difficult for tourists to find accommodation or else forces them to pay premium prices and squeeze out otherwise regular patrons such as tour groups of events organisers are to capitalise on the ability of events to reduce seasonality, they need actively encouragement to host events during quieter times. The volume of patronage may be lower but the yield will likely be higher. Event strategies may be crafted to the suit the conditions prevailing during the quieter periods.

Key Success Factors

Over the past decade, exaggerated claims have been made about the beneficial impacts arising from hosting major events in cities. However, there is also a growing realisation that the forecast benefits of events are not always realised. Since the costs of staging certain events have the potential to outweigh the benefits many state agencies now require the conduct of, comprehensive post-event evaluations in cases where public funds are provided. To enhance the contribution of events to urban tourism, a number of factors should be considered. Preference should be given to events which are consistent with the prevailing or desired city image or have strong connections with the essence of the place, leading to the prospect of developing a unique selling proposition. The "Glasgow Smiles Better" campaign was based on the city's reputation for friendliness. Such positioning may help to minimise the risk of 'copy cat' events being developed elsewhere, prompting a loss of market share. Involvement by the local population can lead to a genuine sense of ownership on the part of residents as was evident with the success of the volunteer programme during the Olympics in Sydney and the Master Games in Melbourne. Since the majority of event attendees are local residents, positive local sentiment will enhance local attendance and enliven the atmosphere surrounding an event. This, in turn, will make an events more attractive to tourists.

The spatial and temporal dimensions of events should link closely with the needs of the host city. Strong connections to tourism and recreation precincts in the host city will help to maximise the benefits that the city derives from the event. Similarly, pro-active involvement by local authorities is needed to reduce seasonal extremes. Regular communication and a shared understanding are needed between destination marketers and event organisers with a view to streamlining marketing and planning activities.

Effective partnerships can ensure that the appropriate events are suited to the relevant city in terms of image, timing, markets, and infrastructural use. Partnerships should also embrace the private sector, particularly as commercialisation and sponsorship are now Integral components of the viability of most events.

Rural Tourism

The employment situation is unfavourable in rural areas with low possibilities of employment agriculture. Local agricultural product markets are mostly missing, the direct marketing forms has not been established.

Expansion of possibilities to generate alternative and supplementary incomes is one of the main areas of development of rural regions. Rural tourism is an efficient way to increase the income of rural inhabitants.

Definition of Rural Tourism

Expressions of Rural tourism, agro tourism, and village tourism are used many times as synonyms by experts and developers. This fact can be explained with the diverse activities of the area. Countryside hospitality is more or less connected to the agribusiness and this marketing product consists of accommodation services, catering and leisure time services. Rural tourism can be defined as a tourism product, which approach accentuates the importance of supply management and marketing activities. The rural tourism, as an element of the Hungarian tourism supply, as a tourism product, is a complex rural supply of a given settlement (or group of settlements) which involves the special elements of hospitality and attractiveness and these elements are organised into special products. Regional tourism can be characterised as a cooperation of local organisations and service providers operating in a well looked-after rural environment, having a regional attractiveness, serving the resident and nonresident tourists' demands of leisure activities, and providing commercial services for the customers.

Rural tourism is a tourism product that is built for introducing rural regions, and to utilise other attractions and provide diversified services. Tourism provides authentic special emotions for the tourists, alternative income and the preservation of local natural values and culture for the local inhabitants.

Generally businesses of rural tourism were initiated by civil associations. Rural tourism connects tourism products. Rural tourism connects areas of rural leisure activities. Therefore the rural tourism, based on the rural circumstances, is a type of tourism which can be combined with the elements of cultural and active tourism (e.g.: horse riding and hiking).

Synthesising the elements of rural tourism the system of definitions of rural tourism. Economical importance of tourism is not calculated from objective data. There are only expert guesses about the contribution of the tourism to the GDP.

Spa Tourism

Definitions

Mineral water-ground water, which in its natural state contains carbon dioxide and other soluble matter in sufficient concentration to cause effervescence or impart a distinct taste.

There are two primary classifications of hot springs:

Filtration hot springs-geothermally heated mineral water that is initially fed by rainwater that seeps into the earth. As it travels into the earth, it becomes subject to increased energy through natural geothermal heat and is exposed to gases and often a wide variety of minerals from rock and mineral deposits. The water adsorbs the minerals via leaching, is heated by the geothermal source, and then returns to the Earth's surface.

Primary hot springs-geothermally heated mineral water, where direct volcanic activity plays a far greater role in the process of the hot springs formation. One of the fundamental physical distinctions between a filtration spring and a primary spring is the mineral and gas content of the water, such as randon and bromide. Primary springs are often powered by magma chambers, which exist under the Earth's surface, as well as in volcanically active regions.

The geothermal resources in Victoria can be principally classified as filtration springs. There are also different temperature classifications:

- cold springs below 25 degrees Celsius,
- tepid springs 25-34 degrees Celsius,
- warm springs 34-42 degrees Celsius,
- hot springs above 42 degrees Celsius,

The term'spa' comes from the Latin acronym'salus per aquum' meaning water-based therapies.

A number of organisations have endeavoured to define spas in a contemporary context. For instance Intelligent Spas defines 'professional spa treatments' to be' based on authentic therapies and practiced by qualified and knowledgeable personnel'.

The International Spa Association (ISPA) defines 'spa' as' ...entities devoted to enhancing overall wellbeing through a variety of professional services that encourage the renewal of mind, body and spirit'.

This definition clearly implies both health and wellbeing.

Wiliness-has been defined by Mueller and Kaufmann as a' state of health featuring the harmony of body, mind and spirit, with self responsibility, physical fitness/beauty care, healthy nutrition/diet, relaxation/meditation, mental activity/education and environment day spa-a business that provides professionally administered spa services that are offered to clients on a daily basis within appropriate day spa facilities.

Destination spa-spas that provide spa-style treatments with accommodation or spas within accommodation environments.

Natural bathing spa-spa businesses operating within a retreat location, offering extensive use of communal bathing in naturally occurring waters or mud pools with a full range of spa services. May or may not provide on-site guest accommodation.

Related spas-businesses that incorporate spa principles into their philosophy and practices, with minimal water therapy facilities and minimal guest amenities. For example, salon spa, dental spa and nail spa.

For the purposes of this plan, related spas will not be a focus, as the majority of these facilities service the local population and have limited spa and wiliness tourism offerings.

From a tourism perspective, day spa, destination spa and natural bathing spa categories, along with their subcategories, are valuable, particularly when analysing the spa industry.

It was not until the 1990s that spa and wellness tourism began to emerge again across Europe, Asia and North America. Spa and wellness tourism is now a thriving segment of the global tourism industry. Over the past decade, investment in the industry has been substantial in many countries. Much of the investment has been in destinations where geothermal waters and mineral springs are located and where there is a longstanding belief in the healing qualities of these waters.

Across Asia, the growth in spa and wellness tourism has been based around each country's heritage and cultural practices. The use of massage, yoga, reflexology, and meditation as preventative practices are well established in many Asian countries, and are offered at spa resorts throughout the region, which have attracted significant investment. In Europe much of the growth has been in established spa villages, with significant redevelopment of spa facilities in towns such as Bath, Baden Baden and Karloy Vary.

Major spa developments have expanded significantly in recent decades and seen mineral water and geothermal water treatments being incorporated with flotation pools, individual spa baths with essential oils and herbal additives, massage, natural therapies and relaxation programs. Bath houses are also commonly located in tranquil surroundings that enhance the experience and provide stress relief for the mind and body. Hotels and resorts have also responded to consumer demand and invested heavily in the establishment of spa and wellness retreats.

When thinking of vacation alongside the Eiffel Tower, cityscapes, fun and alcohol, images of white beaches, palm trees, sublime mountains, lakes, waterfalls, and green landscapes, in short the natural environment crosses one's mind. Tourism obviously entails a specific relation to 'nature' that underlies historic change. However, this historic relation goes beyond tourism's (positive or negative) ecological impact. It also goes beyond an assumed shallow hedonistic 'search' for the sublime, the beautiful, or the authentic when we look at tourism as a special dimension of everyday life. In this paper I am going to outline some ideas about the advantages of a stronger conceptual relation between environmental and a tourism history informed by anthropology and cultural studies. I will start of with some general thoughts on tourism and how it relates to 'nature' on an everyday life level. In the second part of the paper I will take a conceptual look at spa tourism history to point out different aspects of its tourist-'nature' relation. This will lead me to suggest a stronger inclusion of ideas of the body into environmental history.

Tourism Studies is a field of research that many disciplines touch upon. Above all management and marketing seem to dominate the field, addressing issues like effectiveness of marketing strategies or optimization of processes. More critical approaches such as sociology, anthropology, geography, history and cultural studies have been influential on framing ways of explaining the phenomenon of tourism. Naturally researchers of any disciplines will argue for the importance of the topic: Many let the numbers speak for themselves: The World Tourism Organization speaks of 565m international arrivals in 1995, predicts this number to rise to 1bn by 2010, respectively 1,5bn by 2015 (obviously not considering peak oil) (WTO).

The WTO's statistics reach back only until the beginning of the 1950s; and for the big picture it is not necessary to go back any further, as in 1950 international arrivals laid at less than 20m worldwide; tourism is a child of the 1950s syndrome named as such by Christian Pfister (Pfister). Unsurprisingly the vast majority of arrivals take place in the Americas and Europe, i.e. in distinct economies and more importantly consumer societies.

Scholarly arguments don't circle around whether tourism is or is not an important economic factor, they circle around whether it is the second or third most important economic sector world wide. Accordingly, in the 1960s and 1970s researchers treated tourism first of all as an economic question that seems to sometimes imply quite negative effects for hosting societies, especially "developing countries" (Crick 314-17). Social sciences spoke of new types of colonialism, of "leisure imperialism". And as such, it also has quite an impact on the environment.

The latest most prominent impact in terms of media coverage is certainly air travel, but there have been many other cases where "mass tourist resorts overwhelmed local environmental systems and the capacities of local societies to manage them". The Alps, as Kathleen A Brosnan states in her article on tourism in the Encyclopedia of Environmental history, "provide a well-known example of the large-scale destruction of an ecosystem through vegetation removal to accommodate tourist facilities" (1209-10). Much research is being done nowadays on how to make tourism a more sustainable activity.

However, it has also been acknowledged that tourism can have positive or protective effects on the environment, because of its demand for e.g. "sublime nature" (1207). The creation of national parks, the cleaning and clearing of sights, or the natural environment more generally speaking have been related to tourism in a structural way. Christoph Hennig in fact asserts that the visibility of this double feature of tourism—its demand for nature and its destruction of nature at the same time— makes tourism different from any other societal realm. Hennig's view seems as much oversimplified as Kathleen A. Brosnan's assertion that "the major stimulus for fostering tourism has always been economic".

Tourism is not merely an economic phenomenon that has impacts on the environment or societies. Tourism is also about tourists; about people who move to new places for leisure purposes. But why do they do that? Why would anyone want to lie at the beach for two weeks, climb a mountain or bathe in a hot spring? What does tourism imply in terms of the individual relation to the natural environment? If tourism really is so important in the 20th and 21st century, if vacation and travel divide the year like holidays or even seasons of the year, then this raises the question whether and how people's perception, experience, and views of the natural environment is shaped and organized by modes of tourism and leisure.

Is there for example a connection between the raise of ecological movements and ideas of the natural environment (re)produced through tourism? Is it a coincidence that projects to build hydroelectric power stations have been first blocked and their dedicated spaces have been later turned into national parks, respectively UNESCO World Heritage Sites, such as Hainburg (Austria) and Wachau (Austria)? Was the leisure and tourism value of these spaces only produced through individual protests against their industrial use? The motifs of the environmental movement are certainly more varied than leisure and pleasure, but I believe it is one of them.

The Alps may be a qualified as a destructed ecosystem by some people, but still millions of people enjoy what is sold to them and they assumingly perceive and experience as sublime, authentic and maybe even pristine nature; the destruction does not seem to be visible for many. The everyday relation to the natural environment can thus not merely be deducted from structural processes of conservation or destruction – from positive or negative effects hotel complexes have (Norris). Tourists perceive and experience 'nature' in a specific way that coincides with their mode of being, i.e. with deliberately emphasising extraordinary experiences, relaxation, recreation, etc. There is of course a specific relation to the natural environment embodied in hotel complexes, but it is not the one the actual visitors in the hotel have. They may experience and voice their opinion e.g. on the pollution of the sea caused by sea side resorts, but more probably they will just go out and relish their vacation in different ways, by unreflexively using resources, polluting places, maybe even reflexively cleaning places, by enjoying the panoramic gaze on an alpine road, or just by hiking, lying in the grass and swimming in the sea. The anthropologist Jo Vergunst for example understands 'nature', or natural environment as constructed through the processes of moving, "it is *movement* that ultimately precludes the temporal finalising of how nature is and what it consists of" (Vergunst). The movement hereby is as such a physical act, in which the body touches 'nature' in form of grass, trees, wind, sunlight, etc., all of which have an effect on both how nature is constructed and a physical reality beyond construction, such as sunburn, other bodily conditions or reinforced/created footpaths. While however most studies settled between tourism and environmental history take a look at the structural development and impact of tourism (Brenden; Lemelin), i.e. its effects on resources and pollution (Norris), preservation (O'Neill) and commoditization (M. A. L. Miller) few focus on social histories and everyday experiences.

One of the challenges of the latter might be to bring in material dimensions of the relationship between the individual and the (natural) environment. The reciprocal relation between society and 'nature' that we find when looking at hotel complexes can also be identified on a individual cultural level. Nature hereby retains its agency role towards everyday reality of humans. Avalanches are very obvious example for nature's agency perceived and experienced by Alpine skiing tourists; but also accruing footpaths for hikers, or algae washed ashore on to otherwise clean hotel beaches point to nature's agency perceived by tourists. The meanings and consequences avalanches, accruing footpaths or algae have for tourists and others are however as complex as the mechanisms that lead to these phenomena. In his study on North American colonization Converey Valencius' for example points out that the everyday experience of 'nature' as healthy or unhealthy served as the basis of setting up new settlements (Valencius). In his book it of course remains concealed whether the practice of settling itself might have changed the physicality and the meaning of the land from healthy to unhealthy. However, the everyday perception and experience is thus as much double sided in terms of a nature-culture-relation as a perception implied in more structural approaches: 'nature' organizes 'culture/society' organizes 'nature'.

The way nature is constructed is influenced by the individual's state of being, by the way one engages with the natural environment; by the way it is represented, but also performed and practiced. Tourism is one of those conditions commonly opposed to work. It supposedly indeed makes a difference if one walks through a forest as a forester looking for things to work on or merely for enjoyment and relaxation. The realm I am interested in is the ways 'nature' or 'natural environment' is constructed and included into practices through its experience and perception in spas and cure towns. Spas draw a very special relation between human's everyday life and 'nature'. They use natural elements like water, air, or mud in regulated ways for treating visitors. The visitor's body/mind lies in the centre of its interest, whereat the body/mind becomes the location where culture—the visitor/the body/mind—meets nature—water, mud, air, etc. These are not categories I as a researcher impose on spas, but spa ideology, respectively visitors seem to deploy themselves.

Taking the Waters – Everyday Spa Life and its Relation to 'Nature' : Spas and cure towns unsurprisingly have a very long history (Smith). One immediately thinks of the Roman baths, their precursor the Greek baths, the rise of spa and cure towns in the 19th century, including all the aristocracy, the glamour and the romantic gaze on nature that came with it (Steward)—or non-historians will think of the current revival of spas, that increasingly became bare essentials of top class hotels in the past decade. I am interested in the period beginning after the decline of the romantic 19th century spa, that is, in its more popular reappearance as a leisure and tourist activity in the post World War Two era. Of course the "contemporary leisure-spa" versus the "19th century health-spa" distinction is gradual: 19th century spas did have a strong leisure component. However, they do sound a lot more rigid in terms of purpose and daily routine, that emphasise exercise, early risings and sometimes special diets. While this may be so in current cure practices, this is certainly not the case in day and hotel spas. While some of the treatments the latter provide resemble the former, the emphasis indeed rather lies on beautification than on healing. For the moment, the differentiation between different historic epochs is however not essential due to my focus on conceptual dimensions. Both cases are assumingly about things like leisure, relaxation and health where orthodox mainstream medicine reaches its limits. However, closer looks reveal other rationales for getting a treat at a spa.

Spas relate to 'nature' in very diverse ways. Apart from their material throughput that assumingly has little relevance for the visitor (but most probably for the citizen), spas produce a specific nature-culture relation. For one, many spas are situated in rural areas; this location often plays a role for selling the product, whereat borders between 'nature' and culture are sometimes strictly defined architectonically, such as through windows or regulated streams of water running through the facility. In other cases architects have tried to integrate 'nature' through organic style architecture or the use of material considered more natural. Secondly, the experience of nature in general, i.e. not only thermal water, but also the surrounding natural environment seems to be an important element of the spa, especially when framed as opposed to urban life. Thirdly, elements framed as 'natural' are used for treatments. As a 1950s medical guide for visitors to the Austrian cure town Bad Hofgastein suggests, it is most important, that the water used for therapy is "juvenile", and has never seen earth's surface before. This water is most certainly pure as it has never, not even potentially been exposed to any kind of pollution whatsoever. The purity of water is most important as a reason because it backs up very questionable scientific proof of its quality. The same booklet quotes a small series of proofing experiments produced with this juvenile water, the most spectacular having been made with mice and guinea pigs: While the animals would die from an injection of a fatal poison mixed with "water", they would survive when a mixture of poison and "thermal water" was used instead. According to the author this was proof enough to deduct a detoxicating capacity to the water.

There are many other treatments that seem to work in a similar way. Alongside water there is air, heat, mud, sunshine and others. These elements of course underlie change in both material terms and the way they are culturally constructed. Simone Carter for example has traced back in history how sunshine was framed as advancing healing but also illness when leading to sunburn and cancer (Carter). With respect to spa history, the famous English spa town Bath had to close down its spa in 1978 when it was discovered that the water used contained bacteria causing meningitis. It is little surprising that—after the spa had reopened in 2006 only—the "official tourism website for Bath" talks about "natural bacteria" when touching upon this sensitive part of its history (Plus).

While the points of how people relate to nature through spa visits that I made above have been quite comprehensible, the relation to 'nature' through the body needs a little more detailed explanation: The body is crucial to spa visits. Spas involve the visitor's body in all the different activities visitors can follow. Water, mud, sunshine etc. only unfold their effects through touching, penetrating or saturating the body. Environmental history has according to Christopher Sellers not paid much attention to the body (Sellers), despite its pioneer position that would take forward theoretical concepts of the body due to environmental history's "dual obligation" to include the body's nature and culture, that is positivist and constructionist positions. Six years after Christopher Sellers article was published, Susan D. Jones in 2005 still expresses the body as a possible future topic of environmental history (Jones). In contrast the social sciences as much as social history has gradually focused on the body (Howson; Lorenz). In tourism studies the issue only received attention to some degree since the 1990s, largely as a reaction to John Urry's seminal, but narrow focus on the tourist gaze (Urry). According to him it is most importantly the gaze at sights that frame tourist experiences. Tim Edensor, David Crouch and others on the other hand focus rather on practices and performances of tourism as of being per se embodied (Edensor; Crouch; Crouch and Desforges). To bury one's feet in the sand is as important for the experience of beach as gazing at it (Game). The concept of the body thus involves two dimensions: the history of the body (as a positivist but discursive object) and the embodied history (as a subject).

Both dimensions are of interest in the spa, because the body in the spa is where nature-culture relations are constructed. If thermal water is more natural, more pure and juvenile, and if one swallows and digests this water, then what effect does this have on the body? Does it purify the body, does it make the body more 'natural'? Furthermore, can this very strong individual focus on the body during spa visits be understood as a focus on 'human nature'? The answers to these questions have certainly changed over time, especially since going to the spa serves every time less classical health purposes but reaching conditions of wellbeing.

As the questions asked above imply, spa treatments are partly about purifying and cleansing the body, or more broadly speaking, the self. It is about purification, catharsis and asceticism—not at once, but to different degrees in different eras. It is therefore quite evident to take a closer look at concepts of purity and pollution. According to Mary Douglas seminal work "Purity and Danger" (Douglas), pollution results from matter (dirt) being "out of place", i.e. according to her structuralist approach there are only two ontological conditions of being: order and disorder. However, I would argue that order in everyday life does not equal purity. On the contrary, order rather seems to be normal—a rather unreflected condition of being, while purity and pollution seem to be liminal conditions that one can only reach temporarily. For example when I stay in a hotel room, I might first notice any little spot of dirt. But once I stayed for a few nights, these spots become normal, they loose their danger and disappear from reflexive awareness. Similarly Michael Thompson talks about rubbish becoming invisible, hidden away in drawers as useless and valueless stuff, until its value increases again. This highly constructivist approach of course has limited value when it comes to including analysis on what effects rubbish has on the environment. The reason I am mentioning it is because it is indeed essential for people's behaviour towards dirt and pollution. Judith Okely has excellently illustrated this circumstance in a section of her study on the "Traveller-Gypsies". According to her research the 'Gypsies' consider the 'Gorgois" (the 'non-Gypsies') use of sinks (in trailers) as polluting, because different things—dishes, the body, laundry, etc.—Intermingle there. Instead of using sinks, they thus use a whole set of buckets. It is a similar taboo to use the same bucket for different things to clean, as it is for most Europeans to use the same (clean) dish first for serving a cat or dog and then—after cleaning it—for serving oneself. I thus agree with Mary Douglas that pollution does not necessarily have a material base. However, I do follow William Miller's argument, that some materials inherently induce feelings of disgust or pollution.

The value of using Mary Douglas' approach lies in its universal conceptual applicability. Her definition suits Aristotle's concept of catharsis as much as Bruno Latour's analysis of the modern scientific nature-culture division as a quest for order and cleanliness.

The realm of purity, cleansing and pollution always consists of different interrelated issues. With respect to spas these issues can serve as an epistemological guideline: 1) What is the dirt that pollutes the body? Is it culture, is it society; is it the order of normality? 2) How does nature work as a cleansing agent? What does this imply for the way people understand nature? 3) What is the condition of purified bodies? How is it related to the cleansing agent?

Concluding Remarks

Tourism is a topic of environmental history, and nature-culture/society relations in history are issues in studies of tourism. It is therefore only obvious to establish stronger connections between the two fields of research in terms of the theoretical approaches and topics of interest they imply. It is worthwhile to not only see tourism as an impact from outside, but to include tourists and their everyday interest in the natural environment, which is shaped and organized by their condition of being tourists. Tourism is not just the place where resources are consumed or pollution is caused. Tourism seems to have a much wider impact on the way people understand, discursively construct and negotiate what nature is, what meaning it has and consequently how it needs to be treated. Furthermore, the focus on tourists can open up new topics and insights for environmental history, as shown with my conceptual outline on spa tourism. Spas produce, support and create special relations to the natural environment for and through their visitors. They accentuate the body as a location over which the 'culture'-'nature' dichotomy is negotiated. Treating spa tourism as an embodied environmental history from below can thus provide insights on how concepts of nature, i.e. natural environment, and 'human nature' have changed in everyday lives.

The other way around tourism history could profit from environmental historic approaches, that do not only understand 'nature' or the natural environment as mere background or stage where tourism takes place, that do not just understand the natural environment as a sight tourists engage with, but also as a more active part shaping a relation between humans and the rest of the world.

The Successful Destination

The World Tourism Organisation (WTO) sees local tourist destinations as central contributors to the process of development and delivery of tourism products. Therefore, tourist (or tourism) destination is identified as a fundamental unit of analysis. According to WTO, "a local tourism destination is a physical space in which a visitor spends at least overnight. It includes tourism products such as support services and attractions, and tourism resources within one day's return travel time. It has physical and administrative boundaries defining its management, and images and perceptions defining its market competitiveness. Local destinations incorporate various stakeholders often including a host community, and can nest and network to form larger destinations" (WTO, Working Group on Destination Management).

Destinations are often regarded as specific geographical area: a country, an island, or a town. Buhalis (2000) addresses the destination concept from the strategic perspectives of destination marketing and management. He argues that "...traditionally, marketing (literature) concentrates on increasing visitation and treats tourism like any other commodity.

This approach fails to recognise the unique needs and limitations of each destination as well as their particular geographical, environmental and sociocultural characteristics". However, "...it is increasingly recognised that a destination can also be a perceptual concept, which can be interpreted subjectively by consumers, depending on their travel itinerary, cultural background, purpose of visit, educational level, and past experience.

Often, destinations are artificially divided by geographical and political barriers, which fail to take into consideration consumer preferences or tourism industry functions (e.g. Alps shared by France, Austria, Switzerland, and Italy)" (Ibid). Destination branding approach allows to work with consumer perceptions and preferences, creating and controlling the image of a tourist destination. Buhalis (2000) suggests the "destinations are amalgams of tourism products, offering an integrated experience to the consumers", and this *amalgam* of tourism products and services offered by a destination is consumed by tourists under the *brand name* of the destination during their period of stay. So, in other words, "a destination can be regarded as a combination (or even as a brand) of all products, services, and ultimately experiences provided locally.

Destination "Brand" Definition

"A Destination Brand is a name, symbol, logo, word, mark or other graphic that both identifies and differentiates the destination;

furthermore, it conveys the promise of memorable travel experience that is uniquely associated with the destination; it also serves to consolidate and reinforce the recollection of pleasurable memories of the destination experience"

Visitor Attractions

A tourist attraction is a place of interest where tourists visit, typically for its inherent or exhibited cultural value, historical significance, natural or built beauty, or amusement opportunities. Some examples include historical places, monuments, zoos, aquaria, museums and art galleries, botanical gardens, buildings and structures (e.g., castles, libraries, former prisons, skyscrapers, bridges), national parks and forests, theme parks and carnivals, living history museums, ethnic enclave communities, historic trains and cultural events. Many tourist attractions are also landmarks.

Tourist attractions are also created to capitalise on unexplained phenomena such as a supposed UFO crash site near Roswell, New Mexico and the alleged Loch Ness monster sightings in Scotland. Ghost sightings also make tourist attractions.

Ethnic communities may become tourist attractions, such as Chinatowns in the United States and the black British neighbourhood of Brixton in London, England.

In the US, owners and marketers of attractions advertise tourist attractions on billboards along the side of highways and roadways, especially in remote areas. Tourist attractions often provide free promotional brochures and flyers in information centres, fast food restaurants, hotel and motel rooms or lobbies, and rest areas.

While some tourist attractions provide visitors a memorable experience for a reasonable admission charge or even for free, others can have a tendency to be of low quality and to overprice their goods and services (such as admission, food, and souvenirs) in order to profit from tourists excessively. Such places are commonly known as tourist traps. A 'tourist destination' means a permanently established attraction or facility which:

(a) attracts or is used by visitors to an area;

(b) is open to the public without prior booking during its normal opening hours; and

(c) is recognised by the Wales Tourist Board.

It is this definition which is adopted in this policy as the definition of a tourist attraction or facility for direction signing purposes.

General Criteria for All Tourist Destinations

In order to be considered eligible for the provision of tourist signs a tourist destination must satisfy the following general criteria:-

(i) be a tourist destination as defined at 2.1 above.

(ii) be accredited or recognised by an appropriate national quality assurance scheme.

(iii) have produced and distributed to appropriate outlets a promotional leaflet which shall indicate opening times and a preferred route to the destination.

(iv) provide adequate on-site parking facilities or have in place alternative off-site parking arrangements within a reasonable walking distance of the destination.

In addition to the above there is specific guidance issued by the Welsh Assembly Government (TD 52/04 of the Design Manual for Roads and Bridges) regarding the provision of tourist direction signing on the all-purpose and motorway trunk road network which in Denbighshire comprises the A55, A494 and A5. The main points contained in this guidance are summarised briefly in Appendix A.

Specific Criteria for Particular Types of Tourist Destinations

Traditional Tourist Attractions e.g. Visitor Centres, Theme Parks, Museums, Historic Buildings, Parks and Gardens, Natural Attractions (i.e. nature reserves, beaches etc.) Where appropriate these should be accredited by the 'Visitor Attraction Quality Assurance Scheme' VAQAS or a recognised national or regional scheme of this sort.

Tourist Routes e.g. Leisure Drives, Country Tours, Cycleways In order to be considered for signing these shall be subject to a formal Road Safety Audit carried out by an appropriately qualified person approved by the Traffic Authority. The route should as far as possible avoid main traffic routes and unsuitable minor roads. The route must be supported by a readily available promotional leaflet which shall describe or preferably map the route and the points of interest located along it. Adequate facilities such as toilets, picnic areas and refreshments should be available at regular intervals along the route.

Leisure/Entertainment Facilities e.g. Sports Centres, Golf Courses, Concert Venues, Theatres, Cinemas Such facilities would normally be signed with standard directional signing however the provision of tourist signs would be considered providing this policy and the appropriate criteria can be satisfied.

Tourist Facilities e.g. Hotels, Public Houses, Guesthouses, B & B's, Restaurants, Holiday Parks, Picnic Sites, Tourist Information Centres These should be recognised by the National Quality Assurance Scheme and in the case of Holiday Parks accredited by the British Graded Holiday Parks Scheme.

There will be a presumption against signing Hotels, Public Houses, Guesthouses, B & B's and Restaurants in urban areas where tourists would expect to find such facilities and where to do so could quickly result in a proliferation of signs. The only exception to this would be where the Traffic Authority is satisfied that exceptional traffic management and/or road safety reasons exist to justify signing.

Touring Caravan and Camping Sites

These Must be licensed under the Caravan Sites and Control of Development Act 1960 and/or the Public Health Act 1936, have a minimum of 20 pitches for casual overnight use and should be accredited by an appropriate quality assurance scheme e.g. The Caravan Club or The Camping and Caravanning Club.

Retail Establishments: e.g. Retail Parks, Shopping Centres, Individual Retail Outlets and Shops, Garden Centres Retail establishments will not be eligible for signing with tourist signs. If in the opinion of the Traffic Authority there are good traffic management and/or road safety reasons to justify signing then the option of standard directional signing may be considered.

Craft Centres/Workshops: To be eligible for signing such destinations will need to be able to demonstrate to the Traffic Authority that their function is not primarily retail.

Cultural Tourism

'Cultural tourism' (or culture tourism) is the subset of tourism concerned with a country or region's culture, specifically the lifestyle of the people in those geographical areas, the history of those peoples, their art, architecture, religion(s), and other elements that helped shape their way of life. Cultural tourism includes tourism in urban areas, particularly historic or large cities and their cultural facilities such as museums and theatres. It can also include tourism in rural areas showcasing the traditions of indigenous cultural communities (i.e.

festivals, rituals), and their values and lifestyle. It is generally agreed that cultural tourists spend substantially more than standard tourists do. This form of tourism is also becoming generally more popular throughout the world, and a recent OECD report has highlighted the role that cultural tourism can play in regional development in different world regions. Cultural tourism has been defined as 'the movement of persons to cultural attractions away from their normal place of residence, with the intention to gather new information and experiences to satisfy their cultural needs'.

Destinations

One type of cultural tourism destination is living cultural areas. For an indigenous culture that has stayed largely separated from the surrounding majority, tourism can present both advantages and problems. On the positive side are the unique cultural practices and arts that attract the curiosity of tourists and provide opportunities for tourism and economic development. On the negative side is the issue of how to control tourism so that those same cultural amenities are not destroyed and the people do not feel violated. Other destinations include historical sites, modern urban districts, theme parks and country clubs, coastal or island ecosystems, and inland natural areas.

Key Principles

Destination Planning

As the issue of globalization takes place to this modern time, the challenge of preserving the few remaining cultural community around the world is becoming hard. In a tribal based community, reaching economic advancement with minimal negative impacts is an essential objective to any destination planner. Since they are using the culture of the region as the main attraction, sustainable destination development of the area is vital for them to prevent the negative impacts (i.e. destroying the authentic identity of the tribal community) due to tourism.

Management Issues

Certainly, the principle of "one size fits all" doesn't apply to destination planning. The needs, expectations, and anticipated benefits from tourism vary greatly from one destination to another. This is clearly exemplified as local communities living in regions with tourism potential (destinations) develop a vision for what kind of tourism they want to facilitate, depending on issues and concerns they want to be settled or satisfied.

Destination Planning Resources

Planning Guides

It is important that the destination planner takes into account the diverse definition of culture as the term is subjective. Satisfying tourists' interests such as landscapes, seascapes, art, nature, traditions, ways of life and other products associated to them-which may be categorized cultural in the broadest sense of the word, is a prime consideration as it marks the initial phase of the development of a cultural destination.

The quality of service and destination, which doesn't solely depend on the cultural heritage but more importantly to the cultural environment, can further be developed by setting controls and policies which shall govern the community and its stakeholders. It is therefore safe to say that the planner should be on the ball with the varying meaning of culture itself as this fuels the formulation of development policies that shall entail efficient planning and monitored growth.

Local Community, Tourists, the Destination and Sustainable Tourism

While satisfying tourists' interests and demands may be a top priority, it is also imperative to ruminate the subsystems of the destination's *(residents)*. Development pressures should be anticipated and set to their minimum level so as to conserve the area's resources and prevent a saturation of the destination as to not abuse the product and the residents correspondingly. The plan should incorporate the locals to its gain by training and employing them and in the process encourage them to participate to the travel business. Keep in mind that the plan should make travellers not only aware about the destination but also concern on how to help it sustain its character while broadening their travelling experience.

Planning Tools

Sources of Data: The core of a planner's job is to design an appropriate planning process and facilitate community decision. Ample information which is a crucial requirement is contributed through various technical researches and analyses. Here are some of the helpful tools commonly used by planners to aid them:

1. Key Informant Interviews.
2. Libraries, Internet, and Survey Research.
3. Census and Statistical Analysis.

4. Spatial Analysis with Geographical Information System (GIS) and Global Positioning System (GPS) technologies.

Key Institutions

Participating structures are primarily led by the government's local authorities and the official tourism board or council, with the involvement of various NGOs, community and indigenous representatives, development organizations, and the academe.

Case Studies: Mountainous Regions of Central Asia and in the Himalayas

Tourism is coming to the previously isolated but spectacular mountainous regions of Central Asia, the Hindu Kush and the Himalayas. Closed for so many years to visitors from abroad, it now attracts a growing number of foreign tourists by its unique culture and splendid natural beauty. However, while this influx of tourists is bringing economic opportunities and employment to local populations, helping to promote these little-known regions of the world, it has also brought challenges along with it: to ensure that it is well-managed and that its benefits are shared by all.

As a response to this concern, the Norwegian Government, as well as the UNESCO, organized an interdisciplinary project called the Development of Cultural and Ecotourism in the Mountainous Regions of Central Asia and the Himalayas project. It aims to establish links and promote cooperation between local communities, national and international NGOs, and tour agencies in order to heighten the role of the local community and involve them fully in the employment opportunities and income-generating activities that tourism can bring. Project activities include training local tour guides, producing high-quality craft items and promoting home-stays and bed-and-breakfast type accommodation.

Religious Tourism

Religious tourism, also commonly referred to as faith tourism, is a form of tourism, whereby people of faith travel individually or in groups for pilgrimage, missionary, or leisure (fellowship) purposes. North American religious tourists comprise an estimated $10 billion of this industry. Religious tourism comprises many facets of the travel industry including.

Pilgrimages-In religion and spirituality, a pilgrimage is a long journey or search of great moral significance. Sometimes, it is a journey to a shrine of importance to a person's beliefs and faith. Members of many major religions participate in pilgrimages. A person who makes such a journey is called a pilgrim. Buddhism offers four sites of pilgrimage. The Buddha's birthplace at Lumbini, the site where he attained Enlightenment at Bodh Gaya, where he first preached at Sarnath, and where he achieved Parinirvana at Kusinagara.

The Holy Land acts as a focal point for the pilgrimages of the Abrahamic religions such as Judaism, Christianity, Islam and the Bahai Faith.

In the kingdoms of Israel and Judah, the visitation of certain ancient cult-centres was repressed in the 7th century BCE, when worship was restricted to YHWH at the temple in Jerusalem. In Syria, the shrine of Astarte at the headwater spring of the river Adonis survived until it was destroyed by order of Emperor Constantine in the 4th century.

In mainland Greece, a stream of individuals made their way to Delphi or the oracle of Zeus at Dodona, and once every four years, at the period of the Olympic games, the temple of Zeus at Olympia formed the goal of swarms of pilgrims from every part of the Hellenic world.

When Alexander the Great reached Egypt, he put his whole vast enterprise on hold, while he made his way with a small band deep into the Libyan desert, to consult the oracle of Ammun. During the imperium of his Ptolemaic heirs, the shrine of Isis at Philae received many votive inscriptions from Greeks on behalf of their kindred far away at home.

Although a pilgrimage is normally viewed in the context of religion, the personality cults cultivated by communist leaders ironically gave birth to pilgrimages of their own. Prior to the demise of the USSR in 1991, a visit to Lenin's Mausoleum in Red Square, Moscow can be said to have had all the characteristics exhibiting a pilgrimage—for Communists. This type of pilgrimage to a personality cult is still evident today on people who pay visits of homage to Mao Zedong, Kim Il Sung, and Ho Chi Minh.

Pilgrimage Centres in Various Times and Cultures

Antiquity

Many ancient religions had holy sites, temples and groves, where pilgrimages were made.

- Karnak, Egypt.

- Thebes, Egypt.
- Kurukshetra, India
- Delphi, Greece. Oracle.
- Dodona, Epirus, Greece. Oracle.
- Ephesus Temple of Diana, Turkey.
- Baalbek Lebanon.
- Jerusalem, Israel.

Bahá'í Faith

Baha'u'llah, the founder of the Baha'í Faith, decreed pilgrimage to two places in his book of laws, the Kitab-i-Aqdas: the House of Baha'u'llah in Baghdad, Iraq, and the House of the Bab in Shiraz, Iran. He, later, prescribed specific rites for each of these pilgrimages in two other religious texts. Later, 'Abdu'l-Baha designated the Shrine of Baha'u'llah at Bahji, Israel as a site of pilgrimage, for which there are no rites. Since Baha'ís do not have access to the original two places designated as sites for pilgrimage, Baha'i pilgrimage currently consists of visiting the holy places in Haifa, Acre, and Bahji at the Baha'í World Centre in Northwest Israel. Baha'is can apply to join an organized nine-day pilgrimage where they are taken to visit the various holy sites, or attend a shorter three-day pilgrimage.

Buddhism

Tibetans on a pilgrimage to Lhasa; they are kowtowing every few steps of the way.

Gautama Buddha spoke of the four sites most worthy of pilgrimage for his followers to visit:

- Lumbini: birth place (in Nepal),
- Bodh Gaya: place of Enlightenment,
- Sarnath: (formally Isipathana) where he delivered his first teaching,
- Kusinara: (now Kusinagar, India) where he attained mahaparinirvana (died).

Other pilgrimage places in India and Nepal connected to the life of Gautama Buddha are: Savatthi, Pataliputta, Nalanda, Gaya, Vesali, Sankasia, Kapilavastu, Kosambi, Rajagaha, Varanasi.

Other famous places for Buddhist pilgrimage in various countries include:

- India: Sanchi, Ellora, Ajanta.
- Thailand: Sukhothai, Ayutthaya, Wat Phra Kaew, Wat Doi Suthep.
- Tibet: Lhasa (traditional home of the Dalai Lama), Mount Kailash, Lake Nam-tso.
- Cambodia: Angkor Wat, Silver Pagoda.
- Sri Lanka: Polonnaruwa, Temple of the Tooth (Kandy), Anuradhapura.
- Laos: Luang Prabang.
- Myanmar: Bagan, Sagaing Hill.
- Nepal: Bodhnath, Swayambhunath.
- Indonesia: Borobudur.
- China: Yung-kang, Lung-men caves. The Four Sacred Mountains
- Japan: Kansai Kannon Pilgrimage, Chugoku 33 Kannon Pilgrimage, Shikoku Pilgrimage, Mount Koya.

Christianity

Christian pilgrimage was first made to sites connected with the birth, life, crucifixion and resurrection of Jesus. Surviving descriptions of Christian pilgrimages to the Holy Land date from the 4th century, when pilgrimage was encouraged by church fathers like Saint Jerome. Pilgrimages also began to be made to Rome and other sites associated with the Apostles, Saints and Christian martyrs, as well as to places where there have been apparitions of the Virgin Mary.

Missionary Travel

A missionary is a member of a religious group who works to convert those who do not share the missionary's faith; someone who proselytizes. The word "mission" is derived from the Latin *missioninimus* (nom. *missio*), meaning "act of sending" or *mitto, mittere*, literally meaning "to send" or "to dispatch",. It functions as the equivalent of the Greek-derived word "apostle" from *apostolos*, meaning "a delegate, specially, an ambassador of the Gospel; officially a commissioner of Christ ["apostle"] KJV-apostle, messenger, one that is sent. "Strong's Exhaustive Concordance of the Bible"

In Christian cultures the term is most commonly used for Christian missions, but it applies equally to any proselytizing creed or ideology. Buddhism launched 'the first large-scale missionary effort in the history of the world's religions' in the 3rd c. BC Christian missions

Since the Lausanne Congress of 1974, a widely accepted definition of a Christian mission has been "to form a viable indigenous church-planting movement." Recognizing justice as being at the heart of the Gospels, many modern missionaries now promote the development of western government, education and economic structure in the place of pre-existing local systems and tradition. Missionaries can be found in many countries around the world.

Biblical Mandate

Jesus instructed the apostles to make disciples: This reference is understood by Christian missionaries as the Great Commission to engage in missionary work.

Catholic Missions

The New Testament missionary outreach of the Christian church from the time of St. Paul was extensive throughout the Roman Empire. During the Middle Ages the Christian monasteries and missionaries such as Saint Patrick, and Adalbert of Prague propagated learning and religion beyond the boundaries of the old Roman Empire. In the 7th century Gregory the Great sent missionaries including Augustine of Canterbury into England. During the Age of Discovery, the Roman Catholic Church established a number of Missions in the Americas and other colonies through the Augustinians, Franciscans and Dominicans in order to spread Christianity in the New World and to convert the Native Americans and other indigenous people. At the same time, missionaries such as Francis Xavier as well as other Jesuits, Augustinians, Franciscans and Dominicans were moving into Asia and the far East. The Portuguese sent missions into Africa. These are some of the most well-known missions in history. While some of these missions were associated with imperialism and oppression, others (notably Matteo Ricci's Jesuit mission to China) were relatively peaceful and focused on integration rather than cultural imperialism.

Much contemporary Catholic missionary work has undergone profound change since the Second Vatican Council, and has become explicitly conscious of Social Justice issues and the dangers of cultural imperialism or economic exploitation disguised as religious conversion. Contemporary Christian missionaries argue that working for justice is a constitutive part of preaching the Gospel, and observe the principles of inculturation in their missionary work.

As the church normally organizes itself along territorial lines, and because they had the human and material resources, religious orders—some even specializing in it—undertook most missionary work, especially in the early phases. Over time a normalised church structure was gradually established in the mission area, often starting with special jurisdictions known as apostolic prefectures and apostolic vicariates. These developing churches eventually intended 'graduating' to regular diocesan status with a local episcopacy appointed, especially after decolonization, as the church structures often reflect the political-administrative reality.

Orthodox Missions

The Eastern Orthodox Church, under the Orthodox Church of Constantinople was vigorous in its missionary outreach under the Roman Empire and continuing Byzantine Empire, and its missionary outreach had lasting effect, either founding, influencing or establishing formal relations with some 16 Orthodox national churches including the Romanian Orthodox Church, the Georgian Orthodox and Apostolic Church and the Ukrainian Orthodox Church (both said to have been founded by the missionary Apostle Andrew), the Bulgarian Orthodox Church (said to have been founded by the missionary Apostle Paul). The two ninth century saints Cyril and Methodius had extensive missionary success in Eastern Europe. The Byzantines expanded their missionary work in Ukraine after a mass baptism in Kiev in 988. The Serbian Orthodox Church had its origins in the conversion by Byzantine missionaries of the Serb tribes when they arrived in the Balkans in the 7th century. Orthodox missionaries also worked successfully among the Estonians from the 10th to the 12th centuries founding the Estonian Orthodox Church.

Under the Russian Empire of the 19th century, missionaries such as Nicholas Ilminsky moved into the subject lands and propagated Orthodoxy, including through Belarus, Latvia, Moldova, Finland, Estonia, Ukraine, and China. The Russian St. Nicholas of Japan took Eastern Orthodoxy to Japan in the 19th century. The Russian Orthodox Church also sent missionaries to Alaska beginning in the 18th century, including Saint Herman of Alaska, to minister to the Native Americans. The Russian Orthodox Church Outside Russia continued missionary work outside Russia after the 1917 Russian Revolution, resulting in the establishment of many new dioceses in the diaspora, from which numerous converts have been made in Eastern Europe, North America and Oceania.

First Protestant Missions

Among the first Protestant missionaries were John Eliot (missionary) and contemporary ministers including John Cotton and Richard Bourne, who ministered to the Algonquin natives that were co-located with the Massachusetts Bay Colony in the middle 17th century. Quaker missions were established soon after this in several late 17th century colonies.

The Danish government included Lutheran missionaries among the colonists in many of its colonies, Bartholomaeus Ziegenbalg in Tranquebar India in the late 17th century. But the first organized Protestant mission work was carried out beginning in 1732 by the Moravian Brethren of Herrnhut in Saxony Germany (*die evangelische Brüdergemeine*). While on a visit in 1732 to Copenhagen for the coronation of his cousin King Christian VI the Moravian Church's patron, Nicolas Ludwig, Count von Zinzendorf got to know a slave from the Danish colony in the West Indies. When he returned to Herrnhut with the slave, he inspired the inhabitants of the village—it was fewer than 30 houses then—to send out "messengers" to the slaves in the West Indies. The first missionaries landed in St. Thomas in December, 1732. Work soon was started in another Danish colony, Greenland. Within 30 years there were Moravian missionaries active on every continent, and this at a time when there were fewer than 300 people in Herrnhut. They are famous for their selfless work, living as slaves among the slaves and together with the native Americans, the Delaware and Cherokee Indian tribes. Today the work in the former mission provinces of the worldwide Moravian Church is carried on by native workers. The fastest growing area of the work in Tanzania in Eastern Africa. The Moravian work in South Africa inspired William Carey and the founders of the British Baptist missions. Today 7 of every 10 Moravians are in a former mission field and belong to a race other than Caucasian. Like other missionary denominations, Protestant missionaries have been accused of cultural imperialism and have often been associated with a colonial power.

Evangelical Church Missions

With a dramatic increase in efforts since the 1900s, and a strong push since the *Lausanne I: The International Congress on World Evangelization* in Switzerland in 1974, evangelical groups have focused efforts on sending missionaries to every ethnic group in the world. While this effort has not been completed, increased attention has brought larger numbers of people distributing Bibles, Jesus videos, and establishing evangelical churches in more remote, less Christianized areas.

Internationally, the focus for many years in the later 20th century was on reaching every "people group" with Christianity by the year 2000. Bill Bright's leadership with Campus Crusade, the Southern Baptist International Mission Board, The Joshua Project, and others brought about the need to know who these "unreached people groups" are and how those wanting to tell about a Christian God and share a Christian Bible could reach them. The focus for these organizations transitioned from a "country focus" to a "people group focus." (From "What is a People Group?" by Dr. Orville Boyd Jenkins: A "people group" is an ethnolinguistic group with a common self-identity that is shared by the various members. There are two parts to that word: ethno and linguistic. Language is a primary and dominant identifying factor of a people group. But there are other factors that determine or are associated with ethnicity.). What can be viewed as a success by those inside and outside the church from this focus is a higher level of cooperation and friendliness among churches and denominations. It is very common for those working on international fields to not only cooperate in efforts to share their gospel message but view the work of their groups in a similar light. Also, with the increased study and awareness of different people groups, western mission efforts have become far more sensitive to the cultural nuances of those they are going to and those they are working with in the effort.

Over the years, as indigenous churches have matured, the church of the "Global South" (Africa, Asia and Latin America) has become the driving force in missions. Korean and African missionaries can now be found all over the world. These missionaries represent a major shift in Church history. Brazil, Nigeria, and other countries have had large numbers of their Christian adherents go to other countries and start churches. These non-western missionaries often have unparalleled success because they need few western resources and comforts to sustain their livelihood while doing the work they have chosen among a new culture and people.

The British Missionary Societies

The London Missionary Society was an extensive Anglican and Nonconformist missionary society formed in England in 1795 with missions in the islands of the South Pacific and Africa. It now forms part of the Council for World Mission. The Anglican Church Missionary Society was also founded in England in 1799, and continues its work today. In 1809 the *London Society for Promoting Christianity Amongst the Jews* was founded, which pioneered mission amongst the Jewish people. It continues today as the Church's Ministry Among Jewish People. All these organisations spread through the extensive 18th and 19th century colonial British Empire, establishing the network of churches that largely became the modern Anglican Communion.

Jehovah's Witnesses Missionaries

Jehovah's Witnesses are known for their missionary activities. Typically, all adult Witnesses are expected to spend time every week "witnessing" in their area. Depending on the civil law in the respective country, this may take the form of proselytizing door to door, distribution of magazines and other literature such as *The Watchtower* and *Awake!* or responding to the questions of passersby. They also conduct home Bible studies with interested persons. While all baptized Jehovah's Witnesses engage in missionary work, the branch office of the Christian Congregation of Jehovah's Witnesses, will appoint full-time missionaries. Regular Pioneers are appointed to serve in a local congregation and spend an average of 70 hours a month preaching. Special pioneers are appointed to serve in isolated areas where preaching might be limited. Foreign missionaries are appointed to serve in another country after they have completed a 5 month course at the Watchtower Bible School of Gilead in Patterson, New York. They devote an average of 130 hours a month. They consider this activity as obedience to the teachings of Jesus Christ in.

Latter-day Saint Missionaries

The Church of Jesus Christ of Latter-day Saints is one of the most active modern practitioners of missionary work. Young men between the ages of 19 and 26 (usually beginning at the age of 19) are encouraged to prepare themselves to serve a two-year, self-funded, full-time proselytizing mission. Young women and retired couples may serve missions as well. Young women who desire to serve as missionaries serve at an older age, 21 or older, and often for only one and a half years. Missionaries typically spend one to three months in a Missionary Training Centre where they study the scriptures, learn new languages, and otherwise prepare themselves to teach the Gospel and understand the culture in which and the people among whom they will be living. The LDS Church has about 53,000 missionaries worldwide.

Islamic Missions

Dawah means to "invite" (in Arabic, literally "calling") to Islam, estimated to be the second largest religion next to Christianity. From the 7th century it spread rapidly from the Arabian Peninsula to the rest of the world through the initial Arabic conquests, and subsequently with traders and explorers after the death of the Prophet Muhammad. Initially, the spread of Islam came through the dawah efforts of Muhammad and those who followed him. After his death in 632 CE, much of the expansion of the empire came through conquest, such as that of North Africa and later Spain (Al-Andalus), and the Islamic conquest of Persia putting an end to the Sassanid Empire and spreading the reach of Islam to as far East as Khorasan, which would later become the cradle of Islamic civilization during the Islamic Golden Age and a stepping-stone towards the introduction of Islam to the Turkic tribes living in and bordering the area.

The missionary movements peaked during the Islamic Golden Age, with the expansion of foreign trade routes, primarily into the Indo-Pacific and as far South as the isle of Zanzibar and the South-Eastern shores of Africa.

With the coming about of the tradition of Sufism, Islamic missionary activities have increased considerably. The mystical nature of the tradition had an all-encompassing aspect, a property many societies in Asia could relate to. Later, with the conquest of Anatolia by the Seljuk Turks, missionaries would find easier passage to the lands then formerly belonging to the Byzantine Empire.

In the earlier stages of the Ottoman Empire, a Turkic form of Shamanism was still widely practiced in Anatolia, which soon started to give in to the mysticism offered by Sufism. The teachings of Jalal ad-Din Muhammad Rumi, who migrated from Khorasan to Anatolia, are good examples to the mystical aspect of Sufism.

During the Ottoman presence in the Balkans, missionary movements were also taken up by people from aristocratic families hailing from the region, who had been educated in Constantinople or any other major city within the Empire, in famed madrassahs and kulliyes. Most of the time, such individuals were sent back to the place of their origin, being appointed important positions in the local governing body. This approach often resulted in the building of mosques and local kulliyes for future generations to benefit from, as well as spreading the teachings of Islam.

The spread of Islam towards Central and West Africa has been prominent but slow, until the early 19th century. Previously, the only connection was through Transsaharan trade, of which the Mali Empire, consisting predominantly of African and Berber tribes, stands as a strong proof of the early Islamization of the Sub-Saharan region. The gateways prominently expanded to include the aforementioned trade routes through the Eastern shores of the African continent. With the European colonization of Africa, missionaries were almost in competition with the European Christian missionaries operating in the colonies.

The Muslim population of the US has increased greatly in the last one hundred years, with much of the growth driven by widespread conversion. Up to one-third of American Muslims are African Americans who have converted to Islam during the last seventy years. Conversion to Islam in prison, and in large urban areas has also contributed to its growth over the years.

Missionaries and Judaism

Despite some inter-Testamental Jewish missionary activity, contemporary Judaism states clearly that missionary activities are not a priority.

Most Jews share a strong distaste for all missionary activity by practitioners of all religions, a tradition which stems from years of Jewish persecution at the hands of (mostly Christian) missionaries.

Modern Jewish teachers repudiate proselytization of Gentiles in order to convert them. The reason for this is that Gentiles already have a complete relationship with God via the Noahidic covenant; there is therefore no need for them to become Jewish, which requires more work of them. In addition, Judaism espouses a concept of "quality" not "quantity". It is more important in the eyes of Jews to have converts who are completely committed to observing Jewish law, than to have converts who will violate the Abrahamic covenant into which they have been initiated.

On the other hand, most Jewish religious groups encourage "Outreach" to Jews alienated from their own heritage owing to assimilation and intermarriage. Some movements encourage Jews to become more observant of Jewish religious law (known as halakha). Those people who do become religious are known as *baalei teshuva*. The large Hasidic group known as Chabad Lubavitch has internationally promoted such "outreach." Others, such as the National Jewish Outreach Program do the same in North America. In recent times, members of the American Reform movement began a program to convert to Judaism the non-Jewish spouses of its intermarried members and non-Jews who have an interest in Judaism. Their rationale is that so many Jews were lost during the Holocaust that newcomers must be sought out and welcomed. This approach has been repudiated by Orthodox and Conservative Jews as unrealistic and posing a danger. They say that these efforts make Judaism seem an easy religion to join and observe when in reality being Jewish involves many difficulties and sacrifices.

Eastern Religions

The first missions were sent by the Indian religions, in particular Buddhism.

Buddhist Missions

Buddhist proselytism at the time of king Ashoka, according to his Edicts.The first Buddhist missionaries were called "Dharma Bhanaks". The Emperor Ashoka was a significant early Buddhist missioner. In the 3rd century BC, Dharmaraksita-among others-was sent out by emperor Ashoka to proselytize the Buddhist tradition through the Indian Maurya Empire, but also into the Mediterranean as far as Greece. Buddhism was spread among the Turkic people during the 2nd and 3rd centuries BC into modern-day Pakistan, Kashmir, Afghanistan, eastern and coastal Iran, Uzbekistan, Turkmenistan and Tajikistan. It was also taken into China brought by An Shigao in the 2nd century BC. The use of missions, formation of councils and monastic institutions influenced the emergence of Christian missions and organizations which had similar structures formed in places which were formerly Buddhist missions. During the 19th and 20th centuries, Western intellectuals such as Schopenhauer, Henry David Thoreau, Max Müller and esoteric societies such as the Theosophical Society of H.P. Blavatsky and the Buddhist Society, London spread interest in Buddhism. Writers such as Hermann Hesse and Jack Kerouac, in the West, and the hippie generation of the late 1960s and early 1970s led to a re-discovery of Buddhism. During the 20th and 21st centuries Buddhism has again been propagated by missionaries into the West such as the Dalai Lama and monks including Lama Surya Das. Tibetan Buddhism has been significantly active and successful in the West since the Chinese takeover of Tibet in 1959.

Non-religious Missionaries

The original meaning of the word "missionary" is not specifically religious, but refers instead to anyone who attempts to convert others to a particular doctrine or program.

- Leisure (fellowship) vacations.

- Faith-based cruising.
- Crusades, conventions and rallies.
- Retreats.
- Monastery visits and guest-stays.
- Faith-based camps.
- Religious tourist attractions.

Sacred travel, or metaphysical tourism, spiritualized travel, is a growing niche of the travel market. It attracts New Age believers, primarily middle-aged women, and involves tours and travel to "spiritual hotspots" on the Earth. Destinations are often ancient sites where there is a mystery concerning their origin or purpose, such as Machu Picchu in Peru, The Pyramids of Egypt, or Stonehenge in England. Some Christian sites such as the locations of the Black Madonnas and the Rosslyn Chapel in Scotland are also popular. These travellers see the journey as more than just tourism and take the trips in order to heal themselves and the world. Part of this may involve rituals involving, (supposedly), leaving their bodies, possession by spirits (channelling), and recovery of past life memories. The travel is considered by many scholars as transcendental, a life learning process or even a self-realization metaphor.

Retail Shopping

Shopping is the examining of goods or services from retailers with the intent to purchase at that time. Shopping is an activity of selection and/or purchase. In some contexts it is considered a leisure activity as well as an economic one.

Shopping in Ancient Societies

Shopping can be traced back to many civilisations in history. In ancient Rome, there was Trajan's Market with tabernas that served as retailing units. Shopping lists are known to be used by Romans as one was discovered by Hadrian's wall dated back to 75-125 AD and written for a soldier.

The Shopper

Florida woman shopping at a Mall, as a member of a "shoptilyoudrop" club To many, shopping is considered a recreational and diversional activity in which one visits a variety of stores with a premeditated intent to purchase a product. "Window shopping" is an activity that shoppers engage in by browsing shops with no intent to purchase, possibly just to pass the time between other activities, or to plan a later purchase. To some, shopping is a task of inconvenience and vexation. Shoppers sometimes go though great lengths to wait in long lines to buy popular products as typically observed with early adopter shoppers and holiday shoppers. More recently compulsive shopping is recognised as an addiction. Also referred as shopping addiction, "shopaholism" or formally oniomania, these shoppers have an impulsive uncontrollable urge to shop. The term "retail therapy" is used in a less serious context. In the last years in the United States there are private clubs that promote the so called "Shoptilyoudrop" fever during holiday seasons (like Christmas), even with competences between members. These clubs argue that the competences are good for relaxation from work stress. Indeed, the American TV promoted a Shop till You Drop series in the 1990s.

Shopping Venues

Shopping Hubs

A larger commercial zone can be found in many cities, downtowns or Arab city souks. Shopping hubs, or shopping centres, are collection of stores; that is a grouping of several businesses. Typical examples include shopping malls, town squares, flea markets and bazaars.

Stores

Stores are divided into multiple categories of stores which sell a selected set of goods or services. Usually they are tiered by target demographics based on the disposable income of the shopper. They can be tiered from cheap to pricey.

Some shops sell second-hand goods. Often the public can also sell goods to such shops. In other cases, especially in the case of a non-profit shops, the public donates goods to these shops, commonly known as thrift stores in the USA or charity shops in the UK. In giveaway shopes goods can be taken for free. In antique shops, the public can find goods that are older and harder to find. Sometimes people are broke and borrow money from a pawn shop using an item of value as collateral. College students are known to resell books back though college textbook bookstores. Old used items are often distributed though surplus stores.

Many shops are part of a *shopping centre* that carry the same trademark (company name) and logo using the same branding, same presentation, and sell the same products but in different locations. The shops may be owned by one company, or there may be a franchising company that has franchising agreements with the shop owners often found in relation to restaurant chains. Various types of retail stores that specialise in the selling of goods related to a theme include bookstores, boutiques, candy shops, liquor stores, gift shops, hardware stores, hobby stores, pet stores, pharmacys, sex shops and supermarkets. Other stores' such as big-box stores, hypermarkets, convenience stores, department stores, general stores, dollar stores sell a wider variety of products not horizontally related to each other.

History of Modern Shopping

Fairs and markets have a long and history that started when man felt the need to exchange goods. People would shop for goods at a weekly market in nearby towns. Then shops began to be permanently established. Shops were specialized, e.g. a bakery, a butchery, a grocer. Then supermarkets appeared. There have been three major phases in the shopping/trading world in the last 100 years. In a way, these link up into a full circle.

1. Customers would be served by the shopkeeper, who would retrieve all the good on their shopping list. Shops would often deliver the goods to the customers' homes.
2. Customers have to select goods, retrieve them off the shelves using self service, and even pack their own goods. Customers deliver their own goods.
3. Customers select goods via the internet. The goods are delivered to their homes as in phase one.

It was 1878 in Dayton, Ohio saloon owner James Ritty was not a happy man. He suspected that members of his staff were stealing from his business by taking customer cash and pocketing it. Unfortunately, Ritty had no way of proving that pilfering was the problem. The next year he did. With the help of his brother, Ritty invented and patented the first mechanical cash register, named " Ritty's Incorruptible Cashier. The last ten years have been a wild time on the Internet, especially when it comes to online shopping. The e-commerce industry has seen rapid growth, a shake out of the market due to security concerns, and finally, a rebirth thanks to new technologies and innovative ways to shop.

Home Shopping

With modern technology such as television and telephone and the Internet, users could be described as *home shopping* through online retail stores. Electronic commerce and business-to-consumer electronic commerce systems in combination of home mail delivery systems make this possible. Typically a consumer could make purchases through online shopping, channels, mail order, etc. Sometimes peddlers and ice cream trucks pass through the neighbourhood offering services and goods. Also, neighbourhood shopping takes place through various garage sales found in United States. Online shopping has completely redefined the way people make their buying decisions; they have access to a lot of information about a particular product which can be looked at and evaluated, at any given time. Online shopping allows the buyer to save the time which would have been spent travelling to the store or mall.

Shopping Time

Some business have shopping hours but some are open round-the-clock. Some nations regulate the operation of businesses for religious reasons and do not allow shopping on particular days or dates.

Shopping Seasons

Shopping seasons are periods where a burst of spending occurs-typically near holidays in the United States, where Christmas shopping is the biggest shopping spending season. Some famous target dates are Black Friday and Cyber Monday. Some religions regard such spending seasons against their religion and dismiss the practice. Many question the over-commercialization and the response by stores who downplay the shopping season often cited in the Christmas controversy or War on Christmas. The National Retail Federation (NRF) also highlights the importance of back-to-school shopping for retailers which comes second behind holiday shopping, when buyers often buy clothing and school supplies for their children. In 2006, Americans spend over $17 billion on their children, according to a NRF survey.

Pricing and Negotiation

The pricing technique used by most retailers is cost-plus pricing. This involves adding a markup amount (or percentage) to the retailers cost. Another common technique is *manufacturers suggested list* pricing. This simply involves charging the amount suggested by the manufacturer and usually printed on the product by the manufacturer. In Western countries, retail prices are often so-called *psychological prices* or *odd prices*: a little less than a round number, e.g. $ 6.95. In Chinese societies, prices are generally either a round number or sometimes some lucky number.

This creates price points. Often prices are fixed and displayed on signs or labels. Alternatively, there can be price discrimination for a variety of reasons. The retailer charges higher prices to some customers and lower prices to others. For example, a customer may have to pay more if the seller determines that he or she is willing to. The retailer may conclude this due to the customer's wealth, carelessness, lack of knowledge, or eagerness to buy. Price discrimination can lead to a bargaining situation often called *haggling*, a negotiation about the price. Economists see this as determining how the transaction's total surplus will be divided into consumer and producer surplus. Neither party has a clear advantage, because the threat of no sale exists, whence the surplus vanishes for both.

Gastronomic Tourism

Since the 1960s, interest in wine and food – as illustrated through cooking programmes on television and radio and sales of cookbooks – has become a significant component of popular culture in the developed world. Indeed, the consumption of wine and food is an important part of contemporary lifestyles, often indicating social status and the extent of cultural capital. The changed consumption of wine and food in western society is also marked by an increase in eating out or purchasing takeaways, this occurring at a time when not only are there more cookbooks and cooking shows on television than ever before, but also fewer and fewer people actually know how to cook. As a significant component of contemporary lifestyles it should therefore be of little surprise that specific forms of wine and food consumption have also become an important part of tourism. This chapter will use a case study from New Zealand to highlight key characteristics of the gastronomic tourism niche.

Defining the niche Clearly we all have to eat, whether at home or at holiday. However, food and wine has historically tended to be in the background of the tourist experience as part of the overall hospitality service that is provided for travellers. Yet, increasingly, wine and food has become a focal point for travel decisionmaking and the hallmark attraction of a number of destinations around the world.

Food tourism is defined by Hall and Mitchell (2001: 308) as 'visitation to primary and secondary food producers, food festivals, restaurants and specific locations for which food tasting and/or experiencing the attributes of specialist food production region are the primary motivating factor for travel'. Wine tourism is a subset of food tourism, being defined as visitation to vineyards, wineries, wine festivals and wine shows, for which grape wine tasting and/or experiencing the attributes of a grape wine region are the prime motivating factors for visitors. Such definitions do not mean that any trip to a restaurant is food tourism; rather the desire to experience a particular type of food or the produce of a specific region or even to taste the dishes of a particular chef must be the major motivation for such travel. Indeed, such is the need for food to be a primary factor in influencing travel behaviour and decision-making that as a form of special interest travel, food tourism may possibly be regarded as an examples of culinary, gastronomic, gourmet or cuisine tourism that reflects consumers for whom interest in food and wine is a form of 'serious leisure'

Although there is substantial overlap between these concepts, subtle differences in interpretation do exist. Gourmet tourism usually occurs in terms of visits to expensive and/or highly rated restaurants, wineries and festivals. There is a tendency for such products to be expensive and exclusive. Gastronomic or culinary tourism suggests a wider interest in food and wine, that may include expensive products, but which is also typically related to interest in the broader dimensions of wine and food and the cultures and landscapes that produce them. Cuisine tourism is similar in scope but instead reflects special interests in specific types of cuisine, whether national or regional. In all three categories, visits to adjunct products such as cooking schools or specialist tours (whether accompanied or self-guided) is important. Such definitional distinctions are also significant because they also alert the reader to the potential dimensions of the food and wine tourism market. However, for all these categories described so far as part of food tourism, food and wine will rank as the main or a major travel motivator. Although food and wine are also significant elements of what is usually described as rural or urban tourism, they are not major motivations for travel; instead food and wine (or beer or whisky) become a part of the overall attractiveness of a particular location and the rural or urban tourism experience. Nevertheless, the sales of food to such tourists may also be significant from the perspective of individual firms and regions as whole.

The emergence of food and wine tourism A lay perspective on food and wine tourism might suggest that food and drinks have always been a part of the tourism experience. Indeed, that is true, but accounts suggest that it was not until the early to mid-nineteenth century, with the invention of the restaurant and the commodification of cuisines into regional and national categories and as a result of the medium of cookbooks and codification of cooking styles, that food and wine became a travel product in its own right.

However, the number of travellers who were food and wine tourists at this time was extremely small, not only because of lifestyle interest but also because of the time and monetary costs of mobility. However, improvements in technology allowed not only people to travel further in a shorter period of time but also allowed foodstuffs to do the same. It is therefore perhaps of no great surprise that the designation of the first wine trails and roads in Germany in the late 1920s coincided with the growth of automobile ownership and the development of autobahn out from the larger cities. Reflexive interest in food also began to grow in the immediate post-Second World War period as not only did the range of foodstuffs available to households in western countries also grow rapidly because of the end of rationing and further improvements in transport technology but, so of course did the movement of people.

One of the key understandings of the tourism-food and tourism-wine relationships is that when people travel they take their 'tastebuds and stomachs' with them and, when they return home, some of the new acquired tastes may then influence their food consumption in terms of choice of restaurant and selection of what is purchased to eat at home. Arguably, demand for the wide range of cuisines to be found in restaurants in the developed world is as much a function of travel and interest in 'the other' as it is the mobility of migrant or ethnic populations.

The rise of celebrity chefs and celebrity restaurants that has occurred since the late 1970s has served to reinforce not only the potential attraction of such restaurants, but also the role of the media with respect to food and drinks in making cuisine a major element of contemporary western lifestyle. Nowadays, the 'kind' of food and wine.

Gastronomic Tourism' Catching up Globally

A comparatively new kind of tourism, what may be called gastronomic tourism, is gaining popularity across the world. In gastronomic tourism, food and beverages are the main factors that motivate a person to travel to a particular destination.

Studies conducted into the new phenomenon have shown that food plays, consciously or unconsciously, an important part in the holiday experience of a good number of travellers.

Tourism authorities around the world are now recognizing the potential of gastronomic tourism as a powerful instrument to identify and promote places, regions or even entire countries. Global trends have identified that the so-called gastronomic tourists are looking for a more participatory style of holiday experience, which satisfies their interest in food and beverages and contributes to their personal development and social status. Analysts have noticed a shift from 'passive observation' to 'interaction and involvement' in tourists, whereby the visitor comes into close contact with locals and their way of life rather than be a mere spectator. As food and beverages are increasingly becoming one of the main reasons for travel, several countries are attempting in a big way to combine food, beverage and culture into a total tourism experience – which should be authentic and reflecting the local and unique flavours of a particular country.

A good case in point is the World Cuisines Show 2008 (WCS '08), to be held in Singapore, on July 25-27, 2008. The World Cuisines Show 2008 is intended to be a global marketplace where countries around the world gather under one roof to showcase their national cuisines and cultural activities. Tourism authorities from over 130 countries have been invited to participate in this inaugural international event.

Other Site Attractions

A tourist attraction is a place of interest where tourists visit, typically for its inherent or exhibited cultural value, historical significance, natural or built beauty, or amusement opportunities.

Some examples include historical places, monuments, zoos, aquaria, museums and art galleries, botanical gardens, buildings and structures (e.g., castles, libraries, former prisons, skyscrapers, bridges), national parks and forests, theme parks and carnivals, living history museums, ethnic enclave communities, historic trains and cultural events. Many tourist attractions are also landmarks.

Tourist attractions are also created to capitalise on unexplained phenomena such as a supposed UFO crash site near Roswell, New Mexico and the alleged Loch Ness monster sightings in Scotland. Ghost sightings also make tourist attractions. Ethnic communities may become tourist attractions, such as Chinatowns in the United States and the black British neighbourhood of Brixton in London, England.

In the US, owners and marketers of attractions advertise tourist attractions on billboards along the side of highways and roadways, especially in remote areas. Tourist attractions often provide free promotional brochures and flyers in information centres, fast food restaurants, hotel and motel rooms or lobbies, and rest areas.

While some tourist attractions provide visitors a memorable experience for a reasonable admission charge or even for free, others can have a tendency to be of low quality and to overprice their goods and services (such as admission, food, and souvenirs) in order to profit from tourists excessively. Such places are commonly known as tourist traps. World Heritage Sites are the planet's outstanding attractions, the greatest monuments from the past. They are contemporary tourism magnets and national icons that continue to influence present values. They are treasures in the: fullest and deepest sense. They must be managed in such a way that they are preserved for future generations and at the same time presently made accessible to the public for its education and enjoyment. Finding the proper balance between the two demands is the difficult and important task of World Heritage Site managers.

They include archaeological sites, ruins, or intact structures still in use day or adapted for a new use. In contrast to natural heritage sites which were formed by natural forces, cultural heritage sites contain the physical evidence of outstanding examples of human creativity or of important historic events. They proved a unique record of momentous achievements that puts the witness in direct c tact with an otherwise invisible time. Only in a few cases around the world is there sufficient national allocated for educating and hiring staff for the professional care, maintenance and presentation of these great places. Yet glamorous pictures of World Heritage Sites are used in national tourism marketing efforts, and visitors flock to them. To ism earns hard currency and is the darling of national finance ministers. Conservation, however, is usually the last line-item to be included in national budgets and the first line-item to be cut.

In the context of modern developments in world tourism, this imbalance of concerns requires immediate redress. In the year 1991, there were 450 mi lion international tourist arrivals worldwide. In the year 2000, the figure is expect d to rise to 650 million. The pressure on World Heritage Sites can only be expect d to increase. When they were built, most of these sites were not meant for numbers of people, and certainly they were not meant to accommodate large numbers of tourists.

The management of World Heritage Sites is a crucial issue. This be is devoted to helping the managers of World Heritage Sites accomplish annual purpose: to conserve the site given to their care, and to provide meaningful and considerate access to as many visitors as the site can allow. In order to do this site managers must work in partnership with professionals in the fields of planing, community development and tourism.

Events

Definition

An events tourism visitor is defined as a domestic overnight traveller aged 15 years or above who participates in the following activities in the ACT;

- Attends festivals/fairs or cultural event, or
- Attends an organized sporting event.

Introduction: Events are an important motivator of tourism, and figure prominently in the development and marketing plans of most destinations. The roles and impacts of planned events within tourism have been well documented, and are of increasing importance for destination competitiveness. Yet it was only a few decades ago that 'event tourism' became established in both the tourism industry and in the research community, so that subsequent growth of this sector can only be described as spectacular.

Equally, 'event management' is a fast growing professional field in which tourists constitute a potential market for planned events and the tourism industry has become a vital stakeholder in their success and attractiveness. But not all events need to be tourism oriented, and some fear the potential negative impacts associated with adopting marketing orientation. As well, events have other important roles to play, from community-building to urban renewal, cultural development to fostering national identities— tourism is not the only partner or proponent. In this paper the nature, evolution and future development of 'event tourism' are discussed, pertaining to both theory and professional practice. Emphasis is placed on

The Event Perspective

Planned events are spatial–temporal phenomenon, and each is unique because of interactions among the setting, people, and management systems—including design elements and the program.

Much of the appeal of events is that they are never the same, and you have to 'be there' to enjoy the unique experience fully; if you miss it, it's a lost opportunity. In addition, 'virtual events', communicated through various media, also offer something of interest and value to consumers and the tourism industry; they are different kinds of event experiences. Planned events are all created for a purpose, and what was once the realm of individual and community initiatives has largely become the realm of professionals and entrepreneurs.

Despite the fact that special events have become key components of the tourism development strategy for many regions, the amount of research that has been conducted within the field of special events does not reflect its importance. It is unlikely that the substantial growth rate that the field of special events has experienced in recent years is sustainable and an understanding of consumer patronage in relation to special events will be crucial for the development and promotion of events in the future. This study seeks to help address these shortcomings.

In seeking to understand the field of special events, a model that involved the perspectives of six major parties was proposed. The fundamental aim of this study was to explore one of these perspectives, namely, that of consumers. This perspective was then used as the basis for a proposed consumer decision making model in relation to visitor attractions, including special events, that underpinned the second part of the thesis. The first part of this study sought to conceptualise systematically, special events from a consumer perspective and to conduct a comparative methodological assessment of three approaches to market segmentation in terms of their ability to explain consumer behaviour in relation to special events. The three approaches used were personal values, psychographics and demographics.

A comprehensive and systematic literature review was conducted to identify the attributes that could be used to categorise an event as 'special'. Based upon this review, a schema of event categories was proposed as well as a listing of the core and qualifying attributes that could be used to describe each of the special event categories. A set of definitions for each of the main special event categories was then developed. In order to operationalise the term 'special event', primary research was then conducted to identify the attributes that consumers believed were important in describing a special event. Several distinct measuring techniques, including elicitation, attribute rating and conjoint analysis, were used in the questionnaire for this part of the study, in an effort to derive a comprehensive view of the consumer understanding of special events and to facilitate the convergent validation of the various techniques.

It was found that there were four principal attributes that consumers used to describe a special event, these being: the number of attendees, the international attention due to the event, the improvement to the image and pride of the host region as a result of hosting the event, and the exciting experience associated with the event. The study also found a high degree of convergence between the techniques used. The second part of this study sought to understand and predict consumer behaviour in relation to visitor attractions in general, and special events in particular. This further developed the consumer perspective that was the key underlying theme of the thesis. In the second part of this study, 500 randomly selected Melbourne residents were asked to indicate their visit behaviour in relation to a range of visitor attractions including special events. Three dimensions of visit behaviour were measured in order to overcome limitations noted in earlier studies. The visit dimensions used were actual visitation, visit interest and visit intention. This enabled analysis of respondents' visit behaviour on three dimensions to be assessed at both the generic level and at the individual attraction level. Being an origin-based study, unlike most of the studies that have been conducted in this field which have been destination-based, enabled consumers and non-consumers alike to be considered. Although the consumer decision making model, referred to earlier, which was used in this part of the study, included a range of variables thought to impact upon the consumer decision process, the focus of this thesis was on the comparative abilities of personal values, psychographics and demographics to explain consumer behaviour. Personal values were measured in the questionnaire via the List of Values (LOV) and psychographics were measured using a battery of AIO statements (Activity, Interest and Opinion). Assessing the explanatory power of three techniques on three dimensions of visitation to a wide range of visitor attractions enabled a systematic evaluation to be conducted that was more methodologically rigorous than many of the other studies that have been reported in this field.

The Growth and Promotion of 'Dark Tourism'

Cemeteries have a strange and macabre attraction for the curious and the morose. The dark symbolism of granite headstones, monuments, and crypts, viewed by some with sorrow and grief, is often no more than a part of a sightseeing itinerary for the general populace.

Pere-LaChaise in Paris, France, a burial place for such notable figures as Maria Callas, Modigliani, Jim Morrison, Edith Piaf, Chopin, and Gertrude Stein, is thought to be the most visited cemetery in the world. When first established in 1804 by Napoleon Bonaparte, the cemetery attracted few funerals and fewer visitors due to its remote location. In an effort to exploit the potential profit from tourism, marketing strategists moved the remains of Moliere and the legendary lovers Heloise and Abelard to a more accessible site. As more famous people were interred in Pere-LaChaise, it soon became a much sought-after burial place. In the rows and divisions of gravesites for the rich and famous, there is only one monument that remains unknown.

Today, tourists come each year to view the grand mausoleums, private chapels, and elaborate tombs of the people who made history. Crowds of melancholics and incurable romantics, grief seekers, and even so-called professional mourners arrive by the thousands to Pere-LaChaise. Aside from the ghoulish pleasure they may receive, there is little cause in most cases for quiet reflection and no apparent connection with the dead. Cemetery tourism, oddly enough, does seem to provide a great deal of satisfaction for many in reliving the excitement and passion of long ago. Some tourists bring the appropriate flowers, wreaths, or other tributes, while others simply follow tradition, leaving lipstick kisses on the headstone of the infamous and flamboyant Oscar Wilde. Since the cemetery is quite large, with over 300,000 burial sites and five World War I memorials, navigational maps are provided for tours of the premises. Visitors and tourists bring lunch on family outings and holiday treks and enjoy the roasted chestnuts and sausages sold just outside the cemetery gates. At times, the Vienna Philharmonic Orchestra and choir singers perform at open gravesites, adding the customary funeral music to the burial ritual. Pere La-Chaise is open Monday through Friday, 8:00 a.m. to 6:00 p.m., Saturday from 8:30 a.m. to 6:00 p.m., and Sunday from 9:00 a.m. to 6:00 p.m. Admission is free.

In a less remarkable, distant corner of Vienna, Austria, lies the tranquil Friedhof der Namenlosen, the Cemetery of the Nameless. The first to be buried here were the bodies of strangers who perished and washed ashore in the floods of the Danube in the mid to late 1800's. Most of the 500 victims were so badly decomposed, it was impossible to identify them. A few simple crosses and broken stones reflect the tragedy and sorrow of accidental death, murder, and unrequited love. After 1940 when the last funeral was held, few visitors returned to grieve their loss. The Cemetery of the Nameless has no elaborate headstones, few living flowers, and few words in memoriam. Candles no longer burn for these ghosts of the past who rest amid the rocks and boulders now covered with brambles and thorns. No names of famous people can be found, no music can be heard, and no professional speakers orate, and yet, the symbolism of the Cemetery of the Nameless haunts us in its neglect and isolation. There is no admission charge to this lonely place where grief is far too overwhelming to contemplate.

In the movie Before Sunrise, the two lovers meet on a train to Vienna, a city, according to Freud, that has a peculiar obsession for death and melancholia. In one night of wandering the streets of the city, they discover life, love, and romance. Their attraction for each other and eagerness to share the past continues to grow as each carefree hour goes swiftly by. In their visit to the Cemetery of the Nameless, we sense the longing of a woman to recapture her youth and innocence, as she recalls a similar visit as a child. The scene of nostalgia and romantic illusion leaves us with a feeling of sadness, as we wonder if love too is subject to time and as unpredictable as life itself. The cemetery is somehow symbolic of opportunities missed and the reality of knowing that some things are truly lost and forgotten, only to be buried in the memories of yesterday. It has been said that cemetery tourism for some is an "aphrodisiac for necrophilia," for others, a temporary feeling of sentimentalism and grief, but for many, it is just another form of entertainment. Cemetery tourism has become far more than a popular tourist attraction; it is, in reality, an institution.

Dark tourism (also black tourism or grief tourism) is tourism involving travel to sites associated with death and suffering. Thanatourism, derived from the Ancient Greek word *thanatos* for the personification of death, is associated with dark tourism but refers more specifically to violent death; it is used in fewer contexts than the terms dark tourism and grief tourism. This includes castles and battlefields such as Culloden near Inverness, Scotland, Chernobyl in ex USSR, or Bran Castle, Poienari Castle in Romania; sites of disaster, either natural or man made such as Ground Zero in New York; prisons now open to the public such as Beaumaris Prison in Anglesey, Wales; and purpose built centres such as the London Dungeon. The best-known destination for dark tourism is the Nazi extermination camp at Auschwitz in Poland.

9

The Hospitality Sector

Introduction

The hospitality sector includes all businesses that provide food, beverages, and/or accommodation services, and convention centres. It includes hotels, restaurants, pubs, bars and clubs, contract catering, etc. This industry has grown at a considerable pace in the last few years. However, at present, it is one of the badly hit industries due to the economic recession. The global energy efficiency market in the hospitality sector includes all the revenues generated by implementation of energy efficient equipment and consultation services provided for the hotels and restaurants, worldwide.

Hospitality is the relationship between a guest and a host, or the act or practice of being hospitable, that is, the reception and entertainment of guests, visitors, or strangers, with liberality and goodwill. Hospitality frequently refers to the hospitality industry jobs for hotels, restaurants, casinos, catering, resorts, clubs and any other service position that deals with tourists. Hospitality is also known as the act of generously providing care and kindness to whoever is in need.

Meaning of Hospitality

The word hospitality derives from the Latin *hospes*, which is formed from *hostis*, which originally meant a 'stranger' and came to take on the meaning of the enemy or 'hostile stranger' (cristal-hostilis) + pets (polis, poles, potentia) to have power. The meaning of "host" can be literally read as "lord of strangers." Furthermore, the word *hostire* means equilize/ compensate.

In the Homeric ages, hospitality was under the protection of Zeus, the chief deity of the Greek pantheon. Zeus was also attributed with the title 'Xenios Zeus' ('xenos' means stranger), emphasizing the fact that hospitality was of the utmost importance. A stranger passing outside a Greek house could be invited inside the house by the family. The host washed the stranger's feet, offered him/her food and wine, and only after he/she was comfortable could be asked to tell his/her name.

The Greek concept of sacred hospitality is illustrated in the story of Telemachus and Nestor. When | Telemachus arrived to visit Nestor, was unaware that his guest was the son of his old comrade Odysseus. Nonetheless, Nestor welcomes Telemachus and his party lavishly, thus demonstrating the relationship between *hostis*, "stranger," and *hostire*, "equalize," and how the two combine in the concept of hospitality.

Later, one of Nestor's sons slept on a bed close by Telemachus to take care that he should not suffer any harm. Nestor also put a chariot and horses at Telemachus' disposal so that he could travel the land route from Pylos to Sparta rapidly, and set his son Pisistratus as the charioteer. These illustrate the two other elements of ancient Greek hospitality, protection and guidance.

Based on the story above and its current meaning, hospitality is about compensating/equalizing a stranger to the host, making him feel protected and taken care of, and at the end of his hosting, guiding him to his next destination.

Contemporary Usage

In the contemporary West, hospitality is rarely a matter of protection and survival, and is more associated with etiquette and entertainment. However, it still involves showing respect for one's guests, providing for their needs, and treating them as equals. Cultures and subcultures vary in the extent to which one is expected to show hospitality to strangers, as opposed to personal friends or members of one's in-group.

The hospitality service industry includes hotels, casinos, and resorts, which offer comfort and guidance to strangers, but only as part of a business relationship. The terms hospital, hospice, and hostel also derive from "hospitality," and these institutions preserve more of the connotation of personal care. Hospitality ethics is a discipline that studies this usage of hospitality.

In the western context, with its dynamic tension between Athens and Jerusalem, two phases can be distinguished with a very progressive transition: a hospitality based on an individually felt sense of duty, and one based on "official" institutions for organized but anonymous social services: special places for particular types of "strangers" such as the poor, orphan(s), ill, alien, criminal, etc. Perhaps this progressive institutionalization can be aligned to the transition between Middle Ages and Renaissance.

Hospitality Around the World

Biblical and Middle Eastern

In Middle Eastern Culture, it was considered a cultural norm to take care of the strangers and foreigners living among you. These norms are reflected in many Biblical commands and examples. Perhaps the most extreme example is provided in Genesis. Lot provides hospitality to a group of angels (who he thinks are only men); when a mob tries to rape them, Lot goes so far as to offer his own daughters as a substitute, saying "Don't do anything to these men, for they have come under the protection of my roof.".

The obligations of both host and guest are stern. The bond is formed by eating salt under the roof, and is so strict that an Arab story tells of a thief who tasted something to see if it was sugar, and on realizing it was salt, put back all that he had taken and left.

Hospitality in Celtic Cultures

Celtic societies also valued the concept of hospitality, especially in terms of protection. A host who granted a person's request for refuge was expected not only to provide food and shelter to his/her guest, but to make sure they did not come to harm while under their care.

A real-life example of this is rooted in the history of the Scottish Clan MacGregor, from the early seventeenth century. The chief of Clan Lamont arrived at the home of the MacGregor chief in Glenstrae, told him that he was fleeing from foes and requested refuge.

The MacGregor welcomed his brother chief with no questions asked. Later that night, members of the MacGregor clan came looking for the Lamont chief, informing their chief that the Lamont had in fact killed his son and heir in a quarrel. Holding to the sacred law of hospitality, the MacGregor not only refused to hand over the Lamont to his clansmen, but the next morning escorted him to his ancestral lands. This act would later be repaid when, during the time that the MacGregors were outlawed, the Lamonts gave safe haven to many of their number.

Hospitality in India

India is one of the oldest civilizations on earth, and like every culture has its own favourite stories including quite a few on hospitality. That of a simpleton readily sharing his meager morsels with an uninvited guest, only to discover that the guest is a God in disguise, who rewards his generosity with abundance. That of a woman who lovingly cooks up all the Khichdi she can afford, for everyone who is hungry...till one day when she runs out of food for the last hungry person to whom she offers her own share, and is rewarded by the god in disguise with a never ending pot of Khichdi. Most Indian adults having grown up listening to these stories as children, believe in the philosophy of "Atithi Devo Bhava", meaning the guest is God. From this stems the Indian approach of graciousness towards guests at home, and in all social situations.

Cultural Value or Norm

Hospitality as a cultural norm or value is an established sociological phenomenon that people study and write papers about. Some regions have become stereotyped as exhibiting a particular style of hospitality. Examples include:

- Minnesota nice.
- Southern hospitality.

Hospitality ethics

The term "Hospitality Ethics" is used to refer to two different, yet related, areas of study:

1. The philosophical study of the moral obligations that hold in hospitality relationships and practices.
2. The branch of business ethics that focuses on ethics in commercial hospitality and tourism industries.

Whereas Ethics goes beyond describing what is done, in order to prescribe what *should* be done; Hospitality Ethics prescribes what should be done in matters related to hospitality. Hospitality theories and norms are derived through a critical analysis of hospitality practices, processes, and relationships; in various cultures and traditions; and throughout history. Ultimately, hospitality theories are applied, and put to practice in commercial and non-commercial settings.

As a standard of conduct, hospitality has been variously considered throughout history as a law, an ethic, a principle, a code, a duty, a virtue, etc. These prescriptions were created for negotiating ambiguous relationships between guests, hosts, citizens, and strangers. Despite its ancient origins and ubiquity amongst human cultures, the concept of hospitality has received relatively little attention from moral philosophers, who have tended to focus their attention on other ethical concepts, e.g. good, evil, right, and wrong.

Yet hospitality as a moral imperative, or ethical perspective, preceded many other prescriptions for ethical behaviour: In ancient Middle Eastern, Greek and Roman cultures, the Ethic of Hospitality was a code that demanded specific kinds of conduct from both guests and hosts. One example: Chivalry required men of station to offer food and lodging to any men of station that requested it.

In many ways, these standards of behaviour have survived into the present day in the commercial hospitality industry, where descendents of the ancient ideas continue to inform current standards and practices.

Hospitality Ethics in Practice

Ethics in commercial hospitality settings. Applied ethics is the branch of Ethics which investigates the application of our ethical theories and judgments. There are many branches of Applied Ethics: Business ethics, professional ethics, medical ethics, educational ethics, environmental ethics, and more.

Hospitality Ethics is a branch of Applied Ethics. In practice, it combines concerns of other branches of Applied Ethics, such as business ethics, environmental ethics, professional ethics, and more. For instance, when a local hospitality industry flourishes, potential ethical dilemmas abound: What effect do industry practices have on the environment? On the host community? On the local economy? On citizens' attitudes about their local community; about outsiders, tourists, and guests? These are the kinds of questions that Hospitality Ethics, as a version of Applied Ethics, might ask.

Since Hospitality and tourism combine to create one of the largest service industries in the world, there are many opportunities for both good and bad behaviour, and right and wrong actions by hospitality and tourism practitioners. Ethics in these industries can be guided by codes of conduct, employee manuals, industry standards (whether implicit or explicit), and more.

Though the World Tourism Organization has proposed an industry-wide code of ethics, there is presently no universal code for the hospitality industry. Various textbooks regarding ethics in commercial hospitality settings have been published recently, and are currently used in hospitality education courses.

The concept of Hospitality Exchange, also known as "accommodation sharing", "hospitality services" (short "hospex"), and "home stay networks", refers to centrally organized social networks of individuals, generally travellers, who offer or seek accommodation without monetary exchange.

History

In 1949, Bob Luitweiler founded the first hospitality service called Servas Open Doors as a cross national, non-profit, volunteer run organization advocating interracial and international peace. In 1965, John Wilcock set up the Traveller's Directory as a listing of his friends willing to host each other when travelling. In 1988, Joy Lily rescued the organization from imminent shutdown, forming Hospitality Exchange. In 2000, Veit Kuhne founded Hospitality Club, the first Internet-based service. In 2004, Casey Fenton started Couch Surfing, now the largest hospitality exchange organization.

How they Work

Generally, after registering, members have the option of providing very detailed information and pictures of themselves and of the sleeping accommodation being offered, if any. The more information provided by a member improves the chances that someone will find the member trustworthy enough to be their host or guest. Names and addresses may be verified by volunteers. Members looking for accommodation can search for hosts using several parameters such as age, location, sex, and activity level.

Home stays are entirely consensual between the host and guest, and the duration, nature, and terms of the guest's stay are generally worked out in advance to the convenience of both parties. No monetary exchange takes place except under certain circumstances (e.g. the guest may compensate the host for food). After using the service, members can leave a noticeable reference about their host or guest. Instead of or in addition to accommodation, members also offer to provide guide services or travel-related advice. The websites of the networks also provide editable travel guides and forums where members may seek travel partners or advice. Many such organizations are also focused on "social networking" and members organize activities such as camping trips, bar crawls, meetings, and sporting events. Some networks cater to specific niche markets such as students, activists, religious pilgrims, and even occupational groups like police officers.

Benefits

Monetary Savings

As these networks provide accommodation at no charge, monetary savings can be significant.

Local Contact

Hospitality exchange gives travellers the chance to experience what life is like for people living in other places. In addition, making interpersonal connections and fostering understanding of different cultures may in the long run also be important to international relations. During hospitality exchanges, hosts may show off their local knowledge and exciting places "off the tourist map". Not only may travellers get a distinct experience, but they will also get a feel for the everyday lives of local residents.

Reciprocity

These systems foster richer and more convenient travel experiences not so much on the premise of altruism, but on the basis of social exchange theory. Implicit in the agreement to host travellers is the ability to ask to be hosted by them in the future. If one enjoys having interesting guests in their home, this works out well for both parties. It works comparatively better if you are visited by travellers from a locale you find particularly attractive. Thus, hosting someone from New York City in Gainesville, Florida seems to be an unbelievable opportunity. Moreover, if you are a Westerner visiting someone in a developing country, your stay might be the only way that this individual or family could afford a trip to a rich nation. This may mean more than just a relaxing vacation for such disadvantaged parties.

Ecological Sustainability

Accommodation sharing reduces the demand for hotels, which, depending on the location can be detrimental for the environment.

Drawbacks

Lack of Guarantee: There is no contractual agreement between users in these systems. Reservations are made, but if they are for some reason broken, there is no higher authority to which one could plead for a refund or other compensation. The only repercussion will be the poor rating you give that user and your only consolation will be that your warning will deter others from visiting or hosting them. For those who feel insecure unless their travel arrangements are written in stone before departure, this system will not be comforting.

Potential Interpersonal Conflict or Awkwardness

There is a chance that guest and host will not get along. Perhaps there will be scheduling or ideological conflicts. Maybe you will find that hosts or visitors have misrepresented themselves. Perhaps the experience will not live up to your expectations. Intense interpersonal communications in advance and a flexibility once you have arrived is your best bet. These experiences require additional planning and courtesy towards the demands of your host. Thus, your living conditions, length of stay, and overall experience will be circumscribed by the living conditions you enter into.

Digital divide and demographic segregation: As use of these services generally requires access to the internet and knowledge of the English language, the sample population found in searches of these databases is really much less diverse than a geographical representation of worldwide users might suggest.

Security

Staying in someone's house, or inviting people into your house leaves open the possibility of being taken advantage of.

The Structure of the Accommodation Sector

The Nature of Demand for Accommodation Facilities

The tourism industry for the economy of Jordan is significant. Tourism is the largest export sector and second largest private sector employer and producer of foreign exchange. Moreover, it contributes to more than US$800 million to the national economy and accounts for approximately 10% of the country's gross domestic product.

Jordan's prime destinations: Petra, Wadi Rum and the Dead Sea are directly dependent on the rich natural and cultural resources in the area. However, Jordan has been subject to environmental pressure from tourism due to unsatisfactory performance in protecting the environment. It is therefore crucial for the sustainability of the country to protect and preserve these natural sites. In light of this, the present study focused on three main objectives for the Jordanian Tourism Industry: to assess the current situation, to assess the environmental impacts caused and to develop methods to encourage the improvement of the environmental performance of the tourist accommodation sector.

The Distribution of Accommodation

Environmental Issues

'Environmental' issues have emerged as hot subjects in economic discussions since the early 1970. So far, the term has usually been used to the analysis of exhaustible and productive resources. Lately, it is being also applied to amenity use of natural resources and in investigating the economic role of the environment and the associated causes and effects of its degradation and overuse, pollution etc.

The basic lesson that we have learnt from the environmental economics is that the environment can not be perceived as separate from other resources. Most human activities affect it and in turn changes in its state have economic repercussions. It is therefore important that economic decisions take into account the welfare of the future generation. Accordingly, greater awareness of interdependence of the environment, economic activity and quality of life raises political, social and scientific issues in addition to those that are directly economic.

Tourism is almost wholly dependent on the environment. Natural resources and man made resources (historic cities, heritage buildings and sites, monuments etc.) constitute the primary source of tourism. Any degradation of the primary sources is likely to lead to a decline of tourism. Therefore, their analysis within economics is particularly relevant to tourism.

Key Environmental Issues

International business and holiday tourism travel, according to the World Trade Organization (WTO, 2006) has grown at the rate of 5,4 percent and total 826 million arrivals. The domestic tourism is estimated to be ten times bigger. Major economic, environmental and social impacts follow this mass movement. In addition to the primary sources, tourists require the secondary supportive sources such as accommodation, transport facilities, shops, restaurants and other facilities which entail physical changes and expansion in general economic activity.

Like other economic activities, tourism consumes resources. Today, tourism is one of the major economic activities in the world. It contributes roughly 6 per cent of the world income. Naturally, it has a marked impact on the demand for exhaustible and renewable resources. It generates significant wastes and thus disposal problems. The operation of tourism firms reflects the market driven characteristics of other economic sectors. Extended tourism expansion or concentration in certain destinations has neglected the long term dependence of the industry on environment and led over exploitation of natural resource base and the generation of non-priced effects.

The environmental effects, widely defined, include cultural and social elements, and are probably the biggest problem of tourism. Areas where overcrowding and overdevelopment occur are often relatively small and possess fragile environments. At peak season visitors can outnumber the resident population. Hosts, tourism firms are seldom aware of the unintentional damage being caused to monuments, paintings, ecosystem. Other effects are more deliberate, e.g. off-road use of vehicles. Excess numbers also increases the demand for secondary resources, water, energy which might be scarce at certain destinations. Loss of flora and fauna occurs due to tourism expansion. The influx of tourists with a different life-style, large financial resources, and non-indigenous services can not only disturb existing economic life but also can destroy the cultures.

These problems have been recognized by many involved in tourism and have become issues of concern. The attainment of sustainable tourism has been seen as the urgent need. It would imply balanced commercialization, resource conservation, waste disposal management, pollution control, etc. Attention has to be diverted on 'ecotourism'.

Environmental impact of tourism is most visible in tourist destinations. But effects are also visible at points of origin and transit. For example, the output of aircrafts, ferries, buses, cars equipment and promotional material consumes productive and energy resources and generates waste in origin areas while travel creates pollution in the atmosphere and adversely effects the environment of areas traversed. These problems have come to be increasingly addressed in the 1990s, but serious efforts to mitigate them have lacked. This in part is reflection on the government's failure to seriously commit to pursue the environmental policies and in part lack of comprehension by the business companies of the environmental issues and objectives.

Economic analysis of resource use and their costs has been expressed in terms of opportunity cost, i.e. the benefits lost by not using them for an alternative use. The guiding principle has been the benefits must outweigh the costs. Given the nature of environmental issues, economists have used cost-benefit analysis (CBA) as a suitable framework for the assessment of monetary and nonmonetary costs and benefits, as well as large capital outlays, over a long period over which costs and benefits accrue. Another method used method is the planning balance sheet analysis (PBSA). The method was devised in the 1950s to overcome the fact that many cost benefits are not easily measured in money terms. Using the ranks according to criteria thought to be the 'best' multi-criteria analysis (MCA) has also been developed. Mathematical approach in decision making between alternatives is the analytic hierarchy process developed and used by Saaty (1987).

Issues in Tourism

Very often mentioned and discussed issues in tourism generally refer to:

- Sustainable development.
- Sustainable tourism.
- Maximum sustainable income.
- Resources conservation.
- Recycling.
- Market failures.

Sustainable Development

Sustainability of economic development has become the catchword since Brundtland Commission Report was published in 1987 and Rio Declaration in 1992 defined a set of principles that define actions and agreements in which biodiversity, climate change, forest management and conservation were accorded prominence along with a priority to be given to the poorest sections of population. The essence of sustainable development is to manage world economies in such a way that the present needs should be met without impairing the capacity to meet the future needs. The implication of such a strategy is that the growth rates will have to be moderated. Moreover, it has been stressed that quality of life, that can not be measured in monetary terms, should be taken into account. Reductions in adverse externalities such as chemical pollution, noise levels, air and water quality etc. should be taken as measures. Further, the cost of production should be inclusive of social and environmental costs.

The main issue associated with sustainable development is how to reconcile economic development and growth with open access public good and nature of the natural environment which consequently suffers from detrimental externalities. We feel that in a sense sustainable development, although initially partial only, can be achieved through various types of sustainability, e.g. sustainable agriculture, sustainable cities, sustainable ecological systems and sustainable tourism.

Sustainable Tourism

Sustainability should be the cornerstone of the development of tourism since the natural environment constitutes most of its primary resource base. Moreover, with growing awareness of both tourists and residents, firms and governments are under increased pressure to take concrete action to attain sustainability. In tourism sector experts as well as governments are trying to enforce the concept of 'viable tourism' as sustainability in the commercial sense that business is profitable and will survive.

So far, the concrete measures taken by firms confine to the conservation of energy and materials and minimization of wastes as a means of cutting their costs and thus increase revenues and profits. Firms have also taken the concern of tourists and residents alike that tourism should be environmentally responsible. In order to achieve such effect firms need to comply with environmental regulations and standards. However, there is no coherent strategy on sustainability because the past incentives have generated tourism expansion only. Because of a largely fragmented structure of tourism the issue remains complex and only the public sector has the potential to resolve.

Tourist Transport

Tourism and Air Transport industry are complement each other. Tourism depends on transportation to bring visitors, while the transportation industry depends on tourism to generate demand for its services. The growth in tourism industry directly reflects onto the air transportation. Over the last 25 years, the number of international tourists has more than doubled. The expansion of international tourism has a large impact on the discipline of transport geography.

Transport is the cause and the effect of the growth of tourism. To start with, the improved facilities have stimulated tourism, and the expansion of tourism has stimulated transport. Accessibility is the main function behind the basics of tourism transport. In order to access the areas that are mainly aimed, tourists will use any transportation mode. However, air transport is the main mode for international tourism. Air transport plays a dominant role in inter-regional movements of tourists, which normally entails travel over long-distance. Growth rates of international air traffic are pegged with growth rates of international tourism. Attractive package tours, competitive airfare attract more and more tourist day by days, therefore both the industry is expanding rapidly.

Transport policies and decisions of governments can make a big difference in the destinations available to tourists, for instance the Suvarnabhumi airport Bangkok, Thailand. Air transport is far advance than the transport mode. Air transport has revolutionized the geographical aspect of distances; the most remote areas can now be attained, any journey around the world can be measured in terms of hours of travelling. With jet that, can reach up to 1950 km/hrs, international tourism is no longer an on going adventure.

About 6.7 million jobs worldwide are in tourism industry directly supported by the spending of foreign visitors arriving by air. Taking into account both the overseas visors and work force employed it can be said that the Industry is giant in shape "The worlds largest industry of Travel and Tourism". How big the airline industry and its market share are an example will give you a clear image-in a statistics it shown that, American Airlines saves US$40,000 in a year by eliminating one olive from each salad served in first class only.

In the modern world, travelling is more centred to the annual holidays and can be fairly well predicted. The demand in international and even national transport infrastructures implies a very large number of people who wants to move in an efficient, fast and inexpensive manner. It requires heavy investments and complex organization. Well-organized terminals and intelligently planned schedules are essential in promoting effective transportation facilities for tourists, notably since the industry is growing at a fast rate.

Tourism dominantly takes place in Europe and North America. Travelling has always been an important feature of society. First the explorers travelled the world to learn more about geographical regions, potential markets and to exploit resources. As time moved on as transportation became more reliable definitely the air transportation, travelling became a mundane activity taking place in an organized environment, tourism. The importance of tourism as an economic activity has increased dramatically in recent years.

The travel and tourism industry employs 72 million people worldwide. Global tourism expenditure is estimated to be nearly US$

3 trillion. Tourism accounts directly for 3.8% of worlds GDP. Tourism is expected to maintain its growth by 2014, the World Travel and Tourism Council expects the torsion industry to employ more than 84 million people globally.

Tourism as an Up coming Industry

The World Tourism Organization (UNWTO) forecasts that international tourism will continue growing at the average annual rate of 4 %. By 2020 Europe will remain the most popular destination, but its share will drop from 60 % in 1995 to 46 %. Long haul will grow slightly faster than intraregional travel and by 2020 its share will increase from 18 % in 1995 to 24 %. With the advent of e-commerce, tourism products have become one of the most traded items on the Internet. Tourism products and services have been made available through intermediaries, although tourism providers (hotels, airlines, etc.) can sell their services directly. This has put pressure on intermediaries from both online and traditional shops.

It has been suggested there is a strong correlation between Tourism expenditure per capita and the degree to which countries play in the global context. Not only as a result of the important economic contribution of the tourism industry, but also as an indicator of the degree of confidence with which global citizens leverage the resources of the globe for the benefit of their local economies.

Space tourism is expected to "take off" in the first quarter of the 21st century, although compared with traditional destinations the number of tourists in orbit will remain low until technologies such as a space elevator make space travel cheap.

Technological improvement is likely to make possible airship hotels, based either on solar-powered airplanes or large dirigibles. Underwater hotels, such as Hydropolis, expected to open in Dubai in 2009. On the ocean tourists will be welcomed by ever larger cruise ships and perhaps floating cities. Some futurists expect that movable hotel "pods" will be created that could be temporarily erected anywhere on the planet, where building a permanent resort would be unacceptable politically, economically or environmentally.

International Travel Tips

1. Check the latest travel advice for your destination and subscribe to receive free e-mail notification each time the travel advice for your destination is updated.

2. Take out appropriate travel insurance to cover hospital treatment, medical evacuation and any activities, including adventure sports, in which you plan to participate.
3. Before travelling overseas register your travel and contact details online or at the local Australian embassy, high commission or consulate once you arrive, so we can contact you in an emergency.
4. Obey the law Consular assistance cannot override local laws, even where local laws appear harsh or unjust by Australian standards.
5. Check if you require visas for the country or countries you are visiting or transiting. Be aware that a visa does not guarantee entry.
6. Make copies of your passport details, insurance policy, traveller checks, visas and credit card numbers. Carry one copy in a separate place to the originals and leave a copy with someone at home.
7. Check with health professionals for information on recommended vaccinations or other precautions and find out about overseas laws on travelling with medicines.
8. Make sure your passport has at least six months validity and carry additional copies of your passport photo with you in case you need a replacement passport while overseas.
9. Leave a copy of your travel itinerary with someone at home and keep in regular contact with friends and relatives while overseas.

High Fliers

* To beat jetlag, book an overnight flight or one that arrives in the evening when travelling east so you can either catch your sleep on the flight or as soon as you get in to your destination.
* To prevent the swelling of feet as is wont to happen on long flights, walk in the aisle at intervals and try not to take off your shoes.
* Refrain from OD-ing on the free booze when on a flight, as too much alcohol causes dehydration. Tank up instead on aqua-pura.
* When making flight reservation, remember to request for special meals if you have any food restrictions.

* After September 11, airlines follow very strict security procedures. So make sure you reach the airport for check in well before departure time. Its best to check with the airline regarding how much in advance you should be at the airport.
* If your baggage does not arrive on the same flight as you, fill out a Property Irregularity Report (PIR), with a description of the baggage, a list of contents and address to which it should be forwarded. If your baggage does not arrive at all, place a claim with the airline within 21 days.
* Overbooking is a fact of life in the airline industry. If you are not in a particular hurry to get to your destination then volunteer to give your seat up and take the next flight. The airline will provide you a hotel room and other frills, so you can end up having an extended vacation at the airlines expense!
* Do not accept any package from a stranger.
* For a smooth ride on a plane, choose the seats located near the wings as if the plane hits an air pocket, this is where you will get the least amount of bumps.
* If you are planning to watch the in flight movie, choose the fourth or fifth row from the screen to avoid getting a neck cramp.
* If you are prone to motion sickness, take an anti sickness pill before the flight. The pill won't help much, if you have it after you have started feeling sick!
* Abide by the list of items prohibited on board and carry most items like skis/cues/walking canes/sticks/Swiss knives in checked in baggage-this smoothens the check-in process plus avoids the risk of confiscation and unnecessary delays.
* Last and this is equally important-report any unattended items in the airport or aircraft to the nearest airport or airline personnel.
* Keep track of the weather at your destination and be prepared, especially if you are going to a hurricane prone area.

Heartbreak Hotel

* Make your hotel reservations in advance, especially if you are visiting a place in peak season. You don't want to be caught without a roof over your head!

* Negotiating room tariffs over the phone? Call the hotel twice to confirm the rates. Note down the name of the person you have talked to and request a written/faxed confirmation. This way you can be sure that you will not be wrongly billed by the hotel.
* Don't depend solely on the hotel's alarm service. Carry your own little alarm clock to catch an early morning flight or that pre-dawn sightseeing trip.
* When you check into your hotel, ask the reception to give you a card with the hotel's name address and telephone number. This will come in handy if you get lost or forget the name of your hotel.
* Check whether your hotel has a hair-dryer, iron, coffee percolator, etc., to avoid carrying these gadgets and also making it easy to skip the 110/220 conversion problem when travelling to foreign countries.

Most hotels frown on guests doing their own laundry in the bathrooms, but if you do need to wash some smalls, carry a length of nylon twine to improvise a clothesline.

The Airline Business

An airline provides air transport services for passengers or freight, generally with a recognized operating certificate or license. Airlines lease or own their aircraft with which to supply these services and may form partnerships or alliances with other airlines for mutual benefit.

Airlines vary from those with a single aeroplane carrying mail or cargo, through full-service international airlines operating hundreds of airplanes. Airline services can be categorized as being intercontinental, intra continental, domestic, or international and may be operated as scheduled services or charters.

Delag, *Deutsche Luftschiffahrts-Aktiengesellschaft* was the world's first airline. It was founded on November 16, 1909 with government assistance, and operated airships manufactured by The Zeppelin Corporation. Its headquarters were in Frankfurt. The five oldest non-dirigible airlines that still exist are Australia's Qantas, Netherlands' KLM, Colombia's Avianca, Czech Republic's Czech Airlines and Mexico's Mexicana. KLM first flew in May 1920 while Qantas (for the Queensland and Northern Territory Aerial Services Limited) was founded in Queensland, Australia in late 1920.

The DC-3, often regarded as one of the most influential aircraft in the history of commercial aviation, revolutionized the aviation industry.

Tony Jannus conducted the United States' scheduled commercial airline flight on 1 January 1914 for the Saint Petersburg-routes, Braniff Airways, American Airlines, Delta Air Lines, United Airlines (originally a division of Boeing), Trans World Airlines, Northwest Airlines, and Eastern Air Lines, to name a few. Service during the early 1920s was sporadic: most airlines at the time were focused on carrying bags of mail. In 1925, however, the Ford Motor Company bought out the Stout Aircraft Company and began construction of the all-metal Ford Trimotor, which became the first successful American airliner. With a 12-passenger capacity, the Trimotor made passenger service potentially profitable. Air service was seen as a supplement to rail service in the American transportation network. At the same time, Juan Trippe began a crusade to create an air network that would link America to the world, and he achieved this goal through his airline, Pan American World Airways, with a fleet of flying boats that linked Los Angeles to Shanghai and Boston to London. Pan Am and Northwest Airways were the only U.S. airlines to go international before the 1940s. With the introduction of the Boeing 247 and Douglas DC-3 in the 1930s, the U.S. airline industry was generally profitable, even during the Great Depression. This trend continued until the beginning of World War II.

Development Since 1945

In October 1945, the American Export Airlines became the first airline to offer regular commercial flights between North America and Europe. Shown here is Am Ex Boeing 377 *Stratocruiser* in 1949.

As governments met to set the standards and scope for an emergent civil air industry toward the end of the war, the U.S. took a position of maximum operating freedom; U.S. airline companies were not as hard-hit as European and the few Asian ones had been. This preference for "open skies" operating regimes continues, within limitations, to this day.

World War II, like World War I, brought new life to the airline industry. Many airlines in the Allied countries were flush from lease contracts to the military, and foresaw a future explosive demand for civil air transport, for both passengers and cargo. They were eager to invest in the newly emerging flagships of air travel such as the Boeing Stratocruiser, Lockheed Constellation, and Douglas DC-6. Most of these new aircraft were based on American bombers such as the B-29, which had spearheaded research into new technologies such as pressurization. Most offered increased efficiency from both added speed and greater payload.

In the 1950s, the De Havilland Comet, Boeing 707, Douglas DC-8, and Sud Aviation Caravelle became the first flagships of the Jet Age in the West, while the Soviet Union bloc had Tupolev Tu-104 and Tupolev Tu-124 in the fleets of state-owned carriers such as Czechoslovak ESA, Soviet Aeroflot and East-German Interflug. The Vickers Viscount and Lockheed L-188 Electra inaugurated turboprop transport.

The next big boost for the airlines would come in the 1970s, when the Boeing 747, McDonnell Douglas DC-10, and Lockheed L-1011 inaugurated widebody ("jumbo jet") service, which is still the standard in international travel. The Tupolev Tu-144 and its Western counterpart, Concorde, made supersonic travel a reality. Concorde first flew in 1969 and operated through 2003. In 1972, Airbus began producing Europe's most commercially successful line of airliners to date. The added efficiencies for these aircraft were often not in speed, but in passenger capacity, payload, and range. Airbus also features modern electronic cockpits that were common across their aircraft to enable pilots to fly multiple models with minimal cross-training.

The deregulation of the American airline industry increased the financial troubles of the iconic airline which ultimately filed for bankruptcy in December 1991.

1978's U.S. airline industry deregulation lowered barriers for new airlines just as a downturn occurred. New start-ups entered during the downturn, during which time they found aircraft and funding, contracted hangar and maintenance services, trained new employees, and recruited laid off staff from other airlines.

As the business cycle returned to normalcy, major airlines dominated their routes through aggressive pricing and additional capacity offerings, often swamping new startups. Only America West Airlines (which has since merged with US Airways) remained a significant survivor from this new entrant era, as dozens, even hundreds, have gone under.

In many ways, the biggest winner in the deregulated environment was the air passenger. Indeed, the U.S. witnessed an explosive growth in demand for air travel, as many millions who had never or rarely flown before became regular fliers, even joining frequent flyer loyalty programs and receiving free flights and other benefits from their flying. New services and higher frequencies meant that business fliers could fly to another city, do business, and return the same day, for almost any point in the country. Air travel's advantages put intercity bus lines under pressure, and most have withered away.

By the 1980s, almost half of the total flying in the world took place in the U.S., and today the domestic industry operates over 10,000 daily departures nationwide.

Toward the end of the century, a new style of low cost airline emerged, offering a no-frills product at a lower price. Southwest Airlines, JetBlue, AirTran Airways, Skybus Airlines and other low-cost carriers began to represent a serious challenge to the so-called "legacy airlines", as did their low-cost counterparts in many other countries. Their commercial viability represented a serious competitive threat to the legacy carriers. However, of these, ATA and Skybus have since ceased operations.

Thus the last 50 years of the airline industry have varied from reasonably profitable, to devastatingly depressed. As the first major market to deregulate the industry in 1978, U.S. airlines have experienced more turbulence than almost any other country or region. Today, American Airlines is the only U.S. legacy carrier to survive bankruptcy-free.

The Airline "Bailout"

Congress passed the Air Transportation Safety and System Stabilization Act (P.L. 107-42) in response to a severe liquidity crisis facing the industry in the aftermath of the September 11th terrorist attacks. Congress sought to compensate carriers for both the cost of the four-day federal shutdown of the airlines and the incremental losses incurred through December 31, 2001 as a result of the terrorist attacks. Congress expressly sought to preserve a viable, safe, and efficient air transportation system. In recognition of the essential national economic role of a healthy aviation system, Congress authorized partial compensation of up to $5 billion in cash subject to review by the Department of Transportation and up to $10 billion in loan guarantees subject to review by a newly created Air Transportation Stabilization Board (ATSB). The applications to DOT for reimbursements were subjected to rigorous multi-year reviews not only by DOT program personnel but also by the Government Accountability Office and the DOT Inspector General.

Ultimately, the federal government provided $4.6 billion in one-time, subject-to-income-tax cash reimbursements to 427 U.S. air carriers, including numerous charter and cargo carriers. (Passenger carriers operating scheduled service received approximately $4 billion, subject to tax.) In addition, the ATSB approved loan guarantees to six airlines totalling approximately $1.6 billion. Data from the Treasury Department show that taxpayers eventually recouped the $1.6 billion and a profit of $339 million from the fees, interest and stock associated with loan guarantees.

European Airline Industry

The Imperial Airways Empire Terminal, Victoria, London. Trains ran from here to flying boats in Southampton, and to Croydon Airport.

The first countries in Europe to embrace air transport were Finland, France, Germany, the Netherlands and the United Kingdom. KLM, the oldest carrier still operating under its original name, was founded in 1919. The first flight (operated on behalf of KLM by Aircraft Transport and Travel) transported two English passengers to Schiphol, Amsterdam from London in 1920. Like other major European airlines of the time, KLM's early growth depended heavily on the needs to service links with far-flung colonial possessions (Dutch Indies). It is only after the loss of the Dutch Empire that KLM found itself based at a small country with few potential passengers, depending heavily on transfer traffic, and was one of the first to introduce the hub-system to facilitate easy connections.

France began an air mail service to Morocco in 1919 that was bought out in 1927, renamed Aeropostale, and injected with capital to become a major international carrier. In 1933, Aeropostale went bankrupt, was nationalized and merged with several other airlines into what became Air France.

In Finland, the charter establishing Aero O/Y (now Finnair, one of the oldest still-operating airlines in the world) was signed in the city of Helsinki on September 12, 1923. Junkers F 13 D-335 became the first aircraft of the company, when Aero took delivery of it on March 14, 1924. The first flight was between Helsinki and Tallinn, capital of Estonia, and it took place on March 20, 1924, one week later.

Germany's Lufthansa began in 1926. Lufthansa, unlike most other airlines at the time, became a major investor in airlines outside of Europe, providing capital to Varig and Avianca. German airliners built by Junkers, Dornier, and Fokker were the most advanced in the world at the time. The peak of German air travel came in the mid-1930s, when Nazi propaganda ministers approved the start of commercial zeppelin service: the big airships were a symbol of industrial might, but the fact that they used flammable hydrogen gas raised safety concerns that culminated with the Hindenburg disaster of 1937. The reason they used hydrogen instead of the not-flammable helium gas was because the United States was the only source of helium and at the time the Americans refused to deliver helium to Germany.

The British company Aircraft Transport and Travel commenced a London to Paris service on August 25, 1919, this was the world's first regular international flight. The United Kingdom's flag carrier during this period was Imperial Airways, which became BOAC (British Overseas Airways Co.) in 1939. Imperial Airways used huge Handley-Page biplanes for routes between London, the Middle East, and India: images of Imperial aircraft in the middle of the Rub'al Khali, being maintained by Bedouins, are among the most famous pictures from the heyday of the British Empire.

In Soviet Union the Chief Administration of the Civil Air Fleet was established in 1921. One of its first acts was to help found Deutsch-Russische Luftverkehrs A.G. (Deruluft), a German-Russian joint venture to provide air transport from Russia to the West. Domestic air service began around the same time, when Dobrolyot started operations on 15 July 1923 between Moscow and Nizhni Novgorod. Since 1932 all operations had been carried under the name Aeroflot. By the end of the 1930s Aeroflot had become the world's largest airline, employing more than 4,000 pilots and 60,000 other service personnel and operating around 3,000 aircraft (of which 75% were considered obsolete by its own standards). During the Soviet era Aeroflot was synonymous with Russian civil aviation, as it was the only air carrier. It became the first airline in the world to operate sustained regular jet services on 15 September 1956 with the Tupolev Tu-104.

Deregulation

Deregulation of the European Union airspace in the early 1990s has had substantial effect on structure of the industry there. The shift towards 'budget' airlines on shorter routes has been significant. Airlines such as EasyJet and Ryanair have grown at the expense of the traditional national airlines.

There has also been a trend for these national airlines themselves to be privatised such as has occurred for Aer Lingus (Ireland) and British Airways. Other national airlines, including Italy's Alitalia, have suffered-particularly with the rapid increase of oil prices in early 2008.

Asian Airline Industry

India was one of the first countries to embrace civil aviation. One of the first Asian airline companies was Air India, which had its beginning as Tata Airlines in 1932, a division of Tata Sons Ltd. (now Tata Group). The airline was founded by India's leading industrialist, JRD Tata. On October 15, 1932, J. R. D. Tata himself flew a single engined De Havilland Puss Moth carrying air mail (postal mail of Imperial Airways) from Karachi to Bombay via Ahmedabad. The aircraft continued to Madras via Bellary piloted by Royal Air Force pilot Nevill Vincent. Tata Airlines was also one of the world's first major airlines which began its operations without any support from the Government.

Philippine Airlines was founded on February 26, 1941, making it one of Asia's oldest carriers and also the oldest operating under its current name. The airline was started by a group of businessmen led by Andres Soriano, hailed as one of the Philippines' leading industrialists at the time. The airline's first flight was made on March 15, 1941 with a single Beech Model 18 NPC-54 aircraft, which started its daily services between Manila (from Nielson Field) and Baguio, later to expand with larger aircraft such as the DC-3 and Vickers Viscount.

With the outbreak of World War II, the airline presence in Asia came to a relative halt, with many new flag carriers donating their aircraft for military aid and other uses. Following the end of the war in 1945, regular commercial service was restored in India and Tata Airlines became a public limited company on July 29, 1946 under the name Air India. After the independence of India, 49% of the airline was acquired by the Government of India. In return, the airline was granted status to operate international services from India as the designated flag carrier under the name Air India International.

On July 31, 1946, a chartered Philippine Airlines (PAL) DC-4 ferried 40 American servicemen to Oakland, California from Nielson Airport in Makati City with stops in Guam, Wake Island, Johnston Atoll and Honolulu, Hawaii, making PAL the first Asian airline to cross the Pacific Ocean. A regular service between Manila and San Francisco was started in December. It was during this year that the airline was designated as the flag carrier of Philippines.

During the era of decolonization, newly-born Asian countries started to embrace air transport. Among the first Asian carriers during the era were Cathay Pacific (founded in September 1946), Orient Airways (later Pakistan International Airlines; founded in October 1946), Malayan

Airlines (later Singapore and Malaysian Airlines; founded in 1947), Garuda Indonesia in 1949, Japan Airlines in 1951, and Korean Air in 1962.

Latin American Airline Industry

TAM Airlines is the largest airline in Latin America in terms of number of annual passengers flown.

Along the first countries to have regular airlines in Latin America were Colombia with Avianca, Chile with LAN Chile (today LAN Airlines), Dominican Republic with Air Dominicana, Mexico with Mexicana de Aviacion, Brazil with Varig, and TACA as a brand of several airlines of Central American countries (Honduras, El Salvador, Costa Rica, Guatemala and Nicaragua). All the previous airlines started regular operations before World War II.

The air travel market has evolved rapidly over recent years in Latin America. Some industry estimations over 2000 new aircraft will begin service over the next five years in this region.

These airlines serve domestic flights within their countries, as well as connections within Latin America and also overseas flights to North America, Europe, Australia, Africa and Asia. Just one airline, LAN (Latin American Networks) has international subsidiaries: Chile as the central operation along with Peru, Ecuador, Argentina and some operations in the Dominican Republic.

The main hubs in Latin America are Sao Paulo and Rio de Janeiro in Brazil, Bogota in Colombia, Caracas in Venezuela, Guayaquil in Ecuador, Lima in Peru, Mexico City in Mexico, Buenos Aires in Argentina, Santiago in Chile and Santo Domingo in the Dominican Republic.

Regulatory Considerations

National

Pakistan International Airlines Boeing 747-300. The Government of Pakistan is the majority stake-holder in the country's flag carrier.

Many countries have national airlines that the government owns and operates. Fully private airlines are subject to a great deal of government regulation for economic, political, and safety concerns. For instance, the government often intervenes to halt airline labour actions in order to protect the free flow of people, communications, and goods between different regions without compromising safety.

The United States, Australia, and to a lesser extent Brazil, Mexico, the United Kingdom and Japan have "deregulated" their airlines. In the past, these governments dictated airfares, route networks, and other operational requirements for each airline. Since deregulation, airlines have been largely free to negotiate their own operating arrangements with different airports, enter and exit routes easily, and to levy airfares and supply flights according to market demand.

The entry barriers for new airlines are lower in a deregulated market, and so the U.S. has seen hundreds of airlines start up (sometimes for only a brief operating period). This has produced far greater competition than before deregulation in most markets, and average fares tend to drop 20% or more. The added competition, together with pricing freedom, means that new entrants often take market share with highly reduced rates that, to a limited degree, full service airlines must match. This is a major constraint on profitability for established carriers, which tend to have a higher cost base.

As a result, profitability in a deregulated market is uneven for most airlines. These forces have caused some major airlines to go out of business, in addition to most of the poorly established new entrants.

International

Singapore Airlines Airbus A380 lands at Changi Airport. The Singapore Airlines was the first international airline to operate the A380, the world's largest passenger airliner.

Groups such as the International Civil Aviation Organization establish worldwide standards for safety and other vital concerns. Most international air traffic is regulated by bilateral agreements between countries, which designate specific carriers to operate on specific routes. The model of such an agreement was the Bermuda Agreement between the US and UK following World War II, which designated airports to be used for transatlantic flights and gave each government the authority to nominate carriers to operate routes.

Bilateral agreements are based on the "freedoms of the air," a group of generalized traffic rights ranging from the freedom to overfly a country to the freedom to provide domestic flights within a country (a very rarely granted right known as cabotage). Most agreements permit airlines to fly from their home country to designated airports in the other country: some also extend the freedom to provide continuing service to a third country, or to another destination in the other country while carrying passengers from overseas.

In the 1990s, "open skies" agreements became more common. These agreements take many of these regulatory powers from state governments and open up international routes to further competition. Open skies agreements have met some criticism, particularly within the European Union, whose airlines would be at a comparative disadvantage with the United States' because of cabotage restrictions.

Economic Considerations

Juan Trippe, the founder of Pan American World Airways, surveying his globe. The collapse of Pan Am, an airline often credited for shaping the international airline industry, in December 1991 highlighted the financial complexities faced by major airline companies.

Historically, air travel has survived largely through state support, whether in the form of equity or subsidies. The airline industry as a whole has made a cumulative loss during its 120-year history, once the costs include subsidies for aircraft development and airport construction.

One argument is that positive externalities, such as higher growth due to global mobility, outweigh the microeconomic losses and justify continuing government intervention. A historically high level of government intervention in the airline industry can be seen as part of a wider political consensus on strategic forms of transport, such as highways and railways, both of which receive public funding in most parts of the world. Profitability is likely to improve in the future as privatization continues and more competitive low-cost carriers proliferate.

Although many countries continue to operate state-owned or parastatal airlines, many large airlines today are privately owned and are therefore governed by microeconomic principles in order to maximize shareholder profit.

Ticket Revenue

Airlines assign prices to their services in an attempt to maximize profitability. The pricing of airline tickets has become increasingly complicated over the years and is now largely determined by computerized yield management systems. Because of the complications in scheduling flights and maintaining profitability, airlines have many loopholes that can be used by the knowledgeable traveller. Many of these airfare secrets are becoming more and more known to the general public, so airlines are forced to make constant adjustments.

Most airlines use differentiated pricing, a form of price discrimination, in order to sell air services at varying prices simultaneously to different segments. Factors influencing the price include the days remaining until departure, the booked load factor, the forecast of total demand by price point, competitive pricing in force, and variations by day of week of departure and by time of day. Carriers often accomplish this by dividing each cabin of the aircraft (first, business and economy) into a number of travel classes for pricing purposes.

A complicating factor is that of origin-destination control ("O&D control"). Someone purchasing a ticket from Melbourne to Sydney (as an example) for AU$200 is competing with someone else who wants to fly Melbourne to Los Angeles through Sydney on the same flight, and who is willing to pay AU$1400. Should the airline prefer the $1400 passenger, or the $200 passenger plus a possible Sydney-Los Angeles passenger willing to pay $1300? Airlines have to make hundreds of thousands of similar pricing decisions daily.

The advent of advanced computerized reservations systems in the late 1970s, most notably Sabre, allowed airlines to easily perform cost-benefit analyses on different pricing structures, leading to almost perfect price discrimination in some cases (that is, filling each seat on an aircraft at the highest price that can be charged without driving the consumer elsewhere).

The intense nature of airfare pricing has led to the term "fare war" to describe efforts by airlines to undercut other airlines on competitive routes. Through computers, new airfares can be published quickly and efficiently to the airlines' sales channels. For this purpose the airlines use the Airline Tariff Publishing Company (ATPCO), who distribute latest fares for more than 500 airlines to Computer Reservation Systems across the world.

The extent of these pricing phenomena is strongest in "legacy" carriers. In contrast, low fare carriers usually offer preannounced and simplified price structure, and sometimes quote prices for each leg of a trip separately.

Computers also allow airlines to predict, with some accuracy, how many passengers will actually fly after making a reservation to fly. This allows airlines to overbook their flights enough to fill the aircraft while accounting for "no-shows," but not enough (in most cases) to force paying passengers off the aircraft for lack of seats. Since an average of S! of all seats are flown empty, stimulative pricing for low demand flights coupled with overbooking on high demand flights can help reduce this figure. This is especially crucial during tough economic times as airlines undertake massive cuts to ticket prices in order to retain demand.

Operating Costs

Full-service airlines have a high level of fixed and operating costs in order to establish and maintain air services: labour, fuel, airplanes, engines, spares and parts, IT services and networks, airport equipment, airport handling services, sales distribution, catering, training, aviation insurance and other costs. Thus all but a small percentage of the income from ticket sales is paid out to a wide variety of external providers or internal cost centres. Moreover, the industry is structured so that airlines often act as tax collectors. Airline fuel is untaxed because of a series of treaties existing between countries. Ticket prices include a number of fees, taxes and surcharges beyond the control of airlines. Airlines are also responsible for enforcing government regulations. If airlines carry passengers without proper documentation on an international flight, they are responsible for returning them back to the original country.

Analysis of the 1992–1996 period shows that every player in the air transport chain is far more profitable than the airlines, who collect and pass through fees and revenues to them from ticket sales. While airlines as a whole earned 6% return on capital employed (2-3.5% less than the cost of capital), airports earned 10%, catering companies 10-13%, handling companies 11-14%, aircraft lessors 15%, aircraft manufacturers 16%, and global distribution companies more than 30%. (Source: Spinetta, 2000, quoted in Doganis, 2002) In contrast, Southwest Airlines has been the most profitable of airline companies since 1973.

The widespread entrance of a new breed of low cost airlines beginning at the turn of the century has accelerated the demand that full service carriers control costs. Many of these low cost companies emulate Southwest Airlines in various respects, and like Southwest, they are able to eke out a consistent profit throughout all phases of the business cycle.

As a result, a shakeout of airlines is occurring in the U.S. and elsewhere. United Airlines, Continental Airlines (twice), US Airways (twice), Delta Air Lines, and Northwest Airlines have all declared. Some argue that it would be far better for the industry as a whole if a wave of actual closures were to reduce the number of "undead" airlines competing with healthy airlines while being artificially protected from creditors via bankruptcy law. On the other hand, some have pointed out that the reduction in capacity would be short lived given that there would be large quantities of relatively new aircraft that bankruptcies would want to get rid of and would re-enter the market either as increased fleets for the survivors or the basis of cheap planes for new startups. Where an airline has established an engineering base at an airport then there may be considerable economic advantages in using that same airport as a preferred focus (or "hub") for its scheduled flights.

Assets and Financing

Airline financing is quite complex, since airlines are highly leveraged operations. Not only must they purchase (or lease) new airliner bodies and engines regularly, they must make major long-term fleet decisions with the goal of meeting the demands of their markets while producing a fleet that is relatively economical to operate and maintain. Compare Southwest Airlines and their reliance on a single aeroplane type (the Boeing 737 and derivatives), with the now defunct Eastern Air Lines which operated 17 different aircraft types, each with varying pilot, engine, maintenance, and support needs.

A second financial issue is that of hedging oil and fuel purchases, which are usually second only to labour in its relative cost to the company. However, with the current high fuel prices it has become the largest cost to an airline. While hedging instruments can be expensive, they can easily pay for themselves many times over in periods of increasing fuel costs, such as in the 2000–2005 period.

In view of the congestion apparent at many international airports, the ownership of slots at certain airports (the right to take-off or land an aircraft at a particular time of day or night) has become a significant tradable asset for many airlines. Clearly take-off slots at popular times of the day can be critical in attracting the more profitable business traveller to a given airline's flight and in establishing a competitive advantage against a competing airline.

If a particular city has two or more airports, market forces will tend to attract the less profitable routes, or those on which competition is weakest, to the less congested airport, where slots are likely to be more available and therefore cheaper. Other factors, such as surface transport facilities and onward connections, will also affect the relative appeal of different airports and some long distance flights may need to operate from the one with the longest runway.

Airline Partnerships

A Japan Airlines Boeing 777-300 with special Oneworld livery. Oneworld is the third largest airline alliance after Star Alliance and Sky Team.

Code sharing is the most common type of airline partnership; it involves one airline selling tickets for another airline's flights under its own airline code. An early example of this was Japan Airlines' code sharing partnership with Aeroflot in the 1960s on flights from Tokyo to Moscow: Aeroflot operated the flights using Aeroflot aircraft, but JAL sold tickets for the flights as if they were JAL flights. This practice allows airlines to expand their operations, at least on paper, into parts of the world where they cannot afford to establish bases or purchase aircraft. Another example was the Austrian-Sabena partnership on the Vienna-Brussels-New York JFK route during the late '60s, using a Sabena Boeing 707 with Austrian colours.

Since airline reservation requests are often made by city-pair (such as "show me flights from Chicago to Düsseldorf"), an airline who is able to code share with another airline for a variety of routes might be able to be listed as indeed offering a Chicago-Düsseldorf flight. The passenger is advised however, that Airline 1 operates the flight from say Chicago to Amsterdam, and Airline 2 operates the continuing flight (on a different aeroplane, sometimes from another terminal) to Düsseldorf. Thus the primary rationale for code sharing is to expand one's service offerings in city-pair terms so as to increase sales.

A more recent development is the airline alliance, which became prevalent in the 1990s. These alliances can act as virtual mergers to get around government restrictions. Groups of airlines such as the Star Alliance, Oneworld, and SkyTeam coordinate their passenger service programs (such as lounges and frequent flyer programs), offer special interline tickets, and often engage in extensive codesharing (sometimes systemwide). These are increasingly integrated business combinations—sometimes including cross-equity arrangements—in which products, service standards, schedules, and airport facilities are standardized and combined for higher efficiency. One of the first airlines to start an alliance with another airline was KLM, who partnered with Northwest Airlines. Both airlines later entered the SkyTeam alliance after the fusion of KLM and Air France in 2004.

Often the companies combine IT operations, buy fuel, or purchase airplanes as a bloc in order to achieve higher bargaining power. However, the alliances have been most successful at purchasing invisible supplies and services, such as fuel. Airlines usually prefer to purchase items visible to their passengers to differentiate themselves from local competitors. If an airline's main domestic competitor flies Boeing airliners, then the airline may prefer to use Airbus aircraft regardless of what the rest of the alliance chooses.

Environmental Impacts

MODIS tracking of contrails generated by air traffic over the southeastern United States on January 29, 2004.

Aircraft engines emit noise pollution, gases and particulate emissions, and contribute to global warming and global dimming, even though it is one of the least-polluting forms of travel in the world.

Modern turbofan and turboprop engines are considerably more fuel-efficient and less polluting than earlier models. However, despite this, the rapid growth of air travel in recent years contributes to an increase in total pollution attributable to aviation, offsetting some of the reductions achieved by automobiles. In the EU greenhouse gas emissions from aviation increased by 87% between 1990 and 2006.

CO2 emissions from the jet fuel burned per passenger on an average 3200 kilometres (1992 miles) airline flight is about 353 kilograms (776 pounds). Loss of natural habitat potential associated with the jet fuel burned per passenger on a 3200 kilometres (1992 miles) airline flight is estimated to be 250 square meters (2700 square feet).

In the context of climate change and peak oil, there is a debate about possible taxation of air travel and the inclusion of aviation in an emissions trading scheme, with a view to ensuring that the total external costs of aviation are taken into account.

The airline industry is responsible for about 11 percent of greenhouse gases emitted by the U.S. transportation sector. Boeing estimates that biofuels could reduce flight-related greenhouse-gas emissions by 60 to 80 percent. The solution would be blending algae fuels with existing jet fuel:

- Boeing and Air New Zealand are collaborating with leading Brazilian biofuels maker Tecbio and Aquaflow Bionomic of New Zealand and other jet biofuel developers around the world.
- Virgin Atlantic and Virgin Green Fund are looking into the technology as part of a biofuels initiative.

Call Signs

Each operator of a scheduled or charter flight uses an airline call sign when communicating with airports or air traffic control centres. Most of these call-signs are derived from the airline's trade name, but for reasons of history, marketing, or the need to reduce ambiguity in spoken English (so that pilots do not mistakenly make navigational decisions based on instructions issued to a different aircraft), some airlines and air forces use call-signs less obviously connected with their trading name. For example, British Airways uses a *Speedbird* call-sign, named after the logo of its predecessor, BOAC, while SkyEurope used *Relax*.

Airline Personnel

The various types of airline personnel include: Flight operations personnel including flight safety personnel.

- Flight crews, responsible for the operation of the aircraft. Flight crew members include:
  - o Pilots (Captain and First Officer: some older aircraft also required a Flight Engineer and or a Navigator).
  - o Flight attendants, (led by a purser on larger aircraft).
  - o in-flight security personnel on some airlines (most notably El Al).
- Groundcrew, responsible for operations at airports. Ground crew members include:
  - o Aerospace and avionics engineers responsible for certifying the aircraft for flight and management of aircraft maintenance.
    - — Aerospace engineers, responsible for airframe, powerplant and electrical systems maintenance,
    - — Avionics engineers responsible for avionics and instruments maintenance,
  - o Airframe and powerplant technicians.
  - o Electric System technicians, responsible for maintenance of electrical systems.
  - o Avionics technicians, responsible for maintenance of avionics.
  - o Flight dispatchers.
  - o Baggage handlers.

- Ramp Agents.
- Gate agents.
- Ticket agents.
- Passenger service agents (such as airline lounge employees).

• Reservation agents, usually (but not always) at facilities outside the airport.

Airlines follow a corporate structure where each broad area of operations (such as maintenance, flight operations(including flight safety), and passenger service) is supervised by a vice president. Larger airlines often appoint vice presidents to oversee each of the airline's hubs as well. Airlines employ lawyers to deal with regulatory procedures and other administrative tasks.

Industry Trends

The pattern of ownership has gone from government owned or supported to independent, for-profit public companies. This occurs as regulators permit greater freedom and non-government ownership, in steps that are usually decades apart. This pattern is not seen for all airlines in all regions. The overall trend of demand has been consistently increasing. In the 1950s and 1960s, annual growth rates of 15% or more were common. Annual growth of 5-6% persisted through the 1980s and 1990s. Growth rates are not consistent in all regions, but countries with a de-regulated airline industry have more competition and greater pricing freedom. This results in lower fares and sometimes dramatic spurts in traffic growth. The U.S., Australia, Canada, Japan, Brazil, Mexico, India and other markets exhibit this trend. The industry has been observed to be cyclical in its financial performance. Four or five years of poor earnings precede five or six years of improvement. But profitability even in the good years is generally low, in the range of 2-3% net profit after interest and tax. In times of profit, airlines lease new generations of airplanes and upgrade services in response to higher demand. Since 1980, the industry has not earned back the cost of capital during the best of times. Conversely, in bad times losses can be dramatically worse. Warren Buffett once said that despite all the money that has been invested in all airlines, the net profit is less than zero. He believes it is one of the hardest businesses to manage.

As in many mature industries, consolidation is a trend. Airline groupings may consist of limited bilateral partnerships, long-term, multi-faceted alliances between carriers, equity arrangements, mergers, or takeovers. Since governments often restrict ownership and merger between companies in different countries, most consolidation takes place within a country. In the U.S., over 200 airlines have merged, been taken over, or gone out of business since deregulation in 1978. Many international airline managers are lobbying their governments to permit greater consolidation to achieve higher economy and efficiency.

The International Air Transport Association (IATA) is an international industry trade group of airlines headquartered in Montreal, Quebec, Canada, where the International Civil Aviation Organization is also headquartered. IATA's mission is to represent, lead and serve the airline industry. IATA represents some 230 airlines comprising 93% of scheduled international air traffic. The Director General and Chief Executive Officer is Giovanni Bisignani. Currently, IATA is present in over 150 cou History

IATA was formed in April 1945, in Havana, Cuba. It is the successor to the International Air Traffic Association, founded in The Hague in 1919, the year of the world's first international scheduled services. At its founding, IATA had 57 members from 31 nations, mostly in Europe and North America. Today it has about 230 members from more than 140 nations in every part of the world.

Mission: IATA's stated mission is to represent, lead and serve the airline industry.

Price Setting

One of its core functions is to act as a price setting body for international airfare. In an arrangement going back to 1944, international fare prices have been set through bilateral governmental agreements rather through market mechanisms. Airlines have been granted a special exemption by each of the main regulatory authorities in the world to consult prices with each other through this body. Originally both domestic and international aviation were highly regulated by IATA. Since 1978 in US and later in Europe, domestic deregulation highlighted the benefits of open markets to consumers in terms of lower fares and companies in terms of more efficient networks. This led to the formation of bilateral "open skies" agreements that weakened IATA's price fixing role. Negotiations are underway since 2003 to create a completely deregulated aviation market covering European and US airspace.

In recent years the organisation has been accused of acting as a cartel, and many low cost carriers are not full IATA members. The European Union's competition authorities are currently investigating the IATA. In 2005, Neelie Kroes, the European Commissioner for Competition, made a proposal to lift the exception to consult prices. In July 2006, the United States Department of Transportation also proposed to withdraw antitrust immunity. IATA teamed with SITA for an electronic ticketing solution.

For fare calculations IATA has divided the world in three regions:

1. South, Central and North America.
2. Europe, Middle East and Africa. IATA Europe includes the geographical Europe and Turkey, Israel, Morocco, Algeria and Tunisia.
3. Asia, Australia, New Zealand and the islands of the Pacific Ocean.

Other Activities

IATA assigns 3-letter IATA Airport Codes and 2-letter IATA airline designators, which are commonly used worldwide. ICAO also assigns airport and airline codes. For Rail&Fly systems, IATA also assigns IATA train station codes. For delay codes, IATA assigns IATA Delay Codes.

IATA is pivotal in the worldwide accreditation of travel agents with exception of the U.S., where this is done by the Airlines Reporting Corporation. Permission to sell airline tickets from the participating carriers is achieved through national member organisations. Over 80% of airlines' sales come from IATA accredited agents. IATA administrates worldwide the Billing and Settlement Plan (BSP) and Cargo Accounts Settlement Systems (CASS) that serve as a facilitator of the sales, reporting and remittance of accredited travel and cargo agencies. Both settlement programmes are ruled by standards and resolutions.

IATA regulates the shipping of dangerous goods and publishes the IATA Dangerous Goods Regulations manual, a globally accepted field source reference for airlines' shipping of hazardous materials.

IATA coordinates the Scheduling process which govern the allocation and exchange of slots at congested airports worldwide, applying fair, transparent and non-discriminatory principles. In consultation with the airline and airport coordinator communities, IATA manages and publishes the industry standards in the Worldwide Scheduling Guidelines (WSG) intended to provide guidance on managing the allocation of slots at airports.

IATA maintains the Timatic database containing cross border

passenger documentation requirements. It is used by airlines to determine whether a passenger can be carried, as well as by airlines and travel agents to provide this information to travellers at the time of booking.

IATA publishes standards for use in the airline industry. The Bar Coded Boarding Pass (BCBP) standard defines the 2-Dimensional (2D) bar code printed on paper boarding passes or sent to mobiles phones for electronic boarding passes.

IATA publishes the IATA Rates of Exchange (IROE) four times per year, used with the Neutral Unit of Construction (NUC) fare currency-neutral construction system that superseded the older Fare Construction Unit (FCU) system in 1989.

In 2004, IATA launched Simplifying the Business-a set of five initiatives which it says will save the industry US$6.5 billion every year. These projects are BCBP, IATA e-freight, CUSS (common use self-service), Baggage Improvement Programme (BIP) and the Fast Travel Programme.

In 2003, the IATA Safety Operational Audit (IOSA) was launched with the aim to serve as a standard and worldwide recognized certification of airlines' operational management. The IOSA certification has now become an mandatory requisite for all IATA member airlines.

IATA is member of the Air Transport Action Group (ATAG).

Countries covered through 101 offices around the globe.

International Civil Aviation Organization

The International Civil Aviation Organization (ICAO), a major agency of the United Nations, codifies the principles and techniques of international air navigation and fosters the planning and development of international air transport to ensure safe and orderly growth. Its headquarters are located in the *Quartier International* of Montreal, Canada.

The ICAO Council adopts standards and recommended practices concerning air navigation, its infrastructure, Flight inspection, prevention of unlawful interference, and facilitation of border-crossing procedures for international civil aviation. In addition, the ICAO defines the protocols for air accident investigation followed by transport safety authorities in countries signatory to the Convention on International Civil Aviation, commonly known as the *Chicago Convention.*

The ICAO should not be confused with the International Air Transport Association (IATA), a trade organization for airlines also headquartered in Montreal, or with the Civil Air Navigation Services Organisation (CANSO), an organization for Air Navigation Service Providers (ANSP's) with its headquarters at Amsterdam Airport Schiphol in the Netherlands.

Statute

The 9th edition of the Convention on International Civil Aviation includes modifications from 1948 up to year 2006. The ICAO refers to its current edition of the Convention as the *statute*, and designates it as ICAO Doc 7300/9. The Convention has 18 Annexes. These Annexes are listed by title in the article Convention on International Civil Aviation.

Standards

The ICAO also standardizes certain functions for use in the airline industry, such as the Aeronautical Message Handling System AMHS; this probably makes it a standards organization. The ICAO defines an International Standard Atmosphere (also known as ICAO Standard Atmosphere), a model of the standard variation of pressure, temperature, density, and viscosity with altitude in the Earth's atmosphere. This is useful in calibrating instruments and designing aircraft.

The ICAO standardizes machine-readable passports worldwide. Such passports have an area where some of the information otherwise written in textual form is written as strings of alphanumeric characters, printed in a manner suitable for optical character recognition. This enables border controllers and other law enforcement agents to process such passports quickly, without having to input the information manually into a computer. ICAO publishes Doc 9303, Machine Readable Travel Documents, the technical standard for machine-readable passports. A more recent standard is for biometric passports. These contain biometrics to authenticate the identity of travellers. The passport's critical information is stored on a tiny RFID computer chip, much like information stored on smartcards. Like some smartcards, the passport book design calls for an embedded contactless chip that is able to hold digital signature data to ensure the integrity of the passport and the biometric data.

Codes Registered with ICAO

Both ICAO and IATA have their own airport and airline code systems. ICAO uses 4-letter airport codes and 3-letter airline codes. In the continental United States, the ICAO codes are usually the same as the IATA code, with a prefix of "K" — LAX is KLAX. Canada follows a similar pattern, where a prefix of "C" is usually added to an IATA code to find the ICAO code — YEG is CYEG. In the rest of the world, the codes are unrelated, as the IATA code is phonic and the ICAO code is location-based; for example, Charles de Gaulle Airport has an ICAO code of LFPG, and an IATA code of CDG.

ICAO is also responsible for issuing alphanumeric aircraft type codes that contain 2-4 characters. These codes provide the identification that is typically used in flight plans. An example of this is the Boeing 747 that would use (depending on the variant) B741, B742, B743, etc.

ICAO provides telephony designators to aircraft operators worldwide. These consist of the three-letter airline identifier and a one- or two-word designator. They are usually, but not always, similar to the aircraft operator name. For example, the identifier for Aer Lingus is EIN and the designator is Shamrock, while Japan Airlines International is JAL and Japan Air. Thus, a flight by Aer Lingus numbered 111 would be written as "EIN111" and pronounced "Shamrock One Eleven" on the radio, while a similarly numbered Japan Airlines flight would be written as "JAL111" and pronounced "Japan Air One Eleven". ICAO maintains the standards for aircraft registration ("tail numbers"), including the alphanumeric codes that identify the country of registration.

Regions and Regional Offices

ICAO World Headquarters, Montreal, Canada

The ICAO has seven regional offices serving nine regions:

1. Asia and Pacific, Bangkok, Thailand.
2. Middle East, Cairo, Egypt.
3. Western and Central Africa, Dakar, Senegal.
4. South America, Lima, Peru.
5. North America, Central America and Caribbean, Mexico City, Mexico.
6. Eastern and Southern Africa, Nairobi, Kenya.
7. Europe and North Atlantic, Paris, France.

Leadership

List of Secretaries General

- Albert Roper (France) (1944-1951).
- Carl Ljungberg (Sweden) (1952-1959).

- Ronald MacAllister Macdonnell (Canada) (1959-1964).
- Bernardus Tielman Twigt (Netherlands) (1964-1970).
- Assad Kotaite (Lebanon) (1970-1976).
- Yves Lambert (France) (1976-1988).
- Shivinder Singh Sidhu (India) (1988-1991).
- Philippe Rochat (Switzerland) (1991-1997).
- Renato Claudio Costa Pereira (Brazil) (1997-2003).
- Taieb Cherif (Algeria) (2003-2009).
- Raymond Benjamin (France) (2009-present).

List of Council Presidents

- Edward Pearson Warner (United States) (1947-1957).
- Walter Binaghi (Argentina)(1957-1976).
- Assad Kotaite (Lebanon) (1976-2006).
- Roberto Kobeh Gonzalez (Mexico) (2006-Present).

Emissions from international aviation are specifically excluded from the targets agreed under the Kyoto Protocol. Instead, the Protocol invites developed countries to pursue the limitation or reduction of emissions through the International Civil Aviation Organisation (ICAO). ICAO's environmental committee continues to consider the potential for using market-based measures such as trading and charging, but this work is unlikely to lead to global action. It is currently developing guidance for states who wish to include aviation in an emissions trading scheme (ETS) to meet their Kyoto commitments, and for airlines who wish to participate voluntarily in a trading scheme.

Emissions from domestic aviation are included within the Kyoto targets agreed by countries. This has led to some national policies such as fuel and emission taxes for domestic air travel in the Netherlands and Norway respectively. Although some countries tax the fuel used by domestic aviation, there is no duty on kerosene used on international flights.

ICAO is currently against the inclusion of aviation in the European Union Emissions Trading Scheme (EU ETS). However, the EU is pressing ahead with its plans to include aviation from 2011.

Investigations of Air Disasters

ICAO has conducted just two investigations involving air disasters. Both incidents involved passenger airliners shot down while in international flight over hostile territory. The first incident occurred on February 21, 1973, during a period of tension which would lead to the Israeli-Arab "October war", when a Libyan Arab Airlines Flight 114 was shot down by Israeli F-4 jets over the Sinai Peninsula. The second incident occurred on Sept. 1, 1983, during a period of heightened Cold War tension, when a Soviet Su-15 interceptor shot down a straying Korean Air Lines Flight 007 just west of Sakhalin Island. KAL 007 was carrying 269 people.

Air Transport Regulation

Introduction To The Model Civil Aviation Safety Act And Model Regulations

[State] is a Signatory to the Convention on International Civil Aviation (Chicago Convention, signed at Chicago on 7 December 1944). Under Article 12 of the Convention, [State], as a Contracting State, is obligated to adopt measures to insure safety through conformity with international standards in its safety oversight obligations. The fundamental elements of national safety oversight are legislation establishing and empowering a civil aviation authority in [State], and the promulgation of specific operating regulations for civil aviation.

The Model Civil Aviation Safety Act and the Model Regulations are published to assist the government of [State] in carrying out its aviation safety oversight responsibilities. The Model Civil Aviation Safety Act and the Model Regulations provide primary information sufficient to allow [State] to meet its overall safety oversight responsibilities and to emphasize [State]'s commitment to aviation safety. Under Articles 37 and 38 of the Chicago Convention, [State] has agreed to conform to the standards and recommended practices (SARP) presented by the International Civil Aviation Organization (ICAO) in a series of ICAO Annexes addressing subjects ranging from the licensing of airmen to the shipment of dangerous goods by air. Each ICAO Annex sets forth ICAO standards, which are the minimum standards required for operation in international aviation by aircraft registered in a Contracting State. Recommended practices set forth in each ICAO Annex, while not mandatory, provide information about what standards should be adhered to in order to insure aviation safety.

Model Civil Aviation Safety Act

The Model Aviation Safety Act (Act) provides a legal basis for the establishment of a Civil Aviation Authority, or CAA in [State], referred to in the Model Statute and the Model Regulations as the "Authority." The Act establishes the Authority under the Director of Civil Aviation, and defines both the duties and the authority granted the Director under the law of [State]. Subchapters I through IV address the organization, administration, general powers, and duties of the Authority. Subchapter V requires the registration of aircraft in [State] and makes the maintenance of a system of recordation of such registration a matter of law. Subchapter VI sets forth the statutory bases for safety regulation by the Authority, including the certification of aviation personnel and entities, the duties required of aviation operators and airmen, the power of inspection granted the Authority and prohibitions applicable to all citizens of [State] respecting aviation. Subchapter VII sets forth the civil and criminal penalties that may be imposed by the Authority for violations of the law or the regulations, and Subchapter VIII establishes the procedure that is to be followed by the Authority in enforcement action. Statutory authority for the economic regulation of air operators is also necessary, but due to the variation in national systems, no such language is provided in this Model Civil Aviation Safety Act. It is recognized that most Signatories to the Chicago Convention may already have a civil aviation law. The purpose of the Model Civil Aviation Safety Act is to provide the basis for review and modification of existing law, where such review and modification is deemed necessary by [State].

Model Regulations

The Model Regulations present ICAO standards as regulatory requirements for aircraft expected to operate internationally from and into [State]. Where applicable, ICAO recommended standards are included for completeness. Each model regulation presents the standards and recommended practices in the appropriate ICAO Annex supplemented by sections from the United States Federal Aviation Regulations (14 CFR) and/or the European Joint Aviation Requirements (JAR). Supplementation by 14 CFR or JAR allows efficient implementation of the basic ICAO standards and recommended practices, based upon the experience gained by the FAA and the JAA. In some instances, modern regulatory practice in aviation either exceeds the ICAO Annex requirements or regulates in areas not yet addressed by the ICAO. Where Model Regulations exceed the requirements of a specific ICAO Annex, or address an area not covered by the ICAO Annex, those model regulations will be based upon the appropriate provisions of 14 CFR and the JAR. Modern aviation practice presents complex situations to an Authority. These model regulations attempt to address the present situation faced by most countries, with aircraft operating both within the country and in international aviation. One of the assumptions underlying the Model Regulations is that most aircraft registered in [STATE] will have the range to operate in both local and international aviation. Simplicity in the regulation of civil aviation under such circumstances supports the consistent application of ICAO rules throughout the aviation community within [State].

In most cases, a modern Authority must account for a number of different situations while regulating its aviation community. The key to satisfactory assurance of safety and accountability is the use of efficient and effective means of communication and data transfer. The Model Regulations assume that the following situations will be present in [State], and in most Contracting States:

- there are aircraft registered in [State] that were designed and manufactured in another Contracting State;
- there are aircraft registered in [State] that were designed in one Contracting State and manufactured in another Contracting State;
- [State] may have Air Operator Certificate (AOC) holders who operate aircraft registered in another Contracting State, which may have different states of design and manufacture;
- [State] may have AOC holders who are part of a regional consortium, with operations and maintenance facilities in a neighbouring country;
- [State] international air carriers may operate in countries requiring pilot's licenses with terms and conditions additional to those required by ICAO Annex 1, and which differ from one country or region to another;
- [State] may host air operators and/or aviation repair facilities that are required to follow the regulations of another country or region in addition to those of [State];

The Model Regulations are presented in eleven Parts. Part 1, *General Policies, Procedures and Definitions*, sets forth the basic rules of construction and application of the regulations, definitions applicable to more than one Part, and the rules governing the administration of licenses and certifications. Of special interest are the Implementing Standards that accompany each Part. These Implementing Standards provide detailed requirements that support the intent of a regulation presented in a Part, but gain the force and effect of the governing regulations only if specifically referred to in the governing regulation. Implementing Standards are used in the Model Regulations to allow an Authority the flexibility to incorporate new practices or procedures as they become available without the procedures required for promulgation of legally binding regulations.

Part 2 addresses the licensing of personnel. Article 32 of the Chicago Convention requires [State] to issue certificates of competency and licenses or validate such certificates or licenses issued by other Contracting States to the pilot of every aircraft and to other members of the operating crew of every aircraft engaged in international navigation. The basis of this obligation is the goal of promoting and conducting safe and regular aircraft operations through the development and implementation of internationally acceptable certification and licensing processes. If the same process is extended to domestic operations, [State] can ensure the overall safety of aircraft operation through unification of licensing requirements. ICAO Annex 1, Personnel Licensing, presents the broad international specifications for personnel licensing agreed upon by Contracting States. Most of the specifications in ICAO Annex 1 are not given in enough detail to satisfy the day-to-day management of a country's personnel licensing activities. Part 2 of the Model Regulations presents detailed requirements for the general rules of licensing and detailed requirements for the certification of airmen, pilots, non-pilot flight crewmembers, and airmen, such as mechanics, who are not flight crew. Part 2 also presents medical standards for the granting of licenses and certification, and for the administration of medical examinations. The licensing and medical standards are based upon ICAO Annex 1, as well as both 14 CFR and the JAR.

Part 3 of the Model Regulations addresses the certification and administration of Aviation Training Organizations (ATO). No ICAO Annex presently covers international standards for an ATO. Consequently, Part 3 relies heavily upon regulations presented in 14 CFR and the JAR. The use of an ATO for the training and qualification of airmen is common in modern aviation, most particularly as operators upgrade their aircraft inventory and airmen transition to new aircraft. The interrelation between ATO requirements under Part 3 and the licensing and certification requirements of Part 2 is plain. Even if [STATE] does not have an ATO located in the country, the requirements for ATO operation do apply to the standards required for adequate training for qualification for a [STATE] certification. Thus, [STATE] citizens who receive training from a foreign ATO should be trained by an ATO meeting [STATE] standards. This situation will be encountered when a [STATE] holder of an Air Operator Certificate (AOC), such as a national airline, is part of a regional consortium with AOC holders from other Contracting States in the region, and the consortium has established an ATO in only one of the regional Contracting States. The regulations set forth in Part 3 allow for this situation.

Part 4 of the Model Regulations set forth the requirements for registration of aircraft in [State], and governs the application of nationality and registration marks. This Part is derived from ICAO Annex 7.

Part 5 of the Model Regulations presents regulatory requirements for the airworthiness of aircraft expected to operate in [State] using the standards and recommended practices in ICAO Annexes 6 and 8 supplemented by sections from 14 CFR and the JAR. Part 5 is designed to address the complex situation faced by most countries today respecting the airworthiness of aircraft operating within the country and in international aviation. In most such cases, there are aircraft registered in [State] that were designed and manufactured in another Contracting State, and aircraft registered in [State] that were designed in one Contracting State and manufactured in another Contracting State. In addition, [State] may have AOC holders who operate aircraft registered in another Contracting State, with different states of design and manufacture. Additionally, [State] may have AOC holders who are part of a regional consortium, with maintenance facilities in a neighbouring country. Proper airworthiness of aircraft registered in [State] is the result of communication. The Model Regulations require all persons operating [State] registered aircraft to notify the Authority when certain events occur. The Authority is required to open lines of communication with the State of Design and/or the State of Manufacture, so that the Authority can receive all safety bulletins and airworthiness directives for each type of aircraft operating in [State]. Maintenance requirements are set forth in Part 5 for persons who are neither employees of an Approved Maintenance Organization (AMO) nor work for an Air Operator.

Part 6 of the Model Regulations provides regulations for the registration and monitoring of Approved Maintenance Organizations (AMO) in [STATE]. The proper maintenance of aircraft is fundamental to aviation safety, and requires meticulous record-keeping. Modern practice among Contracting States varies. In the United States, persons may be individually licensed, or may be granted maintenance authority as a member of an AMO. Similarly, a United States AOC holder may use an AMO, or may employ a maintenance organization using licensed personnel. In JAA practice, the maintenance organization of an AOC holder must qualify as an AMO in its own right. Whether or not [State] adopts the FAA or JAA approach with their AOC holders, there will be a need for oversight and regulation of AMO's. Maintenance requirements for AOC holders with integral maintenance organizations with no AMO certificate are addressed in Part 9. Many regional airline consortia use common maintenance facilities in one Contracting State. This practice does not relieve [State] from approving the AMO that its AOC holders use. Knowledge of the other Contracting State's AMO licensing and regulating practices will allow the Authority both to communicate with the Authority overseeing the AMO certificate, and to weigh the AMO requirements of the other Contracting State for satisfaction of [State]'s own regulations.

Part 7 of the Model Regulations presents regulatory requirements for instruments and equipment on aircraft expected to operate in [State]. The requirements in Part 7 address three categories of aircraft operations. The sections of Part 7 applicable to all aircraft address minimum requirements, and are noted by the key [AAC] preceding the particular section. It is important to note that the AAC designation applies to all aircraft in the Commercial Air Transport [CAT] and AOC Holder [AOC] categories unless other, more specific regulations supplant the [AAC] requirement. In some instances, certain items such as Mach meters or sea anchors apply only to aircraft with performance characteristics requiring such items. Some [AAC] requirements apply to passenger-carrying aircraft. In such instances, the requirement addresses the operation of any passenger-carrying aircraft, most particularly corporate aircraft, that may have performance and range capabilities matching the type of aircraft operated by commercial air transport entities or AOC holders. Similarly, some equipment specified for [CAT] or [AOC] aircraft have sections keyed as [AAC]. In such instances, if a non-[CAT] or [AOC] aircraft is fitted with such equipment, the equipment characteristics must comply with the applicable sections designated [AAC]. The key [CAT] addresses those aircraft operated commercially, that is, for compensation or hire, within [State] or into or from [State]. [CAT] requirements will apply to [AOC] aircraft unless a section designated as [AOC] supplies a more specific requirement. The key [AOC] applies to AOC holders operating in [State], whether on domestic or international flights. Certain sections, such as those addressing MNPS airspace, may not address airspace contiguous to [State], but anticipate that [State] AOC holder's aircraft may operate through such airspace in the course of commerce. Such requirements are intended to facilitate the integration of [State] AOC holders into such operations. As in other Parts of these Model Regulations, operators of aircraft operated in [State] but registered in another Contracting State must notify the Authority in [State] when alterations, major repairs or major alterations are made to the aircraft. [State] may have unique territorial or geographic features that may affect the operation of aircraft, and must be kept informed of the condition of aircraft operated within its borders. Part 7 includes survival equipment requirements that may apply to [State]. The Authority is encouraged to review geographic areas within [State], and designate those areas requiring specific types of survival equipment.

Part 8 of the Model Regulations presents regulatory requirements for the operation of aircraft in [State], based upon the requirements of ICAO Annexes 6 and 8. Part 8 prescribes the requirements for operations conducted by airmen certificated in [State] while operating aircraft registered in [State], as well as operations of foreign registered aircraft by [State] AOC holders, and operations of aircraft within [State] by airman or AOC holders of a foreign State. Part 8 applies to operations outside of [State] by all [State] pilots and operators unless compliance would result in a violation of the laws of the foreign State in which the operation is conducted. The regulations apply to all aircraft, except where superseded by the more stringent requirements put upon entities engaged on commercial air transport and upon AOC holders.

Part 9 of the Model Regulations sets forth the requirements for persons or entities to be granted an AOC certification from [State]. Part 9 includes regulations concerning the AOC certificate, flight operations management, maintenance requirements, security management, and dangerous goods management. Note that the requirements for an AOC-operated maintenance organization are contained in this part, and shall apply where the AOC does not use the services of an AMO, or does not gain an AMO certification for its maintenance organization.

Part 10 of the Model Regulations prescribes requirements applicable to foreign air carriers. Commercial air transport by a foreign air carrier is the operation of any civil aircraft or helicopter for the purpose of commercial air transportation operations by any air carrier whose Air Operator Certificate is issued and controlled by a civil aviation authority other than [State]. Part 10 does not apply to aircraft and helicopters when used by military, customs, and police services, unless those flights are made for compensation or hire. Part 10 sets forth the requirements for operations specifications, documents to be carried aboard the aircraft, and security and dangerous goods requirements placed upon a foreign air carrier operating into or out of [State].

Part 11 of the Model Regulations sets forth the requirements for aerial work operations, including agricultural aviation, helicopter external load carrying, glider and banner towing, TV and movie operations, sightseeing flights, fish spotting and traffic reporting. Although the requirements of Part 11 appear to address operations internal to [State], in some instances, aircraft registered in [State] will be able to perform aerial work in contiguous states. If such operations can be carried out outside the boundaries of [State], the aircraft must be operated and maintained in accordance with ICAO standards set forth in other Parts of these Model Regulations.

Regional Coordination

The Authority of [State] should consider the benefit of correlating their civil aviation laws and regulations with those of other Contracting States in the region. Correlation of regulations can lead to greater unity of air safety efforts by [State] and its neighbours. This approach can facilitate the safety regulation of commercial consortia operating in a region that includes [State]. The Model Civil Aviation Safety Act and the Model Regulations provide a basis for such correlation.

Deregulation of Air Transport

Deregulation: Deregulation is, in its most simplistic terms, when the government removes certain regulations on businesses, to encourage the industry. The premise behind deregulation is that with fewer regulations impeding operations, businesses will become more competitive. This increased competition will then result in higher productivity levels, increased efficiencies, and lower prices for consumers. There have been some failures in attempts to deregulate certain industries. Most notably, the deregulation of the Savings and Loan industry in the 1980s was perceived as a failure and was subjected to re-regulation in order to balance out the industry. The Savings and Loan scenario is a perfect example of why regulation or deregulation must be handled responsibly and intelligently, taking into account and utilizing sophisticated economic theories to help predict the future results. The Airline Deregulation Act was signed into law on October 28, 1978. The Act was created to remove governmental control and open up the passenger air transport industry to free market forces. As noted above, the desire was to increased efficiencies within the industry by promoting competition, which would hopefully le Deregulation.

Deregulation is, in its most simplistic terms, when the government removes certain regulations on businesses, to encourage the industry. The premise behind deregulation is that with fewer regulations impeding operations, businesses will become more competitive. This increased competition will then result in higher productivity levels, increased efficiencies, and lower prices for consumers. There have been some failures in attempts to deregulate certain industries. Most notably, the deregulation of the Savings and Loan industry in the 1980s was perceived as a failure and was subjected to re-regulation in order to balance out the industry. The Savings and Loan scenario is a perfect example of why regulation or deregulation must be handled responsibly and intelligently, taking into account and utilizing sophisticated economic theories to help predict the future results. The Airline Deregulation Act was signed into law on October 28, 1978. The Act was created to remove governmental control and open up the passenger air transport industry to free market forces. As noted above, the desire was to increased efficiencies within the industry by promoting competition, which would hopefully lead to reduced airfares for consumers.

Given the last three decades of outburst and turbulence in the world economy, there are tremendous and irreversible changes in the structure of production, institutional characteristics, and geographical boundaries of markets and industries around the globe. These changes include the transnationalization of capital and emergence of institutions and networks that are able to carry out the task of production and the distribution of goods and serves beyond the confining borders of nation-states in the complete and connected circuit of *social capital* worldwide. As a result, there has been a remarkable disintegration and re-integration in the structure of firms, industries and markets through the spread of transnational activities. At the present stage of global integration, the centerpieces of global accumulation include, among others, the unifying control over the global labour process, universal and unified access to technology, and the expansion of networks of information, cost-and-revenue-sharing, globalization of product design, and transnationalization of finance capital.

Another side of this epochal transformation pertains to the fast-paced, hyper-competitive, and highly volatile character of economic production and exchange that, in turn, measure the magnitude of global successes and/or failures of capitalism in the contemporary world economy. For our limited purpose here, we shall focus on global alliances in the Air Transport Industry to illustrate attempts at cost-and-revenue-sharing within networks of information sharing and the turbulent impact of hypercompetition. The present globalization, therefore, is the process of continuous integration, disintegration, and re-integration of the world economy in terms of hypercompetition, and fast-paced technological and organizational change beyond the confinement of the nation-states.

Deregulation, introduced in the United States in 1978, has led to dramatic changes in the Air Transport industry. Prior to 1978, The Civil Aeronautics Board (CAB) set airline passenger fares, and entry into the industry and route structures were tightly controlled. Most airlines were party to a multilateral agreement that required they honour tickets issued by other participants. Carriers were mutually reliant upon each other to supply one another feeder traffic. The result was that route licenses by CAB ensured a stability, interdependence of carriers, and reinforced linear route structures. Indeed, before deregulation, fully one-fourth of U.S. domestic passengers were "interlining", or transferring from one carrier to another at major airports to get to their destinations. Upon relaxation of CAB's controls, the strategic vulnerability of the linear route systems operated by the major airlines became clear. New entrants such as People Express, Air Florida, and Midway quickly targeted the profitable high-density city-pair markets.

By 1980, 22 entrants challenged incumbents with low fares, and all but two of the major carriers lost money (HBS, 1995). To compete against lower-cost new entrants, major airlines needed a new source of competitive advantage. One advantage emerged when the major airlines realized that, given their recently acquired choice to enter new markets, there was no benefit in having passengers "interline" if they were able to carry them on their own airplanes for an entire journey. Accordingly, they began to establish nationwide networks. As a result, interlining fell from 25% of passenger traffic prior to deregulation to below less than 10% in 1984.

In building nationwide networks, the most efficient mechanism to overcome the production indivisibilities inherent in the use of large aircraft was to redesign route systems into the now familiar hub and spoke configuration in which routes radiate from a central hub airport to a number of outer spoke airports. According to Hanlon (1996) the main advantage of this system is due to its enhanced number of available city pairs in comparison with direct linking of airports. The value of any hub is directly related to the size of the network it serves. A larger network allows a hub airline to offer a wide range of flights and, by consolidating long-distance travellers from many markets at one sight, integrates what were separate consumer markets into a single captive customer base. In addition, hub creation allowed carriers to increase their local market power and also lower costs from reduced overhead expenses in ground operations. The economic advantages are powerful: hub systems quickly came to dominate the U.S. route system. Prior to deregulation, only five airports served as major traffic hubs. By 1987, there were 30 airports nationwide fulfilling this role.

While the major carriers realized the strategic importance of a nationwide service network, most did not initially have a presence in smaller regional markets. Drawing feeder traffic to their hubs from these regional routes became a strategic imperative. As the hub system evolved, almost all the hub airlines formed alliances with commuter and regional carriers to increase traffic feed. Regional airlines were happy to oblige: they also benefited from an ever-increasing number of city pairs they could offer their customers. Oum, Park and Zhang (2000) note that a similar pattern of hub building occurred in Canada and the European Union following the deregulation of their markets.

Hub airlines coordinated and managed the commuter's flight schedules, provided reservation services, and shared airport and ground handling facilities. Notwithstanding these efforts vis-a-vis independent regional carriers, alliances would often fracture as the regionals played one competitor against another. To solidify their relationship with the regional airlines, American, Continental, Air Canada and others purchased majority stakes in their feeder airlines.

One indication of the increasing importance of the domestic "network" in the industry is the relative rise of regional airlines in the last twenty years. A passengers enplaned from regional airlines has increased by more than five-fold during the 1981-2001 period. Revenue passenger miles have increased by more than twelve fold in the same period. Available-seat-miles increased by more than 100% from 1993 to 2001. The evolution of the role of the regional airline is also underscored by changes in the range of markets they serve and their fleet composition. The length of an average trip on a regional airline more than doubled in the 1981-2001 period, as has the seating capacity of the regional fleet. These trends are a sharp departure from the industry as a whole.

It also became apparent to national carriers that a true national network required more than one hub. Hub set-up required enormous financial investments ($100-$150 million) and time (up to 10 years) to build the terminals and acquire strategically located gates (HBS, 1995). A far quicker way to achieve multiple hub airports was to acquire a competitor's hub. Indeed, the merger wave that occurred in the industry in the mid-1980s is mostly explicable by strategic efforts to realize the full potential of the new route structure: via the acquisition of either feeder airlines or strategic hubs. These acquisitions. The steady increase in ownership concentration in the industry over the period is also the result of this business strategy. By the end of the 1980s, consolidations led to 8 airlines controlling 92% of U.S. air traffic (HBS, 1995). Parallel to these changes in the route structure and ownership concentration there emerged the change in the composition of the capital stock—aircraft—in the industry. The development of hub systems resulted in the addition of flights to small cities around the major hubs. This, in turn, increased the demand for small-and medium-sized aircraft. One case in point is the changing product-mix ordered from Boeing, among the world's largest aircraft manufacturers. In orders for Boeing's aircraft, is divided into five product categories: single-aisle short-range (SASR), single-aisle mid-range (SAMR), twin-aisle mid-range (TAMR), twin-aisle long-range, and twin-aisle, twin-deck long-range (TDLR). The increasing importance of the single aisle mid-range aircraft. The trend is clearer when the additional seating capacity of the ordered aircrafts are considered. As presented, the majority of planned additional seating capacity is on SAMR aircraft. These versatile machines, including some models of the Boeing 737 and the Boeing 757, are to economically serve smaller cities and the regional hubs of the hub route structure. Yet, having a range of 5000-10,000 kilometres, and a seating capacity of 125 to 250, they provided needed flexibility and were assigned to all but the longest point-to-point routes.

Not captured in the Boeing data is the sharp increase in the number of jets in the U.S. regional fleet. Regional jets, introduced in the late

1980's, are small planes that fly shorter distances and have fewer seats than their counterparts: large mainline jets. Being the industry leaders, however, the jets manufactured by Canada's Bombardier and Brazil's Embrear, have a range up to 1300 miles and seating capacity of 50 to 70. The turboprop aircrafts they are replacing usually are confined to flights of up to 350 miles, with seating capacity for only 20 to 40 passengers. By the end of 2001, some 800 regional jets were in operation in the U.S., as opposed to only 137 in 1997, while the number of regional aircraft remained roughly constant at 2300 level.

Similar changes are also occurring in Europe. In particular, the advantage of building hub systems was clear to European airlines as well, although limits on international ownership meant consolidation within one's own national borders. During the 1980's, acquisition of British Caledonia by British Airways is one example. Some large European carriers also purchased minority stakes in smaller European airlines in order to solidify their positions at certain hub airports. Lufthansa purchased a minority position in Interflug—the (formerly) East German airline. Swissair purchased a share of the Zurich based Crossair. British Airways took control of 40% of Brymon Airlines, a commuter carrier. KLM purchased two Dutch commuter airlines (Cityhopper, Netherlines) and took a minority stakes in a British commuter (Air UK). And Air France was aggressive in acquiring or taking minority stakes in French commuter airlines (UTA, Air Inter).

The elaborate hub system, and the route structure that goes with it, played as a unifying framework that allowed a continuous access to arrival and departure points by both the major airlines and their regional affiliates and thus provided a ready platform to lunch a multiplied line of service by all involved. This indeed constitutes as a *de facto* or "social" (collective) capital for a particular alliance and, perhaps, a potential platform for future alliances. However, provision of such a structure embodies the double-edged sword of competition. Given the fierce competitive environment within the industry, having access to such an extensive hub system by already low-cost regional airlines, has led to a further competitive struggle between major U.S. carriers and the smaller airlines within the same alliances. This has given the regional airlines an intra-alliance competitive advantage, in addition to the inter-alliance competition, a norm in the industry. One indication of this is the relatively rapid increase in the revenue passenger miles generated by the regional airlines, when compared with their major airlines counterparts, as discussed above.

Global Alliances

As hub systems came to dominate domestic markets in the U.S. and Europe, the airlines began to rely heavily on inter-continental alliances to expand their networks, increase customer service, and generally to increase the value of their domestic hubs. This pattern is occurring globally. For U.S.-based airlines, international enplanements climbed 112% between 1986 and 1999, more than twice the growth in domestic travel. In 2000, international travel was 8.5% of total enplanements, compared to 6% in 1986.

The underlying economic advantages of the hub system operate in international as well as domestic markets. Because of the advantages of network size, carriers have sought to expand their operations geographically and thereby gained significant competitive advantage. Strategically, exploiting the hub system internationally required carriers to plan on a global basis. Most international routes, however, remain governed by bilateral Air Service Agreements (ASAs) between governments. These agreements designate such matters as the types of applicable fares, the authorized carriers on certain routes, and the type of plane and allowable flight frequency. As such, they provide a protected source of economic profits for those carriers with rights to the routes. For example, more than half of the business of large European carriers is in longer-haul international routes covered by bilateral agreements, yet more than two-thirds of the revenue of U.S. carriers is derived from the competitive, domestic arena accounting, in part, for European airlines ability to weather the recent downturn in the global industry.

Recently, the U.S. has been proposing new ASAs called "Open Sky Agreements". These imply no limits on the number of airlines that may be designated by country, unrestricted capacity, frequency of flights, unlimited ability to change aircraft type, and, finally, full pricing freedom unless both governments object. Since the first open skies pact was reached between the U.S. and the Netherlands in 1992, 57 agreements have emerged.

The Open Sky Agreements and deregulation introduced around the globe have, to varying degrees, opened previously protected national and regional markets to penetration by new competitors. Some airlines, notably Northwest and KLM, and United and Luthhansa were given anti-trust immunity and took advantage of "Open Skies" to engage in unprecedented cooperation. Never the less, no nation has to date opened its markets to carriers from all countries. This limitation has carriers ally with, rather than purchase or attempt to directly challenge foreign carriers in their own hubs.

Alliances offer a form of consolidation without having to seek authority for the full cross-national mergers that most governments have refused to allow. As Pekar, Jr. (2001) points out, alliances fall between "transactional conventional sourcing and servicing arrangements at one extreme to acquisitions and mergers at the other." Importantly, they allow a firm to acquire (or capture) core capabilities from a foreign firm that directly advance its competitive position—gate access, route network, customer base, etc.—without having to invest in new airport facilities and aircraft or acquiring other assets that are unnecessary from a strategic point of view. It is important to point out that these advantages accrue to both parties within the alliance. Indeed, we believe that alliances are ultimately undermining the position of major carriers and portend realignment of the industry.

Despite all this, alliance growth in recent years has been notable. Air Florida and British Island formed the first international alliance in 1986. As firms learned of the success of the initiative, it was quickly emulated throughout the industry. The most recent figures available number 579 alliances involving 220 major international airlines. Most international alliances have initially been formed between European and North American airlines. In the early 1990s, however, Asia Pacific airlines began to join the alliances. From Europe, North America, and Asia-Pacific, alliances have recently extended into new regions in Africa and Latin America. The gradual expansion of what would become the Star Alliance, the worlds largest, suggests the Alliance's rapid development of its global reach.

Bibliography

Andrew, N; Flanagan, S & Ruddy, J: *Tourism Destination Planning*, Dublin, Dublin Institute of Technology, 2002.

Apostolopous, Y and Leivadi, S: *Sociology of Tourism, The: Theoretical And Empirical Investigations*, London, Retailed, 1996.

Ashworth, G J and Dietvorst, A G J: *Tourism and Spatial Transformations: Implications For Policy and Plan*, Wallingford, CAB International, 1995.

Ashworth, Greg and Larkham, P J: *Building a New Heritage: Tourism, Culture & Identity in the New Europe*, London, Routledge,1994.

Baum, Tom: *We're all Going on a Summer Holiday: Images of Tourism Past and Person*, Buckingham, University of Buckingham, 1995.

Beeho, A & Prentice, R: *Conceptualising The Experiences of Heritage Tourists*, 1997.

Beeton, Sue:: *Film-Induced Tourism*, Clevedon, Channel View, 2005.

Belie et al.: *Tourism and the Inner City: An Evaluation of / Impact of Grant Assist*, London, HMSO, 1990.

Benefice, Brian G, and Cooper, Chris: *Geography of Travel and Tourism*, The, London, Heinemann, 1987.

Bolshevism, Germy: *Coping with Tourists: European Reactions to Mass Tourism*, Oxford, Berghahn Books, 1995.

Boniface, Priscilla and Fowler, Peter: *Heritage and Tourism: In the Global Village*, London, Retailed, 1993.

Bosselman, Fred P: *In The Wake of the Tourist: Managing Special Places in Eight Countries*, Washington, DC, Conservation Foundation, The, 1978.

Briguglio, L and Vella, Leslie: *Competitiveness of the Maltese Islands in Mediterranean in Tourism*, Chichester, John Wiley, 1995.

Brown, Dona: *Inventing New England: Regional Tourism in the Nineteenth Century*, Washington DC, Smithsonian Institution, 1995.

Brunt, Paul: *Market Research in Travel and Tourism*, Oxford, Butterworth Heinemann, 1997.

Burkart, A and Medlik, S: *Management of Tourism*, The, London, Heinemann, 1975.

Chambers, Erve: *Native Tours: The Anthropology of Travel and Tourism*, Prospect Heights, Waveland Press, 2000.

Chandler, Harry and Carter, John: *Chandler's Travels: A Tour of the Life of Harry Chandler*, London, Quiller Press, 1985.

Clark, Colin: *Tourist Services and Guidance: Heritage and Information*, Strasbourg, Council of Europe Press, 1989.

Coccosis, Harry and Nijkamp, Peter: *Sustainable Tourism Development*, Aldershot, Avebury, 1995.

Cohen, Erik: *Towards a Sociology of International Tourism*, 1972.

Dann, Graham M S: *Language of Tourism*, The, Wallingford, CAB International, 1996.

Davidson, R and Maitland, R: *Tourism Destinations, London*, Hodder and Stoughton, 1997.

Davidson, Rob: *Travel and Tourism in Europe*, Harlow, Addison Wesley Longman, 1998.

Ecotec: *Calderdale: Tourism Impact Study*, Calderdale, ECOTEC/Calderdale Council, 1990.

Edensor, Tim: *Tourists at the Taj*, London, Retailed, 1998.

Edgell, David L: *International Tourism Policy, New York*, Van Nostrand and Reinhold, 1990.

Elliott, James: *Tourism: Politics and Public Sector Management*, London, Retailed, 1997.

Fairgrieve, James: *Geography in School*, London, University of London Press, 1926.

Foster, Douglas: *Travel and Tourism Management*, London, Macmillan Educational, 1985.

Frechtling, Douglas C: *Practical Tourism Forecasting*, Oxford, Butterworth Heinemann, 1996.

Gamble, P. R: *The Educational challenge for Hospitality and Tourism Studies*, Tourism Management, 13, 1992.

Ghimire, Krishna: *The Native Tourist*: Mass Tourism within Developing Regions, London, Earthscan, 2001.

Goeldner, C. R: *The Evaluation of Tourism as an Industry and a Discipline, Paper Presented to*, International Conference for Tourism Educators, Guildford, University of Surrey, 1988.

Gunn, Clare and Var, Turgut: *Tourism Planning*, London, Retailed, 2002.

Hall, C Michael *Tourism Planning: Policies, Processes and relationships*, Harlow, Prentice Hall, 2000.

Hall, Colin and Jenkins, John: *Tourism and Public Policy*, London, Retailed, 1995.

Hall, Colin Michael: *Tourism and Politics*: Policy, Power, & Place, Chichester, Wiley, 1994.

Harrison, Lyndon: *Tourism Means Jobs*, Chester, Lyndon Harrison, 1996.

Harron, S and Weiler, B: *Ethnic Tourism*, Belhaven/Wiley, 1992.

Inkpen, G: *Information Technology for Travel and Tourism*, Harlow, Addison Wesley Longman, 1998.

Inskeep, Edward *National and Regal Tourism Planing*: Methodologies & Case Studies, London, Routledge/WTO, 1994.

Irwin, William *The New Niagara: Tourism, Technology, And the Landscape of Niagara Fal*, University Park, PA, University of Pennsylvania, 1996.

Jack, G and Phipps, A: *Tourism and Intercultural Exchange: Why Tourism Matters*, Clevedon, Channel View, 2005.

Jakle, John: *Tourist, The: Travel in Twentieth Century North America,* University of North Nebraska, 1985.

Jennings, Gayle: *Tourism Research*, Chichester, Wiley, 2001.

Judd, D R: *Promoting Tourism* in US Cities, 1995.

Karski, A: *Urban Tourism* - A Key to Urban Regeneration?, 1990.

Kotler, Philip et al: *Marketing Places: Attracting Investment, Industry & Tourism etc*, New York, free press, 1993.

Labarge, Margaret Wade: *Medieval Travellers: The Rich and Restless*, London, Hamish Hamilton, 1982.

Laws, Eric: *Tourist Destination Management: Issues, Analysis & Policies*, London, Routledge, 1995.

Leed, Eric J: *Mind of the Traveller, The: From Gilgamesh to Global Tourism*, New York, 1991.

MacCannell, Dean: *Tourist, The: A New Theory of the Leisure Class*, London, Macmillan, 1976.

Machin, Alan: *Retracing the Steps: Tourism as Education, Janus*, Fin, ATLAS / FUNTS, 2001.

Opperman, Martin and Chon, Kye-Sung: *Tourism in Developing Countries, London*, International Thomson Business Press, 1997.

Patullo, Polly: *Last Resorts: The Cost of Tourism in the Caribbean*, London, Cassell, 1996.

Pearce, Douglas: *Tourism Today: A Geographical Analysis*, Harlow, Longman, 1995.

Pearce, P L: *Social Psychology Of Tourist Behaviour*, The, Oxford, Pergamon, 1982.

Peters, M: *International Tourism*, London, Hutchinson, 1969.

Ringer, Greg: *Destinations: Cultural Landscapes of Tourism*, London, Routledge, 1998.

Ritchie, Brent: *Managing Educational Tourism*, Clevedon, Channel View, 2003.

Robinson, H: *Geography of Tourism*, A, London, Macdonald and Evans, 1976.

Robinson, M, Evans, E & Chalazion, P: *Tourism and Cultural Change, Sunderland*, Business Education Publishers Ltd, 1996.

Rogers, H Anthea and Slinn, Judy A: *Tourism: Management of Facilities*, London, Pitman: M & E, 1993.

Schwaninger, M: *Trends in Leisure and Tourism for 2000 - 2010*, Prentice Hall, 1989.

Scottish Tourist Board: *Visitor Attractions: A Development Guide*, Edinburgh, Scottish Tourist Board, 1991.

Seaton, A V et al: *Tourism: The state of the Art*, Chichester, John Wiley, 1994.

Shaw, G and Williams, A: *Tourism and Tourism Spaces*, London, Sage, 2004.

Stevens, Terry: *Island Tourism*: Malta, , WTO, 1993.

Trench, R: *Travellers in Britain*, London, Aurum, 1990.

Tribe, John *Corporate Strategy for Tourism, London*, International Thomson Business Press, 1997.

Urry, John: *Tourist Gaze*, The, London, Sage, 1990.

Van den Berg et al: *Urban Tourism: Performance and Strategies in Eight European Cities*, Aldershot, Avebury, 1995.

Van Harssel, Jan: *Tourism: An Exploration*, New York, Prentice Hall, 1994.

Veal, A: *Leisure and Tourism*: Policy and Planning, Wallingford, CABI, 2001.

Wahab, S A: *Tourism Management*, Tourism International Press, 1975.

Walle, Alfred H: *Cultural Tourism*: A Strategic Focus, Boulder, Co, Westview Press, 1998.

Wilkinson, Paul: *Tourism Policy and Planning: As Studies from the Caribbean*, Elmsford New York, Cognizant Communications Corporation, 1997.

Yale, Pat: *From Tourist Attractions to Heritage Tourism*, Huntingdon, Elm, 1991.

Zarkia, Cornelia: *Philoxenia: Receiving Tourists*-but *not Guests-on a Greek Island*, Oxford, Berghahn Books, 1996.

Index

A

Accounting Systems, 150.
Achievements, 198, 202, 279.
Adventure Tour, 216, 226.
Adventure Tourism, 24, 28, 104.
Arrangements, 38, 117, 264, 301, 328, 333, 335.
Associations, 154, 225, 229, 233, 242.

B

Benchmarking, 149, 160.
Business Travel, 23, 88, 111.

C

Coastal Tourism, 235.
Collaboration, 166, 169.
Communications, 55, 293, 310.
Computer Reservation Systems, 312.
Constitution, 22.
Cruise Industry, 37.
Cultural Environment, 258.
Cultural Tourism, 6, 8, 20, 28, 123, 190, 257.
Customers, 5, 14, 24, 110, 125, 132, 134, 189, 200, 202, 206, 207, 209, 211, 216, 217, 218, 220, 222, 230, 234, 242, 273, 275, 335.

D

Dark Tourism, 8, 285.
Demands, 11, 36, 91, 94, 111, 122, 153, 156, 157, 170, 183, 187, 200, 215, 227, 242, 258, 279, 293, 314.
Destination Management, 253.
Destination Planning Resources, 258.
Development Project, 182.
Development Strategy, 175, 281.

E

Economic Growth, 31, 34, 146, 166, 199.
Economic Impact of Tourism, 143, 148.
Economic Policy, 38.
Educational Tourism, 7, 8.
Environmental Auditing, 212, 225.
Environmental Conservation, 233.
Environmental Impact, 198, 201, 205, 215, 221, 295.
Environmental Management, 19, 200, 214, 215, 230.
Environmental Protection, 39, 166, 206.
Evidence, 41, 107, 182, 194, 206, 279.
Evolution of Marketing, 86.
Export Strategy, 175, 176.

F

Federal Government, 305.
Forms of Tourism, 2, 6, 29, 31, 210.

G

Gastronomic Tourism, 275, 278.
Global Tourism, 39, 146, 188, 244, 298.
Global Warming, 316.
Growth of Tourism, 33, 35, 38, 86, 153, 159, 297.
Guidance Protecting, 163.

H

Hospitality Industry, 286, 290.
Hotel Industry, 10, 78.
Human Resource Management, 214.

I

Industry Initiatives, 163.
Instruments, 95, 172, 173, 314, 317, 322, 330.
Interest Tourism, 8.
International Civil Aviation Organization, 310, 319, 321, 325.
International Monetary Fund, 175.
International Tourism Demand, 9.
International Tourism Receipts, 1, 3, 101.
International Tourist Market, 144.
International Tourists, 18, 75, 93, 111, 297.
Investments, 20, 104, 111, 153, 176, 199, 212, 221, 232, 240, 298, 336.

L

Leaders, 21, 208, 260.
Leadership, 53, 74, 95, 228, 266, 324.
Local Economic Development, 28.

M

Maintenance, 46, 50, 119, 148, 165, 185, 194, 199, 200, 203, 205, 280, 304, 314, 317, 318, 326, 327, 329, 330, 332.
Management Decisions, 144, 148.
Management Systems, 214, 215, 224, 225, 281, 311.
Market Research, 40.
Marketing Approach, 95, 191.
Marketing Efforts, 95, 123, 280.
Marketing Plan, 141.
Marketing Resources, 124.
Motivations, 8, 41, 122, 135, 170, 211, 227, 277.

N

National Policy, 30.
Nature Tourism, 28, 81, 217.
Niche Tourism, 6.

O

Observations, 52, 238.
Occupations, 119.
Operations Management, 332.
Outdoor Recreation, 80.

P

Package Holiday, 90, 91, 216.
Philosophy, 243, 289.
Planning Tourism Development, 200.
Politics, 135, 136, 140, 141, 194.
Powers, 56, 57, 62, 109, 311, 326.
Product Development, 130, 226, 229, 231.
Production, 5, 14, 34, 35, 36, 49, 86, 87, 105, 145, 151, 180, 181, 188, 204, 210, 211, 219, 222, 232, 233, 236, 276, 296, 334, 335.
Promote Sustainable Tourism, 169, 173.
Property, 183, 268, 301.

Protection, 28, 39, 162, 166, 176, 198, 199, 203, 206, 221, 226, 228, 286, 287, 288.
Provision, 24, 33, 38, 39, 104, 105, 106, 111, 117, 120, 203, 204, 218, 224, 255, 256.

R

Rafting, 25.
Relationship, 34, 80, 85, 105, 106, 160, 179, 180, 194, 198, 207, 221, 222, 247, 269, 286, 287, 336.
Religious Tourism, 6, 259, 260.
Resource Management, 179, 214, 225.
Responsible Tourism, 169, 198, 217.
Restaurants, 14, 23, 71, 72, 80, 86, 87, 89, 118, 149, 156, 162, 211, 219, 235, 240, 254, 256, 276, 277, 278, 279, 286, 294.
Rural Tourism, 28, 241, 242.

S

Safari, 229.
Seaside Resorts, 6, 12, 70, 72, 73, 236.
Security, 40, 81, 101, 159, 222, 274, 293, 300, 317, 332.
Sex Tourism, 159, 160, 174, 227.
Small Business, 31.
Society, 2, 4, 22, 34, 35, 50, 52, 53, 56, 86, 138, 164, 207, 219, 247, 252, 267, 270, 275, 298.
Sociocultural Impact of Tourism, 155.
Space Travel, 9, 299.
Sports Events, 23.
Sports Tourism, 79.
Supply Chain Management, 210, 212, 223, 224, 228.
Sustainable Development, 7, 85, 117, 163, 169, 170, 171, 173, 191, 231, 296.
Sustainable Management, 162.
Sustainable Tourism, 7, 8, 84, 85, 106, 107, 146, 162, 163, 167, 168, 169, 171, 172, 173, 174, 186, 199, 203, 205, 210, 212, 213, 220, 225, 226, 227, 231, 232, 295, 296.

T

Target Market, 125.
Technology, 5, 7, 20, 33, 37, 40, 46, 55, 78, 92, 113, 114, 136, 145, 187, 189, 274, 277, 317, 334.
Tour Operator, 14, 86, 87, 109, 110, 139, 210, 211, 212, 215, 216, 221, 222, 231, 232.
Tour Packages, 110.
Tourism Activities, 19, 37, 103, 116, 170, 175, 177, 182, 198, 199, 202, 204, 205, 213, 220.
Tourism Business, 23, 86, 87, 153.
Tourism Chain, 206.
Tourism Demand, 9, 14, 121, 122, 136, 137, 139, 140, 141, 142, 156, 187, 236.
Tourism Destinations, 98, 102, 108, 110, 111, 112, 160, 167, 220.
Tourism Development, 8, 38, 39, 40, 92, 93, 102, 150, 152, 153, 157, 161, 162, 167, 169, 182, 184, 199, 200, 204, 205, 231, 281.

Tourism Establishments, 101 150.
Tourism Facilities, 164, 172 189, 200, 201.
Tourism Flows, 96, 102, 146.
Tourism Industry, 2, 6, 9, 23, 29, 32, 40, 75, 78, 81, 83, 86, 87, 93, 94, 95, 104, 106, 115, 121, 127, 136, 139, 142, 144, 146, 155, 163, 164, 165, 166, 167, 168, 169, 171, 175, 176, 177, 181, 182, 183, 187, 196, 197, 201, 203, 204, 205, 209, 212, 215, 239, 244, 253, 280, 281, 293, 297, 298, 299.
Tourism Infrastructure, 30, 170, 200.
Tourism Marketing, 79, 86, 87, 94, 126, 130, 138, 140, 280.
Tourism Markets, 6, 91, 106, 134, 169, 221.
Tourism Organisation, 78, 145, 174, 175, 253.
Tourism Planning, 39, 200.
Tourism Policy, 105, 201.
Tourism Promotion, 38, 151.
Tourism Satellite Account, 149, 150.
Tourism Supply, 118, 209, 210, 211, 220, 223, 225, 242.
Tourism Sustainability, 106, 109.
Tourist Accommodation, 293.
Tourist Attractions, 10, 11, 12, 13, 30, 31, 76, 80, 186, 219, 235, 239, 254, 271, 279.
Tourist Destination, 17, 18, 30, 32, 94, 179, 180, 229, 235, 253, 255.
Tourist Movements, 12.
Tourist Product, 10, 14, 15, 16, 19, 26, 27, 31, 139.
Tourist Traffic, 145.
Trade, 4, 11, 12, 41, 43, 56, 70, 94, 95, 97, 103, 107, 116, 117, 119, 120, 146, 152, 154, 156, 159, 160, 165, 172, 176, 177, 208, 212, 221, 236, 268, 269, 294, 317, 319, 322.
Traditions, 11, 20, 21, 26, 39, 63, 117, 146, 155, 158, 160, 162, 180, 257, 258, 289.
Transport Technologies, 37.
Transportation, 1, 16, 19, 35, 38, 44, 45, 52, 55, 74, 77, 88, 89, 152, 204, 216, 233, 235, 297, 298, 303, 305, 316, 320, 332.
Travel Agents, 14, 75, 114, 206, 320, 321.
Travel Industry, 140, 189, 202, 260.
Treatment, 4, 18, 27, 57, 60, 61, 64, 67, 68, 69, 106, 140, 166, 177, 299.

U

Urban Tourism, 75, 76, 77, 235, 236, 240, 277.

W

Water Sports, 24, 25, 149.
Wildlife Tourism, 6.
World Bank, 176, 199.
World Tourism, 1, 2, 3, 9, 12, 78, 83, 86, 96, 144, 145, 146, 147, 174, 175, 225, 233, 245, 253, 290, 299.

□□□